CANTELON'S
CASUAL
COMMENTARY

CANTELON'S CASUAL COMMENTARY

A 21ST CENTURY GUIDE TO
THE LIFE OF JESUS
FOR THE INTERNET GENERATION

JAMES CANTELON

Published by Wordzworth
www.wordzworth.com

To Kathy,
my sweet wife and constant friend.

CONTENTS

Books of the Bible & Abbreviations

A

Ac – Acts
Am – Amos

C

1Ch – 1 Chronicles
2Ch – 2 Chronicles
Cl – Colossians (or Col)
1Co – 1 Corinthians
2Co – 2 Corinthians

D

Da – Daniel
Dt – Deuteronomy

E

Ec – Ecclesiastes
Ep – Ephesians (or Eph)
Er – Ezra (or Ezr)
Es – Esther (or Est)
Ex – Exodos
Ez – Ezekiel

G

Ga – Galatians
Ge – Genesis

H

Hb – Habakkuk
He – Hebrews (or Heb)
Hg – Haggai
Ho – Hosea

I

Is – Isaiah

J

Ja – James
Jb – Job (or Job)
Jd – Jude
Je – Jeremiah
Jg – Judges (or Jdg)
Jl – Joel
Jn – John
1Jn – 1 John
2Jn – 2 John
3Jn – 3 John
Jo – Jonah (or Jon)
Js – Joshua (or Jos)

K

1Ki – 1 Kings
2Ki – 2 Kings

L

La – Lamentations
Le – Leviticus (or Lv)
Lk – Luke

M

Ma – Malachi
Mi – Micah
Mk – Mark
Mt – Matthew

N

Na – Nahum
Ne – Nehemiah
Nu – Numbers

O

Ob – Obadiah

P

1Pe – 1 Peter
2Pe – 2 Peter
Ph – Philippians
Pm – Philemon (or Phm)
Pr – Proverbs
Ps – Psalms

R

Re – Revelation
Ro – Romans
Ru – Ruth

S

1Sa – 1 Samuel
2Sa – 2 Samuel
So – Song of Solomon

T

1Th – 1 Thessalonians
2Th – 2 Thessalonians
1Ti – 1 Timothy
2Ti – 2 Timothy
Ti – Titus (or Tt)

Z

Ze – Zechariah
Zp – Zephaniah

NIV – New International Version
KJV – King James Version
NKJV – New King James Version
RSV – Revised Standard Version

(All quotations are NIV unless otherwise noted.)

PREFACE

Cantelon's Casual Commentary is a reflection on a life journey as much as it is a "Guide to the Life of Jesus for the 21st Century". I was raised in a pastor's home. Indeed, I often facetiously say that I cut my teeth on a church pew. My great-grandfather, grandfather, and father were all preachers of the Gospel, as were three great-uncles and two uncles. Our three adult children are pastors. I and one of my cousins are preachers. One might call pastoring "the family business".

I had been pastoring for eleven years when the totally unexpected occurred. I was invited by Israeli government officials in 1981 to plant an international church in Jerusalem. This of course is a story in itself. Suffice to say it was an offer I couldn't refuse.

The ensuing seven years were an adventure – moving our young family to Jerusalem, adapting to a foreign culture saturated by both secular and biblical history, learning to speak Hebrew, getting our children into the Jerusalem school system, adjusting to the weekly and yearly rhythms of sabbaths and holy celebrations, and (as we had been mandated) planting what is now known as the "King of Kings" church in the heart of the city (*kkcj.org*). (King of Kings Church today has a multifaceted signature both in Israel and around the world).

While immersed in all this I also travelled once a week into Southern Lebanon where, armed with a military pass and a semi-automatic rifle (!) supplied by the commander of the army, I did two eight hour shifts broadcasting out of the war zone known by the locals as the "Valley of the Springs". Among other things I learned first hand what it was like to be under barrages of Katyusha and mortar rocket fire. The battles between the Israeli armed forces and the PLO militia entrenched in Beaufort Castle looming over our humble radio station were intense.

Israel quickly became our adopted country. It is very small geographically, so over time our family got to know every nook and cranny. We loved it. To this day we refer to Jerusalem lovingly as our home town.

So, as I wrote this commentary, it was with a three-dimensional perspective. I know Jesus' country. I can see it, smell it, feel it. More than historical or theological my sense of Israel and the Gospels is visceral. This, I think, makes this commentary unique.

I hope you enjoy it as much as I did in the writing.

Shalom!

James Cantelon

INTRODUCTION

I'm pretty sure that most of us think of the Gospel of Jesus as the "story" of Jesus. And it is. But, if we look at the meaning of "gospel" in history, it isn't.

It has a facinating family tree. "Gospel" finds its roots in "euangelion" (Gk), "basar" (Heb), "euangelium" (Lat), "god-spell" (Anglo-Saxon), and is also related to "logos" (Gk) and "dabar" (Heb), so a word study can be quite a journey. In that this book is a "casual" work I do not want to follow an etymological rabbit trail, but a cursory overview will be helpful.

"Basar" (Heb) means "to publish, bear good news" of military encounters (Is. 52:7; Ps. 40:9; 68:11; 96:2). The essential nuance is that of a messenger doing a marathon run from a battle scene with news of God's victory over the enemy. The people are ready to hear and rejoice (although bad news can bring great sorrow – see 1Sa. 4:12-18).

"Euangelion" (Gk) refers to an announcement or proclamation of good news. Like "basar" it's a message of victory. An evangelist ("evangelistes") is the messenger (derived from "angelos"), the announcer of gladness. But, what's very interesting about "euangelion" is that it is an oral, not a written, proclamation. It is "the Gospel of God" (Mk. 1:14; Ro. 1:1; 1Th. 2:2,9) which He himself proclaims (Ac. 10:36; 13:26; Ro. 1:1; Tt. 13), and through it He calls all people to himself (2Th. 2:14).

Closely tied to these words is the Hebrew noun "dabar" ("back, background") which has a number of applications ("speech, thing, commandment, event, account, cause..."). It sometimes refers to what is done, and sometimes it's a report (proclamation, announcement) of what is or has been done. A classic usage of "dabar" is in the name of the Book of Chronicles in the Old Testament – "the book of the words (acts) of the times" ("sepher dibré ha-yamim"). Dabar is a revelatory work of God. In that sense "the word of the Lord" would "come upon" a prophet, or indwell him/her (2Ki. 3:12) – "the word of the Lord is in him", referring to Elisha. This word was "right" and "true" (Ps. 33:4), "eternal... firm in the heavens" (Ps. 119:89) and "a lamp unto my feet and a light unto my path" (Ps. 119:105). The prophet Jeremiah employed similes to describe dabar: "like a fire" and "a hammer that breaketh the rock in pieces" (23:29). The "Gospel of God" has the fearsome potential to consume and destroy. But, in its revelatory capacity "dabar" throws the present into historical relief, providing the "background" or "what lies behind" God's declared word. It brings light and context to his will.

The Greek word "logos" runs parallel to "dabar" both in meaning and in its relation to "gospel". In the Greek Old Testament (Septuagint) "logos" is used to translate "dabar" and usually denotes "word". In the New Testament logos has several applications, not the least being "the word of the Lord", that is, the revealed will of God which is seen as revealed in Christ (1Th. 4:14-18; Ac. 8:25; 13:49; 15:35,36; 16:32; 19:10; 1Th. 1:8; 2Th. 3:1). This "word" (message, proclamation) is given with God's full authority and empowerment. The "logos" in John's gospel is God himself (Jn. 1:1). In this sense Jesus *is* the Gospel. He is the word spoken from the beginning (vv.1,2). What is more, he is "the power of God and the wisdom of God" (1Co. 1:24), "our peace" (Ep. 2:14), "the culmination of the law" (Ro.10:4), "our righteousness, holiness and redemption" (1Co. 1:30), and "the great I am" (Jn. 6:35; 8:12; 10:7,11; 14:6; 15:1). He is the word that God proclaims of himself.

After Jesus' baptism and testing in the wilderness Luke records his first public reading of the scriptures in his home synagogue in Nazareth. It was a powerful, polarizing moment where Jesus essentially proclaimed that he was the personification of God's good news:

> *"The Spirit of the Lord is on me,*
> *because he has anointed me*
> *to proclaim good news to the poor.*

He has sent me to proclaim freedom for the prisoners
and recovery of sight for the blind,
to set the oppressed free,
to proclaim the year of the Lord's favor."

—Lk. 4:18 19

This reading from Isaiah's 61st chapter captured the essence of the Gospel. The messianic era foreshadowed by the prophet could come only through the agency of Messiah. Jesus was he. He would usher in an era of redemption and salvation.

Jesus declared that those who embraced God's proclamation were blessed, "But blessed are your eyes because they see, and your ears because they hear" (Mt. 13:16). Not only did they hear but they saw divine activity in history. Indeed the Gospel was/is rooted in history. The empty tomb in Jerusalem was/is the pivot point of salvation history. Because of the resurrection the "good news" was truly "glad tidings". The Gospel:

1. created faith (Ro. 1:16,17)

2. brought salvation and life (1Co. 15:2)

3. brought judgement (Ro. 2:16)

4. revealed God's righteousness (Ro. 1:17)

5. brought fulfillment of hope (Cl. 1:5,23)

6. brought peace (Ep. 2:17; 6:15)

7. reconciled Jew and Gentile (Ep. 3:1-9)

8. brought "life and immortality to light" (2Ti. 1:10)

9. produced rebirth and new life (1Pe. 1:23-25).

Even as God's proclamation had accomplished all this, it was also more than a done deal. It was/is a work in progress. The "message of the cross" (past tense) was seen as "foolishness to those who are perishing" (present tense), "but to us who are being saved" (continuous present/ future) "it is the power of God" (1Co. 1:18). St. Paul made it clear that God had begun his good work in the believers but it was not yet completed (Ph.1:6; Cl. 1:23). The good news from heaven had been sealed by the death and resurrection of Jesus, and had been empowered by the outpouring of the Spirit at Pentecost, but the immaturity of the believers could see them sliding back (Cl. 1:22, 23), so they were to be vigilant because "the Day of the Lord" or "the Day of the Son of Man" was awaiting those who were "holy in his sight, without blemish and free from accusation." In this sense the full Gospel was "here but not yet". Christians were/are being saved for the final victory of Christ (Re. 11:15-18).

This means that God's proclamation of salvation for all believers is merely preliminary work "that in the coming ages he might show the immeasurable riches of his grace in kindness toward us in Christ Jesus" (Ep. 2:7 RSV). The full impact of our salvation will not be revealed until the glory of Jesus is both revealed and manifested (Lk. 17:30; Ro. 8:18; 1Co. 1:7; 2Th. 1:7; 1Pe. 1:5,7,13; 4:13; 5:1; Cl. 3:4; 1Jn. 3:2). So God's goal in his powerful word from heaven was/is twofold:

1. the removal of sin and all it produces (Lk. 4:18,19; Is. 61)

2. the investiture of righteousness, peace, and joy in the Holy Spirit in all believers (Ro. 14:17).

These realized goals will be/are being accomplished through Christ and will create a newborn body of saints who will inherit the coming Kingdom of Heaven. Thus, the Gospel is not only the story of Jesus, but it is the proclamation of God the Father's victory over sin, decay and death. The "song of God's servant Moses and of the Lamb" says it all:

"Great and marvelous are your deeds,
Lord God Almighty.
Just and true are your ways,
king of the nations.

Who will not fear you, Lord,
and bring glory to your name?
For you alone are holy.
All nations will come
and worship before you,
for your righteous acts have been revealed."

—REVELATION 15:3,4

As you can see, "Cantelon's Casual Commentary" is predicated on and rife with the scriptures. I'm hoping (assuming?) that you'll have a Bible close at hand. This is a book you'll want to journey through, *slowly*. In many ways I've tried to paint a picture even as I casually explore the life of Jesus. It's a "broad brush" effort. As such it may provide a stimulus for further study on your part. There are a lot of excellent authors out there. You'll want to read much more from those who are skilled in the finer points. Consider "Cantelon's Casual Commentary" as a primer for an adventure in learning about the greatest man who ever lived.

THE GOSPEL OF MATTHEW

INTRODUCTION

Matthew ("Matatiya" – Heb – "gift of Yahweh") was one of the twelve disciples (Mk. 3:18; Mt. 10:3; Lk. 6:15; Ac. 1:13). A tax collector in Capernaum (Jesus' adopted home town), he was apparently also known as "Levi" (Mk. 2:14; Lk. 5:27). Some of the early church fathers and many scholars to this day have expressed doubt as to whether Matthew was Levi, or Levi was Matthew, or even suggest that he has been confused with "James the son of Alphaeus" (a "casual" commentary will not plumb those depths…). Nevertheless, early church tradition saw Matthew as author of the first gospel.

As a tax collector for the Roman occupiers he was vilified by his fellow Jews. He was a turncoat, a traitor, a "Benedict Arnold", in that he not only was squeezing his countrymen on behalf of the Romans for their hard-earned cash, but was also surcharging in order to line his own pockets. In a town of subsistence living blue collar fishermen he was rich.

This in itself was enough to warrant his social stigmatization. He would never be awarded Capernaum's "Man of the Year".

Most commentators agree that Matthew's priority in writing was to demonstrate that the life, teaching, and overall ministry of Jesus satisfied the messianic expectations of the Old Testament prophets. The fulfillment of prophecy was a major concern for the Jews, thus it's believed that Matthew's target readership was Jewish. The fact that in Matthew the denunciation of Pharisaical Jews in particular is so distinct, suggests to me that the author had felt the sting of his social isolation by the religious citizens of Capernaum. His ostracization had been both for his turncoat tax gathering and his perceived flouting of oral tradition (shunned at the synagogue?). Regardless, Matthew chose to record incidents and teachings that demonstrated (as one old theologian put it) the "diametrical contrast between Christ and Pharisaism". He understood Jesus' universal message, a new wineskin that would stretch beyond the religious and cultural confines of Palestine. The anger of the Pharisees, their fulminating frustration, and taking offense at Jesus' words, were some of the first stretch marks that would culminate in crucifixion in the short term, and the Gospel reaching the broader world in the long term.

Matthew's book can be analyzed in three main divisions:

1. Jesus' early life (cc.1,2).

2. Jesus in the Galilee (cc.3-18).

3. Jesus in Judea and Jerusalem (including his crucifixion and resurrection) (cc.19-28).

It is not an exhaustive record of Jesus' life, but (as is the case with the other gospels) a mere taste of the myriad acts and teachings of Christ. Matthew's fellow disciple put it well, "Jesus did many other things… If every one of them were written down, I suppose that even the whole world would not have room for the books that would be written" (Jn. 21:25).

THE STORY BEGINS 1:1–4:25

Jesus' Ancestors 1:1–17

Nobody enjoys reading genealogies. That is, unless you're a genealogist! The Bible has several, and most of us, when confronted by one, tend to roll our eyes and press the delete button. It seems irrelevant. But, in Jesus' day, genealogies were taken with great seriousness. A genealogy was seen as a pedigree. It proved purity of lineage. Jesus' culture, of course, was Jewish, and no one could call himself/herself a "Jew" if there was any foreign blood in their veins. The "Chosen People" had chosen DNA. They were exclusive.

What's more, with the critical component of religious observance in Jewish culture, those who served them spiritually, the priests, had to have an unbroken DNA record right back to the first priest, Moses' brother Aaron. And the priest's wife had to have pure Jewish blood at least five generations back. The priests had to prove their acceptability as God's servants by this exacting physical and spiritual rigor. Nothing else would do. Indeed, Jerusalem's ruling council of seventy elders, the "Sanhedrin" made sure of it. They kept and assiduously checked the genealogical records. There was no "gray area" when it came to being a Jew. Interestingly, in modern Israel there is a very strict adherence to pedigree in the Ministry of Immigration. If you arrive at Ben Gurion Airport in Tel Aviv with papers proving your Jewish heritage, you are given citizenship immediately... It was founded as a Jewish state and Israel works hard at keeping the "bloodlines" pure. But, no papers – no citizenship. Case closed. Appeal as much as you have energy for, to the Ministries of Immigration and Interior, but you'll lose. A pedigree is a pedigree.

This emphasis on genealogical purity was even harsher when it came to the centuries-long Jewish expectation of a future messiah. His pedigree had to go back all the way to Abraham, and more specifically, he had to be a "son of David". This is why Matthew starts his genealogy of Jesus with, "Abraham was the father of Isaac..." Messiah's family history had to be built on this exclusive bedrock.

It is surprising to the modern reader to discover in doing a little historical study that most people in Jesus' day were illiterate. There were many scrolls in the synagogues and courts of law, but no books, as we know them today. And, all of those religious and legal works were written and copied by *hand*. So, when a rabbi taught there were few, if any, note-takers. Learning was done by memorization.

This is why Matthew's genealogy of Jesus is recorded in three groups of fourteen people each. Each group of fourteen is a summary, and they're listed in orderly fashion to assist memorization. The theologians call this literary device a "mnemonic".

So, the first group of fourteen traces Jesus' genealogical history from Abraham to King David (vv.1-6). The second moves from David to the Babylonian exile (vv.7-11). And the third progresses from Babylon to "Jesus who is called Messiah" (vv.12-16). And that is Matthew's point precisely – Jesus is Messiah, child of Abraham, Son of David, Son of God.

This critical heritage was of huge import to later biblical writers. Listen to Peter, as he speaks to thousands in Jerusalem on the Day of Pentecost in Acts 2:29-36:

> *"Fellow Israelites, I can tell you confidently that the patriarch*
> *David died and was buried, and his tomb is here to this day. But*
> *he was a prophet and knew that God had promised him on oath*
> *that he would place one of his descendants on the throne. Seeing*
> *what was to come, he spoke of the resurrection of the Messiah, that*
> *he was not abandoned to the realm of the dead nor did his body*
> *see decay. God has raised this Jesus to life, and we are all witnesses*
> *of it… Therefore let all Israel be assured of this: God has made this*
> *Jesus, whom you crucified, both Lord and Messiah."*

Or, Paul, in Romans 1:2-4, where he refers to,

> *"the gospel he (God) promised beforehand through his prophets*
> *in the Holy Scriptures regarding his Son who as to his earthly*
> *life was a descendant of David, and who through the Spirit of*
> *holiness was appointed the Son of God in power…"*

Then there's John in the Revelation, 22:16, where Jesus says,

*"I, Jesus... am the Root and Offspring of David
and the bright Morning Star."*

But the common people, those illiterate, impressionable laborers, farmers, and shop-keepers, also had their say:

*"Could this be the Son of David?" (Mt. 12:23).
"A Canaanite woman from that vicinity came to him, crying out,
'Lord, Son of David, have mercy on me!'" (Mt. 15:22).*

Perhaps the ultimate declaration, albeit not from the apostles, nor the people, was the voice of the demonic spirits, no better illustrated than by Luke 4:33, 34:

*"In the synagogue there was a man possessed by a demon,
an impure spirit. He cried out at the top of his voice, 'Go away!
What do you want with us Jesus of Nazareth? Have you
come to destroy us? I know who you are – the Holy One of God!'"*

This is what Matthew wants to stress – Jesus is Son of Abraham, Son of David, Son of Man, Son of God. He *is* the Messiah. Thus the genealogy.

But, before moving on, there is something powerfully ironic in this genealogy. In contradistinction to almost all other Jewish records, Matthew's includes women! Here are their stories.

In Genesis 19:30-38 we read about Lot's daughters. Lot, Abraham's nephew, had settled in Sodom, which at that time was a fertile valley. The moral climate of Sodom was sexually out of control, and there was a decided hedonism characterized by pride, gluttony, laziness, and the neglect of the poor (Ez. 16:49). God decided to destroy it, but gave Lot and his family angelic warning. He, his wife, and daughters fled. While camping in a cave in the mountains outside of a small town called

Zoar, something happened that greatly offends modern sensibilities. Lot's daughters slept with their father.

Why? Well, for one thing women in that day found their value in their capacity to bear and raise children (sons especially). Here Lot's daughters were, stuck in a cave, with the whole world (as they thought it) destroyed. They did not want the human race to end with them. So, since their father was the only living male, they chose a deliberate and "practical" course of action. This had nothing to do with sexual pleasure. It was all about keeping the race alive.

As it turned out, both became pregnant, and bore two future enemies of Israel – Moab (Moabites) and Ben-Ammi (Ammonites).

In Ge. 38:1-3 the narrative of Judah and Tamar is written. Judah was the fourth-born to Jacob's first wife Leah. He was the "father" of the future Israelites who later took on his name to describe their territory – the southern kingdom of Judah – and their national/ethnic designation: "Jews". As you read the Genesis account you realize that this story summarizes events over the course of 15-20 years. It reads like a soap-opera.

Judah's era was what modern Israelis refer to as "meyode primitivi" (very primitive). It was a raw time of battles between ethnic clans, ongoing struggles with health and nature, short life-spans, and more sorrow than joy. Rape and pillage were common, as was the view of women as sex-objects and wombs for sons. They had the status of prized animals in many cases. Sexual morality had faint profile. It was a man's world, and it was the strong man who prevailed.

Judah was such a man. He ruled his household with inviolable authority. What he wanted he got. What he commanded was obeyed. His word was his will. In this account we read about his marriage to a Canaanite woman, daughter of a man named Shua. She gave Judah three sons, Er, Onan, and Shelah. There appears to have been a gap of several years between the last two.

Judah married Er to a young Canaanite woman named Tamar. Their marriage was short-lived. Er died. So Judah ordered his next son, Onan to have sex with Tamar in order "to raise up offspring for your brother." This was what we know as "levirate marriage" (more on that later). Onan complied with his father's command but not fully. Whenever he ejaculated he withdrew ("coitus interruptus") and "spilled his semen on the ground." He "knew the child would not be his." We're told, "what he did was wicked in the Lord's sight", and so God is credited with his death.

So the patriarch consigns Tamar to widowhood – a fate worse than death in that culture – and tells her to wait until Shelah is old enough to father children. Tamar submits to Judah's instruction and goes home, disgraced, to live with her parents.

Shortly thereafter Judah himself is widowed. Then, after the mourning period, he sets out to find his workers who are shearing his sheep. Tamar hears that her father-in-law is on the road. She quickly discards her widow's garments, dresses as a prostitute, and intercepts him. He propositions her. She accepts, but demands a "pledge" or "IOU" that will guarantee Judah's compliance in sending her a "goat" for payment. He gives her his "seal and its cord", and the "staff in his hand". This was quite extravagant – It would be like surrendering your driver's license and credit cards. Judah was already awash in guilt, apparently.

A few months later Judah is told, "Your daughter-in-law Tamar is guilty of prostitution and as a result she is now pregnant." Judah responds angrily, "Bring her out and have her burned to death!" When she is confronted she coolly replies, "I am pregnant by the man who owns these" and she produces the seal and staff of Judah. Judah embarrassed, replies, "She is more righteous than I, since I wouldn't give her my son." Tamar, exonerated, gives birth to twins Perez and Zerah. Perez becomes a progenitor of the kings of Judah. Truly, "God moves in mysterious ways."

Then there's the story of Ruth. An entire, but brief, book of the Old Testament tells us about her. A Jewish man Elimelek ("My God is king") with his wife Naomi ("Pleasant") migrate from Bethlehem to the region of Moab because of a famine. In Moab, shortly after, Elimelek dies. His widow is left with two sons and both marry Moabite women one of whom is Ruth. About ten years later both sons die leaving Naomi, Ruth and Orpah without male protection. The Bethlehem famine ends and Naomi decides to go back to her hometown and extended family. Orpah stays in Moab, but Ruth determines to accompany her and care for her.

It's at this point that Ruth, resisting Naomi's entreaties to stay with her own Moabite people, makes the timeless statement: "Don't urge me to leave you or to turn back from you. Where you go I will go, and where you stay I will stay. Your people will be my people and your God my God. Where you die I will die and there I will be buried. May the Lord deal with me, be it ever so severely, if even death separates you and me" (Ru. 1:16,17). So the two of them return to Bethlehem, Naomi changing her name to "Mara" ("bitter"), "Call me Mara, because the Almighty has made my life very bitter. I went away full but the Lord has brought me back empty" (1:20, 21).

As it turns out (read Ruth for the fun, romantic account) Ruth marries Naomi's wealthy relative Boaz. It's a scandal because Ruth is a foreigner. Moab (descended from one of Lot's daughters) is an enemy, "unclean", an alien. But Boaz marries her nonetheless, and becomes the protector, the "kinsman redeemer" for Naomi and Ruth. Most importantly, however, the scripture tells us that Ruth bears a son to Boaz and, Naomi took the child in her arms and cared for him. The women living there said, 'Naomi has a son!' And they named him Obed. He was the father of Jesse, the father of David. Then harking back to Judah and Tamar's son Perez, the Bible says,

"This then, is the family line of Perez:
Perez was the father of Hezron,
Hezron the father of Ram,
Ram the father of Amminadab,
Amminadab the father of Nahshon
Nahshon the father of Salmon,
Salmon the father of Boaz,
Boaz the father of Obed,
Obed the father of Jesse,
and Jesse the father of David." (Ru. 4:18-22)

And, as Matthew's genealogy tells us, King David became the ancestral father of Jesus.

And, as Matthew's genealogy tells us, King David became the ancestral father of Jesus.

Then, there is another woman to consider. Bathsheba was a Hittite woman, wife of Uriah one of King David's military leaders. While Uriah was on duty, David seduced Bathsheba, then had Uriah killed. To maintain whatever honor David could have salvaged from such a sinful, tawdry act, he married Bathsheba. She eventually gave birth to King Solomon. And wonder of wonders, she is listed as one of Jesus' progenitors!

So, Matthew's genealogy includes four non-Jewish "Mothers of Messiah". Absolutely astonishing for the culture and messianic expectation of the time. But, there are two more! A prostitute and a virgin.

The prostitute was the Canaanite woman, Rahab, who aided two Israelite spies in the well-known Jericho story (Joshua ch.2). It is conjectured by some biblical historians that Salmon may have been one of those two Israelite spies. The fact that she is mentioned in Ja. 2:25 and He.11:31 suggests that her profile was very much alive in Matthew's day. Interestingly, rabbinic legend portrays eight prophets, including Jeremiah and his scribe Baruch, among her descendants. Nevertheless, Matthew includes her in Jesus' pedigree as great-great-great grandmother of King David.

And the virgin? Well, there's only one – Mary, the unmarried but betrothed mother of Jesus. Only fourteen or fifteen years of age at the time of her "visitation" by the angel Gabriel, she stands out as the singularly most famous and revered woman in history. She is the last of six "mothers of Messiah": Lot's daughter, Tamar, Rahab, Ruth, Bathsheba, Mary. Such an unlikely sextet!

Before moving on, just a word about "levirate marriage".

In De. 25:5-10 we read this:

"If brothers are living together and one of them dies without a son his widow must not marry outside the family. Her husband's brother shall take her and marry her and fulfill the duty of a brother-in-law to her. The first son she bears shall carry on the name of the dead brother so that his name will not be blotted out from Israel.

"However, if a man does not want to marry his brother's wife, she shall go to the elders at the town gate and say, 'My husband's brother refuses to carry on his brother's name in Israel. He will not fulfill the duty of a brother-in-law to me.' Then the elders of his town shall summon him and talk to him. If he persists in saying, 'I do not want to marry her,' his brother's widow shall go up to him in the presence of the elders, take off one of his sandals, spit in his face and say, 'This is what is done to the man who will not build up his brother's family line.' That man's line shall be known in Israel as The Family of the Unsandled."

The word "levir", from the Latin "brother-in-law", is derived from the Hebrew, "have". At that time in history, not just the Israelites, but many other ethnic peoples believed that the only form of "immortality" a man would have would be "patrilineal" succession and bequeathing of property to a son. A man who died without a son was summarily excised from memory. So his brother was expected to marry his brother's widow and give her a son who would bear the departed brother's name and inherit his property.

The Book of Ruth sees the custom of levirate marriage in very flexible terms. When the closest male relative refuses to "redeem" Naomi's property, her next-in-line kinsman, Boaz, chooses to do so. And he gives Naomi a son by marrying her daughter-in-law Ruth (Naomi being too old to become pregnant). In this way Boaz becomes "Kinsman Redeemer" and fulfills the levirate duty as well. The whole point, of course, was lineage and inheritance – to say nothing of genealogy.

JESUS' EARLY LIFE 1:18–2:23

Jesus' Birth 1:18–25

Matthew's account of Jesus' birth is blunt and to the point, lacking Luke's beguiling detail. Matthew seems to rush into the messianic narrative, impatient to recount Jesus' powerful, earth-shaking ministry. So he summarizes the story of the incarnation. But the words he does use are charged with meaning.

The word Matthew employs to depict Joseph and Mary's marital status is "betrothed" or "engaged" in the Greek. The NIV translates it as "pledged". We modern readers need a little help with this, because Joseph is referred to as Mary's "husband", not "fiancé".

In those days marriages were arranged by the parents and/or a matchmaker. From her earliest memory Mary would have known that Joseph was her intended husband. Their "betrothal" was totally binding, and could be broken only by death or "divorce". When the day came where within a year she would be married she would call Joseph her "husband" and he would call Mary his "wife". But, there would be no sexual union until he "took her into his house" after that twelve-month period. If, on the other hand, a man were marrying a widow, that trial period was reduced to one month.

So, even though Joseph and Mary were not yet married, Matthew tells us in v.19, "Because Joseph her husband was faithful to the law, and yet did not want to expose her to public disgrace, he had in mind to divorce her quietly."

Joseph was "law-abiding", a righteous man. He was also kind. He didn't ask questions or confront Mary with her extra-marital pregnancy. He simply decided to protect her dignity and privately divorce her. Impressive.

We don't know how far the divorce proceedings had progressed, but at some time in the process, "an angel of the Lord appeared to him in a dream and said, 'Joseph, son of David, do not be afraid to take Mary home as your wife, because what is conceived in her is from the Holy Spirit.'" The angel goes on to say, "She will give birth to a son, and you are to give him the name Jesus, because he will save his people from their sins." No other man in history had or has received such a message. It's amazing, indeed a testament to Joseph's spiritual fine-tuning, that he accepted this dream-word uncritically.

"From the Holy Spirit" are the key words. The angelic messenger announced a supernatural creation of life. Just as the Almighty had called the universe into existence, He was now calling the Redeemer of that fallen space-time created order into being here on planet Earth. And, God being God, this creative act was entirely within his capacity to do.

Only a supernatural act could qualify the developing embryo to be called "Immanuel" (v.23), "God with us", or as one rabbi put it, "God tabernacled with us." The Apostle John, one of Matthew's fellow disciples of Jesus, put it this way, "The Word became flesh and made his dwelling among us." (Jn. 1:14). This miraculously conceived baby was to become "God made flesh".

> *Only a supernatural act*
> *could qualify the developing*
> *embryo to be called "Immanuel",*
> *"God with us".*

Then, without any nativity narrative, Matthew hastily tells us the noble Joseph abstained from sex with his wife until she "gave birth to a son" named "Jesus".

The Wise Men 2:1–12

There are four points of interest in these twelve verses: Bethlehem, the Wisemen (or "Magi"), the Star, and Herod the Great.

Bethlehem literally means "house of bread". In Micah 5:2 the prophet adds "Ephratah" to Bethlehem which reads, "House of Bread twice blessed". Perhaps Micah, under the inspiration of the Holy Spirit, was thinking of the double blessing in terms of Bethlehem being not only "the city of David" (1Sa. 16:1; 17:12, 20:6), but also the birthplace of Israel's Messiah. In most messianic writing, Bethlehem was the expected birthplace of David's "anointed" son, so Micah writes in that tradition. We know from scripture that Jacob buried Rachel near Bethlehem (Ge. 35:19,20; 48:7) – indeed "Ramat Rachel" is now a thriving neighborhood on the outskirts of Jerusalem with Rachel's tomb still very much in evidence. And, we also know that Ruth and Boaz lived there (Ru. 1:22). It was, and is, a small town, situated on low lying hills, surrounded by steep valleys on the north, and wide plains on the east. Its hills are scored with cave-pocked fertile terraces. Although sleepy-looking, Bethlehem "breathes" with history and messianic significance.

Traditionally the Magi are believed to have been Medes from Medea. This territory, the ancient name for Northwest Iran, covers most of what we know today as Azerbaijan and Kurdistan. Magi were mainly a tribe of priests, but they have also been seen in a multitude of roles as philosophers, teachers, holy men, doctors, soothsayers, interpreters of dreams, truth seekers, and astrologers. As astrologers, especially, they believed that a "star" could be the "counterpart" or "angel" ("fravashi") of a great ruler. Perhaps they were acquainted with the Jewish expectation that the Messiah would be identified by a "star out of Jacob" (Nu. 24:17). They were driven by astrological mystery and eschatological hope. We don't know how many made the long trek to Bethlehem, but the three gifts presented to Jesus suggest there were three.

Then there's the star. There have been many attempts to explain this phenomenal aberration. Some commentators refer to Halley's comet (11 BC), or to the conjunction of Saturn and Jupiter (7 BC). Others talk of the Egyptian "dog star" (Sirius) that rose at sunrise.

My view on the star is heavily influenced by v.10, "When they saw the star they were overjoyed", or as the KJV puts it, "When they saw the star, they rejoiced with exceeding great joy." The Greek word for "exceeding" is "sphodia" which means "excessive" or "violent". Why the excess of joy? After all this "star" had accompanied them for over a year of travel. Could it be that once it led the Magi to Jerusalem, it dimmed, or left them altogether? If it did disappear they would have been both perplexed and disturbed. They hadn't seen the new "king" yet. Was the journey and the expense in vain?

The fact that it reappeared to lead them from Jerusalem to Bethlehem (a mere 5 miles) indicates that it may have been a bright light only hundreds of feet above and in front of them. Halley's Comet or Saturn and Jupiter would never be able to direct anybody for such a short distance. It may have been a supernatural phenomenon like the "pillar of cloud by day" and the "pillar of fire by night" (Ex. 13:21) that led the children of Israel out of Egypt to the Promised Land. After all, if God is God, the supernatural is his stock-in-trade.

The Jewish messianic hope, four hundred years "back-burnered" by prophetic silence, was beginning to percolate again.

And, to add a bit of historical context, at that time there was a synergy of both religious and secular hope, or expectation, that a kingly figure would emerge from somewhere in the Mediterranean basin and rule the world. The Jewish messianic hope, four hundred years "back-burnered" by prophetic silence, was beginning to percolate again. Josephus, the Jewish historian, wrote: "about that time one from their country should become governor of the habitable earth." And the Roman historians Suetonius and Tacitus also bear witness to this Mediterranean-centric hope for universal reign. It was an eschatological "perfect storm".

Enter Herod. Called "the Great" because he was a great builder, he was nonetheless one of the most pathetic persons of his day. For one

THE GOSPEL OF MATTHEW

thing he was desperately insecure. Much of this was rooted in his "half-breed" status, half Jew and half Idumean. He had Edomite blood in his veins. As such he was looked down upon by his Jewish subjects. And, as is often the case, his insecurity fed a troubling paranoia. In old age he became a "murderous old man" murdering his wife Mariamne, her mother Alexandra, three of his sons: Antipater, Alexander, Aristobulus, all seventy of the Sanhedrin, three hundred court officers, and countless others. The Roman Emperor Augustus said it was safer to be Herod's pig than Herod's son. Appointed governor in 47 BC, he became "king" in 40 BC and reigned until 4 BC. He was the only Roman ruler of Palestine to keep the peace. Part of his success was due, no doubt, to his generous care of the poor. But it was he who in the Christmas story ordered "the slaughter of the innocents" in Bethlehem.

Egypt 2:13–15

This is the second time an angel gave instructions to Joseph. As husband and protector of Mary and the baby, he was told to "take the child and his mother and escape to Egypt." This was to avoid Herod's murderous intent.

We read a couple of sentences like this and tend to "watch" the action like we do a movie. The scenes shift from moment to moment, from place to place, and sometimes from time zone to time zone in the flash of an editor's cut. But, we need to slow down here. It takes at least twelve hours to drive from Tel Aviv to Alexandria. (Joseph's likely destination would not only take days of walking, but would require amazing fortitude.)

Egypt was a haven for Jews over the centuries. Alexandria alone housed about one million Jews in the first century. And every town and village in Egypt had Jewish citizens. In Egypt a Jewish immigrant would find synagogues, markets, housing, and food that provided a seamless transition. Ironically, a Jew could feel "at home" in Egypt. Yes, the Exodus had been about escape from Egypt, "out of Egypt I called my son" (Ho. 11:1), but Matthew applies that ancient word to what was happening with the Christ-child. With his parents he would emigrate to Egypt and later migrate back to Palestine. For a time, Egypt was the Messiah's protector.

Infanticide 2:16–18

It's surprising that Herod's paranoia had not fuelled more efficient "intelligence gathering", in that he sent no police with the Magi, nor did he commission any of his officials to "follow the star" to Bethlehem. He simply asked the magi to let him know once they had found the baby king. But, in his rage at being deceived by the Magi, his paranoia and cruelty kicks into gear and he orders every male child of two years or under in the Bethlehem region to be killed. None of our Christmas traditions include this unspeakable tragedy. We focus on the one baby. We forget the others.

Matthew captures the sorrow and heartbreak of the mothers by quoting Jeremiah 31:15:

> *"A voice is heard in Ramah,*
> *weeping and great mourning,*
> *Rachel weeping for her children*
> *and refusing to be comforted,*
> *because they are no more."*

Rachel, of course, was the much-loved second wife of Jacob, and the mother of Joseph and Benjamin. One of Joseph's sons was named Ephraim, and Ramah, centuries later, was an Ephraimite town not far from Jerusalem. When Jeremiah penned these words he was probably thinking of Israel being exiled to Babylon, but Matthew sees a proper double meaning. The exalted sounds of the angelic announcement of Jesus' birth is followed a year or so later by the wailing of the bereaved. A stark juxtaposition to say the least.

Egypt to Nazareth 2:19–23

Joseph, like his patriarchal namesake, was a "dreamer". Here in these four verses of scripture we read of a third, then a fourth, directive dream Joseph receives from the Lord. The third instructs him to go back to Israel. The fourth moves him and his young family on to the region of the Lower Galilee to a town called Nazareth. It was here that Jesus lived the next thirty years of his life, working as a carpenter side-by-side with his mentor, Joseph. We can only imagine the conversations, the family meals, the fellowship with friends and neighbors, that helped shape the emerging Messiah.

Nazareth was, and in many ways still is, an inconsequential, nondescript town. Situated on a range of hills overlooking the Jezreel Valley, its only distinction was its proximity to international trade routes. It was a frontier town, out of the mainstream, and marked with a peculiar accent. Indeed Nazareth and Nazarenes were looked on with scorn by the Jewish world to the south of them. "Can anything good come out of Nazareth?" was a common slight. So even the moniker "Jesus of Nazareth" had a certain innuendo – yes he was from Nazareth, but he was also "from Nazareth", not to be taken seriously. (It took more than a bit of getting used to being called "Notzrim" when I and my family first moved to Jerusalem in 1981. I was often introduced by my Israeli friends to others as a "Notzri" (Christian). Not much good out of that town. I always felt slightly diminished). Nevertheless that's where Jesus grew up, and that's what makes Nazareth a name of honor to this day. He was "called a Nazarene".

JOHN THE BAPTIST 3:1–12

Jesus' cousin John (the "Baptist" as he became known) was just a few months older and unlike Jesus had spent most of his young adult life in the desert. In fact he had become a bit of a "wild man" in the sense that his clothing, diet, and ministry were offensive to city dwellers. Smelling like the camel whose hair he had fashioned into a shirt, eating whatever he could find ("locusts and wild honey"), and preaching cutting sermons against priests, tax-collectors, and soldiers, he seemed a throwback to the prophets of Israel's ancient history.

Calling to the city and town folk to join him in the desert he baptized them in the Jordan River, a symbol of the "cleansing" of repentance. But, when Pharisees, Sadducees, tax-collectors, and soldiers came to hear him, he excoriated them referring to them as snakes fleeing a grassfire. Why was he so hard on them? For one, they were collaborators with the Roman occupiers. The priestly class (Pharisees and Sadducees) had compromised temple worship, the tax-collectors were working for the occupiers (and gouging their own people with surcharges), and the soldiers were enforcing occupation law (although some commentators see them as insurgents who because of their poor pay were forcing their own people to support them). John and Jesus ministered in a tumultuous time. The people's hopes for a peaceful, triumphal messianic era were all but dashed, and all they could expect was subjugation by foreign powers. They grumbled and rumbled. Chaos was a heartbeat away.

John and Jesus ministered in a tumultuous time.

Indeed, just a few kilometers from John's baptismal site, was a hermitic sect called the "Essenes". They lived in a settlement built among the mountains bordering the southwest shore of the Dead Sea. Totally ascetic, they lived a harsh lifestyle reflective of their sun-scorched environment, studying the ancient Hebrew texts of the Torah and writing end-time treatises. A simple diet, constant prayers, and stringent discipline were matters of course. So too were daily baptisms (or "mikvot"), ceremonial immersions in water they collected during winter storms and preserved in cisterns. Little wonder many commentators see John the Baptist as one of these desert holy men.

For sure his lifestyle was similar to theirs. And his message had parallel aspects as well. These Essenes saw themselves as "end-time" heralds of a coming war between "the Sons of Darkness and the Sons of Light". The end was near. Their urgent task was to call people out of the morally bankrupt towns and cities to become cleansed soldiers in the last battle.

Like the Essenes, John preached "The Kingdom of Heaven has come near", or, "is at hand". Repentance was not just a cleansing from past sins, but a preparation for the coming kingdom. And part of that preparation was to "prepare the way for the Lord". In ancient times work crews toiled sometimes for weeks in the hot sun, smoothing out a path on the stony ground for the chariots and carriages of a royal procession as a king or emperor made a "state visit". In John's view the king was coming.

The king needed a "path prepared". So John set about preparing that path. His message was essentially this:

1. Repent!

2. No excuses – even the claim of Abrahamic pedigree is not enough.

3. Demonstrate your repentance through acts of righteousness.

4. Don't delay – "the axe is already at the root of the trees".

5. The king is coming, and his advent will be terrible for those who have not been prepared.

"He will baptize you with the Holy Ghost…", signifying supernatural cleansing, and "with fire", which will consume all the unrighteous and unjust "chaff" smothering Israel. The "threshing floor" will be swept clean. This king will play hardball.

JESUS' EARLY MINISTRY 3:13–4:25

Jesus' Baptism

The big question here is "Why?". Why would the sinless Son of God intentionally submit to John's baptism of repentance? Some commentators suggest it betrayed a dawning awareness on Jesus' part that he was special. Others say he did so because he was anticipating a "word from Heaven". Still others suggest he began his public ministry by taking on the sins of mankind (thus the need for baptism) and ended it by dying for those sins. Even John himself wonders "Why?". He tried to stop Jesus with "I need to be baptized by you." (The word "need" in the Greek suggests a "gap" – thus, "There is a gap in my ministry. It's not complete"). Regardless, the mystery is only partially solved by Jesus' response, "It is proper for us to fulfill all righteousness." What does he mean by that?

In the Old Testament scriptures the word for righteousness is "zedek" or "tzadkah". It refers to the fulfillment of mankind's relationship with God. As such it is both a present and an ongoing process that will see fulfillment ultimately in heaven. Righteousness is a space/time characteristic of those who have an "eternal" worldview. Jesus took on space/time limitations in the incarnation. In that context he saw himself as "Son of Man". As such he must "fulfill" his relationship with the Father. He knew the Father was at work in John's "fore-running" ministry. He also knew he was about to be severely tested by Satan. The baptism was synchronous with a process that would ultimately result in the cross and an empty tomb.

God's pleasure at Jesus' submission to John's baptism was immediately expressed by the descent of "the Spirit of God" alighting on Jesus like a "dove", with the loving assertion, "This is my Son whom I love; with him I am well pleased." There is an interesting nuance to the word "this" in the Greek. It suggests "this one". It's as though the Spirit saw two outstanding men standing in the Jordan, but He put his "finger" on Jesus: "This is the one. Of the two he is the One." Jesus was to live a singular life from that point on.

Jesus Tested in the Wilderness 4:1–11

Immediately after the Father had singled Jesus out as his son, Jesus was "led by the Spirit" into the wilderness for forty days of testing. This is often referred to as the "temptation" but the Greek suggests "testing". Whereas "temptation" bears the nuance of being tempted to sin, "testing" possesses a more positive tone. Jesus was, then and always, sinless. The point of the testing here was his "new" status as "my Son". Satan hoped to capitalize on any deep-seated insecurity that Jesus might have about his exalted position (thus, the "*if* you are the Son of God"). Satan, of course, wasted his breath.

Satan's testing was double-pronged. He tried not only to underscore Jesus' (non-existent) insecurity but also to encourage him to misuse his power and rights as "Son of God". So he pushed Jesus in three directions:

1. Use your power to meet your physical needs.

2. Force God's hand to stop a suicidal leap from the "pinnacle of the temple" thereby setting yourself up as a force (and even "tempting" the Father to send protective angels).

3. Avoid the knobby little hill called "Calvary" and short-cut your way to political dominance in the world – a kingdom without a cross.

Satan's testing was double-pronged.

Jesus met each of these diabolical ideas with scripture, all from Deuteronomy chapters 6-8. Satan even quoted scripture himself (Ps. 91:11,12)! But the battle was won even before it began. Satan slunk away, defeated. Jesus was now ready to preach.

Jesus' Ministry Begins 4:12–25

John the Baptist's imprisonment precipitated Jesus' "withdrawal" from Nazareth to Capernaum in the Galilee. The region was known as "the Galilee of the Gentiles", looked down upon by the citizens of Judea, but critical to international trade as it was on the trade route between Egypt and Damascus (called "the Way of the Sea"). As such it was cosmopolitan and alive with the bustle of camel caravans and the colorful languages and fashions of the outside world. For Jesus this was a critical move

– he left his provincial home town Nazareth and established "worldly" Capernaum as his ministry base – as it was often said, "the world comes through Galilee". Jesus placed his hand on the pulse of the world's heart-beat, and brought Good News to the people.

Jesus had a succinct message, "Repent for the Kingdom of Heaven has come near." This was a novel message for the Gentiles, but had a familiar ring for any Jewish person. Whenever a Jew recited the "Great Shema" ("Hear O Israel, the Lord our God, the Lord is One") he took upon himself the "yoke of the kingdom" (De. 6:4-9; 11:13-21; Nu. 15:37-41). This confession of faith, recited every Sabbath in the synagogues of Judah, was pregnant with hope, a hope of a time when Israel's messiah would rule the world from Jerusalem. Even though they were under the yoke of Rome they dreamed of a day when another yoke, the yoke of freedom, would see them working with Messiah to bring righteousness and justice to the world.

The First Disciples 4:18–22

Like his cousin John, Jesus too had need of followers, or "disciples". These were not "hangers-on" but leaders-in-the-making. Jesus knew that unlikely as they were they would nonetheless change the world. But, they certainly didn't appear to be world changers. Indeed, the first four were two pairs of brothers, all of them fishermen. And, if the catch in "Kinneret" (Sea of Galilee) was like it is today, they were experts in catching sardines! There is no mention of their qualifications, education, or predisposition to spiritual matters. They were just "there" and Jesus said, "Follow me". So Simon, Andrew, James, and John dropped everything and did just that – "immediately", says Matthew. Amazing! Could it be that the word had spread about the dove and voice from heaven a few weeks previously at Jesus' baptism? Or was it that John the Baptist's disciples had told their acquaintances that Jesus was the next big thing? We don't know. All we do know is that Jesus' invitation was irresistible.

The DNA of Jesus' Ministry 4:23–25

The Galilee provided a doorway to the greater Roman province of Syria. Its territory essentially comprised northern Palestine, bounded by the Jordan River on the east, the Mediterranean ocean on the west, and the mountains of Lebanon on the north. From Mount Hermon, 10,000 feet above sea level in the north, the "upper Galilee" descended in plains and marshland ("Lake Hula") to the "lower Galilee" four-hundred feet below sea level where the "Sea of Galilee" sat in resplendent beauty. Then, as it descended further, following the course of the Jordan (the "Down-rusher"), it gave way to the Jordan Valley, and ultimately the Dead Sea, fifteen-hundred feet below sea level. The Galilee of Jesus' time was essentially 40 miles from north to south, and 25 miles east to west. Heavily treed, well watered with streams from the northern mountains, and fertile with black volcanic soil, it was a great exporter of olive oil, vegetables, and fish. Cut off from Jerusalem by Samaria, it stood culturally alone, producing rugged farmers, fishermen, and tradesmen – the "salt of the earth" laborers who spoke with a rich accent, seemingly unperturbed by their alienation from the Jewish city-dwellers in Jerusalem. When it was asked, "Can anything good come out of Nazareth?", those elite urbanites might just as well have asked, "Can anything good come out of Galilee?" The Galileans ignored this snobbery and kept fishing.

As Jesus called disciples to follow him, he concurrently began to minister to the needs of the Galileans. He "proclaimed the Good News of the Kingdom" by preaching and teaching in the synagogues, and he demonstrated the Good News by healing the sick.

The synagogues were a natural place for Jesus to preach and teach. Brought up with a home synagogue in Nazareth, he was culturally tuned to local synagogues as centers of worship, education, and the administration of civil law. They were like local town halls, schools, and religious community centers. Most towns had several. Jerusalem in Jesus' time had close to five hundred. As a preacher Jesus was uncompromising in announcing the inevitability of the Kingdom of Heaven. As a teacher he expounded on the meaning and significance of that inevitability. And, as a healer, he championed deliverance from suffering. Little wonder he drew crowds.

The Sermon on the Mount 5:1–7:29

The "Mount of Beatitudes" provides one of the most beautiful vistas in all of Israel. Beginning at the northern shore of the Sea of Galilee, it slopes upward to a height about four hundred feet above the water. It is called a "mountain" but in fact is one of several foothills leading from the "Lower Galilee" to the "Upper Galilee", culminating about thirty miles to the north in majestic Mount Hermon, ten thousand feet above sea level. Standing at the top of this storied foothill you look down on an awesome sight. Immediately below is Capernaum and Tabgha (where Jesus multiplied the loaves and fish) with the entire expanse of the Sea of Galilee glittering in the sunlight. From this prospect you see why the Israelis call the lake "Kinneret", for it truly is harp-shaped. About twelve miles long and six wide, the lake is bordered by the mighty Golan Heights on the east, and the "Horns of Hittim", a towering outcropping of jagged heights, on the west. Just a bit south of the Hittim horns is Tiberias, one of Israel's four "sacred" cities. This is where much of the Talmud was written over the course of hundreds of years. Immediately on the right, about five kilometers away and one hundred meters higher than where you're standing, is the ancient town of Safat, another of Israel's sacred cities, the home of the "Kabalah", the handbook of ancient Jewish mysticism. Today it's a favorite Jewish tourist destination, rife with artists' studios, and colorful old synagogues.

There are two constructions on the crown of the Mount: one is a Catholic nunnery, the other a beautiful chapel built with funds supplied by the Italian dictator Benito Mussolini. No one knows why he built it, but it may have been an effort to leave a "good taste" with the historical record of his life. Sweeping down the hill to the very edge of the lake is a citrus orchard redolent with fragrance and peace. Between the mount and Safat on the west, the rocky slope is festooned with luscious green grass (in season) and herds of sheep. The entire setting is idyllic.

Adjacent to the chapel is a small grove of tall eucalyptus trees shading a fascinating outcropping of twelve basalt rocks "placed" in a circle of about thirty feet in diameter. This circle slopes downward with the contour of the mount and looks like the rocks were deliberately placed as some kind of monument. The rocks stick out of the ground at a height of two to three feet. There, in the shade of the eucalyptus trees, I imagine Jesus sitting down, his disciples lounging against the rocks as "lawn chairs", and "opening his mouth" to teach. Such a pastoral picture for the greatest "pastoral" sermon of all time!

The Poor in Spirit v.3

Jesus prioritized the poor. His "mission statement" was Isaiah 61 – "to preach good news to the poor…" (see Lk. 4:16-21). He made it clear that God the Father loves the poor because of their total dependency upon him. What's more, it stood to reason that if "God so loved the world" his love had to begin with the weakest link. Otherwise there would be a material prerequisite for entry into the Kingdom of Heaven. With love for the poor as priority, the Lord precluded any socio-economic barrier to entry. The invitation was "whosoever will may come".

No doubt, as he cast his eyes beyond the reclining disciples he looked at some of the "hangers-on" who had followed them up the hill. The "halt, lame, and blind" would have been there, looking beseechingly at Jesus, hearing his words but impatient for the sermon to end so that he would heal them. Some stared out of empty, hollow eyes, so crippled by poverty that they had hardly made it up the hill. There were widows, orphans, both young and old, and ragged folk in various modes of disrepair. They were the very people Jesus had come to save.

But at the moment his concern was the coaching, the mentoring of his chosen twelve. He makes it clear, however, just in case any of them saw the hangers-on as intruding, that the Gospel was to be preached first and foremost to the desolate.

"Blessed are" is translated by some theologians as, "O The blessedness of…!" The exclamation relates to how God sees those in need. The "blessed" ones live in the heady presence of God's grace and faithfulness. They are on his radar. He knows their names and he is looking out for them. Because of this focus from the Lord they are truly blessed. They are in much greater shape, even in poverty (!), than the rich without God. Those who live beyond the pale of God's grace and faithfulness are to be pitied.

The "blessed" ones live in the heady presence of God's grace and faithfulness.

According to the "Etymological Dictionary" the English word "bless" comes from old English, "bletsian", "to consecrate, make holy" and the Proto-Germanic, "blodison", "to hallow with blood" – originally to sprinkle blood on an altar. Both Latin and Greek words for "bless" indicate a "speaking well of", or "praising". In the Hebrew, "barak" means "to bend the knee", or "worship, praise, or invoke blessings". Over time, the old English "bless" morphed into "bliss" to describe the state of someone who is blessed. So, the ancient preacher who said, "To bless is to bleed," was not far from the mark. He, of course, was applying the meaning to Christ's sacrifice on the cross. For his part, Jesus stresses the blessedness of the poor by declaring that they are privileged citizens in the Kingdom of Heaven. The greatest earthly mansion can't compare.

By the way, I don't see "in spirit" as a qualifier. The fact is that poverty has a huge oppressive impact. It not only dulls the eyes, and depresses the heart, but it wounds the spirit, sometimes to the point where all hope is gone. Abject poverty and buoyant happiness are mutually exclusive. So, when the poor cry out to their maker it's as though their blood cries out from the earth. God's first reflex is to respond with grace and healing. The Kingdom of Heaven awaits.

The Mourners v.4

Here we have what an old theologian called, "a deep doctrine of sin, a high doctrine of joy." St. Paul's, "O wretched man that I am…" is followed by, "I thank God through Jesus Christ our Lord…" (Ro. 7:24,25). Comfort comes to those who mourn.

Jesus is addressing both those who've been bereaved and those whose poverty has driven them to spiritual despair. Whatever the source of the mourning, the sorrowing soul has been driven to the deep. The mourner has "a broken and a contrite heart," which, as we know from scripture, "the Lord will not despise" (Ps. 51:17). The sorrow of repentance is eclipsed by the joy of forgiveness. There is no greater comfort. A crushing weight has been lifted from the soul.

The Meek v.5

I wonder if Jesus was thinking of Psalm 37 as he spoke these words. King David was reflecting on the apparent freedom of the wicked as they prospered with impunity. The godly tend to "fret" (v.1) and resent (v.8) the easy affluence of the evildoers. But David tells the righteous soul to "chill" and be patient. It's only a matter of time (v.10) and the ungodly will perish. The only sustainable way to long-term peace and prosperity is "meekness". The teachable, moldable, righteous and just soul will "inherit the earth" (v.11). The meek will prevail.

Those who Crave Righteousness v.6

Ps. 37 is not alone. Again and again the Old Testament speaks of the short shelf-life of the godless rich, and the long, everlasting future that awaits the virtuous poor. The young virgin Mary captured it in what we now know as "The Magnificat" when she said, "God has filled the hungry with good things, and the rich He has sent empty away" (Lk. 1:53).

The poor are hungry for righteousness. We're talking about a *real* hunger and thirst – a healthy, hearty spiritual appetite. It's something that transcends our predisposition to failure, and even in the grip of moral or spiritual iniquity, there is a deep visceral longing for the highest good. One commentator astutely observed it's like being "haunted by goodness." And, just like our hunger and thirst for food and water has to be satisfied on a daily basis, so too must our spiritual craving. Indeed, our need for righteousness is an indicator of health. Otherwise we are in decline, suffering, as Robert Louis Stevenson put it, "the malady of not wanting." Bring your hunger and thirst to the table, Jesus is saying. There's more than enough to satisfy your deepest longing.

The Merciful v.7

First a word from Shakespeare, and then Jesus' brother James:

> *"The quality of mercy is not strain'd*
> *It droppeth as the gentle rain from Heaven*
> *Upon the place beneath: it is twice blest;*
> *It blesses him that gives and him that takes:*
> *'Tis mightiest in the mightiest: it becomes*
> *The throned monarch better than his crown."*
> —MERCHANT OF VENICE, ACT 4, SC 1

And,

> *"Judgment without mercy will be shown to anyone*
> *who has not been merciful. Mercy triumphs over judgment."*
> —JAMES 2:13

Then there's the old French proverb: "to know all is to forgive all." In the Hebrew the word "hesed" ("mercy") has the nuance of "walking in the other person's shoes." It denotes "pity plus loving action." And, without doubt, as Shakespeare suggests, the merciful have on at least one occasion (if not several) been shown mercy. You receive it, you give it. Self-righteousness and pride are eclipsed by mercy received. The merciful seldom, if ever, judge others.

The merciful seldom, if ever, judge others.

With these words, Jesus proclaimed a counter-cultural view of human relations. In his time the Romans despised pity, and the Stoics dismissed compassion. The Pharisees were strident and grating in their self-righteousness – "Woe to you, teachers of the law and Pharisees, you hypocrites! You give a tenth of your spices – mint, dill, and cumin. But you have neglected the more important matters of the law – justice, mercy and faithfulness... you blind guides!" (Mt. 23:23,24). In their view if you suffered in any way it was because you had sinned. They were very much like "Job's comforters", or "Job's wife". Jesus, unlike them, has a Father who loves to forgive, and he loves those who do likewise.

The Pure in Heart v.8

I was raised on the Canadian prairies, son of a preacher who pastored small town churches. His congregants were subsistence farmers, all poor and semi-literate. My view of church buildings was limited. Most of them weren't even purpose-built houses of worship. They were converted halls, barns, and abandoned store-front buildings. A couple of them even had wood shavings for flooring. So you can imagine my amazement when, years later, I first saw a cathedral.

I was in Toronto on a high-school band trip. During some free time I was walking downtown and came upon St. James Cathedral. I marveled at its beauty, the "frozen poetry of church architecture," as Christopher Wren described it. I noted the large, intricate, but muted windows, and wondered why they were so darkly colored. Then I walked in!

The sanctuary was brilliantly awash in the light bursting through the stained glass. Awesome pictures of Jesus, the disciples, and the saints shone down from above. The contrast between the outside and inside view took my breath away. I had walked into kaleidoscopic brilliance, almost revelatory in its impact. It was stunning.

This "outside-inside" juxtaposition is rather like what Jesus is talking about in this beatitude. For those on the outside God is a study, an object for analysis, an impassive steady structure for muted praise (if any should be required), but not inspiring or even noteworthy. For those on the inside He is a riot of colors, sensory overload, an overwhelming presence casting us on our faces in reverence. These "insiders" are the "pure in heart".

With the pure in heart there is no spiritual astigmatism. They may, like all of us, "see through a glass darkly" (1Co. 13:12), but what they do see they see clearly. Indeed, in Jesus' words, they see God.

Long before Jesus the Psalms expressed the genius of the pure in heart:

"Who may ascend the mountain of the Lord?
Who may stand in his holy place?
The one who has clean hands and a pure heart,
who does not trust in an idol
or swear by a false god." (Ps. 24:3,4)

"Surely God is good to Israel,
to those who are pure in heart." (Ps. 73:1)

"Cleanse me with hyssop, and I will be clean;
wash me, and I will be whiter than snow." (Ps. 51:7)

The pure in heart are free. Free from over-analysis of their faith. Free from lies. Free from secret agendas. Their hearts are singular, unconflicted:

"Unite my heart to fear Thy name." (Ps. 86:11)

The pure in heart "has no desire for falsehood, and has not sworn to a lie" (Ps. 24:4). They are without guile. Little wonder the eyes of their pure hearts "see God".

The Peacemakers v.9

In Israel the standard "Hello" is "Shalom" ("Peace"). The standard "Goodbye" is "Shalom". Ironically, "peace" is not the standard state of the atmosphere in Israel, or anywhere else in the Middle East for that matter. But "shalom" is the heart's cry of the world. Imagine the blessed state of the nations if there were genuine peace! This is why God blesses those of his children who make peace. It is near to his heart.

A peacemaker is proactive. He/she has no time for appeasement. There's no room for passive acquiescence. The peacemaker "makes" peace. And, in most cases, that active effort involves the art of reconciliation. This is what God has done, and is doing through Christ: "For God was pleased to have all his fullness dwell in him, and through him to reconcile to himself all things, whether things on earth or things in heaven, by making peace through his blood, shed on the cross" (Cl. 1:19,20). Indeed, someone who makes peace is doing what God is doing.

In his last supper conversation with his disciples Jesus said, "my peace I give unto you".

The Bible clearly calls Jesus "The Prince of Peace". At his birth the angelic chorus proclaimed "peace on earth", and in his last supper conversation with his disciples Jesus said, "my peace I give unto you" (Jn. 14:27). In the course of his ministry Jesus prioritized the poor – poverty is at the root of so many conflicts, so Jesus, the Prince of Peace, sought to banish it. So must we.

Persecuted because of Righteousness vv. 10–12

Rather than do a word study on "righteousness" (which he could have done), Jesus qualifies its meaning as that which is done "on my account" or "because of me" (v.11b). He is looking ahead and anticipates the push-back the disciples will suffer as they "go into all the world and preach the Gospel." In fact history tells us most of them died martyrs deaths "because of [him]."

They became martyrs not just because of their radical rabbi, but also because of the worldview that he taught and lived. Jesus was all about "the Kingdom of Heaven". This worldview brought with it an unheard of culture, a values "transplant", a collateral uprooting of religiosity, offensive to both Pharisees and Sadducees. It demanded resistance by the established order. It needed to be squashed. So start by squashing the founder and his followers. Jesus knew that the first to be eliminated would be he.

Jesus links persecution "because of me" with "reward in heaven". Make that "great" reward. There are at least two nuances here:

1. Suffering for Jesus does not necessarily bring material gain or comfort. Most, if not all, of those who have died because of their witness for Christ in history did so penniless. This "earth" does not reward saints. "Heaven" does.

2. Reward rejects a mercenary attitude on the one hand, and the obligation of compensating meritorious service ("not by works of righteousness that we have done, but *according to his mercy* he saved us…") on the other hand. The ultimate reward is, and will be, entry into the Father's presence. Any other reward is eclipsed by that ultimate prospect. And, in space and time, God's love is the best reward for anything done in Christ's name.

A Summary Comment

Many years ago I had the honor of interviewing John R. W. Stott for a television show. I brought my copy of his classic, "The Message of the Sermon on the Mount" to the studio. He graciously signed it. As we waited for the crew to make the final lighting adjustments, we talked about the "sermon". I'll never forget his summary of the beatitudes. I can't quote him directly, but this is what I remember of what he said:

The first four beatitudes are about our attitude towards God:
We are poor in spirit, our bankrupt souls are dependent on him;
we mourn the corruption of our fallen nature, but in meekness
offer moldable hearts to the work of the Holy Spirit; and in all
of this we find ourselves constantly hungry and thirsty for Jesus.

The last four beatitudes are about our attitude towards
our neighbor: we refuse to judge; we have no secret agenda
which will exalt ourselves and diminish the other guy;
we will make peace, not war; and we'll suffer hardship
to tell our world that the Kingdom of Heaven awaits.

Stott made it clear that these were "preaching points". Which they are. But they're worth remembering.

Salt and Light vv. 13–16

You don't have to be a scientist. All you do is Google the question, "Can salt lose its saltiness?" The answer is clear. "Sodium chloride is readily water-soluble, so if this crude salt were exposed to condensation or rain water, the sodium chloride could be dissolved and removed, and the salt could in effect lose its saltiness" (askascientist.co.uk). I start with this because there has been debate by Bible commentators over the years as to the permanence of saltiness. Some say salt is salt and will always be salty, others say it can deteriorate. Jesus is vindicated on this count by the scientists. Salt *can* decay.

Salty salt, of course, both preserves and provides flavor. And, just as a little bit of light will dispel darkness, a little bit of salt will prevent food from rotting. Both are indispensable to sustainable life on earth.

Jesus looks his little band of blue-collar followers in the eye and says, "You are going to save the world from rottenness and darkness. And, you're going to make life on earth worth living." Preserve, enlighten, and flavor the world? Yes. That's what his disciples will do.

Looking over to his right, seeing the town of Safat on the mountainside, he says his followers will be as conspicuous in the world as a city built on a hill. Their light will shine. Their influence will permeate like salt. They will become critical players on the world stage. Really?

Yes, really. History has proven Jesus' words true. And, apart from a bit of Constantine here and there, Jesus' followers have not impacted the world through money or power. Rather, their influence has been that of distinctiveness, not conformity. They have been champions of counter-culture, the ultimate expression being the eschatological "Kingdom of Heaven". Unworldly vision begets unworldly action. And, God is glorified.

But, Jesus warns them to stay salty and well lit. No room for shrinking violets. And, no doubt he foresaw imprisonment and cruel death for many of them. This old world has a way of pushing back.

So, before shifting to Jesus' words about "fulfilling the law" a short recap of the preceding words:

1. We are blessed (beatitudes vv.1-12).

2. We serve (salt and light vv.13-16a).

3. God is glorified (v.16b).

The New Law vv. 17–20

Later in his writing about Jesus, Matthew (9:17) recalls Jesus saying, "Neither do people pour new wine into old wineskins. If they do, the skins will burst; the wine will run out and the wineskins will be ruined. No, they pour new wine into new wineskins, and both are preserved." Radical leaders often use this saying as a rationale for destroying all vestiges of a former era. They see their scorched-earth policy as the only way to effecting change. And, many of these revolutionaries have seen their actions as divinely ordained.

Jesus would vilify such superficial and destructive zeal as much as he criticized the intransigence of the established old order of pharisaic righteousness. Both radical and reactionary are guilty of blindness. The issue ultimately is not old versus new. Rather it is the new growing out of the old. New branches from old roots producing new fruit.

New wine never comes from new vines. I quote an article entitled, "When it comes to grape vines, old is gold" (Toronto Globe and Mail, April 03, 2012):

Old vines yield more concentrated fruit, resulting in richer wines with more sumptuous balance. [Age] can mean 30 years. In Australia, California, and Spain, the cutoff is more like 50 or 60... a few California producers, with vineyards planted 80-100 years ago, have adopted the designation 'ancient vines'... the oldest dating back more than 150 years."

Every spring we see the principle of new growing from old born out in the budding of trees and plants that have been dormant throughout winter. It's always a wonder. Miraculous even. In every way those youthfully green new leaves are the "fulfillment" of the old root system which has not only stood the test of time but feeds it in the present. And, ironically, it's these new leaves that enable the photosynthesis giving ongoing life to the old roots. You can't have one without the other.

Jesus proclaimed the "springtime" of God's dealings with Israel after a four hundred year drought of hearing from the Lord. His "green leaf" message had full regard for the ancient stock and vine of the Law and the Prophets. Indeed, as he put it, "Do not think that I have come to abolish the Law or the Prophets; I have not come to abolish them but to fulfill them" (v.17). His words were to bring photosynthetic new life to the great principles of old Sinai. Indeed, he presents a "New Sinai", in bursting color. But he does not do so at the expense or eradication of the old, "For truly I tell you, until heaven and earth disappear, not the smallest letter, not the least stroke of a pen, will by any means disappear from the Law until everything is accomplished" (v.18).

In Jesus' time the "Law" was understood by most Israelites as the "oral" or "scribal" law, the expansion/reduction of the Mosaic Law into thousands of rules and regulations. The oral had great impact because that was how a largely illiterate culture was taught and retained God's commands. As such it was rife with man-made legalisms that burdened, rather than released, the spirit of man. This was the "law" that Jesus, and later the Apostle Paul, took umbrage with. This was the petri dish which incubated repression rather than liberation. It was the fungus growing on the stately stock of the Ten Commandments.

Jesus saw manmade constructions as a "relaxing… liberalizing… watering-down… setting aside" (various translations of v.19) of the pure gold of God's law. Rabbi Hillel, the liberal, was as guilty of the "fungification of the Law" as much as Rabbi Shamai, the conservative. Both liberal and conservative schools were codifying, thereby legislating, something that was living and breathing with the pulse of God's love for the world. Jesus fulfills the law by excising the legal and personifying the heart of God. As the Apostle John said, "God is love". And love is *always* alive, dynamic, not static. Jesus changed a negative into a positive. The old "Thou shalt not" became "Blessed are they that…". Law morphed into love. St. Paul put it this way, "Love is the fulfilling of the Law" (Ro. 13:10).

New vs. Old vv. 21–48

So, now that Jesus had put pharisaic righteousness into perspective, he proceeded to describe the "new wine" proceeding from both Old Testament Law and Oral Law. He starts with murder and anger.

Murder and Anger vv. 21–26

You will notice as you read from 5:21 through to the end of the chapter, that each paragraph begins with, "You have heard that it was said…" This, of course, was how the illiterate and unlearned had been taught the law. Both the Old Testament Law and the scribal (Oral) Law were read and/or spoken to the people. Their knowledge was based on hearing. Jesus gives them an "earful" of what lies behind what they have heard.

Of course you should not murder, says Jesus, but that horrific outcome is rooted in something that precedes it: anger. Both epithets,

"Raca!" and "You fool!" expose a low view of neighbor. In modern parlance it is utter disdain that spews "empty head! blockhead! numbskull! you stupid! apostate fool! outcast! scoundrel! foreigner!" These accusations are bathed in contempt and "justify" murder in the view of the murderer. This low life is expendable! The world is better without them! They deserve to die! This outrage sharpens the knife. Indeed the thrust of the weapon requires the impetus that anger provides.

Those who heard these words, like us who read them, pause. We're all guilty of anger. It may not have overcome us yet, but the potential is there to lash out at someone. So Jesus calls for pre-emptive action.

Israel's means of atonement ("at-*one*-ment") was blood sacrifice. As the penitent brought his lamb to the altar he would press his hands down on the lamb's head conferring his guilt to the helpless animal. He would make a statement of confession, something like, "I confess my wrongdoing, let this act be for my covering." Then the animal was slain, the blood poured out on the altar, and the priest declared absolution.

Jesus says, before you are reconciled to God you must be reconciled to your "brother" or "sister". The anger must be dealt with. Deal with it by confessing to the object of your anger, and then confess it to God. The Lord can then forgive. The cumulative effect of unconfessed anger resulting in murder, will be avoided. One cannot love God and hate neighbor. It is out of synch with heaven's heartbeat.

What is more, Jesus says, if you deal with your anger in God's way, you will avoid not only murder but also the possibility of a costly lawsuit. Be practical as well as spiritual.

Adultery and Lust vv. 27–30

To be clear, the Old Testament injunction against adultery is about more than sex. Mainly it's about property. As grating as we may find patriarchy today, the fact is that the Old Testament Israelite culture was totally patriarchal. The man was king. His wife/wives, his children, his entire household were, in their entirety, his property. He could divorce his wife at will. He could even sell his children, just as he might sell an ox. His dwelling compound was his own little fortress. Any break in by a thief was not just an intrusion but an assault against the owner's sovereignty. Thus, any man who seduced, raped, and/or flirted with another man's wife, was engaging in an act of war against that man. He was a thief, a brigand, a careless wrecker of another man's peace. He was worthy of death by stoning.

So, even the "look" at another man's wife was suspect. Adultery doesn't happen spontaneously. It's a process – the look, the casual contact, the "confidential" comment, the flattery, the "innocent" meeting for coffee – adultery is built incrementally. But it all starts with "the look".

> ## *Adultery doesn't happen spontaneously. It's a process.*

In the Greek "the look" can suggest a "lusting after", that is, a conscious intent to have sex – a deliberate cultivation of the woman. The process will end in bed. But then, that end will be but the beginning of the disintegration of the woman's marriage, the upsetting of her husband's peace, the fracturing of a family. In Jesus' view adultery was a relational tumor, a cancer that would quickly metastasize, destroying lives forever.

To emphasize his point Jesus uses both euphemism and hyperbole. The offending "eye" should be plucked out and the "right hand" (read "private parts" – by some. Google "Origen and Matthew 19:12") should be cut off. Now, Jesus didn't want to have a bunch of dismembered disciples following him about, but he exaggerated for the sake of emphasis. Abuse someone else's marriage at your peril!

Divorce vv. 31 & 32

Here in the twenty-first century we live in an era of disposable relationships. Nearly one in two marriages ends in divorce. We accept it, even though it is often painful. And, increasingly, young couples are choosing cohabitation without the legal trappings of marriage. It's a way of avoiding red tape when the inevitable break up occurs. The breakup *will* occur. Or, so we believe. Very few expect to marry for life.

So it's a bit of a jolt to read Jesus' prohibition of divorce. It seems harsh. But let's look at the context.

Marriage, as a social contract, was under siege in Jesus' day. In many ways this reflected a clash of cultures, Jewish, Roman, and Greek. And in the Jewish context there was the added conflict of the perennial liberal/conservative divide. The liberal school under the leadership of Rabbi Hillel, sided with the Greco/Roman view that marriage could be dissolved easily, and for any reason. The conservative school, under Rabbi Shamai, was counter-culture. It contended that there was only one cause justifying divorce – adultery.

Remember that it was a man's world. The liberal view of Hillel, the convenience divorce of Greece and Rome, and the syntheses of these cultural norms all led to a man-sided approach. Shamai, although accused of legalism, sided with the woman. He did not want to see women with no rights, especially when it came to the protection and nurture she deserved as a mother and home-maker. Her rights must be recognized and defended. Moses and Jesus agreed. A woman was not a "throw-away".

Indeed, the whole point of Moses providing a "certificate of divorce" to the woman (De. 24:1) was to protect her from the former husband returning and forcing her back into marriage. The divorce certificate was her defence against being treated like property. It meant she had the legal right to say "no".

She had other rights as well. In Exodus 22:10 Moses delineates the basic rights she had as either concubine or wife. The man was required to provide her with "food... clothing... marital rights." If these were not provided she had the right to divorce *him*, although, as history proved, it would be a difficult road.

In Mt. 19:3-9 Jesus was "tested" by the Pharisees with the question, "Is it lawful for a man to divorce his wife for any and every reason?" King Herod, who ruled during Jesus' life, had divorced his wife Herodias, and, as I've already pointed out, there was a great polarity of thought within Judaism itself. The Essenes were celibates, the Hillelites were liberals – a man could divorce his wife for burning his dinner! And the Shamai-ites were ultra-conservative – no divorce except for adultery. If Jesus was rigid he would offend Herod and the school of Hillel. If he was lenient he would fall out with the school of Shamai. So it was a "test" indeed.

His answer took the wind out of everyone's sails. In essence he says, "Marriage was/is God's creation." The two sexes are complementary. The intent of marriage is to leave the family in which one was raised ("leave his father and mother") and establish one's own. The unit is not the individual, but the family. God is not only creator of the institution, but He is part of it. You must not break it up.

"OK! OK!," said his interlocutors, but Moses allowed divorce. Why else would he command that a certificate of divorce be given to the woman? Jesus responded by saying that Moses did not "command" it. He "permitted" or "suffered" (Greek) it. Why? Because the culture was "hard".

Then he warns them that divorce for "any reason" is not on the table. In fact only "sexual immorality" is reason for divorce. Apart from that exception, a man is not free to remarry. And the same principle applies to a woman. Jesus says in Mk. 10:12, if she takes the initiative and divorces her husband "for any reason" (implied) she too commits adultery if she remarries.

The critical issue here is both the protection of the woman (in a man's world) and the family. Anything that fractures the family is seen as an evil. Divorce is a kind of self-imposed relational schizophrenia. God "hates" it (Ma. 2:16 RSV).

To appreciate God's hatred of divorce one must examine Ma. 2:10-16. I know this is a "casual commentary", not given to academic analysis of the text, but it must be said that this passage is very difficult to interpret from the Hebrew. It leaves room for diverse opinions.

Divorce is a kind of self-imposed relational schizophrenia. God "hates" it.

Malachi starts the argument by declaring that Israel has one God and a unique covenant. Israel will be his people and He will be their God. But they have become disloyal to their national family (v.10), their spiritual family (vv.11,12), and their marriage partners (vv.13-16). These grim realities are all evidenced by their idolatry, mixed marriages, adultery, and divorce. In God's view, as Malachi presents it, there is continuity and spiritual unity implicit in covenant with God and covenant in marriage. Idolatry and adultery destroy covenant. God hates them both, just as he hates the end result.

So, as Jesus sees it, the marriage covenant is inviolable. Because God is present in every wedding, divorcing your partner at a latter stage suggests that the fracture extends to heaven itself.

This does not mean that divorce is the "unpardonable sin". Today, as in Jesus' day, there are/were all kinds of "extenuating circumstances". God the Father "pitieth his children" in their distresses, and provides for their healing. But, what Jesus is doing here is declaring the ideal. When the "real" destroys the "ideal" he would be the first to say, "mercy trumps judgement". But a word to the wise: when you marry keep the back door closed.

Oaths vv. 33–37

Human nature being what it is, we humans tend to "look out for Number One." We seek advantage over our neighbor. We hide our agendas. We tell half-truths. And often, we lie. To protect ourselves from the other guy we bring in an outside authority. Business is done via contract. If we default we are subject to that objective rule. We live under law. The influence of self-interest is so pervasive we have got to be watched.

Often in ancient times contracts were either "sanctified" by or completely based on oaths. An oath invoked a higher, sacred, or valued "other" that became party to the transaction. Even so, the oath-takers often hedged their secret intentions. A lot of double-dealing was done in the name of deity.

This is why the Lord instructed Israel to never "take the name of the Lord in vain."

"Do not swear falsely by my name and so profane the name of your God. I am the Lord" (Le. 19:12). "You shall not misuse the name of the Lord your God…" (Ex. 20:7). In Jewish thought the name of God was binding. To abuse his name by invoking it without follow-through was seen as blasphemous.

So, when it comes to truth it must, as one old theologian put it, "stand before God undraped" by any subterfuge. An oath must never be a cover for deceit.

Jesus simply says, "Yes is yes. No is no." God is omnipresent so there is no need to invoke his presence in a contract. As Jesus' half-brother James put it, "Above all, my brothers and sisters, do not swear – not by heaven or by earth or by anything else. All you need to say is a simple "Yes" or "No". Otherwise you will be condemned" (Ja. 5:12).

Let your word "be your bond". This doesn't mean we shouldn't sign contracts. What it does mean is that our signature is a witness to our integrity. We must never forget that our name is attached to His.

Retaliation vv. 38–42

Revenge is not vengeance. Revenge is vindictive. Vengeance, on the other hand, is retributive justice. Revenge is subjective; vengeance is objective. That's why the victims of an injustice cannot avenge – only a court of law, or better yet, God himself, can bring vengeance. "Vengeance is mine; I will repay," says the Lord" (Ro. 12:19; see also He. 10:30). Only God can right the balance when an injustice has upset the equilibrium of his people. This is why "tit for tat" doesn't work. The "eye for an eye" principle, by the way, was designed to mitigate the escalation of conflict. If someone took your eye, all you were allowed to do was to take theirs. To take two eyes, or an arm or a leg, was unjust. Only equality of loss would do.

"Vengeance" is part of the legal terminology of the Bible. According to the "Interpreter's Dictionary of the Bible" it is "the restoration of wholeness, integrity, to the community, by God or man." There is, however, a blurring of the lines from time to time in Scripture between vengeance and revenge. But in the main the cries to God for vengeance are "cries for redemption, restoration, health and healing…". Retributive justice in the "final judgement" will be harsh, but it will "right the balance". Justice ultimately will be done.

Essentially what Jesus is saying here is that we are not to take the law into our own hands. Wrong done to us by an "evil" person does not justify our doing a wrong in return. Indeed, when wrong is met with wrong, the cycle of injustice only gains momentum. This is what fuels feuds.

So Jesus does what he sometimes does: he utilizes hyperbole. Someone strikes your right cheek? Let him hit you on the left as well. Someone wants to sue the shirt off your back? Give him your coat, too. Nip the revenge reflex in the bud. Let God sort things out in the end.

The same principle applies to "occupation stresses". The people of Jesus' time were under duress due to the Roman forces occupying their country. Any soldier could order you to carry his kit. If he did so, carry it twice as far as he expected. And, be generous with those in need who ask a favor. Not to the point of impoverishing yourselves, but always show compassion. This way you don't bear a grudge. Personal animosity will be cut off before it can take root.

Love & Hatred vv. 43–48

The love of enemies is the ethical bottom line of the Sermon on the Mount. It seems impossible – as does being "perfect" in v. 48. Mind you, to *love* your enemy *is* possible, in that love is essentially volitional.

On the other hand, to *like* your enemy is virtually impossible because "like" is solely emotional. To love is to do. To like is to feel. Love is unconditional. Like has conditions.

Jesus calls on us to "pray for" our enemies. This is hard to do. Indeed an ancient preacher named Chrysostom called prayer for our enemies, "the very highest summit of self-control". But it can be done. To love is a choice, and we *can* choose to add value by prayer and/or deeds directed to the betterment even of those "evil" ones who "persecute" us. The embattled Coptic Christians of Egypt have modeled this in the early twenty-first century in their response to violent persecution by so-called Islamic State terrorists. In their case love is expressed via forgiveness. What spiritual maturity!

This is what "perfect" in v. 48 refers to – maturity. The Greek word used is "teleios" which means "functional" or "mature", no loose ends. A man is teleios if he fulfills the purpose for which he was created. We can never attain to the moral or spiritual perfection of our Creator, but we can, like him, fully function as He intended us to do from the beginning. Any "perfection" assigned to us of the moral and spiritual kind will be solely "Christ in us, the hope of glory." But, just as Christ died for us "while we were yet enemies" so too we can "die" for our neighbor, be he friend or enemy. This is "teleios".

Alms, Prayer & Fasting 6:1–18

Showing Off v.1

In the Jewish culture of the time there were three religious core values: alms giving, prayer, fasting. All three could be done in secret but they also could be done publicly with great show of piety. One could give to the beggar, and beseech heaven with theatrical flourish, and fast with slumped shoulders, unwashed face, soiled clothing and bad breath. In every case attention was paid to the pious pilgrim by the people, with little or no notice in heaven. Jesus casts such displays as counter-productive. They may impress the public, he says, but your Father will not be pleased.

How NOT to Give vv. 2–4

The goal, Jesus is implying, is uncalculating generosity. But to get there one needs to know a few things.

First of all, "alms" meant "righteousness". Or, as the Greek suggests, "rightwiseness". In the Jewish culture almsgiving and righteousness were equivalent. In the Hebrew language "tzadkah" (righteousness) is used for both. Righteousness was identified with "mercifulness" and in most cases associated with giving money to the poor. A much quoted aphorism of the rabbis was, "Greater is he who gives alms than he who offers sacrifices." Another was, "He who gives alms in secret is greater than Moses." The ideal, indeed the ultimate, occurred when the donor gave and the recipient received "blindly". This way only God received the glory.

This secrecy in giving presents a bit of a conundrum, however. Elsewhere Jesus instructs us to "let your light shine before men, that they may see your good works, and glorify your Father who is in heaven." How does one do both? Secret and open at the same time? Seems undoable. Many theologians agree that what Jesus is saying is that we should be open in our love for neighbor but indifferent to their praise or even their opinion. When we give, we give "as unto the Lord". Or, as one of those theological thinkers put it, "show when tempted to hide; hide when tempted to show." The endgame of the process is glory to God.

We should be open in our love for neighbor but indifferent to their praise or even their opinion.

"Hypocrites" steal glory from God. They relish public recognition. Jesus had a dim view of them. The word "hypocrite" comes from the Greek "pharisaios". In turn the Greek root has an etymological parent in the Aramaic word "pera" meaning "to separate". But there are added nuances to the word – for instance, a hypocrite could be an actor in a Greek play, playing a part, feigning a personality or character that was not his own.

As is often the case with language and culture there is a blurring of the lines over time. For example, the "Pharisees" and the "Sadducees" emerged as differing religious sub-cultures in the latter half of the second century before Christ. Their sectarian DNA, however, can be seen as far back as the return of the exiles from Babylon around 537 BC. Once situated again in Judea, they became known as the "Hasideans" and the "Hellenizers". The Hasideans (or, "Hasids" as they are known to this day in modern Israel) were focused on strict adherence to the Law of Moses (and oral law later known as the Talmud), while the Hellenizers (or, "Sadducees" as they were later known) were committed to liberalizing Judaism and assimilating the values of Greek culture. The Sadducees essentially were a political sect, the Hasidim ("Pious Ones") a religious. But there was one issue that found them in agreement: they both felt threatened by Jesus. His life and teaching was antithetical to theirs, and in their world of theological and moral absolutes Jesus was not just counter-culture, he was dangerous. "What if the whole world goes after him?" they spluttered. "He's got to be stopped."

So, while they "trumpeted" their alms, Jesus called for total secrecy. His word about the left hand not knowing what the right hand is doing is intriguing. It may have been a proverbial statement, but it could have referred to the Jewish practice of offering gifts at the altar in the Temple with the right hand. The best instincts of the soul were seen as "right-handed", while the more pedestrian inclinations were seen as "left-handed". So there should be no mix of motives in charity, says Jesus. Keep your gifts close to the chest. When you do, your omniscient Father will take notice. Any "reward" is up to Him.

General Comments on Prayer vv.5–8

I wonder if Jesus was thinking of Ecclesiastes 5:2 at this point: "God is in heaven and you upon earth, therefore let your words be few."

It is clear that prayer has little to do with volume, public visibility, or pious repetitions. Nor does it function as an information bureau ("who can instruct the Lord as his counselor?" Is. 40:13). Rather, it is secret, intimate, and more about listening than talking. It's a time to hear the Lord speak. So, get into your own room, close the door, and be quiet.

Remember, "your Father knows what you need before you ask." He is not, nor will he ever be, a means to our own ends. Prayer is a two-way conversation – mostly "his" way.

The Lord's Prayer vv. 9–13

There are so many excellent works on The Lord's Prayer that anything I write may seem redundant. But, here in the twenty-first century it doesn't hurt to take another look. Our "internet culture" has its own lens. First of all, a general analysis sees seven areas of focus in the prayer:

1. God's nature
2. God's kingdom
3. God's will
4. Daily needs
5. Forgiveness
6. Testing
7. Deliverance from evil

It covers all the bases.

Our Father in Heaven v.9

Right off the top the pronoun puts things in perspective. There is no "I, me, or mine". Rather it's "we, us, and ours". God is the Father of all, not a household deity.

"Our" reminds us that we have no inside track to God peculiar to us but our access is shared by every man and woman of faith throughout history. Ours is a family faith. And, as his children, we have the right to address our Heavenly Father as "Abba" (Hebrew). This is the equivalent of "Daddy" in English. To this day, my three children, even though adults, call me "Abba". Growing up in Jerusalem, attending Israeli schools, they naturally referred to me that way. It's an endearing term. I like it.

Jesus' reference to God as Father would not have surprised his audience. In the Jewish scriptures God had claimed "Israel as his son…" (Ex. 4:22) and had blessed and chastened him time and again throughout a tumultuous history. The use of the term was common in Jewish prayers, and even though these prayers and liturgies were usually expressed in the synagogues, the everyday Israelite had a sense that a Heavenly Father overshadowed his people with protective wings.

"In Heaven" might just as easily be read as "perfect". In an imperfect world there was hope on the part of some in Israel that an unblemished moral order and place of rest existed beyond the grave. This was a place free of sorrow, sickness, and alienation. It was a place of perfection, a place where God dwelt.

"Hallowed" meant "let your name be held holy", or, "glorify your name". Holy, of course, referred to that which in its perfection was apart or separate from a fallen world. It suggests transcendence, awe, respectful fear, and even a touch of dread. God is not to be approached casually. He is the Creator of heaven and earth. He has the keys of life and death. He builds and tears down by a word from his mouth. When approaching him in prayer we are to do so with humility and caution. Our lives are in his hands.

"Your name" is a subject all of itself. I'm tempted to write an essay here, but space won't permit. Rather I'll make a few summary observations.

In the biblical view there is nothing more holy on this space/time spaceship we call earth than the name of the "Holy One of Israel". His name evokes his presence. So much so that Orthodox Jews to this day will not pronounce it. One cannot pronounce YHWH and live. So, when reading the Torah aloud in synagogue, YHWH is pronounced ADONAI, which means "Lord". If, in everyday conversation one refers to the Lord, one employs HA-SHEM, which means "The Name". Even in script one writes G-D rather than GOD. The Name is everything, and it is holy. Indeed, this is why Jerusalem is called "The Holy City". God has placed his name there – "The city that bears my Name" (Je. 25:29).

Our hallowed Father has our backs. Blessed be his Name!

Language limits us. Our descriptive efforts are stigmatized due to our "dark glasses" (1Co. 13:12). Here, in this prayer, Jesus hints at the mystery engaged by our words. The Apostle John captures that mysterious adventure with the words, "Herein is love, not that we loved God, but that he loved us, and sent his son to be the propitiation for our sins" (1Jn. 4:10). Our hallowed Father has our backs. Blessed be his Name!

Thy Kingdom come, Thy will be done v.10

Jesus couldn't have been clearer in expressing the purpose of his ministry: "I must proclaim the good news of the Kingdom of God… because that is why I was sent" (Lk. 4:43). The "Kingdom" was everything.

In one sense this terminology was readily understood by his audience – they all expected a future "Day of The Lord" where Messiah would establish his kingdom and rule from his throne in Jerusalem. This was their "eschatological" hope.

But in another sense the Kingdom was an abstraction. It represented the rule of God in the eternal realm. As such it was (and is) beyond the reach of human comprehension. The only grip the people could make on it was philosophical. And, philosophy has its limits.

But time and again Jesus stressed the nearness of the Kingdom, even declaring that the Kingdom was "within" his disciples and "among" them, personified in himself (check out the scores of Kingdom references in a concordance, or on the internet). Yet, they didn't get it. Even after his resurrection Jesus' disciples were asking, "Lord, will you at this time restore the Kingdom to Israel?" (Ac. 1:6). Their nationalistic prejudice trumped their grasp of the vast kingdom horizon. The power and scope of culture very easily dims the eyes.

The Kingdom is where God's "will" is done – "Thy will be done, on earth as it is in heaven". The omniscient Father who sees all, factors what he sees into his sovereign rule. This is why "God willing" (Deus Vult) has always been the heavenly qualifier for Christian choice. If we're out of synch with heaven we're out of synch with everlasting life.

It should be said that "Thy will be done" is a great safeguard against getting our own way. Why? Because we are self-absorbed. We want wealth, ease, recognition, and flawless health. One theologian suggests that, "if God were a devil, perhaps the most devilish torment he could plan for us would be to give us our own wish." Often our prayers are an exercise in manipulation, "finessing" God to our will, which of course is tantamount to making God in our own image. Jesus himself, in his most trying moment, prayed in the Garden of Gethsemane, "Not my will, but thine be done." That sentence captures the essence of prayer. Our personal agenda must yield to that of our Maker. And what is his agenda? "The Kingdom of God is… righteousness and peace and joy in the Holy Ghost" (Ro. 14:17).

Our Daily Bread v.11

We've briefly looked at the first three of six petitions referencing God's name, kingdom, and will. Now we're going to look at our need for bread, forgiveness, and victory over evil. Daily bread comes first. If there is no bread there is no life.

I'm no Greek scholar (nor are you, probably), but with a little digging in a Greek lexicon or two one can come up with a pretty good idea of what "daily bread" referred to. First of all, bread and physical provision are relatively synonymous. Daily is a bit more elusive in that it could mean "sufficient bread" or "bread for sustenance", but likely means "bread for this day and next", enabling Christians to "be not anxious" about tomorrow. The Lord wants us to live free from worry when it comes to our physical needs.

This petition is a recognition of our vulnerability and dependency. It is not a passive request. Daily bread means daily labor – we've got to bend our backs. But we bend them dependent on God's provision of life in the seed, fertility in the soil, and the faithful cycles of sun and rain. Without these we are food insecure, indeed we are in danger of death. So, as the Lord incrementally metes out his provision, we declare "to God be the glory!" and we seize the day.

Forgiveness v.12 (see also vv.14 & 15)

Our sinfulness is assumed in scripture, "All have sinned and fall short of the glory of God" (Ro. 3:23). And as the Apostle John put it, "If we say we have no sin, we deceive ourselves, and the truth is not in us" (1Jn. 1:8). But our sinfulness is not assumed in our twenty-first century secular culture. Indeed the word "sin" is rarely if ever used. "Mistake" maybe. But "sin"?

The thing about the word "sin" is that it implies (requires) accountability. This grates in our new millennial culture. We're highly individualistic and independent. We "do our thing" – they "do theirs". We stay out of each other's hair, connect via social media, and get on with life. In our world accountability is tantamount to judgement. "Judge not that ye be not judged," once a biblical value, has now become secularized.

So here is a short lesson on sin as it is defined by five exotic Greek words:

1. "Hamartia" means "missing the target" (at least you took aim!).

2. "Parabasis" means "stepping across the line" (on purpose or by accident).

3. "Paraptoma" means "slipping across" or "swept away".

4. "Anomia" means "lawlessness, breaking the law".

5. "Opheilema" means "failure to pay what is due, failure of duty" – This is the word used in Jesus' prayer.

The use of "opheilema" suggests that the translation "debts" is fairly accurate. An unpaid debt is seen as a "sin of omission". Whereas "trespass" is seen as a "sin of commission". In either case the sins are against God or neighbor, and we are accountable to both for our inaction or action. Our behavior always has a domino effect. As the old adage says, "No man is an island."

"As we forgive" is more accurately translated "as we have forgiven". The assumption is that in invoking the forgiveness of God we've already swept our house clean in terms of any dustup we may have had or injustice suffered with our neighbor. Jesus won't countenance any prayer for divine forgiveness on any other terms. Indeed in vv.14&15 he says, "For if you forgive other people when they sin against you, your Heavenly Father will also forgive you. But if you do not forgive others their sins, your Father will not forgive your sins." Unlike our Father in Heaven, we cannot forget sins against us (see Is. 38:17; Mi. 7:19), but we can forgive. To forgive is an act of the will. So even while the memory of an injustice and/or a hurt remains, we can choose to forgive and move on. This is why Jesus, in 5:43, calls us to love our enemies. We can do so because love is volitional. If he had insisted that we "like" our enemies we'd all be miserable failures.

Essentially "forgive" means "to send away". We ask the Lord to send away our missing the target, our step across the line, our slip, our lawlessness, our failure to pay the debt. He forgives because of his grace, our renewal is the product of undeserved favor. And he expects us in a "quid-pro-quo" manner to be graceful with our neighbors. This way our souls are healed.

Temptation and The Evil One v.13

Let's be clear right off the top. God never entices us to do evil. Biblically and historically (until about the 17th century) "tempt" meant "test". In the Old Testament scriptures we see God testing men and (a nonstarter) men testing God. A test was meant to bring out the best (or reveal the evil if there was no best). The temptation Jesus was talking

about was probably the enticement to deny God in response to persecution. If we were to paraphrase we might pray, "Lord, keep us from
the rack."

The nefarious designer/operator of the rack is none other than "the
evil one". Satan, the "adversary", is hard at work "seeking to kill and
destroy". Jesus sees us as sheep fully vulnerable to the ravages of this
predator. We need divine protection. Jesus says, "Pray for it." Later,
Jesus' disciple John reminds us that sometimes we need protection from
ourselves – "the lust of the flesh, the lust of the eyes, and the pride of life"
(1Jn. 2:16) are often quite capable of seeing us self-destruct. So one way
or the other – from the outside or the inside – we are conscious of our
weakness. In that critical self-awareness our soul cries for help. Only the
divine sailor can keep our ship afloat in threatening seas.

The Quid pro Quo of Forgiveness vv.14 & 15

I've already referenced these verses commenting on v.12. But to emphasize the point, take a look at Jesus' hyperbolic parable of the unmerciful
servant in ch.18:23-35.

Here's a guy who owes the king ten thousand (!!) bags of gold. The
king wants to settle accounts, but his servant can't repay. Under threat
of being sold into slavery he throws himself on the king's mercy and
the king cancels the debt. Then, even as he's leaving the king's presence,
he sees a fellow servant who owes him a mere hundred silver coins.
He grabs him, chokes him, and demands payment. The fellow who
has just been forgiven a humungous debt throws the poor wretch into
debtors' prison. The other servants report this incident to the king.
And the king, in total outrage, sends the unmerciful fellow to prison
and torture.

Jesus looks his audience in the eye and says, "This is how my
Heavenly Father will treat each of you unless you forgive your brother
and sister from your heart." Whoa! Where do I sign?

Fasting vv.16–18

There is only one fast declared in the Old Testament. On the Day of Atonement the Israelites were to fast (Le. 16:29, 31; 23:27-32; Nu. 29:7), meaning abstinence from food and drink for the twenty-four hour period from sunset to sunset. Later in Jewish history other fasts were added, mainly marking significant passages or disasters. This is why fasting expresses either/or grief and penitence.

Sometimes fasting was personal – a time of "afflicting the soul", and often it indicated pious self-discipline (Pharisees fasted every Monday and Thursday). Fasting's achilles heel, however, was public display.

This is what Jesus warns his disciples against. Just as was the case with almsgiving and prayer, Jesus saw both the value and the danger. Self-satisfaction, showing off, and phony contrition very easily trumped the essential spiritual quality of genuine fasting. Too easily we humans can yield to the "pride that apes humility".

> *The Old Testament prophets made it very clear that fasting provided no smoke screen for unjust/unrighteous behavior.*

So, says Jesus, turn your fast away from human display and look solely to heaven. Let God see your good work. Don't give anyone else even a hint of what you're up to. The Lord will "give back" ("reward") to those who give to him. But don't think for a minute that fasting guarantees a heavenly hearing. The Old Testament prophets made it very clear (See Is. 58:5-12) that fasting provided no smoke screen for unjust/unrighteous behavior.

THE LIFE OF FAITH 6:19–7:12

True Treasure vv.19–21

The issue here is sustainability. As we live our lives we gather wealth, either earthly or heavenly. Earthly treasure is fraught with risk and always ends in total loss. Heavenly treasure, on the other hand, lasts forever. The case is not either/or but the tricky balancing act of both/and. Money is not the problem. It's the love of it that is toxic. So how does one stick-handle through the stresses and temptations of earthly wealth? How to turn it to the advantage of heaven?

We'll see in a moment that the key (v.22) is "singleness" of vision. That is we're to see all treasure on earth as expendable for the Kingdom of Heaven. "My money – Your money" won't do. There should be no guilt, however, in ownership of things like clothing, food, and housing. But, if there is lack of contentment with these provisions, we flirt with covetousness, which is the only sin, other than pride, which is essentially spiritual. If our worldview sees all that we are, and all that we own, as the Lord's, we are in synch with heaven. If, on the other hand, we see our possessions and wealth as our security, we are out of synch. Jesus would have us know that our ultimate, sustainable security is in the Lord. Our "stuff" merely is food for moths, rust, and thieves. The only thing we can take with us when we die is what we give away.

The Bible is strong on this. Far better to be "rich in good works" (1 Ti. 6:18), "rich in faith" (Ja. 2:5), and shareholders in the "unsearchable riches of Christ and his glory" (Ep. 3:8, 16), than to be rich in this world's goods. "Laying up treasure in heaven" is the wise decision. It's the only sustainable treasure. So if we're going to "treasure our treasure" we had better treasure the heavenly.

How then does one lay up treasure in heaven? King Solomon gives us a starting point: "Whoever is kind to the poor lends to the Lord, and He will reward them for what they have done" (Pr. 19:17). Prioritize the poor, especially the orphan and the widow (Ps. 68:5). Compassion and care for the marginalized is a sure sign of the Spirit at work. It's called "justice seeking". And, in combination with "righteousness seeking", it hits the sweet-spot of God's Heart. "I am The Lord who exercises kindness, justice and righteousness on earth, for in these I delight" (Je. 9:24).

The Optic Nerve of the Soul vv. 22–24

In Proverbs we read, "The spirit of man is the candle (or "lamp") of the Lord" (Pr. 20:27). We call it conscience. It's that inner urge to do what is right. It helps us distinguish what is right and what is wrong. It is the light that illumines our path. An undivided, unconflicted conscience will give us clear direction. But if there is double vision we fall into the ditch. Singleness of purpose will enable us to avoid the pitfalls of a double treasure. It will save us from the stresses of a divided heart.

Jesus is calling for spiritual maturity. A child is easily seduced by the glitter and novelty of a toy. The adult, overly influenced by his "inner child", can also be distracted by material things. When distracted we can easily become spiritually blind. We don't just shut our eyes to what is wrong. We embrace it. It's a kind of "double blindness" or "darkness". And even as we fumble about we rationalize. Troubles are common currency for those who strive for gain. There's nothing wrong with profit. Nothing wrong with bigger and better. Or so we tell ourselves. Meanwhile our marriage is neglected, our children emotionally abandoned, and our relationship with God is at a standstill. Money first, God later. Our darkness is "great" indeed. As the Nobel prizewinning singer Bob Dylan put it, "We gotta serve somebody." What will it be? God or money?

So we have a choice between two treasures (earth or heaven) and two visions (or worldview). Do we see a carefree retirement as our "end game"? Or do we see Jesus, the "author and finisher of our faith", the one who will welcome us to our everlasting home with "well done, good and faithful servant…"? There is no neutral position. We all must, and will, choose. Then we live with the consequences.

Anxiety vv. 25–34

The Greek word "mesimnao" means "to be anxious, careful". In the King James Version of the Bible it is rendered "to take thought". As King James' academics worked on Tyndale's translation the word of the day for anxiety or worry was "thought". This old English word had the nuance of "over-careful" or "over-anxious". But the word is just as relevant in our day as then.

It's very common in the twenty-first century to refer to someone as "a controller". And in moments of transparency we will sometimes refer to ourselves as a controller too. We want to be in charge. But when it comes to the future we're hopelessly out of our depth – it is not predictable, nor is it certain. We literally "know not what the morrow bringeth." This uncertainty bathes the controller in constant worry. Indeed as "mesim-nao" suggests, the controller "worries anxiously."

This, of course, is a zero-sum game. No amount of psychological or emotional energy can influence the future. Indeed, this constant anxiety has the power to do only one thing: fuel the worst case scenario with its concomitant feeling of dread. It's truly amazing that so many people in our prosperous western world live "dreadful" lives. Worry paralyzes.

Jesus' teaching can free us from this bondage. First he puts things in perspective – isn't life more than food and the body more than clothing? Well, of course. It's just that we take our physical infrastructure for granted and obsess about feeding and clothing it. And, in our western world where food security and fashion are taken for granted we obsess about "proper" foods and "cool" clothing. Ironically while we fret about these superficial things, a tumor may be silently growing inside, or an aneurism may be about to rupture. Take stock of what really matters, says Jesus. Live simply, but live!

Besides, since we have chosen "treasure in heaven", we live with the heavenly worldview. Heaven's security banishes worry. And, in the natural world birds eat every day without stockpiling. They practice no trade but are nourished without anxiety. What's the point then of straining to see an unseeable future?

Anxiety cannot add a single second to our life's span, but it might subtract several seconds! As for the body, when has worry ever added a centimeter to our height? When has it ever come close to clothing us with the beauty of the wildflowers in the field? When are we going to call it like it is? Worry essentially is distrust of God. We don't really believe that He is in control.

Worry essentially is distrust of God. We don't really believe that He is in control.

"Be not anxious" suggests a trajectory of seeking the wrong thing. "Seek first" puts priority on the Kingdom of Heaven, where "seeking" will result not in dread but in joy. Anxiety will be trumped by peace. Jesus says we should seek the big things (the Kingdom of Heaven being the ultimate) and the little things will follow.

So "Carpe Diem" – Seize the Day. It is vain to borrow trouble from the future. All that does is eviscerate hope and replace it with fear. I'll never forget what an old man once said to me as he lay dying in his hospital room, "You know, Pastor, 95% of everything I worried about over my lifetime never came to pass."

The Censorious Spirit 7:1–5

Jesus really strikes a chord here. The fact is that all of us judge others. It's almost an automatic reflex. We see someone else's behavior, we disapprove, and we pass judgement. Our "court" is always in session.

We act impulsively. We have no regard for "due process". There is no defense attorney. We prosecute and we judge. It's a "kangaroo court", the sentence always punitive. The only winner is us. By disparaging others we exalt ourselves.

And that's the issue. Exalting ourselves at the expense of others is a function of pride. We compare, we compete, and we win. No one is as righteous as we. Never mind that the scales are weighted in our favor.

The Jewish Mishna says, "When you judge any man weight the scales in his favor" (Aboth 1:6). It goes on to say, "Do not judge your fellow until you are in his position" (Aboth 2:5). Ignorance may blind judgement. In Jesus' words there's a huge timber in our own eye as we try to extricate a small bit of sawdust from our neighbor's eye. What's more, when we judge others we are judging ourselves. We are often seeing our own faults in others and judging them vicariously. As the Apostle Paul puts it, "For wherein thou judgest another, thou condemnest thyself; for thou that judgest doest the same things" (Ro. 2:1 KJV). The lazy man is quick to judge others as lazy. The liar is always afraid someone will lie to him.

To censor someone is not the same as assessing the ethical values of their choices. Judgement is one thing, discernment another. Jesus is warning against harsh, destructive judgement, not against objective appraisal. Even Jesus himself, according to the Apostle John, "came not into the world to condemn the world, but that the world through him might be saved" (Jn. 3:17). Ethical discernment is redemptively fueled. Our instinct should err on the side of grace. Be generous.

Pearls before Swine v.6

Some people find this "pearls before swine" comment confusing, if not offensive. How can we call anyone a pig? A little cultural background will help here. In Jesus' day Gentiles were often referred to by the Jews as "dogs" and "pigs". The Gentile was the "great unwashed", a "disbeliever", a heathen. A devout son of Abraham saw himself as separated from the Gentiles by a great gulf. The Jew was a citizen of heaven, the Gentile of hell.

So, in the cultural context, as Jesus is warning against judging others, he is acknowledging that there will be those whose worldview will blind them to lasting values. They will be "unreachable" by the law of Moses. They will trample on Jewish values and savage the believer in the process. So, be discerning. Don't waste your time on someone whose ignorance of the language of heaven renders them deaf to spiritual values.

We can understand only what we can understand. That's why we don't bare our souls to everyone indiscriminately. Use wisdom in our relationships. Reject those who reject the holy. Move on. Don't get stuck.

Confidence in Prayer vv. 7–12

I should call this segment, "Confidence in Prayer for Others". Why? Because of context. Context is so critical in interpretation. Sometimes it's how the passage relates to the broader passage. Sometimes it has to do with the cultural setting, or historical occasion for writing, and even sometimes with who wrote it. Sometimes it's "all of the above". Context in this case has to do with the concluding sentence of the passage.

Jesus starts with "Ask… seek… knock" and concludes with, "So in everything, do to others what you would have them do to you, for this sums up the Law and the Prophets." Is it a stretch to suggest that Jesus is telling us we can have complete confidence in praying for the best for others?

Regardless of the interpretive exercise (some interpreters see this passage as more properly placed by Luke (11:9-13), without the "golden rule"), one cannot misinterpret the "ask… seek… knock" sequence. Each is an action word. "Ask" – define the need; "Seek" – pursue the options; "Knock" – expect a response. These verbs propel the soul forward. And, if that pursuit conforms to the Father's will ("Not my will, but thine be done…" Mt. 26:39), then the petition will be met. There is no room for passivity here. We must engage with the heavenly plan. Especially, if it has to do with seeking the welfare of others.

The "golden rule", of course, is a no-brainer. Whether Confucius ("The rule of reciprocity") or secular wisdom, ("Do as you would be done by"), one sees the wisdom, even if stated negatively, ("Whatsoever thou wouldst that men should not do to thee, that do not thou to them" – Rabbi Hillel). It is, as theologian William Barclay put it, "The Everest of ethics".

The Golden Rule is, as theologian William Barclay put it, "The Everest of ethics".

The Narrow Way vv. 13,14

There has never been a world-class athlete or a winner of an Olympic medal who hasn't chosen a "narrow way" to victory. That "narrowness" for a swimmer means four to six hours in the pool every day for years. For a track athlete it means one's life spent in wind sprints, distance training, weight-lifting, and dieting. Indeed, most world class athletes, in moments of transparency, will mourn the loss of their youth. "While other kids were having fun, sleeping in, and eating whatever they liked, I was in the gym, tired and hungry all the time," one such athlete told me. It's a narrow path to winning gold.

The word translated "narrow" in v.13 is "straight" in the KJV. In Greek the word is "stenos" from the root "stenazo" which means "to groan". Indeed, a derivative is "stenochoria" which is translated "narrowness, anguish, distress". The imagery is inescapable. The "narrow way" runs counter to our natural inclinations. We want to slide. The narrow way insists we climb. Why? Because the prize is so great.

In v.14 "narrow" is another Greek word, "thlibo", which means, "hemmed in like a mountain gorge". Jesus' use of this word suggests the discipline required of those who attain to eternal life. Self-merit, stubborn insistence on pursuing one's own way, or a preference for sin, disqualify the pilgrim. One has to gut it out, risking one's "conventional life", traversing the precipices of the mountainous way if one is to reach the summit. Our breath may be gasps, our legs weak, and our heart pounding, but we'll never command such a view.

The point is: there are two choices in life. Broad way/Narrow way. Which will it be? The Bible resonates with the challenge. "Choose this

day whom you will serve" (Js. 24:15). "Choose life…" (De. 30:15-20).
"Behold, I set before you the way of life and the way of death" (Je. 21:8).
And it's a no-brainer. The Bible says, the "narrow way" is the road to life.
Indeed, in Psalm 1 we see "the way of the righteous" contrasted with "the
way of the wicked". There are two gates, two destinations, two crowds
– the many and the few. We're faced with an inescapable choice. And,
if we choose not to commit, putting the choice off "til later", we are by
our procrastination making the choice. The way of life is on the move,
the way of death is static. The Bible says, "Get moving."

False Teachers vv. 15–20

One thinks of Zephaniah's description of Jerusalem (Zp. 3:1-4) when
reading these words of Matthew. Zephaniah's words: "…her rulers are
ravening wolves who leave nothing for the morning. Her prophets are
unprincipled; they are treacherous people. Her priests profane the sanctuary and do violence to the law."

And, even as these purportedly righteous leaders muddy the water,
"The Lord within her is righteous; He does no wrong. Morning by
morning He dispenses justice, and every new day He does not fail, yet
the unrighteous know no shame" (v.5).

Jesus draws on the world of nature as he deduces an obvious truth, "by
their fruit you will recognize them." Grapes, thorn bushes, figs, thistles,
wolves, sheep – all contribute to the warning: "Watch out for false prophets."
A wolf may disguise himself, a tree can't. Like root, like fruit. Truth matters.

Lip Service vv. 21–23

If you "say", you've got to "do". Or, as we often hear, "you've got to
practice what you preach". If there's a gap between saying and doing,
Jesus will "say", "I never knew you". These are harsh words, putting the
responsibility and accountability of discipleship in clear relief. Saying
"Lord, Lord" is not enough. Jesus insists on *being* Lord.

As for those false prophets who "perform many miracles" in Jesus' name, one of the church "Fathers" by the name of Origen said, "Such curative power is of itself neither good, nor bad, but within the reach of godless as well as of honest people" ("Against Celsus" 3:22). The Apostle Paul, for example, had "hangers-on" in Ephesus who were the seven sons of Sceva, a Jewish chief priest, who would "invoke the name of the Lord Jesus over those who were demon-possessed" (Ac. 19:13-16). These poor fakers heard one of the evil spirits say, "Jesus I know, and Paul I know about, but who are you?" The evil spirit then attacked them, chasing them from the house in terrible shape, "naked and bleeding" (v.16). One should not mess with the spiritual world without the covering of Jesus' lordship. 'Tis a wise person indeed who not only "hears" the words of Jesus, but "puts them into practice", as we read in the next few verses.

The Solid Rock vv. 24–27

In Isaiah 28:17 the Lord says, "I will test you with the measuring line of justice and plumb line of righteousness." Integrity and sustainability are "tested" by life, and only that which is built righteously and justly will prevail. Thus say the Old Testament prophets again and again.

Jesus has stressed this truth in "these words of mine", that is, the teaching of the Sermon on the Mount. "Salt" and "light" are the elements of sustainability in Christian counter-culture. The disciple of Christ "hears" and "does" with obedience as a core value. Indeed, obedience to Jesus is the only safe foundation for life. Because the rain, the wind, and the flash flood will come, revealing either integrity or pretext, sustainability or fragmentation. We're all building a "house". In so doing we face a choice: do we build on rock or on sand? We're all on a journey. Another choice confronts us: do we choose the narrow or the broad way? Tough or easy? Which will it be? If we "halt between two opinions" perhaps we should consider another word from the Lord in Isaiah where he judges the ungodly with "the measuring line of chaos, and the plumb line of desolation" (34:11). Life is serious business.

Who IS this Person?? vv. 28,29

In Jesus' day the rabbis taught "by" authorities from the past. Like any modern academic when writing an essay, they referred to the sayings, writings, teachings of authorities who preceded them. But Jesus quoted no one. He spoke with his own authority "in the present". This approach "dumbfounded" (Greek) them. And it stirred them deeply. True authority has direct access to our hearts. It transcends the merely intellectual. It is "supra-rational", evoking an immediate response. This kind of authority was truly novel. The people had never heard anything and anyone like it. Who *was* this man?

Jesus' Signs & Wonders 8:1–9:34

Three Healings 8:1–17

1. The Leper 8:2-4

This healing of a leper is a fascinating story, not just for what it tells us, but for what it does not tell us. Jesus had just finished a major mentoring session with his disciples on the mountain. And, as mentioned earlier, there must have been many afflicted hangers-on who had accompanied them up the height. Waiting patiently, or impatiently, on the fringe of the teaching circle, were the "halt, the lame, and the blind". They wanted Jesus to get back to healing. And way beyond them, perhaps half-way down the mountain, marginalized and alone, stood a leper. I say "stood", but he may well have been crouching behind a large boulder. As a leper he was more than outcast. He was like a rabid dog. Without doubt some of the unruly crowd had shouted at him, thrown a stone or two in his direction, anything to keep his vile, breath-transmitted disease away.

As Jesus began his descent the leper saw his opportunity. He broke from his hiding place and ran up to meet the Healer. The crowd, angry at and fearful of him, gave way to a safe distance. The leper reached

Jesus, fell at his feet, and breathlessly said: "Lord, if you are willing, you can make me clean." And, in that private, transforming moment Jesus answered, "I am willing, be clean!"

The crowd had dispersed far away from the leper's presence. They saw the encounter, but could not hear the exchange. They couldn't believe what they saw – Jesus *touched* him! They kept their distance as the leper turned around and walked down the hill to Capernaum. They didn't know he'd been healed. They hadn't heard Jesus say, "Don't tell anyone." But for sure they heard all about it that evening or the next day. Jesus had done it again. This time against all social conventions and caution.

Moses had given express commands about leprosy and other defiling skin disorders in Leviticus chapters 13&14. These were rigorous laws of diagnosis and cleansing designed to protect Israel's desert-wandering millions from terrible diseases, leprosy being the worst.

When leprosy was diagnosed, everything the leper owned and touched was to be fumigated. Their clothing, the very hairs of their bodies which had sloughed off onto the ground, even the walls of their tents (and later their houses), had to be cleansed. The leper was exiled to live "outside the camp". Their presence on a street, in a house, or touching another person, rendered all unclean. And, if some unwitting person were to come within proximity of a victim, the leper had to cover his mouth and shout a warning, "Unclean! Unclean!"

The priest was the medical authority. If it appeared that someone had been healed of a skin disorder, he had to go to the priest for medical clearance. And he had to go through a sacrificial cleansing ritual (Le. 14:3-7). Then he was free.

The "wonder" of Jesus' healing of the leper in this story is not so much that he healed him, but that he *touched* him. Jesus seemed impervious to personal risk and common sense. He lived by different rules.

The "wonder" of Jesus' healing of the leper in this story, is not so much that he healed him, but that he touched him.

2. The Centurion's Servant 8:5-13

The wonder of this healing, like that of the leper, goes beyond the eradication of an affliction. In this case the wonder is that a Roman centurion, a Gentile (!), should have greater faith than Jesus had ever seen in any Israelite (including his own disciples!).

"You don't need to come to my house, or touch my paralyzed servant," says the centurion to Jesus, "you just have to say the word. Your authority is enough."

The centurion's faith was not blind. He had perhaps seen Jesus at work, and he certainly was aware of Jesus' reputation. He may even have witnessed the remarkable transformation of the leper as he had exited the priest's home in Capernaum, a clean bill of health in his hand. The centurion put two and two together. "Jesus has authority over illness like I have authority over my one-hundred soldiers. I command. They obey. Jesus commands. Sickness flees. My servant is ill. Jesus can heal him by a word."

The centurion is an example of faith "feeding" reason. Just like a scientist has vision (faith) for a cure, and then applies his reason in the pursuit of it, so too a believer "sees" the healing and then takes steps to the Healer. But the reasonable steps must be preceded by faith. "Ask, seek, knock" are all predicated on the belief that the solution can and will be found. Faith is not the throw of a dice.

3. Peter's Mother-in-law 8:14-17

Jesus probably had a room in Peter's house in Capernaum. He was a permanent "boarder" in his adopted hometown when he wasn't on the road. And, for sure, he knew Peter's mother-in-law very well. She too lived there, and with her daughter, Peter's wife (1Co. 9:5), managed the household. Peter's mother-in-law was Jesus' friend.

Most Bible commentators think her fever was probably malaria. In the Hula Valley just a few miles north in the Upper Galilee, the swampy conditions incubated millions of mosquitoes, many of which carried the malarial parasite. So malaria was all too common in the region. And, as still is the case in many parts of our world, malaria can and does kill people.

So Jesus sees Peter's mother-in-law suffering this horrible fever lying in her bed, he touches her, and she is healed. Then, as if this were just another day in the life of Capernaum, she gets up and "waits on him". And, after supper, he goes outside and heals the sick[1] who have gathered about the house.

The "wonder" of this story may have been that Jesus healed both at home and outside the home. He wasn't a "performer" for the crowds. He cared for those who cared for him.

The Cost of Discipleship 8:18–22 (see Lk. 9:57–60)

When Jesus wasn't bunking in at Peter's house in Capernaum, he stayed wherever he could while itinerating. Technically he was homeless, but we have no record of him ever having no choice but to sleep out of doors. His life was arduous. Walking great distances, engaging huge, demanding crowds, dealing with the "business" of a "road crew" of twelve plus a coterie of several helpers, he was under constant stress. Little wonder he often withdrew to a quiet place in the mountains or by the sea, to rest. Many of those retreats were at night while others slept.

---

[1] The common view of the time was that most illnesses were caused by evil spirits.

So we, perhaps, can understand his abrupt response to an idealistic would-be follower who says, "I will follow you wherever you go." Jesus says, "I'm homeless. Do you want to be homeless?" And more abruptness: "Let the dead bury themselves," he says to another "novitiate" who's just been bereaved. Stunned by these in-your-face words from Jesus, these two would need time to process. Maybe the next day they might have given thought to the core message of Jesus' harshness: the claims of the Kingdom of Heaven take precedence over every other urgency. Followers of Christ must march to the beat of a different drum. It's going to cost.

By the way, in responding to the first man, Jesus refers to himself as "Son of Man". This is the first of thirty-two times that Jesus refers to himself this way in the Gospel of Matthew. It was a term that had both history and significance.

In the Old Testament "ben adam" (Hebrew) connotes the essential frailty of human nature. It presents him as inconsequential. "What is man, that Thou are mindful of him? and the son of man, that Thou visitest him?" (Ps. 8:4). "Put not your trust in princes, nor in the son of man, in whom is no help" (Ps. 146:3). In the Book of Ezekiel the prophet is referred to as "son of man" eighty-seven times. For a man with so many other-worldly visions the term was maybe used by the Lord to remind him that his feet were both made of clay and were still on the ground.

The idea that this earthly term might have heavenly consequences was introduced in the Book of Daniel: "One like the Son of Man came with the clouds of heaven, and was brought to the Ancient of Days… and there was given unto Him dominion and glory and a kingdom" (Da. 7:13). This descriptor occurs in the midst of an apocalyptic vision. Apocalyptic is *very* difficult to understand, let alone interpret, and to my relief I have no inclination to even try in the context of this New Testament commentary (it is *casual* after all!). But it must be said that this "Son of Man" is seen both by the Jewish Talmud and the New Testament as a term full of messianic implications. Jesus' use of it as a self-descriptor was not lost on those who had training in Old Testament eschatology. It's interesting to note, however, that the term has had little play in common use of Christian theological or liturgical language. We tend to think of it mainly as referring to Jesus' human nature. We don't often think of it as either messianic or heavenly. Yet, "Son of Man" had almost equivalent meaning as "Son of God" in some rabbinical schools. It was as though this "son" had one foot on earth even as the other foot was in Heaven. He was both God and man.

More Miracles 8:23–9:8

In these verses we come to a second grouping of miracles that demonstrate Jesus' authority over nature, the spirit world, and even over sin itself. Each is remarkable.

Calming of the Sea 8:23–27

Try Googling "Calming the Storm" by Rembrandt. This classic painting (painted in 1632) was stolen from the Isabella Stewart Gardner Museum in 1990. Some refer to this as "the biggest art heist in US history".

I'm no art critic but the experts tell us that "every line of the painting converges in Christ". And, in the seismic tempest there is a shaft of light breaking through the clouded heavens portraying the proximity of Divine Providence. It's a gripper. Sadly, the painting is yet to be recovered.

Jesus must have been very tired because Matthew tells us he was asleep in this maelstrom of wind and waves. In a panic the disciples woke him up, and Jesus, seemingly oblivious to the raging tumult asks why they are so afraid. It came as a bit of a rebuke. But then Jesus "rebukes" the storm, and all is suddenly calm.

"Whoa! Who is this?" The disciples exclaim, "Even the wind and the waves obey him!" Such authority!

There was a life lesson here for the disciples, but later narratives indicate they didn't readily learn it. The lesson? Jesus has authority over the "slings and arrows of outrageous fortune". He is there in our human vulnerability and helplessness, as he is when life accidents occur. He is Lord over all nature. He hears the calls of the desperate.

Authority over the Spirit World 8:28–34

After this huge nature miracle the disciples steered the boat over to the northeastern shore of the Sea of Galilee. They beached the boat and then began the arduous climb to the mountains above the lake. This was "the region of the Gadarenes", Gentile country. There has been much discussion among scholars as to the name and specific location of the settlement(s) there. Was it Gadara – east of the Sea, sixteen miles from Tiberias, on the northwest side of the Gilead mountains? Or was it Gerassa – in the Gilead district twenty miles east of the Jordan? Then again maybe it wasn't an urban area as such, but was connected to the Girgashites, one of the Canaanite groups that occupied Canaan before the arrival of the Israelites. Regardless, it was in the general area of the Gentile "Decapolis", ten cities that included Bet Shean (a major city about twenty miles south of Tiberias). Today we refer to some of the area as "the Golan Heights". Regardless, the disciples were about to witness a shocking scene.

First, a word or two about demons. This is a study in itself, far beyond the scope of this "casual" commentary. But let me give you a thumbnail sketch of the biblical/cultural view in the history of Israel and the time of Jesus.

The disciples were about to witness a shocking scene.

In early Israelite history the view of "demon" was not necessarily negative. A demon existed within a generic category of "spirits" or even "gods" (small "g"). There was a blurring of later era definitions. Sometimes a "seer" or prophet gave utterance under the influence of a "demon", sometimes a "god", and each could also be described as a "ruach" or "wind". Regardless of the parsing of definitions, the Old Testament view was that Israel was surrounded by demons and spirits, gods of all sorts, most of which were malevolent. But "the God of Abraham, Isaac, and Jacob" was Lord, protector, healer, deliverer, and Father. The Old Testament prophets were clear in their message: Love the Lord God with heart, soul, mind and strength, and all would be well. Satan, the "adversary", and his minions would flee at the invocation of "the Name".

But, the Israelite cultural/spiritual view in the cut and thrust of everyday life saw affliction as the work of evil spirits. Pretty much any illness, be it epilepsy, palsy, paralysis, wasting diseases, etc., were the work of demons. Thus, the spiritual leaders of Israel developed a means to combatting these enemies by invoking the name of the Lord: "I adjure you by the Name..." and the demons were forced to flee because the very act of invocation demanded their departure. Unfortunately, these "adjurations" weren't always successful. This is why in Jesus' healing ministry the people were so amazed at his 100% success rate. Only those who were spiritually aware saw that Jesus never "adjured" nor did he "exorcize". He simply commanded. His authority was more than even "legions" of demons could bear. They were blinded by his light.

Leaping past the Old Testament era, through the 400 year inter-testamental period, to Jesus' day, the relationship between illness and demonic activity wasn't even questioned. Matthew spends no time distinguishing what was or may have been at the root of what some later scholars call "mental illness". As far as Matthew was concerned "lunatic" (KJV) meant "moonstruck" which meant an evil spirit was present (Mt. 4:24; 17:15). And Jesus sometimes would command the spirit to leave, other times he would "heal". The descriptive word was essentially irrelevant. What mattered was the release of the afflicted one from bondage. No oppression, or possession, could stand when Jesus was near. He was totally Master of both the physical and the spirit world. Jesus ruled.

Now, back to the story. Jesus and the disciples, after an arduous climb above the lake, crest the final height and are just catching their breath on the plateau. Suddenly, out of nowhere they hear blood-curdling screams and see two naked wild men running toward them, hair and spit flying, limbs flailing, delirious madness on their faces. And, just as the disciples reflexively assume a defensive posture, the madmen put on the brakes, falling back as if struck by an invisible sword. They've seen Jesus in the group and draw back in total fear.

Demons are compulsive exhibitionists in the presence of the Holy. So immediately, in their terror they cry, "What do you want with us, Son of God? Have you come here to torture us before the appointed time?" No subtlety here. Just abject terror and clear thinking in the presence of their greatest enemy. They know who Jesus is.

There's a touch of irony here. Just a few hours ago the disciples were asking, "What kind of man is this?" as Jesus calmed the storm. Here, the demons are asking, "What do you want with us, Son of God?" The disciples, like the rest of Israel's populace, didn't get it. Right up to the crucifixion, in spite of all that Jesus said and did, the disciples were essentially blind. Even Peter, who later made the great confession, "Thou art the Christ, the Son of the living God" at Caesarea Philippi, denied him three times and ran away when Jesus was arrested in Gethsemane. No, the Twelve didn't get it. But the demons did. And trembled. They knew that Judgement Day, with Jesus as Judge, was on the horizon. The "abyss" awaited.

No, the Twelve didn't get it. But the demons did. And trembled.

In desperation the demons "begged" Jesus, "If you drive us out, send us into the herd of pigs." Jesus answers, "Go", and they go. The whole herd (St. Mark tells us there were 2000!) rushes down the steep bank the disciples have just climbed and drowns in the lake. The swine-herders run in terror to tell all of Gadera what has just happened. Their "report" obviously panicked the town. They must have believed that this Jesus, whom they had never met, was a Destroyer not a Savior. In fear they went out to implore him to do no more damage and leave their region. If they'd had them in their day they would have called the cops. With an understanding look of "no worries" the unwanted Jesus turns and walks back to the boat.

"But hold on!" you might say. "What about those poor pigs? And the owner! How much did he lose? Besides, I thought Jews didn't raise pigs!"

You're right. Pigs were unclean to Jews – unkosher. But remember the Gadarenes were Gentiles. The owners of such a huge herd may have been the half-Jew Herod's family. The Roman Emperor Augustus' comment that it was "safer to be Herod's pig, than his son" implies that Herod may have kept herds of pigs for commercial sale to the Roman army. The soldiers loved bacon! The pigs were living with a death sentence anyway. It's just that they died of drowning rather than being butchered.

One more thing – let's not be too hard on the Gadarenes for rejecting Jesus. In some faintly similar parallel circumstance we might do the same. For example, how often do people, temporarily at least, blame God for the sudden death of a loved one and say, "I don't believe anymore"? How often is our faith shaken when our life is shaken? We want God to be the defender and sustainer of the status quo. So long as everything runs smoothly we claim a comfortable faith. But when a life accident rocks the boat we exclaim, "I'm out of here!"

When Christ is near so is the Kingdom of Heaven. We're forced to embrace the big picture, which always challenges the safe parameters of the status quo. When Christ is near our whole way of life is under scrutiny, and we're conscious of our accountability to God and neighbor. This rankles us. We'd rather be self-absorbed. We want to stay safe within our cultural borders. "We're Gentiles not Jews! What does this Jesus have to do with us? We don't want to be responsible for the poor, the marginalized, the maniacs. And we certainly don't want monetary loss, porcine or otherwise. So go away Jesus. We don't want you in our lives. Nothing personal! Don't call us. We'll call you."

Authority over Sin 9:1–8

Without protest Jesus and the disciples returned to their boat and sailed back to Capernaum, "his own city." As usual, huge crowds awaited him. So, while teaching and healing from the front door (or balcony) of Peter's (probably) house, there was a sudden commotion as four men carried a litter through the crowd. There was a young man on the litter. He was paralyzed.

Ignoring preamble (no "How are you? What seems to be the problem? Can I help?") Jesus says, "Cheer up, son, your sins are forgiven." Jesus assumes a paternal tone, which is a touch surprising in that he had recently turned thirty. Perhaps this young man was in his teens, half Jesus' age. Regardless, Jesus addresses the core issue. Sin, not paralysis, was the boy's problem. The soul's disease had priority.

> *Regardless, Jesus addresses the core issue.*
> *Sin, not paralysis, was the boy's problem.*

I'm no psychologist, but I wonder if there was some connection between this young man's paralysis and the burden of guilt he was carrying for some unnamed sin. There was need for Jesus to cheer him up, apart from some silent depression/torment that had overtaken him. If it had just been low spirits because of his paralysis Jesus might have said, "Cheer up son, you are healed. Get up." No. Jesus knew immediately that this boy's need was spiritual. His physical need was secondary. He strengthened his soul and then his legs.

The religious leaders, of course, were immediately awash in stuttering spittle. "There he goes again! Blaspheming! Only God can forgive sin. This man is a fraud!"

Jesus pushes back. So fellas, what's easier? To forgive sins, or to heal paralysis? He then consigns them to simmering consternation and surly silence by healing the boy. Jesus was the "Son of Man", the unrecognized (by one and all) Messiah. He had authority over illness and sin. The people "marveled". The critics marinated. The boy walked away, free at last.

A New Way 9:9–17

Jesus was obviously different. The people had seen and heard from all kinds of zealots and rabbis in their time. But there was no one like Jesus. Perhaps one of the most glaring evidences of his uniqueness was the character and nature of his disciples and of those whom he seemed to attract. In the main they were blue-collar, marginalized, relatively uneducated "am ha aretz" ("people of the Land"). They seemed to suit him.

The Calling of Matthew 9:9

If Jesus had had one ounce of political correctness he never would have called Matthew to follow him. Matthew was a "publican", a tax collector. He sat in the toll booth in Capernaum collecting taxes for the hated Roman occupiers. Roman businessmen used to bid on the right to collect taxes in various regions and would sub-contract the work to Jewish men like Matthew. Graft and corruption were the name of the game. Both contractor and sub-contractor got their cut before anything was forwarded to the Roman officials. The taxpayers knew this, resented it, but could do nothing about it. What they could do, however, was despise their turncoat countryman who was putting the squeeze on them. The publican was referred to as "the pariah of Palestine". His money was not accepted as alms, and his evidence was not accepted in courts of law. Seen as unpatriotic extortionists, the publicans were outcast and universally hated. One had to have a very strong love for money to put up with this constant vilification and social isolation. You had to get used to eating alone.

So imagine Matthew's shock at hearing "Follow me" from the Son of Man. What? You want me? Nobody wants me! But Jesus nods in the affirmative and invites himself over to Matthew's house for dinner. Oh, by the way, I'll be bringing a few others with me. Matthew rushes home to alert his wife and servants.

Jesus' Bad Company 9:10–13

Matthew the publican was just one of Jesus' marginalized followers and friends. When Jesus showed up for dinner at his new recruit's house there were plenty more shadowy characters. In his gospel, Matthew describes them as fellow "publicans and sinners". These would run the gamut of tax collectors to homeless and street walkers. They were the ones unwelcome at respectable homes. They like Matthew were seen as "unclean".

The Pharisees clustered outside Matthew's "unclean" house were probably those who had witnessed the healing of the paralytic. As the disciples entered, these Pharisees assailed them with comment and question. So how come your master who makes all these holy claims eats with publicans and sinners? Doesn't he know they're unclean? Maybe it's because he's unclean! Nonplussed, the disciples carry on into the house and tell Jesus what the Pharisees are saying.

Didn't they know that mercy trumps everything?

I wonder if he rolled his eyes? He quoted Hosea 6:6, "I desire mercy, not sacrifice" and stated what for him was an obvious truth (and an indirect criticism of the Pharisees), "It is not the healthy who need a doctor, but the sick." The Pharisees were the ones who had "broken the covenant" (Ho. 6:7). Their religious correctness had mummified their souls. Didn't they know that mercy trumps everything?

Jesus Questioned about Fasting 9:14–17

Enter John the Baptist's disciples. Jesus had upset even them! They're all concerned about the baldly unascetic lifestyle of Jesus' disciples. They don't fast! say John's followers. We fast. And so do the Pharisees for that matter. What's up with your guys?

They are referring to the voluntary fasting, not the required fasting on Yom Kippur (Day of Atonement). The Pharisees fasted every Monday and Thursday. Apparently John's disciples did too. They were pious. Jesus and his disciples were not. Why?

It's interesting that even though Jesus was now on the scene teaching and healing, with disciples in tow, John's ministry was still in place. He was beloved by thousands, and followed by many. It could be that the day Jesus went to Matthew's house was a fast day for John's men. This feast would offend on a few levels, not the least being the stark contrast between their ascetic, camel-hair coated leader and this party-goer. They were beginning to have doubts about Jesus. Even John himself was getting worried that he had baptized the wrong man. "Are you the one who is to come, or should we expect someone else?" (11:3). Jesus was too "new" for comfort.

Yes, Jesus says in response, we *are* having a party. It's a wedding party. I'm the bridegroom and these are my guests. We're making merry. But the day will come when I'll be taken away from them. Then they will fast.

To emphasize the point he refers to new wine and old wine skins. New wine ferments and swells. If poured into old wineskins, which have already stretched, the percolating new wine will explode. So new wine needs flexible new wineskins.

The message is clear. Jesus is new wine. The Oral Law which the Pharisees hold high is an old wineskin. Jesus doesn't fit their container. Little wonder these religious leaders are bursting in apoplectic rage. Their wineskin has burst too.

More Miracles 9:18–34

Jesus is hardly finished the first course of the feast when a synagogue leader bursts in, his face drawn with sorrow. What follows is an account of four miracles where Jesus' authority over death, chronic illness, blindness and dumbness is demonstrated.

> *It's amazing how life's unexpected urgencies can cut through our cultural values and petty dogmatics.*

This bereaved "ruler" would have been one of the "parnasim" (pastors) of the Capernaum synagogue. Everyone at the party would recognize him. Undoubtedly he had had to shoulder his way through the angry Pharisees crowding the entrance to Matthew's house. He didn't care what these colleagues said. His daughter was dead. Only Jesus could raise her to life again. It's amazing how life's unexpected urgencies can cut through our cultural values and petty dogmatics. One is pushed beyond the vain parsing of one's theological/philosophical/idealogical "truths" to the adrenalin fueled present reality. You cut to the chase. Help! I need help! Help me please!

Jesus and his disciples responded immediately, getting up from the meal, following the man to his home. On the way, cutting through the milling swarm of both critics and followers, there is a unique, mysterious moment. An anonymous, meek woman almost imperceptibly touches the "hem of his garment". I say imperceptibly because it was. Here Jesus is jostling his way from one house to another, one surrounded by fulminating critics, the other with ululating mourners. Jesus was being touched and elbowed by scores of people. Yet there was something about this contact that stopped him in his tracks. As if he had heard her inward conversation, "If I only touch his cloak, I will be healed", he turns to her and says, "Take heart, daughter, your faith has healed you." Healed of what? Matthew just says "bleeding". Bleeding for twelve years! This was some sort of female affliction. Perhaps a fistula caused by giving birth. But at that moment the bleeding stopped. Twelve years of discomfort and occasional anaemia over. What a relief! She melts into the crowd. We don't even know her name.

If indeed her affliction had been caused by childbirth twelve years previously, her baby would have been born in the same year the synagogue leader's daughter had been born. We don't know her name either. She had died.

Already the hired wailers were wailing, the local musicians were piping mournful minor key tunes. The crowd was restless, some legitimately sad, others there for the customary funeral food. They make way for the man on a mission. He looks at them sternly and orders them away. She's not dead, she's asleep he says to their incredulous ears. Immediately they mock him. So easy to mock. Sir Alfred Lord Tennyson called mockery "the fume of little hearts" ("Idylls of the King, 'Guinevere'"). Some people will give you a piece of their mind no matter how little they have to spare.

Sir Alfred Lord Tennyson called mockery "the fume of little hearts".

Jesus goes into the house. He takes the hand of the little girl as her body lies on the bed. At his touch she awakens, gets up, goes to the door and waves to the crowd. Even as they marvel they slink away, amazed and ashamed of themselves at the same time. Who *is* this man?

Two blind but vocal men followed Jesus as he walked back to Matthew's place. He seemingly ignored their shouts, "Have mercy on us, Son of David!". Perhaps because this was a messianic title he wanted to distance himself from for the time being. He went into the house presumably to resume the feast but also to get away from these vociferous blind men. But they followed him in. Jesus asked what seemed to be an unnecessary question, "Do you believe that I am able to do this?" They answered, "Yes Lord". After all they'd just been caught up in the flurry of the crowd's amazement at the raising of the dead girl. Jesus said, "According to your faith let it be done to you." Even as their eyes opened Jesus warned them to keep this miracle to themselves. Sure thing Lord, they said, and went out telling everyone. Just as it happened with the raising of the synagogue leader's daughter, it happened again, "News of this spread through all that region." The momentum was building to get this man on the throne in Jerusalem *now*!

More fuel was added to the messianic momentum just a few hours later. As Jesus and the disciples exited Matthew's house someone brought a man to him who had been rendered mute by an evil spirit. Jesus drove the demon out and the man spoke. The crowd who in the last several hours had been inundated with amazement upon amazement exclaimed, "Nothing like this has ever been seen in Israel." The miffed, intransigent Pharisees could just croak, "It is by the prince of demons that he drives out demons." Even as the rejoicing of the recently healed blind men was ringing in their ears the Pharisees blinded their own eyes. Their souls were in darkness.

These miracle stories need little explanation. Just one point occurs to me. The question, "Do you believe?" is timeless and universal. Our honest response is usually, "Help thou mine unbelief." But let's remember that faith itself is a gift from God. Its roots run deeper than doubt. When we suffer a faith deficit we simply need to dig deeper.

MARCHING ORDERS FOR THE DISCIPLES 9:35–10:42

Jesus was about to authorize the disciples as preachers and teachers of the Kingdom of God. They were rookies but they had seen Jesus' model of ministry and had also been mentored in many an "in camera" session. They needed to be gently pushed out of the nest.

Matthew provides a two sentence transition. He summarizes Jesus' ministry methodology, comments on the helplessness of the "am ha aretz" (people of the Land), and then launches into ministry marching orders.

The Critical Role of Compassion 9:35,36

Jesus' arduous ministry was fueled by compassion. This word "compassion" is another word for "mercy" in the Old Testament. The Hebrew for mercy is usually "racham", but "chamal, chus, chesed", all with their own nuances, are also used. Generally mercy is a loving act of God as he shows his covenant commitment to Israel. Indeed, I use the word "commitment" intentionally. Israel's claim to God's mercy was predicated on his initiative in promising that he would be "merciful and gracious, slow to anger, and abounding in steadfast love" (Ex. 34:6; Ne. 9:17; Ps's. 86:15; 103:8; 145:8; Jl. 2:13; Jo. 4:2). It was a good thing for Israel that God chose to commit to them in this way. Israel was continually calling on God's mercy again and again as she suffered the collateral damage of her idolatries.

Culturally in everyday Israelite life compassion/mercy were seen as common currency. The closest ties for a Hebrew were found in family. "Family" and "mercy" were equivalent values. One was to show help, love, consideration to family first, then tribe and community. Included within the scope of mercy were children, the aged, poor, orphaned, and widowed. To truly love God one must truly love neighbor. The 'righteousness/justice" call of the Old Testament prophets prevailed – right relationship with God, right relationship with neighbor.

In the New Testament the Greek word for compassion is "splanchnizomai" which means "to be moved in one's bowels". The Greek culture saw the bowels as the seat of turbulent passions such as anger and love. The Hebrews, on the other hand, regarded the bowels as the center of tender affections like kindness, charity, pity and love. Mercy was an inner-feeling, a visceral reflex to someone's deep need. This was the nature of the compassion of Jesus.

The sick and the suffering were continually appealing to Jesus for mercy, "Lord... have mercy!" (Mt. 9:27; 15:22; 17:15; 20:30-34;

Mk. 5:19; 9:22; 10:47; Lk. 17:13; 18:38). And, even as they cried out we see Jesus motivated by what one commentator called "the pain of love" in healing the blind (Mt. 20:34), the leper (Mk. 1:41), teaching the ignorant (Mk. 6:34), raising the dead (Lk. 7:13), and feeding the hungry (Mt. 15:32; Mk. 8:2). Compassion "blindsided" Jesus (just like it should blindside us). And it catalyzed unconditional acts of rescue.

Compassion "blindsided" Jesus (just like it should blindside us). And it catalyzed unconditional acts of rescue.

The Call for Workers 9:34–10:4

Moved by compassion Jesus compares the ministry of the Kingdom to shepherding and farming. There is urgency in each. The shepherd's sheep are being harassed by wild predators and the wheat harvest is rotting in the fields due to the lack of farm workers. Manpower is the issue. Jesus beseeches the disciples to pray for more laborers. Shepherds and farm-hands are at a premium.

At moments like this we get a faint insight into Jesus' personal stress level. He had more than the mentoring of the disciples in mind. He had to get them in the game, yes. But, his mind was way beyond them to a vast horizon. He had been tasked by his Father to redeem the universe. There was (and is) a long way to go.

82

The Twelve Authorized 10:1–4

Jesus is about to send them out two by two. Interestingly Matthew presents them in pairs: Simon and Andrew (brothers), James and John (brothers), Philip and Bartholomew, Thomas and Matthew (some commentators think they too were brothers), James and Thaddeus, Simon the Canaanite and Judas Iscariot. If "Iscariot" means "a man of Kerioth" then we can assume that Judas was a Judean, with a tendency to religious nationalism. Then, some theologians see "Iscariot" as derived from the Aramaic "ishkariya" meaning "the false". Regardless, the name "Judas" is bathed in infamy.

Matthew refers to these men as "apostles". This designation meant they were being "sent" with the authority and commission of the sender. They had authority because they were under authority. Later in the history of the early church it was assumed that an apostle was a member of an elite group: he had seen the risen Christ. This is why the Apostle Paul was included in this select crew: he had seen Jesus in his vision on the road to Damascus, although he referred to himself as "the least of the apostles". And, by the middle of the second century the canon of the New Testament was incrementally being shaped from writings exclusively authored by these apostles. They were the only "authorized version".

Rules of Engagement 10:5–42

What follows is a kind of ministry manual. Unwritten, it is Jesus' verbal description of what lies ahead on the very first evangelism campaign. It's an entry-level charge to ministry rookies.

Israel First 10:5,6

You've got to start somewhere. So start with your own people, the ones with whom you have cultural, spiritual common ground. Tell them your story. Tell them how and why you are followers of Jesus. Then get into the message of the Kingdom. Avoid the mystery religious speculations of the Gentiles, and the spiritually confused theology of the Samaritans. Both groups will only waste your time – for now at least. You're going to learn by doing. The "lost sheep of Israel" will keep you, and those who follow after, busy until the Day of the Lord (v.23b).

The above is my presumptuous and loose paraphrase of Jesus' first instructions. You see his kindness and brotherly love for these rough-hewn Galileans. He knows they're going to enter a ministry context where angels themselves might fear to tread. He wants them to return intact.

The Message, Signs and Wonders 10:7–8

Jesus had introduced his ministry with "Repent, for the Kingdom of Heaven has come near." Now he's investing that message in his disciples. Their sermon outline is brief. And they are to follow up their preaching with miraculous manifestations of the nearness of the Kingdom. All of this they are to do for free.

Travel Guidelines 10:9–15

When reading this passage I'm reminded of the forty years the children of Israel wandered in the wilderness after the Exodus. The food that sustained them came daily as "manna". They weren't allowed to stockpile it. If they did it rotted. Their food security was God himself. Here Jesus tells the new recruits that they are to take what is on their backs. No extras. No extra shirt, no extra sandals, no extra staff, and especially – no money! They are to rely on the benevolence of good people whom they will meet from town to town. When no charity is forthcoming they are to "shake the dust off their feet" and move on. Jesus says it will not go well for those who reject the Gospel of the Kingdom.

The Tough Road Ahead 10:16–42

Even as Jesus instructed his disciples for this first foray into the world with the Gospel of the Kingdom one wonders if his eyes looked beyond the next few months to the great missionary movements that would follow in millennia to come. For the disciples this was to be essentially a "provincial" exercise. But for Jesus, his words imply a "universal" effort that will impact the rest of time.

The similes swirl: sheep, wolves, serpents, doves. As he did with parables Jesus engaged pictures from nature to make his point. In this instance the word pictures point to the total vulnerability he is imposing on his cherished few. He feels a bit like a modern parent who is about to pass the family car keys to a newly licensed daughter. You're going to face multi-lanes of traffic, speeders, idiots, mechanical breakdown, hazards of every kind, road racers... yikes!

Councils, synagogues, governors, kings, Jews, Gentiles – you'll upset them all. They will hate you, Jesus says. The persecution they will face will reflect the persecution of their master – "If they call me Beelzebub, what will they call you?" How about what one Roman ruler in the second century called them? "Haters of mankind."

"If they call me Beelzebub, what will they call you?" How about what one Roman ruler in the second century called them? "Haters of mankind."

His eyes still on the millennia to come, Jesus implies that their work of evangelism will outlive them and the task assigned. Not only will the evangelization of their own people never end, but so will the evangelization of the world. This Gospel witness will be hard at work until the Day of the Lord (v.23b).

In the meantime they should be prepared for international, national, community, and even family dislocations. It is not Jesus' purpose, but the effect of the Gospel of the Kingdom will fracture relationships. Closest to home will be the home itself.

Perhaps Jesus was thinking of his own family. We know his brothers and sisters didn't believe in him. It wasn't till the crucifixion and a post-resurrection appearance to Jesus' brother James that the family believed. And what about the disciples' families? Had Zebedee endorsed his two sons' abandonment of the family fishing nets? Did Peter's wife and mother-in-law get along? Especially in the stress of Peter's delinquency from day to day family provision? Who knows what strain the disciples' families had undergone? In Peter's case what impact did his eventual crucifixion (upside down!) in Rome have on his wife and children? Did any of them carry bitterness to the grave? In any event the Gospel can cut as well as heal. The weight of the cross will crease your shoulders.

VARIOUS CONTROVERSIES 11:1–12:50

When Matthew wrote this gospel the early church was already two or three decades old. The followers of "The Way" (as Christianity was then known) had a young but growing doctrinal signature. They had a fairly high view of themselves, as heavenly citizens (Ph. 3:20), as fruitful (Ro. 8:23), and endowed with a bank of memories (albeit relatively recent) of the manifestation of heaven's powers (He. 6:5). But they lacked cohesion. They were adrift in terms of a universal dogmatic. They were "free wheeling", but slowly gaining stability as apostolic gospels and letters began to circulate. They were like a young driver learning how to negotiate traffic.

So as Matthew, under the inspiration of the Spirit, reflects on his formative following of Jesus, he remembers a kaleidoscope of controversies that emerged in Jesus' ministry. He does so with the hindsight of history, reflection, and the application of these life lessons to the present growing pains of the nascent Christian world.

An Impatient John the Baptist 11:2–19

Jesus' cousin, John the Baptist, was in prison. He had been rudely wrested from his high profile public ministry and thrust into a dungeon, all because he dared criticize Herod's marriage to his brother's wife Herodias. There in the dank darkness John had the unhealthy opportunity to marinate in the injustices he suffered, and to overanalyze his ministry. This gave room to doubt, not the least being his growing uncertainty about what he thought was the pinnacle of his ministry: the baptism of Jesus. He was getting a steady diet of secondhand reports indicating that Jesus, nationally interpreted, was proving to be a disappointment. John and his disciples were expecting the Kingdom *now*. Jesus wasn't delivering. Where was "the axe at the root of the tree"? Where the "consuming fire"? (Mt. 3:10,12). Cutting to the chase, John sends his men to confront his cousin. Are you the one? Or did we get it wrong?

Jesus, somewhat hurt by John's question, refers to two messianic passages from the Hebrew scriptures:

"Then will the eyes of the blind be opened
and the ears of the deaf unstopped...
The Spirit of the Sovereign lord is on me
because the Lord has anointed me
to proclaim good news to the poor.
He has sent me to bind up the brokenhearted,
to proclaim freedom for the captives
and release from darkness for the prisoners,
to proclaim the year of the Lord's favor
and the day of vengeance of our God,
to comfort all who mourn,
and provide for those who grieve in Zion -
to bestow on them a crown of beauty
instead of ashes,
the oil of joy
instead of mourning,

and a garment of praise
instead of despair.
They will be called oaks of righteousness,
a planting of the Lord
for the display of his splendor."

—Is. 35:5; 61:1-3

It would appear that the "crowd" had been in on this interchange. They had heard Jesus' tone as he responded to this not so indirect criticism from the famous prophet. So, in case they misread him, Jesus speaks to them about John.

(Please indulge me as I paraphrase.) So what did you expect when you flocked in your thousands down to John's baptisms? A slender reed blown about by the wind? A courtier in soft clothing? Or a prophet? Yes you wanted to see a prophet but you got more than you bargained for. You got a loud, ear-piercing blast from a shofar (ram's horn) announcing the coming of the Messiah. You got Elijah himself, not as a reincarnation, but as his very voice declaring the Day of the Lord (Ma. 4:5). John is the last of the old order of Old Testament prophets. Indeed he's the greatest of them. But the new order has come. Anyone of this heavenly citizenry supersedes those of the old order. But make no mistake. John represents a sea-change in God's dealing with mankind. His voice has been heard in the heavens.

A showdown was in the works.

Then Jesus went on to observe that even though the new order was in its infancy, there had already been attempts by religious nationalist zealots to violently seize on John's and Jesus' momentum. They were trying to enlist the cousins' followers in a movement to overthrow the Romans and establish a Jewish throne in Jerusalem. Indeed, Jesus already had one of these violent people in his "cabinet", Judas Iscariot. A showdown was in the works.

This coming conflict would be predicated on more than dissatisfaction with Jesus. Misunderstanding of both his message and mission would play a huge role.

Jesus laments the general misrepresentation of both John and himself. He compares the religious culture to children playing a game called "Weddings and Funerals". We played a pipe for you John, but you wouldn't dance. We sang a dirge for you Jesus, but you wouldn't mourn. You're possessed by a grim religious spirit, John. And Jesus, you're a party animal. John is too serious by half. Jesus has no self-discipline.

Jesus' response: Really? The proof of the pudding is in the eating. Nevertheless he knew he would be "despised and rejected of men..." (Is. 53).

Acceptance or Rejection? 11:20–30

Jesus' next words are disturbing, not just for what they say about the three cities near the Sea of Galilee, but for their ramifications for urban culture everywhere. We don't know much about Chorazin (now a small settlement of modern houses on the northern slopes above Capernaum), and we know little more about Bethsaida, the hometown of Peter, Andrew, and Philip. Capernaum on the other hand was the epicenter of Jesus' ministry. At this early stage in the narrative we've already seen a number of miracles performed in his adopted hometown: a nobleman's son, a demoniac, a paralyzed young man, Peter's mother-in-law, a woman with a chronic bleeding, a synagogue leader's daughter and a centurion's servant had already been impacted by Jesus' compassion and healing power. Yet he excoriates all three towns without any specific charges other than their refusal to repent. There must have been something about their urban culture that hardened their hearts.

We've all read articles on the internet celebrating the restorative experience of getting out of the urban rat race to commune with nature. The writers speak of the salubrious impact of fresh air, wildlife, arboreal beauty, peace, and the revival of the soul. They often reference psychological studies that affirm their thesis: cities are bad for one's spirit. I think we all agree.

Cities can be the petri dish for the cultivation of soul-numbing world-liness. The essential toxin of worldly living is independence. We were created to be in fellowship with our Creator and to be solely dependent on his provision through earth and sky. He sees us as his children – dependent ones. City living, however, incrementally inoculates us against these elementary dependencies. We "do business". We negotiate. We commute. We seek convenience and luxury. We marinate in social isolation even while surrounded by thousands of fellow residents. The oceans, the farm, the rivers, and all else that provides us sustenance are wrapped in plastic and tin. We waste away . Little wonder that opioid addiction is pandemic. We've got to escape the physical, emotional, and spiritual boredom and pain that often accompany the loss of God. We're like the walking dead. We need to repent of our secularity and be born again.

The hyperbolic Jesus, whose prophetic words were often like a fist to the jaw, declares that the Gentile cities of Tyre, Sidon, and Sodom would repent "in sackcloth and ashes" if they were to see the miracles these Galilean cities had seen. But no. Maybe familiarity had bred contempt. Indifference can squash the spirit.

Father and Son 11:25–27

Shifting from his denunciation of the lukewarm cities, Jesus in heartfelt gratitude thanks his Father that at least the "babes", the children – meaning the "am ha aretz" (everyday folk), were simply accepting the "hidden things" of the Kingdom by putting their trust in him. But this child-like faith was itself a gift from Jesus, a gift freely given to those who had been walking in darkness. This gift was the outpouring of an exclusive knowledge the son had of the Father. It was "the great light" that had first shone in Bethlehem and was now spreading to the whole world.

An Easy Yoke and a Light Burden 11:28–30

I think we all know that everyone we meet is fighting a battle we know nothing of, and therefore we should be kind. Jesus certainly knew this. So he gives a great invitation to all those who are "weary and heavy laden". "Come unto me and I will give you rest." Whether it be the burden of overweening religious demands, or the crushing weight of secularity, Jesus offers respite. He, like us, is "gentle and lowly of heart", meaning he knows what it is to be compressed by life. He knows that brokenness not only wounds but also makes us malleable. While there is still a spark, a whisper of life, even as you limp with life's bruising, "come unto me". When you do, you'll find your burdens lightened and finally (!) rest for your soul. Why? Because you'll be "yoked" with the Master. He'll do all the heavy lifting.

Disputes and Controversies 12:1–50

The twelfth chapter of Matthew gives us some examples of the push-back Jesus suffered and the religious controversies he engendered. He truly was "despised and rejected of men…"

Lord of the Sabbath 12:1–14

The concept of a "Sabbath" (Hebrew "to cease, abstain, desist, terminate, to be at an end") had a long history, predating the decalogue recorded in Exodus 20. When God fed the wandering Israelites in the wilderness for forty years by daily "raining bread down from heaven" (Ex. 16:4,5), he did so for six days per week. On the seventh he "rested" from this miraculous provision. This provided a model for what later would appear in the Ten Commandments: "Remember the Sabbath day to keep it holy" (Ex. 20:8). The point was to give beleaguered mankind at least one day a week to eat, sleep, and play. God created humans in his likeness, not as animals of labor. A day for creative/re-creative charging of the batteries was in the best interest of all. Indeed it also gave opportunity for praise and worship to the Father. In this sense it became the "Lord's Day", a day when God was uplifted and man's burdens were lightened.

Whereas the scriptures describe a general proscription of labor on the Sabbath, the rabbis spent centuries debating what does or does not constitute a desecration.

But, history shows us that the rabbis made the Sabbath into an exacting institution. Whereas the scriptures describe a general proscription of labor on the Sabbath, the rabbis spent centuries debating what does or does not constitute a desecration. In the Talmud there are thirty-nine categories of forbidden labor: "sowing, ploughing, reaping, binding sheaves, threshing, winnowing, selecting, guiding, sifting, kneading, baking; shearing wool, bleaching, carding, dyeing, spinning, warping, making two thrums, weaving two threads, separating two threads (in the warp), knotting, unknotting, sewing two stitches, tearing for the purpose of sewing two stitches; hunting the stag, slaughtering it, flaying, salting (the flesh), preparing the hide, scraping (the hair), cutting it into pieces; writing two letters of the alphabet, erasing for the purpose of writing two letters; building, demolishing; kindling a fire, extinguishing it; striking with a hammer; transferring an object from one domain to another; (Shab. 7:2).[2]

These general categories of proscription were then parsed by the rabbis into minute do's and don'ts. For instance, here is an extended quote from the talmudic tractate "Shabbat" re: the last category about transferring objects. The first clause of the Mishnah reads: "There are two acts of transferring objects (from one domain to another), and these are enlarged to four as affecting the inside (of the premises) and four as affecting the outside. How is this? The beggar, for example, stands outside and the householder inside, and the beggar stretches forth his hand into the interior and places something in the householder's hand or takes it from his hand and draws it outside. In that event the beggar

---

[2]   **Everyman's Talmud,** Cohen, p. 154, Schocken 1949

is guilty (of an infraction of the Sabbath law) and the householder is free of guilt. If the householder stretched forth his hand and put something into the beggar's hand or drew from it and brought it into the house, then the householder is guilty and the beggar is free of guilt. If the beggar stretched forth this hand into the interior, and the householder takes something out of it and puts something into it, they are both free of guilt. If the householder stretched forth his hand outside and the beggar took something from it or put something into it which the former draws into the house both are guilty."[3]

The above is only a small sample of the myriad of fine-tuned Talmudic requirements. Nevertheless the Talmud is a "joy" to many Orthodox Jews, even as it is an unreasonable man-made burden to others. Still, it ranks second to the Torah is its impact on Judaism and the world, and is to be respected.

Even in Jesus' day there were varying schools of thought with regard to the Oral Law. Two famous rabbis of the time, Hillel and Shammai, represented the polarities – Hillel the hellenistic "liberal", and Shammai the legalistic "conservative". Both were caught up, however, in the religious furor caused by this unorthodox Galilean who had the temerity to heal, and forgive sins, and desecrate the Sabbath. He was such a cause for concern that killing him seemed the only option.

The oral laws re: reaping and threshing were being blatantly ignored by Jesus' disciples as they walked through some grain fields. Stripping off a few heads of grain, rubbing them in their hands, and eating the grain (hard, tooth-breaking work!) was harmless in Jesus' view. But the Pharisees were not amused. (What they were doing following Jesus on that Sabbath walk is beyond me – I wonder if they measured the distance? A Sabbath day's journey according to the Oral law was approximately 3500 feet. Any further than that was a desecration.)

Jesus silenced them by referring to David and his men eating sacred bread (1Sa. 21:1-6), and reminding his detractors that the priests who work the Sabbath in the Temple are technically "profaning the Sabbath".

---

[3]   Ibid p. 155

He goes on to refer to himself as "something greater than the Temple" (a tooth grinder for the Pharisees!) and rebukes/reminds them that mercy trumps sacrifice by quoting Hosea 6:6. I can do what I want, he says, because I am "Lord of the Sabbath".

Later that day they entered the Capernaum (probably) synagogue. This house of worship would be alive with the faithful coming and going. One of the worshippers was a man with "a withered hand".

I imagine this crippled man sidling up to Jesus, an imploring look on his face. The intrepid Pharisees, still dusting themselves off from the walk through the wheat field, saw an opportunity to catch Jesus in a Sabbath desecration. They tacitly acknowledged Jesus' miraculous power even as they asked their trick question: "Is it lawful to heal on the Sabbath?" This question had historical/cultural roots: the ultra conservatives (school of Rabbi Shammai) wouldn't even set a fractured bone on the Sabbath, whereas the Hellenistic liberals (school of Rabbi Hillel) were far more lenient. Jesus' response? He answers the question with a question. Who of you wouldn't rescue one of his sheep from a pit on the Sabbath? A man is far more important than a sheep. So my friend, "Stretch out your hand."

A man is far more important than a sheep.

Jesus was not only demonstrating his lordship of the Sabbath, he was also modeling a profound truth: The Sabbath was made for man, not man for the Sabbath. But this message was lost on the intransigent Pharisees. They left in a cloud of pique. We've got to get rid of this man! They formed a "council" to hatch a murderous plan.

Jesus, the Personification of Israel 12:15–21

Matthew records that Jesus was aware of the plot and chose to "withdraw" from Capernaum. In that the city was surrounded by the greater

Roman province of Syria it is likely that he may have travelled north or northwest into Gentile territory. As always, "great multitudes" followed him and were not disappointed. He "healed them all."

There have been debates and discussions ad infinitum with regard to Jesus' constant, and some would say unsuccessful, warnings to those he healed that they keep their miracle to themselves. What was he thinking? Matthew quotes Isaiah 42 for a start.

We've got to remember that Jesus had the big picture in view. Yes, his compassion for suffering "sheep" led him to heal, but in the grander scheme he was Israel's "suffering servant". And, he wasn't ready to be crowned Messiah. The enthusiastic crowds wanted to take him by force to Jerusalem for coronation, but Jesus knew this was not to be. So put a lid on it, friends. I know you're pumped by your healing, but please, understand the I'm *more* than Messiah, I'm also Israel's Suffering Servant – the one Isaiah speaks about in chapters 42, 49, 50, and 52-53. My throne will not be in Jerusalem. That's too provincial. My throne is in Heaven where I am Lord, not just of the Jews, but of the Gentiles as well. Indeed the salvation of the entire world is my mandate.

Take the time to Google "servant songs". Read up on the background. You'll see that these Isaiah chapters are usually interpreted by Orthodox rabbis as referring to the suffering Israel has undergone in history, and by many Christian theologians as referring to Jesus' passion and death for mankind. To me it's not one or the other, it's "both-and". Yes, these passages refer to Israel, and yes, I think they refer to Jesus. He is the personification of Israel. Jesus/Israel will be the light that the Gentile world will be drawn to. Not just for the light, but for the gentleness of a Servant who will not break a bruised reed, or quench a smoldering candle. This Servant will administer righteousness in a fair and just manner. The world will put their hope in him, and they will not be disappointed.

Jesus' Authority in the Spirit World 12:22–29

We're not told where Jesus was when the events of this passage occurred. Reading Matthew is like watching a well-edited movie. We proceed from scene to scene with little or no transitions. The locations don't blend, they just happen. If you, like me, engage your imagination as you read, you may experience a bit of whiplash. But it's obvious Matthew wasn't concerned with literary flow. He just had a story to tell.

This time it's about a blind and dumb man whose sorry condition is the result of demonic activity. In a short descriptive sentence (v.22) Matthew states the man's condition and Jesus' sudden, unconditional act of healing. The man immediately can see and talk. The people are amazed. In the emotion of the moment they ask, "Could this be the Son of David?" Is this Messiah? The flustered Pharisees stutter, "It's by Beelzebul, the prince of demons, that this fellow drives out demons." Once again Jesus polarized the people.

"Beelzebul" is an ancient divine name derived from the Aramaic "ba'al zebu" meaning "Lord of the High House" or "Lord of the Temple". Ancient texts predating Jesus by 1400 years (the Ras Shamra texts) refer to the Canaanite god Aleman Baal as "Zebul, baal of the earth". "Zebul" in this instance means "exalted one". In 2 Kings 1:2 the writer refers to Beelzebul king of Ekron as "Beelzebub", a huge insult because changing his name this way meant he was "Lord of the flies". The King James Version (KJV) of this Matthew passage employs "Beelzebub", but the Revised Standard Version (RSV) and other versions correct it. Regardless, the Pharisees were essentially accusing Jesus of being satanic.

The text says Jesus "knew their thoughts". This charge caused him great pain and evoked a powerful, blunt response, "You brood of vipers"! Here he was, restoring health, peace, and harmony to broken people and he's accused of being in league with the Devil. A desperate, intolerable charge by his detractors.

It is noteworthy that Jesus entered into no debate with regard to the existence of a kingdom of evil. Nor did he deny that some of the Pharisees had had success in "driving out" demons. His logic was unassailable: Satan cannot cast himself out. Lucifer was not about to self-destruct. As "Prince of the power of the air" he was organized and effective. Indeed he was "a strong man". But he had to flee before the power of "the Spirit of God". Jesus operated in that power. In so doing he demonstrated that "the Kingdom of God" had come to earth.

The Unpardonable Sin 12:30–32

The English playwright and poet John Heywood in 1546 said, "There is none so blind as he who will not see". This insight is usually seen as a reflection of the prophet Jeremiah's accusation of the "descendants of Jacob": "you foolish and senseless people, who have eyes but do not see, who have ears but do not hear" (Je. 5:20,21). This kind of willful blindness is what theologians call "apostasy". A person who denies his intuitive knowledge of God and his accountability thereby, and who will not repent, is beyond the reach of grace. Like the witches in Macbeth if one says, "Fair is foul, and foul is fair", there is no recourse.

> ### *The English playwright and poet John Heywood in 1546 said, "There is none so blind as he who will not see".*

In pastoring I have, on occasion, had tearful congregants in my office afraid they have committed "the unpardonable sin". Their concern, of course, proves they have not committed it. Those who have done so have no remorse. They have deliberately chosen spiritual darkness and persist in their repudiations of the Spirit of God. They will never repent. And they will never be forgiven. The Lord respects volitional unbelief. He won't touch it.

The general steps to apostasy are described in scripture this way:

1. Grieve the Spirit (Ep. 4:30).

2. Resist the Spirit (Ac. 6:10).

3. Quench the Spirit (1Th. 5:19).

This declension results in a willful blindness, a gouging out of one's eyes as it were. It's a blindness that "sees" the light of heaven as counterfeit. It prefers "outer darkness".

The Fruit Tells the Tale 12:33–37

Jesus then took a step back from his defense of his healing ministry to comment on the very Jewish idea that in the long run it is performance that counts. All you can expect from a viper is a hiss. Nothing but bitter words can emanate from hearts full of bitterness. All the "Beelzebub" talk must be accounted for one day (v.36). The tree is known by its fruit. Good fruit – good conduct. Bad fruit – bad conduct. To the Jewish mind words were conduct, the deed of the lips. These slandering Pharisees needed to know that one day they would have to explain the deeds of their lips to the Almighty. And, by extension, so will we.

The Demand for Signs 12:38–42

When Satan tempted Jesus in the wilderness one of the temptations was that Jesus should perform a "sign" of his heavenly status by leaping from the pinnacle of the Temple. The angels would catch him before he hit the Kidron Valley floor and all the world would be convinced that he was the Son of God. In this passage the Pharisees tempted Jesus to give them a similar sign. This, of course, was disingenuous in that they had just seen him heal a blind and deaf man. What is more, if Jesus had indulged them with another miracle they might have turned it against him again, claiming he was doubly empowered by Satan.

Jesus' answer to this "evil and adulterous generation" went way over their heads. He said he'd give them a sign, the sign of "the prophet Jonah". Like Jonah, he would spend three days in the depths. Even as his listeners assumed a confused look , he stretched them even farther by saying that something (someone?) greater than Jonah was present. And while they were gasping at this, they totally fazed out when Jesus said that both Nineveh and the Queen of Sheba were far more spiritually sensitive than they. Nineveh repented and the Queen believed without any "sign". They heard and responded to a message, not some supernatural portent.

Jesus' miraculous works were never intended to authenticate, honor, or justify his messiahship. They were merely evidence of the Kingdom of Heaven "at hand". The ultimate "sign" would be his resurrection. Indeed, it would be the fulcrum of faith for the ages.

Evil Fills Vacuums 12:43–45

Looking past the "evil generation" who had unsuccessfully tempted him, to the recently delivered blind and dumb man, Jesus gave a quick lesson in demonology. The message to the man was very straightforward: When someone indwelt by an evil spirit is delivered through the power of the Spirit of God, that person's "empty house" needs to be refilled by another presence. If he is not filled with the Spirit of God the evil spirit will return in magnified power. It's not enough to be "clean". One has to be indwelt by righteousness. A Hitler enters when a nation deserts belief in God, for no life can stay empty of worship. "You gotta serve somebody" (Bob Dylan). So, serve the Lord.

Jesus' Family 12:46–50

Jesus' apparent dismissal of his family seems harsh, and unlike him. He was compassionate with the crowds; why not with his brothers and sisters? My speculation is that whoever it was who told Jesus that his family were waiting to see him did so with a tone. Perhaps a scold. This, in my mind, might have been blunt enough that Jesus responded in kind. Besides, he had the "thirty thousand foot view". He saw the big picture. He saw beyond his earthly home to the heavenlies. In that context his words resonate. Those of us who live by the core value of "not my will but Thine be done" are relatives of the Son of Man.

"THE KINGDOM OF HEAVEN IS LIKE..." 13:1–58

Jesus had a very simple didactic approach to educating the illiterate masses who crowded around wherever he went. He told stories. His teaching style fit right in with a culture tuned to the oral transmission of scripture: metaphors, similes and (very rarely) allegories, were rife as he taught. The people hung on his words, tales that Matthew calls "parables".

In the Boat 13:1–3a

Matthew tells us that Jesus walked down to the shore of the Sea of Galilee to do a bit of teaching. But the crowd who followed him there was so huge it was forcing him to the water. So he quickly got into one of the fishing boats and pushed off a short distance from shore. Then, with that little bit of breathing space, he began to teach in parables. The gentle upsweep of the stony beach provided a kind of natural amphitheater. With the onshore breeze acting as a sound system of sorts he was clearly heard by everyone. He began with one of his best remembered stories.

Jesus had a very simple didactic approach to educating the illiterate masses who crowded around wherever he went. He told stories.

Parable of the Sower 13:3b–23

This parable is self-explanatory. There is no need to say anything other than that this is a story about soil. The question which springs to mind is, "What kind of soil am I?" What *does* need explanation is Jesus' answer to the disciples' question, "Why do you speak to them in parables?" (v.10).

Jesus responded by quoting Isaiah 6: 9,10. These are words the Lord spoke to a young Isaiah as he rose to God's challenge, "Whom shall I send? And who will go for us?" Isaiah blurted, "Here am I. Send me!" (Is. 6:8). So the Lord said, "Go and tell this people":

"Be ever hearing, but never understanding;
be ever seeing, but never perceiving.
Make the heart of this people calloused;
make their ears dull
and close their eyes.
Otherwise they might see with their eyes,
hear with their ears,
understand with their hearts,
and turn and be healed."

Whoa! What? An astonished Isaiah asks, "For how long Lord?" The Lord answers:

"Until the cities be ruined
and without inhabitant,
until the houses are left deserted
and the fields ruined and ravaged,
until the Lord has sent everyone far away
and the Land is utterly forsaken.
And though a tenth remains in the Land,
it will again be laid waste.
But as the terebinth and oak
leave stumps when they are cut down,
so the holy seed will be the stump in the land."

—VV. 9B-13

Before joining Isaiah in "What??" keep in mind that the Lord speaks out of his omniscience. He is not saying that Isaiah should "callous" the people. What he's saying is that from his perspective in the all knowing eternities he has already seen what the response of a recalcitrant Judah will be to Isaiah's message. There was a culture of disbelief and godlessness in Judah, colorfully captured by Solomon in Proverbs 9:7-9.

"Whoever corrects a mocker invites insults;
whoever rebukes the wicked incurs abuse.
Do not rebuke mockers or they will hate you;
rebuke the wise and they will love you.
Instruct the wise and they will be wiser still;
teach the righteous and they will add to their learning."

The majority of the people will not listen. They will insult, mock, and abuse the messenger. But there will be a small remnant, a "stump" (v.13) still living, still attached to a God-planted root system that bears the sacred DNA. So, Isaiah, speak the message for the stumps' sake.

This is what Jesus is saying. He speaks in parables for the stumps' sake. The forest may rebel and despise the Heavenly One, thereby wasting away, but the "holy seed" will see the stumps putting out new shoots and bearing fruit on the Day of the Lord. The "planting of the Lord" will prevail.

Weeds, Seeds, and Yeast 13:24–43

Jesus went on to tell three more parables. The first was about counterfeit wheat. "Tares" (zizanium – Greek) were a kind of darnel, bearded, growing in wheat fields as tall as wheat and barley, resembling wheat in appearance. The rabbis used to call tares "bastard". Apparently consumption of tares produced sleepiness, nausea, convulsions, and sometimes death. In its early stages the tare looked very much like wheat, but developed a more distinctive look when mature. For a farmer tares were toxic but the only way to get rid of them was at harvest when they could be clearly identified. To rip them up earlier would see genuine wheat destroyed as well.

Later, in Peter's house, Jesus explained the parable describing tares as "everything that causes sin and all who do evil" (v.41). These coexist with the "children of the Kingdom". No point in purging them. Jesus knew that purges usually do at least as much damage as good. He also knew that purges appeal to self-righteous zealots. Indeed, later in history, salvation by extermination appealed to the Nazis. Any attempt to achieve moral, spiritual, or racial perfection is doomed to death by dogma.

Any attempt to achieve moral, spiritual, or racial perfection is doomed to death by dogma.

The parables of the mustard seed and the yeast are often referred to by commentators as a "double parable" because they essentially teach the same truth: small things can grow into large things, and catalysts don't have to be big to have huge effect. The Kingdom of Heaven is like that. Small but massive. Innocuous but earthshaking. Easy to miss at first, impossible to miss later on. One should never "despise the day of small beginnings".

Three More Parables 13:44–50

The companion parables of the hidden treasure and the precious pearl are a commentary on how the Kingdom of Heaven is discovered: some seek it (the treasure) and others stumble on it (the pearl). St. Paul in Romans 10:20 reflected on this when he quoted Isaiah 65:1:

> *"I was sought by those who did not ask for me;*
> *I was found by those who did not seek me…"*

The point is that the Kingdom of Heaven is the "summum bonum", the ultimate good, the everlasting treasure of the soul. One should value it above all else. We are made for it, whether we find it or it finds us. There is no greater home.

The dragnet parable, however, is a warning. The Kingdom of Heaven will not tolerate evil. In that sense it is exclusive. It does not "bless 'em all". It discriminates. It both invites and excludes. Sober stuff.

The Open-minded Teacher 13:51,52

There is a famous rabbinical saying in "Pirkei Avot" (Google it), "Rabbi Eliezer ben Hyrcanus is a plastered cistern which loses not a drop… Rabbi Eliezer ben Arak is a welling spring" (2:8). One defends the past, the other embraces the future.

Jesus is telling us that the truth of the Kingdom of Heaven is not an either/or proposition. Rather, the new revelation is an offshoot of the old. Symbiosis, not antithesis, is the protocol. A teacher of the Kingdom is someone who sees the horizon with eyes fixed on the view even as his feet are firmly planted on the old. He is master of both left and right, liberal and conservative. He will not be put in a box.

Push-back in Nazareth 13:53–58

It looks like Jesus gave his disciples a few days off and travelled alone to Nazareth to visit his family and teach in the synagogue. He probably enjoyed the change of pace.

But it appears that his hometown friends and acquaintances didn't enjoy him. They resisted his teaching and were "offended" by his miracles (so much for "give us a sign"!). Their familiarity with him bred contempt. So he moved on.

FROM HEROD'S BIRTHDAY PARTY TO JESUS' TRANSFIGURATION 14:1–17:27

Herod Antipas was "a piece of work". The son of Herod the Great he was given rulership over Galilee and Perea which constituted a quarter of the Roman province of Syria (thus, he was "Tetrarch"). Herodias, his wife, was daughter to Aristobulus, another son of Herod the Great. She had been married to Philip, yet another son of Herod the Great. So, in this nepotistic, incestuous royal household, she was niece to both her husbands. To add to the intrigue, she had divorced Philip to marry his half-brother Antipas. Little wonder the sensibilities of Antipas' Jewish subjects were offended. John the Baptist in his prophetic ire inveighed against this adulterous marriage, much to the vindictive ire of the guilty Herodias. She determined to destroy John and knew how to manipulate the weak Antipas in order to do it. There's no need to recount the story. It's well known. It is comprised of a Macbeth-like tide of poisonous guilt as background to adultery, drunken ribaldry, a seductive dance, an inebriated promise, a beheading, and a funeral. It reads like a novel, a morality tale featuring darkness (Herod) and light (John). To this day hundreds of thousands of parents have named their sons John. I'm not sure that any parent has ever named his son Herod.

Antipas obviously was haunted by the evil of his action against John. The horrible memory of the still bleeding head on a platter became a silent terror in the night. Banquo's ghost stalked the halls of the Machaerus fortress. Herod would never know peace again. History tells us his life went downhill from that point on.

The 5000 Man Dinner 14:13–21

"When Jesus heard what had happened, he withdrew by boat privately to a solitary place," Matthew recounts. We don't know why Jesus sought solitude. Perhaps it was to grieve the death of his cousin. Maybe he wanted to avoid the furor of the people which followed John's death. Probably it was a bit of both. But as always his retreat was short-lived. The needy crowd followed shortly after. He saw them from afar and "had compassion on them". A massive lineup of sick people formed, and Jesus began his healing work. It went on all day.

As dusk approached, the disciples came to Jesus concerned that the people were hungry. They suggested that Jesus send them away so that they could buy food in the villages before dark. Jesus' response is a bit unusual, "You give them something to eat." He knew they had no food. Even if they had, it would not have come close to the volume needed to feed "five thousand men" *plus* women and children. The overall crowd may have been in the area of ten thousand. One of the disciples found five loaves of bread and two fish volunteered by someone, and that was it. It would appear that this huge crowd had been so focused on their healing needs, and so spontaneous, that no one had taken the time to pack a lunch.

This is the one miracle recorded in all four gospels.

So Jesus takes the bread and the fish, prays, and then instructs his disciples to start the distribution. Once everyone eats, there are twelve baskets of leftovers.

This is the one miracle recorded in all four gospels. It portrayed Jesus' sovereignty over nature, and was both supernatural and creative. Just as his Father had created the universe "ex nihilo" (out of nothing) Jesus created a massive meal out of a boy's lunch. The Lord can make a lot out of a little.

Jesus (and Peter) Walks on the Water 14:22–31

Jesus dismissed the crowd, their stomachs full of food, and he climbed in the dark up to the top of one of the hills above the northern shore of the lake. It could very well have been the "mount" on which he had preached the famous "sermon". Indeed it may have been the "solitary place" that he had sought before the crowd had rushed to him earlier that day.

Matthew says Jesus "constrained" the disciples to get in a boat. There was urgency here. Why? Could it be the need to escape? The pressing demands, the miraculous works, the overall stress of managing a huge mass of people had exhausted him. Indeed, the Gospel of John (ch. 6) tells us that this insatiable throng wanted to take Jesus by force to Jerusalem to be crowned king, *and* they wanted another free meal! He needed to get away from these agendas and a little distance from the disciples would be good too. He needed to be alone. That's why he climbed the mount, grateful for the cover of night.

What follows is the well-known story of Jesus walking on the water. Read it for yourself. What intrigues me about this story is the way-too-late-by-half exclamation of the disciples after the water-walking by Jesus (and Peter!) and the calming of the waves, "Truly you are the Son of God." Hello?? They had just seen Jesus feed thousands with nothing, and over the past several weeks had witnessed countless miraculous healings. Only *now* they get it? Truly astonishing. Yet, how soon they would forget.

Jesus, the Orthodox Jew 14:34–36

In this brief summary of various healings, there is something I don't want you to miss. Like the woman healed of the fistula these hundreds received healing by touching the "fringe of his garment". In Numbers 15:38-40 we read:

"Throughout the generations to come you are to make tassels
on the corners of your garments, with a blue cord on each tassel.
You will have these tassels to look at and so you will remember
all the commands of the Lord, that you may obey them
and not profane yourselves by chasing after the lusts of your
own hearts and eyes. Then you will remember to obey all
my commands and will be consecrated to your God."

The point? Jesus was Jewish. An observant Jew at that. He had tassels on his garment "to remember all the commands of the Lord."

When I was pastoring in Jerusalem (Google "King of Kings Church Jerusalem") I used to attend synagogue services. When I did I wore my prayer shawl. It had tassels, with a blue cord on each corner. This memory trigger is a vital component in Orthodox Jewish practice to this day. It is precious and beautiful. Even though I am not Jewish, I feel the weight of history and profound meaning whenever I wear the shawl. It clothes me in dignity.

Kosher Controversies 15: 1–20

While you're Googling type in "Mishnah". You'll discover that this was the first effort to reduce the "Oral Law" (or, "Oral Torah") to writing. It became a foundational document as the Talmud (commentary on the Torah) was copied over the course of three to four hundred years. In the Jewish faith it is authoritative.

Even though it would be three hundred years or so before the Mishnah was written, the Pharisees are referencing the Oral Law when they question Jesus about the disciples' unhygienic eating habits. The law, as later redacted by the Mishnah (Aboth 1:1) states, "Moses received the (oral) Torah from Sinai and transmitted it to the prophets, and the prophets transmitted it to the men of the Great Synagogue. They said three things: 'Be deliberate in judgement, raise up many disciples, and make a hedge about the Torah.'" (that is, expand the law in such a way that a man cannot even come near to transgression).

Washing the hands before and after eating was part of the "hedge". The priests did it to achieve and maintain holiness, so the conventional wisdom was that this practice must be effective for laymen too. But the Twelve seemed oblivious to this hedge. They broke "the tradition of the elders" with impunity. The Pharisees want to know why.

"Corban" 15:3–9

Jesus began by upbraiding the Pharisees for loopholing the hedge with regard to caring for their parents. The Law required that they should "honor" their parents, especially in the encroaching disabilities and dependencies of old age. But some of the Pharisees were doing an end run around this inconvenient responsibility by directing the time and treasure necessary for their parents' care to God. They called this "Corban" (a gift to God). In this way they spiritualized their neglect, preening their piety even as their parents descended into penury. Jesus saw this as Isaiah 29:13 all over again.

The epicenter of evil behavior is the heart.

Kosher on the Inside 15:10–20

One would think that Jesus was restating the obvious when he made the point that uncleanness comes from the inside not the outside. But no. The power of tradition and its cultural application eclipsed common sense. The epicenter of evil behavior is the heart (v.19). That's where "murder, adultery, sexual immorality, theft, false testimony, slander" come from. But the Pharisees were content to let their clean hands mask their black hearts. They truly were the blind leading the blind.

Jesus and a Gentile 15:21–28

Once again there is a shift of scene, Matthew saying nothing about the arduous trek from Galilee to Tyre and Sidon in Lebanon. Some commentators see this journey away from the Capernaum region as evidence that after the murder of John the Baptist Jesus began to focus on the mentoring of the disciples and the preparation for what awaited them in Jerusalem. What's more, he may have grown tired of the coterie of Pharisees trying to trip him up at every turn. The long hike up to Lebanon would see them falling away and returning to their homes, muttering all the way, hoping Jesus would stay up there in the north, far from any of their towns and villages.

Jesus' reputation as a healer, however, had preceded him. No sooner had he got to the region of Tyre and Sidon than a Canaanite Gentile woman cried out, "Lord, Son of David, have mercy on me!" Jesus gave her the silent treatment. But she kept at it. Her demon possessed daughter needed to be delivered. She was so persistent the disciples urged Jesus to send her away. Instead, Jesus entered into some religious/cultural banter with the woman. It was a unique exchange.

First, Jesus says in her hearing but not for her sake, rather for the sake of the disciples, "I was sent only to the lost sheep of Israel." He said this because he had instructed the disciples earlier (10:6) to limit their ministry to Jews. The disciples expected consistency from him. Ministry to Gentiles was not part of the "mission statement."

The woman ignores this seeming brush off by kneeling before Jesus and pleading, "Lord, help me!" Jesus replied with a cultural proverb, "It is not right to take the children's bread and toss it to dogs."

The disciples would look at each other knowingly, thinking, "he's telling her how it is!" And the woman would expect this cultural rejection. She had been called a "dog" by Jews throughout her lifetime. Gentiles were the offscouring of the earth. But her rejoinder is genius, "Yes it is, Lord," but, "even the dogs eat the crumbs that fall from their master's table." Jesus, totally impressed with her "great faith" instantly heals the stricken daughter.

What was going on here? First, this Gentile woman "flattered" Jesus by referring to him as both "Lord" and "Son of David", each of which was a messianic title. She had no religious tradition anticipating a Messiah, but her need was so great she didn't care. The Jews apparently call him Lord, so I will too, she thought. Second, Jesus says what both his disciples and the woman would expect to hear. I'm a Jew with a ministry to Jews. I'm here in Gentile territory for a break. "Dogs" are not my mission. Amen! said the disciples. But he healed the girl anyway. Not just because of her mother's great faith, but because he wanted to show his disciples that even though he had sent them out with ethnic/provincial strictures he himself was not bound. He had come to heal both Jew and Gentile. Indeed, he had come to heal the world. The Jew and the Gentile were to eat from the same table in the Kingdom of Heaven.

The Four Thousand 15:29–39

The story continues. Here we see Jesus walking back to the wild hills rising above the Sea of Galilee on the northeast. We can assume (correctly, I believe, in that I have travelled myself from Tyre and Sidon down to the Golan Heights) that it took three days. Matthew tells us Jesus was concerned about the food needs of the crowd who had walked with them. Their healing needs eclipsed their meals, but now they were fading from a few days without food (v.32).

Keep in mind that this was a crowd of Gentiles. Four thousand men plus women and children. The Pharisees (of whom there were none) would have been apoplectic to see Jesus and the Twelve mingling and eating (!) with these "unwashed dogs" (to say nothing of "unwashed hands"). But Jesus didn't see ethnic or racial outcasts, he saw needy people made in the image of God. He was called to save them as much as he was called to Jews. He had "compassion for these people." He wanted to feed them.

It's hard to believe the disciples' short memory. "Where could we get enough bread in this remote place to feed such a crowd?" they asked (without embarrassment)! Had they forgotten the miraculous feeding of the 5000? Apparently they had, just as they would what was about to happen with 4000 (see 16:5-11). Even though some time had elapsed it is beyond comprehension that anyone would ever forget that amazing evening when upwards of 10,000 (including women and children) had been fed near the shore of the lake. All you can do is shake your head in wonder. Were the disciples *that* dull?

All you can do is shake your head in wonder. Were the disciples that dull?

Perhaps the key component in this account is that these Gentiles, even before they were fed, were healed of their diseases and "praised the God of Israel". This was far more than the jaundiced Pharisees ever did, who credited Satan, not the God of Abraham, Isaac, and Jacob, for Jesus' miraculous power. It seemed that the only ones who came close to "getting it" were the untutored, blue-collar folk who were just trying to cope with the adversities of life. They came to Jesus unfiltered. All they brought was brokenness.

The Yeast of the Pharisees and Sadducees 16:1–12

Whole tomes of information are available if you choose to research the histories and beliefs of the Pharisees and the Sadducees. All I'll do here is provide a thumbnail sketch, some might say a "caricature", of these groups. But I'll be true to what I've studied.

The Pharisees were the "clean hands" people. They touted the "Oral Torah" with a definite bias to the "outward appearance". They tended to legalism and the apartness or "separateness" that often accompanies a sectarian view of life. They had low tolerance for the Roman occupiers in Jesus' day, even more so for Gentiles in general. They saw themselves as "the holy ones" and, as is often the case with this self-concept, were "holier than thou".

The Sadducees were also Torah people, but not in the oral sense. They eschewed the Oral Torah (Oral Law) and adhered exclusively to the written Torah, the five books of the Law of Moses. They appeased their Roman superiors, embracing a secular, hellenized worldview. As such they were engaged with the State in a kind of exclusive, elite, aristocratic way. They controlled the Temple priesthood, and owned the temple commerce. Time and again their policies and practices clashed with those of the Pharisees.

But Jesus united them in their mutual fear and hatred of his person and ministry. On the subjects of resurrection and the reality of the spirit world they fought tooth and nail (see Acts 23:6-10). Theology polarized them, but Jesus galvanized them.

Once again (12:38) Jesus is asked for a "sign", and once again (12:39) he says the only sign he will give them is the "sign of Jonah". He then turns on his heel and walks away.

Later, after crossing the lake (how many times did Jesus and the Twelve cross that lake?!) he warns the short-term-memory-loss disciples about the "yeast" of the Pharisees and Sadducees. It took them awhile to clue in, but finally they got it. Jesus was warning them against both legalism and secularism. He wanted them to embrace neither the left nor the right, but a highway above them both.

He wanted them to embrace neither the left nor the right, but a highway above them both.

Jesus' Future Glory 16:13–17:13

After a few days back in Galilee, Jesus and the disciples turned their faces north again, walking to the Upper Galilee all the way to the borders with Lebanon and Syria. They stayed in the region of Caesarea Philippi (modern day Banias). This was the staging ground for both a profound statement of faith and an out-of-this-world moment when three of the twelve saw Jesus in his future glory.

Peter's Confession 16:13–20

This was one of the few times Jesus was able to travel without a throng pressing upon him from every side. Matthew doesn't tell us why. So, after a lengthy walk, probably taking a day and a half, Jesus finds a shady place by one of the mountain streams that flow near Caesarea Philippi to stop for refreshment, rest and conversation. We don't know what the subject of the discussion was, but there were more than enough topics from recent teachings and miracles to keep the talk well fuelled. At some point the subject of Jesus' person came up. Jesus picked up on it and asked, "Who do people say the Son of Man is?" "They say you're John the Baptist, or Elijah, or maybe Jeremiah or one of the other prophets," they answered. "And you? Who do you say I am?" Jesus asked. Peter answered, "You are the Messiah, the Son of the living God." Little did he know that this confession would become foundational in the history of the Church.

Jesus reacted with great enthusiasm, calling Peter "blessed", and crediting his spiritual sensitivity and availability to the Spirit of God the Father. He went on to declare that this confession would be the foundation stone upon which he would build his Church, the construction being impermeable to Satan's attacks. He also stated that the disciples would have profound authority on earth to proclaim and perform heaven's will. Then, strangely, he told them to keep his messiahship to themselves.

Perhaps he explained the need for secrecy. He knew that the issue of messiahship would eventually be his undoing. He didn't shrink from this although a timetable needed to be respected – "his time was not yet". But he *did* begin to reveal what was about to happen, much to the distress of the disciples. In fact Peter couldn't take it, and blurted, "Never! This shall never happen to you!" And Jesus, who had a moment before affirmed Peter, commanded with authority, "Get behind me Satan!"

Peter's words were the words of expediency, uttered with a nationalistic bias.

This didn't mean Jesus thought Peter to be Satan, but Peter's words reminded him of the temptation in the wilderness after his baptism by John (Luke 4:13 tells us that Satan, after finishing his tempting of Jesus, "left him until an opportune time"). This may have been one of the "opportune" moments. Peter's words were the words of expediency, uttered with a nationalistic bias. Yes, Peter had spiritual insight, but he also had feet of clay. Satan took the opportunity to exploit him. Jesus didn't flinch.

The drama of the moment wasn't over. Jesus looked the disciples in the eye and warned them that they would one day take up their own crosses. This was the price they would pay for being ambassadors of the Kingdom. They would not be without reward (v.27) but the cost would be great. Then he said something that has occasioned many a debate: "Truly I tell you, some who are standing here will not taste death before they see the Son of Man coming in his Kingdom." I fail to see the difficulty in this statement. What was about to happen next, in my thinking, clearly explains it (and, of course, I'm not alone in this view).

The Transfiguration 17:1–8

It could be that Jesus' purpose in trekking up to the Gentile city of Caesarea Philippi was to get away from the pestering Pharisees, and to have some "down time" to mentor the Twelve. If so, they had six wonderful days camped by the rushing brook springing out of the ground beneath the trees. I have been there many times over the years. Caesarea Philippi (now called "Banias") and Tel Dan (a few miles away) are awash in ice-cold water that emerges at the foot of Mount Hermon. This mountain is approximately ten thousand feet high. In the winter it can have as much as forty feet of snow covering the upper half. The snow melts in late March, sinks into the slopes, and arises as spring water at the mountain's base. These ice-cold streams rush down to the Hula Valley, then to the Sea of Galilee, and finally to the Dead Sea. They are the tributaries of the Jordan River, the "Down Rusher". After six days had passed Jesus took Peter, James and John on a hike up Mount Hermon, a strenuous climb. The view is awesome. But, what they were about to see eclipsed everything.

They stopped somewhere near the summit, Jesus walked a few paces from the three, and then it happened. He was "transfigured" before their very eyes. "Transfigured" in the Greek is "metamorphoo" which means "to change into another form". His person became as "white as light" and if that wasn't enough, "Moses and Elijah" suddenly appeared talking with him – the Law, the Prophets, and the Son of God together in unspeakable glory. It was as though the brilliance of sun, moon, and stars coalesced on these three, time and space standing in silent attention.

In the midst of this sacred moment Peter, the blusterer, blurted, "Lord I will put up three shelters…", his voice dissonant like a donkey's bray. None other than the Father interrupted this inappropriate burst by declaring from the midst of a "bright cloud" descending on the transfigured ones, "This is my Son, whom I love; with him I am well pleased." (Be quiet Peter), and "listen to him"! Peter fell flat on his face, as did the other two. Hopefully Peter then kept quiet. Years later a much wiser and more mature Peter would write, "we did not follow cleverly devised stories when we told you about the coming of our Lord Jesus Christ in power, but we were eyewitnesses of his majesty" (2Pe. 1:16).

Later, Peter and the apostles would understand that the Transfiguration bore witness to the "incarnation". God had indeed broken into space and time through the Son of Man and Son of God. Truly Jesus was "the

Kingdom among men". He was God's "signature" on the "kinosis" of Philippians chapter two. He was who he said he was. All mankind should be silent and "listen to him".

Walking Down the Mountain 17:9–13

After Jesus "touched" (v.7) the prostrate three they gathered themselves, stricken to the core with what they had seen and heard. They began the slow decent to Caesarea Philippi, gaining courage to talk as they walked. Jesus warned them not to say anything about his transfiguration until after he had been "raised from the dead". This reference to resurrection didn't seem to resonate with them. All they could think of was that the Kingdom had been revealed in that bright cloud, totally confounding their view of the expected sequence of events that was to precede its coming. For one thing, established Jewish orthodoxy said that "Elijah must come first" (v.10). They were referring to Malachi's prophecy where the Lord promised, "I will send the prophet Elijah to you before that great and dreadful day of the Lord comes. He will turn the hearts of the parents to their children, and the hearts of the children to their parents" (Ma. 4:5,6).

What was this all about? Hard to say, but we all know that at the root of dysfunctional civil society is the fractured family. We often hear about "sibling rivalry", but there is something we may call "generational rivalry" – the youth "kicking against the goads" of parental authority, the aged immobilized by the intransigence that creeps in like arthritis, slowly fusing the progressive joints they may have had when they themselves were young. What's more, this generational disconnect can have its roots in decades, even centuries, of resistance to long established values. These frayed cords can eventually weaken an entire nation – a "failed state" may be in the making.

Jesus told Peter, James, and John that Elijah had already come in the person of John the Baptist, not as a reincarnation but as Heaven's spokesman announcing to the world that the Kingdom was now among men in the person of the Son of Man and Son of God. The ancient values would again be embraced by the young, and family unity would be restored. But these values would be uncluttered by oral law. As an old preacher in the nineteenth century put it, "Old truths were to be reproclaimed, and cleared from the after-growth of tradition" (E. H. Plumptre). Core values respected and held intra-generationally would be restored under Messiah, producing civil and spiritual peace, catalyzing the day when it could be declared that there was "peace on earth".

The transfigured Christ with his two heavenly companions on the mountain were guarantors of the angels' proclamation over the shepherds' fields that first Christmas Day in Bethlehem.

The transfigured Christ with his two heavenly companions on the mountain were guarantors of the angels' proclamation over the shepherds' fields that first Christmas Day in Bethlehem. Eternal truth has a way of lighting the sky.

Jesus Heals an Epileptic Boy 17:14–20

Stark contrast is the predominant feature of this account. Jesus had healed thousands before he healed this poor boy suffering "seizures". There was nothing unusual about his doing it again. But what does stand out is the juxtaposition of heavenly glory and earthly need. The famous preacher, George A. Buttrick, put it this way: "the rapt theophany of the mountain and the woebegone suffering of the valley." Just having seen Jesus transfigured, Peter and the other two would certainly understand his impatience and frustration at having to limit himself to the entry-level, mustard seed faith of the people. Yes, as St. Paul said, Jesus had to "empty himself" ("kinosis" Ph. 2:6-8), but surely there were moments like this one where it vexed him greatly. But even he had to leave the mountain. Most of life is lived in the valley.

Jesus Foresees Suffering and Death 17:22,23

This is one of three "heads up" warnings Jesus gave his disciples about the suffering and death that awaited him (this one and 16:21; 20:17-19). It may have been part of their conversation as they walked down the Hula Valley toward Capernaum on the shore of the lake. Mark tells us the disciples "did not understand what he meant and were afraid to ask him about it" (Mk. 9:32). Matthew simply says they were "filled with grief".

The Temple Tax 17:24–27

In Exodus 30:13 we read that every male Israelite over the age of twenty was required to pay a "sanctuary tax" of one-half shekel. In Nehemiah's day it was temporarily reduced to one-third (Ne.10:32, 33). In Jesus' day the temple tax collectors did the circuit. Today it was Capernaum. When they came to Peter's house they expected him to pay the tax along with his famous boarder. Jesus' response to the demand seemed out of character. We know he did not perform miracles for his own needs (remember the Temptation in the wilderness). What's more, the disciples were certainly not so poor they couldn't afford a two-day's wage (1/2 shekel) per man. Maybe they were strapped for cash after six weeks walking the Upper Galilee and Southern Lebanon. We don't know. Nor do we know whether or not Jesus was serious about the fish and the coin. Matthew gives no account of this fish being caught. So, most commentators see this as Jesus speaking with "tongue in cheek". While the busy tax collectors hovered like vultures, Jesus' sense of humor was percolating.

RELATIONAL ISSUES 18:1–35

In this chapter Matthew records Jesus' teaching with regard to relational dynamics within the body of believers. He calls this body "the Church" (v.17), but we should not read our concept into the term. Jesus had first used the word "ekklesia" (Greek) back in Caesarea Philippi when Peter made his profession of faith (16:18). The term refers to those "called out of" some larger group of citizens to discuss affairs of state. It was rather like a town council, or board of education, etc. (Ac. 19:39). In this instance ekklesia referred to a "congregation", a group consisting of believers. But it had none of the denominational or dogma dynamics of modern church life. It was simply an "assembly".

The Insatiable Ego 18:1–4

The greatest? Really? Reading this passage reminds me of the famous boxer Muhammad Ali (Cassius Clay) whose mantra for the world to hear was, "I am the greatest!" The disciples want to know who is the greatest? Jesus must have rolled his eyes and bit his tongue. Maybe the exclusion of nine of them for the Transfiguration climb had caused a level of insecurity (and jealousy?). And in the elite circle of the Three the "sons of thunder" may have been ill-disposed to "the rock". We don't know. Regardless, it was a childish question.

> *After all they had seen and heard,*
> *after all the time spent with Jesus,*
> *the disciples still didn't get it.*

Jesus raised the level of the conversation from the childish to the child-like. He called a little child from the fringes of the group, placed her in the centre, and challenged the disciples to "convert" (Greek "strophe"). They had to change their attitude or they were lost – they would "never enter the Kingdom of Heaven" (v.3). They had to "become like little children".

Jesus demonstrated remarkable patience. After all they had seen and heard, after all the time spent with Jesus, the disciples still didn't get it. They were looking for what was in it for them. Ego, greed, self-aggrandizement, all the stuff of the dark side of human nature pushed back against the Master. They adamantly expected to soon be the "cabinet" in Jesus' messianic administration. The sooner the better, they thought. They thought wrong. Prominence in a kingdom whose first condition is self-abnegation is a non-starter.

God's Care for the Child-like 18:5–10

Let's be clear, the child-like are "those who believe in me" (v.6). So, as Jesus goes on to say a lot about children here, he is thinking of them not only in terms of chronology but also innocent faith. Even a hard-bitten adult can be a "child of God" if his heart is pure.

Jesus had a high view of children. They belonged to a special category, "the least of these" (Mt. 25:40). They were humble, vulnerable, dependent and innocent. Their lives were in the hands of adults. As such they were subject to more than occasional abuse. Jesus had zero tolerance for abusers, whether it be physical or spiritual. Anyone who oppresses a child, in Jesus' view, "should have a large millstone hung around his neck and be cast into the sea" (v.6). A child was the archetype of God's creation.

So, as he goes on to speak about these "little ones" he's thinking first of young children, but he's also applying the principle to those of child-like faith. One causes a small child to "stumble" through imprinting them with bad behavior at an early age. For instance, think of the thousands of children every year who are trafficked or pressed into the child-porn underworld. Their malleable minds are imprinted with a low view of behavior, a fearful view of adults, and a blighted view of their self-worth. They are not just damaged, they are emotionally and psychologically crippled. They will walk with a limp for the rest of their lives.

As for the "millstone", it's often the case that guilt or shame at being found out will see a perpetrator casting himself into the "depths". I'm thinking of the star of a popular American show who recently committed suicide after it was discovered that he had fifty thousand pictures and hundreds of videos of little girls as young as three to five years on his laptop.

Jesus employs hyperbole here as he addresses abusers. His exaggeration is far more than a teaching device, rather it betrays his total disdain for anyone who causes a little one to stumble. "Hands" and "eyes" are often the agents of abuse. Jesus says it's better to cut off your hand or gouge out your eye if they cause your own stumbling leading to a child's stumbling. Now, Jesus is fully aware that sin starts in the heart, but he's making a profound point. Heaven has no tolerance for those who cause others to stumble. Better we should sin privately than draw someone else into our selfishness. Having a toxic effect on someone else is to serve the devil – he gets "two for the price of one". Besides, you don't want to mess with angels (v.10).

Parable of the Lost Sheep 18:11–14

This parable stresses a bedrock truth about God the Father: He loves the "little ones" and is not willing that any should perish (2 Pe. 3:9). He will go to any lengths to seek and save the lost. He is relentlessly involved. A lost lamb's hope is lost but for a dedicated shepherd. Its hope is not in merit, nor experience, nor its own strength. It is doomed to death in the darkness. Enter the "everlasting arms" and despair becomes joy, not just for the lamb but also for the Shepherd.

Sin and Forgiveness 18:15–35

This passage begins with reference to the care of "a brother or sister" who sins. Jesus says that a one-on-one meeting about the bad decision should suffice, but if it doesn't one should bring along one or two others as witnesses to a second meeting. If the offending party still is recalcitrant then a public declaration should be made in the assembly of believers. Finally, if still unrepentant, the erring one should be outcast. This excommunication by the body of believers will be respected even in heaven (v.18), because the Lord is present in these decisions, even when made by "two or three" (v.20).

Unfortunately, Jesus' words re: "agreement about anything" (v.19) and "two or three gathered in my name" (v.20) are often taken out of this context of the adjudication of Church discipline. Just another example of how one's interpretation of scripture can lead people to faulty assumptions. What we *can* gather here is that the Lord gives a sinner at *least* two or three opportunities to repent. And when they do repent (even after "seventy-seven" infractions – v. 22) the Lord will forgive. This is the powerful message of what follows.

Jesus tells Peter a story about a senior servant to a king who owed his master a massive amount of money. When called to account he prostrates himself with a pitiful cry for more time. The king shows great mercy and forgives the entire debt. In surprise and relief the groveling servant backs out of the king's presence and on his way from the palace complex he encounters a fellow servant who owes him "a hundred silver coins". Just having been forgiven a debt of hundreds of millions of dollars, you'd expect this man to be fully forgiving of his fellow servant (100 silver coins, by the way, was a huge amount to the likes of Peter – it represented one hundred days labor, enough to provide a meal for twenty-five hundred men). But no. This unforgiving wretch takes the poor fellow by the throat and demands payment, or else. He then "or else's" the man into prison. The king hears about it, reverses his forgiveness of the debt, and has this self-absorbed villain thrown into the same prison.

The lesson is blunt. Forgive and you will be forgiven. Don't forgive and you will not be forgiven. What's more we are to forgive "from our hearts" (v.35). There are to be no trailing remnants of sins done to us. Our suffered injustices cannot come close to the offences we have committed against the Holy One. Our impurity denies us access to the heavenlies. But, the purity of the Lamb of God can become ours if we forgive. Refuse to forgive at your peril.

Goodbye Galilee, Hello Jerusalem 19:1–23:39

Matthew sweeps through a lengthy transition in his history of Jesus' ministry in a mere two sentences (vv.1,2). Jesus leaves the Galilee for Perea (probably detouring through Samaria) healing people on the way. There is a huge watershed here: Jesus *leaves* Galilee for good. He's expanding his ministry from the regional to the national, from the provincial town of Capernaum to the federal capital. Jerusalem will be the setting of his final ministry focus (v.17). It will also be the city where he is crucified, dies, and rises again. O Jerusalem! A lot happens on the way. We don't see Jesus in Jerusalem until chapter 21.

Marriage and Divorce 19:3–12

"Some Pharisees came to test him". Perea was a Gentile region, so there were no resident Pharisees. Either these Pharisees came all the way from Jerusalem to test Jesus, or else this interaction took place somewhere nearer the Holy City. We don't know. What we *do* know is that the issue of marriage and divorce was a big one. No need for me to go over what I've already written – go back to my commentary on 5:31,32.

Blessing Children 19:13–15

Here we see the disciples doing their duty as cabinet-members-in-waiting, micro-managing Jesus' public ministry. In this case they are shooing away young mothers with their infants and toddlers. The disciples saw them as a nuisance – careless, enthusiastic, playful dependents, with no gravitas nor strategic worth in the more important matter of preparing for the messianic Kingdom. So they "rebuke" these little ones. Jesus, in turn, rebukes the disciples. The Kingdom is not an adult enterprise, rather it belongs to "little ones". The disciples must have been both confounded and embarrassed. This put-down from Jesus must have fuelled quite the discussion over dinner that evening.

The Rich Young Man 19:16–26

Here we have the obverse of a child's easy entry into the Kingdom of Heaven. Whereas childlike dependence catalyzes entry, material independence hinders. It is our need of God that fuels our faith.

This rich young man asked Jesus a sincere question: "What good thing must I do to get eternal life?" He framed the question poorly, however. According to Mark 10:18 he called Jesus, "Good teacher". Jesus then asked the young man if he knew the meaning of "good". The older manuscripts of the scriptures say, "Why asketh thou me concerning what is good?" And, how does he know that Jesus is good? Is this mere politeness? Flattery? Perhaps it's merely something of which we're all guilty from time to time: the easy use of an unexamined word.

Regardless they got into a discussion of obedience to the commandments. The young fellow wants Jesus to delineate. Then he adds a new one: sell what you have and give to the poor (knowing this would be the young man's achilles heel). Jesus knew that in spite of his courteous inquiry this young man would not be willing to yield his material security to follow an itinerant, homeless teacher.

Even as the man slunk away, Jesus used what the disciples had overheard as a teaching opportunity. Riches are a barrier to entry into the Kingdom, he said. This struck the disciples. Like all people everywhere in history they saw material security as a good thing. But Peter took the opportunity to press Jesus here: unlike this rich man we've left everything to follow you! What's in it for us? Instead of rebuking him Jesus said, you'll get your reward. One day you *will* be my cabinet, not here in space and time, mind you, but later in the heavenly Kingdom. So lose your bald ambition. To be first you've got to learn to be last.

Unfair Wages, An Ambitious Mother, and Two Blind Men 20:1–28

What follows is a melange of parable, bald-faced maternal self-interest, and miracle. In the middle of it all is Jesus' third prediction of his imminent death. It's a loaded chapter.

A Labor Dispute 20:1–16

Jesus had just summarized the life lesson from the interaction with the rich young man by declaring that, "many who are first will be last, and many who are last will be first." Now he builds on that principle with a parable about workers in a vineyard. Peter's inappropriate question, "What's in it for us?" (v.27), precipitated the story.

The laborers for hire were not Pharisees or Sadducees but "am ha aretz", people of the Land whom the Pharisees dismissed as scum. John tells us the Pharisees said, "there is a curse on them" (Jn. 8:49). They were the unlettered, "unclean", blue collar workers of the day.

The owner of the vineyard was under seasonal pressure. The harvest time for the grapes was short. He had to get the grapes in now. So he went to the early morning gathering place for day laborers and hired everyone there. He would have preferred more but he hired what he could get. The "contract" was one denarius for the working day, which meant morning to night. As the day progressed, the hired hands nearly expiring in the heat, the owner went back three more times to the gathering place to hire more men. The size of the harvest and the shortness of time demanded as many laborers as possible. Finally, at the end of the day, the work was done. He brought the workers together and paid them the agreed wage. The men who had worked twelve hours, of course, expected more money than those who had worked six, three, and one hours. But to their outrage the owner paid everyone one denarius. What?! This isn't fair!

The owner responded to this accusation, "Didn't we agree to a denarius? You've got what we contracted. These later workers also agreed to a denarius. This is my vineyard, my money, to do as I like. I have dealt with you fairly."

This parable starts with, "The Kingdom of Heaven is like..." The simile is teaching the disciples that the doctrine of merit to which we all adhere is both offended and eclipsed by a Sovereign's grace. Like the elder son in the parable of the Prodigal we demand that our faithful, long-suffering work for God gives us rank over "tax collectors and harlots". Jesus says, no, that's not how the Kingdom works. The question is, what is our motive? What is the spirit of our work? Truly, Peter's question had been woefully out of order.

> *The simile is teaching the disciples that the doctrine of merit to which we all adhere is both offended and eclipsed by a Sovereign's grace.*

Another Warning 20:17–19

Jesus led the long, arduous slog through the Jordan Valley to Jericho on the way to Jerusalem. He and the disciples had lots of time to talk. Matthew records a brief but poignant heads-up from Jesus. He warns them that in Jerusalem the religious leaders will condemn him to death, and the Gentiles (Romans) will mock, flog, and crucify him. Then (again something that the disciples don't seem to hear), he will rise again.

A Mother Lobbies Jesus 20:20–28

In this account two of Jesus' "inner circle" of three (James and John) get their mother to present their agenda to Jesus. Dutifully they stood behind her as she knelt down before Jesus, requesting that her two boys be the ones who would sit on the right and left of Jesus when he established his Kingdom. Like Peter they wanted what was "in it for them", but they didn't have the courage, the "chutzpah", to ask for it themselves. Let Mommy do it. And forget this "last shall be first" stuff. We've got the inside track. Jesus had a quick response: "You don't know what you're asking." They had no idea of what lay ahead.

When the other disciples heard about it they were totally "indignant". There must have been a heated exchange. Jesus broke into the mêlée, calmed them down, and then reminded everyone that the hierarchical power and politics view of the world did not apply to the Kingdom. Service, not status, was the key to heavenly approval. The road to greatness was paved with self-denial, not self-exaltation. There's nothing wrong with being small. Sometimes the innocuous incubates the unexpected. Remember the manger in Bethlehem?

Two Blind Men 20:29–34

Two blind men were healed as Jesus and his disciples left Jericho. There was nothing, by now, unusual about this. What does stand out, however, is the totally uninhibited approach they took. They shouted. Again and again. "Have mercy on us, Son of David!" The crowd rebuked them, but no amount of social pressure could deter them. They just kept shouting till Jesus, with compassion, "touched their eyes". There is wisdom in seizing the moment.

Jerusalem 21:1–23:39

These three chapters show the momentum building against Jesus in Jerusalem. They also contain the last collection of his teaching, other than what he says about the end times. It is gripping reading.

The Triumphal Entry 21:1–11

The difficulty of the climb from Jericho to Jerusalem cannot be exaggerated. During the seven years I pastored in Jerusalem I used to drive down to Jericho, through the Jordan Valley to Tiberias on the Sea of Galilee. Then I would climb to the Upper Galilee to Metulla, Israel's northernmost town. From there I would present my Israel Defence Forces pass to the border guards and drive into Lebanon to an abandoned customs house that had been converted into a humble radio station. There I would broadcast country music, the news, weather, and the Gospel to Northern Israel and Southern Lebanon. I'd do two back-to-back shifts and return to Jerusalem the next day. The road from Jericho to Jerusalem was so steep my little Volkswagen would nearly expire. I can't imagine walking it.

But that's what Jesus and the Twelve did. They set their faces toward Jerusalem and started out. The whole region is desert, mountains and valleys (wadis). Dust, heat, and a climb of thousands of feet tested their endurance and resolve. Undoubtedly their first stop was about halfway up at Wadi Qelt, a refreshing valley running with cool, clean water. What relief! Home to St. George's monastery today, this wadi is still a welcome desert refuge from the heat. It's a destination for both Jewish and Arab hikers, an oasis hiding deep between two imposing, barren hills.

Several hours later they would have reached a height near the modern day pilgrim site of the Samaritan's Inn. From there they could look miles over a series of desert mountain ridges and valleys to the heights of Jerusalem on the far horizon. Just about a mile south of the Holy City they reached their destination for the night: Bethphage, the "house of unripe figs" (late season figs that appear unripe but are edible). It was situated on the side of a hill across the valley southeast of Bethany ("house of the poor"), the home of Mary, Martha, and Lazarus.

Bethphage was a vital town in Jewish cultural/spiritual life. The Talmud later saw it as the entry to Jerusalem. Any proper pilgrimage had to start somewhere beyond Bethphage. When pilgrims reached it, although it was on the outskirts of the Holy City, they rejoiced. Their pilgrimage was almost over.

When Jesus' troop arrived they most certainly refreshed themselves at some anonymous friend's house, then Jesus sent two of his disciples over to Bethany to get a donkey and her colt. Matthew tells us this was to fulfill Zechariah's prophecy:

> *"Say to Daughter Zion*
> *see your king comes to you,*
> *gentle and riding on a donkey,*
> *and on a colt, the foal of a donkey."*
>
> —Ze. 9:9

This "king" was to ride a donkey, not a white stallion, with no trappings of royalty, devoid of pomp and circumstance. Ironically, "His rule will extend from sea to sea and from the River to the ends of the earth" (Ze. 9:10). But it would be more than an earthly reign. As Jesus put it in John 18:36: "My kingdom is not of this world... my kingdom is from another place." Long before scientists and astrophysicists coined the word "multiverse" Jesus spoke of "another", a parallel (?) world, from which his Father had sent him to save our world.

Matthew gives precious few details so we have to engage our imagination. Whether it was in the late afternoon that day, or the next morning, Jesus made his entry into Jerusalem. I suspect it was the next morning, how else could such a crowd materialize, supplied with palm branches? Word certainly had spread that the miracle-worker was coming to town. And the "am ha aretz" could hardly wait to welcome their triumphant king. It was about time! He's finally here! We can proclaim him king and the Romans will be routed, the world ruled in heavenly peace! Our day of liberation has come!

"A very great multitude" (KJV) lined the road along the heights of the Mount of Olives down into and up from the Kidron Valley and into Jerusalem through the eastern gate. This procession surrounded by hilariously happy people waving palm branches and flinging their coats down on the road in front of the donkey would have moved slowly. Without the crowds it takes about an hour or so to walk from Bethany into Jerusalem. This ungainly parade probably took two or three hours.

The shout from the crowd was a resounding repetition of "Hosanna!"

In the Hebrew this means, "Save now!" The agenda of the people was clear. Save us! Save us now from the Romans! Save us from the corrupt political and spiritual elite! We want your Kingdom now!

But Jesus was not about to "save now". He had a much larger and challenging task than the mere temporal relief of a sandlot on the outer fringes of Roman rule. He was here to save the world. To do that the "Hosanna" must morph into "Crucify him!" And it did. In very short order the "Triumphal Entry" would soon become the "Big Disappointment".

> *In very short order the "Triumphal Entry" would soon become the "Big Disappointment".*

The Temple Uproar 21:12–17

Hundreds of years before Jesus, the prophet Malachi had written, "The Lord… shall suddenly come to his temple… But who may abide the day of his coming?" (Ma. 3:1,2 RSV). This prophecy may or may not have referred to the sequel to the Triumphal Entry, but the clamor in the temple courts resonated with Malachi's warning.

Jesus attacked. Angered by the extortion and graft of the Sadducees' temple markets he overthrew the kiosks and drove the vendors away. He was attacking something else too: the religious nationalism of the temple culture. "Jerusalem for the Jews" was the common slogan. Jesus, on the other hand, declared, "My house shall be called a house of prayer for all nations" (Mk. 11:17 KJV). The Sadducees had made it a "house of graft". Their motive was greed. Jesus' motive was love for the world.

He then turned the chaos into beauty by healing the lame and the blind right there among the scattered furniture and trappings of the fleeing temple merchants. He recovered by his miraculous love what the priestly caste had destroyed. Nevertheless his "unkingly" behavior had tongues wagging.

An Unfortunate Fig Tree 21:18–22

My challenge here is to avoid the temptation to write an essay on fig trees. It's amazing how the symbolism of the fig emerges again and again in the Hebrew scriptures. Here's a summary.

Way back in Israel's history grapes, pomegranates and figs became the "signature" of the Promised Land. When Moses sent spies from their wilderness wandering into Canaan they returned with "a branch bearing a single cluster of grapes. Two of them carried it on a pole between them, along with some pomegranates and figs" (Nu. 13:23). Moses later described the "good land" into which "the Lord your God is bringing you" as a "land with wheat and barley, vines and fig trees, pomegranates, olive oil and honey" (Dt. 8:7, 8). Later historians and prophets would describe Israel's past and future peace and prosperity this way:

> "During Solomon's lifetime Judah and Israel, from Dan
> to Beersheba, lived in safety, everyone under their own vine
> and under their own fig tree."
>
> —1 Ki. 4:25

> "He will judge between many peoples and will settle disputes for
> strong nations far and wide. They will beat their swords into
> ploughshares and their spears into pruning hooks. Nation will not
> take up sword against nation, nor will they train for war anymore.
> Everyone will sit under their own vine and under their own fig tree."
>
> —Mk. 4:3, 4a

"In that day each of you will invite your neighbor to sit under your vine and fig tree', declares the Lord Almighty."

—ZE. 3:10

One of my favorite places in Jerusalem for the past forty years (seven of which we lived there) is a small fruit and cold drinks stand on the southeast ridge of the ancient Mt. Moriah, overlooking the steep valley of Kidron facing the Arab town of Silwan on the western slope of the Mount of Olives. This idyllic setting is special for three reasons: shade, peace, and view. The kiosk is owned by a kind, hospitable Christian Arab who, like me, is now getting "up in years". I was there recently recording a television series. When I'm there it's like time has stopped and all stress has flown away. In the heat of the day the grape vines and fig trees overshadowing the kiosk are like a natural air conditioner. Sitting on the clean white plastic chairs, placed right on the edge of the ridge, a cold soda in hand, the view of the Mount of Olives across the valley, one feels at peace. All is right with the world. Such is the impact of the fig.

Getting back to the Jewish scriptures, the obverse of God's pleasure in providing his faithful people rest under their fig trees is the destruction of those very figs by a wrathful God due to his children's intransigence:

"He struck down their vines and fig trees..."

—Ps. 105:33

"'I will take away their harvest,' declares the Lord. 'There will be no grapes on the vine. There will be no figs on the tree, and their leaves will wither.'"

—JE. 8:13

"'I will ruin her vines and her fig trees'... declares the Lord."

—HO. 2:12

So, the fig could be cursed as well as blessed. It all depended on Israel's obedience to the God of Abraham, Isaac, and Jacob.

Matthew and the other disciples assumed Jesus was "hungry". But it appears that Jesus was angry. Just having returned to Bethany the day before, he was still troubled by what he had found at the Temple. His cursing of the barren fig tree issued from a deep distress at Jerusalem's barrenness. As the tree wilted the disciples were watching a parable in action. They would not forget the lesson. It was passed on to others, including St. Paul, who passed it on to young Timothy. Christians were to be faithful and bear fruit, "in season and out of season" (1 Ti. 4:12). They were to be "known by their fruit" (Mt. 7:16). It's not enough to be leafy, like so many who are "preachy". You've got to practice what you preach. That's when the fruit will emerge; unless, of course, your preaching is shallow and sectarian.

Jesus followed up the disciples' amazement at the impact of his words on the tree with a comment that must be seen in the broader context of his body of teaching. "Truly I tell you, if you have faith and do not doubt, not only can you do what was done to the fig tree, but also you can say to this mountain, 'Go, throw yourself into the sea', and it will be done. If you believe, you will receive whatever you ask for in prayer" (vv.21, 22). Without context these words seem reckless.

But here's context: "I am the vine; you are the branches. If you remain in me and I in you, you will bear much fruit; apart from me you can do nothing. If you do not remain in me, you are like a branch that is thrown away and withers; such branches are picked up, thrown into the fire and burned. If you remain in me and my words remain in you, ask whatever you wish, and it will be done for you. This is to my Father's glory, that you bear much fruit, showing yourselves to be my disciples" (Jn. 15:5-8).

The contextual caveat is predicated on a huge "If". *If* the disciples "remain in" Jesus' teaching, and "if" his words "remain" in the disciples, *then* they will "bear much fruit" and their requests will be granted. It all boils down to "not my will but *Thine* be done." The branch cannot bear fruit by itself. It must live and grow by the life issuing from the roots. So stop praying to win the lottery.

Various Intrigues, Controversies, and Parables 21:23–23:39

After the juxtaposed chaos and the miraculous of the day before, and a wilted fig tree just an hour or so ago, Jesus was back in the Temple. Immediately a crowd surrounded him, this time to hear him teach. As he taught, some of the priests and temple officials stood on the outer fringes of the group to both hear and criticize. In spite of themselves, they were impressed with his authority. Loathe to admit it to one another they inwardly marvelled at Jesus' authoritative impact. He didn't quote the rabbis of the past. In fact when he did quote anyone or anything it was their own prophets and scriptures. He did so without apology. Indeed, "he taught as one who had authority, and not as their teachers of the law" (Mt. 7:29). He was a didactic phenom.

These Sadduceean elites were threatened by Jesus' authority. So they sought to diminish him both as a teacher and by what he had done to their cozy money-making scheme in the temple courts yesterday demanding his academic/rabbinical credentials. Jesus answered the question with a question of his own. Had they interrogated John the Baptist? If so what was the result? Was he of God or of man? This, of course, forced a conundrum. They had gone to the Jordan to witness John's ministry (Mt. 3:7). They had also accused him of being demon possessed (Mt. 11:8), a claim that probably precipitated huge push-back from the people. So, now, surrounded by fans of both John and Jesus in the Temple they were afraid of inciting a riot by denying John's heavenly mandate. Caution told them to defer. Which they did. So then did Jesus, and he continued the lesson.

Parable of Two Sons 21:28–32

Jesus shifted the lesson in the direction of the suddenly quiet Sadducees. He told them a story about two sons whose father wanted them to work in his vineyard. The first said he would not, the second said he would. But the first son changed his mind and got the work. The other son didn't show. Jesus then asked the Sadducees a grade-school question, "Who did what his father wanted?" The answer was obvious.

The former group had practice with no promise, the latter had promise but no practice.

The meaning of the parable was also obvious. The two "sons" were sketchy groups: a. tax collectors and prostitutes; b. Pharisees and Sadducees. The former group had practice with no promise, the latter had promise but no practice. The teaching? Ultimately obedience (however late or grudging) is the way to God's heart.

Parable of the Wicked Farmers 21:33–43

Jesus was still teaching in the Temple, and the Sadducees were still in the audience. They had been bested in the attempt to discount Jesus' authority and had been embarrassed in front of the crowd. Even as they looked for a face-saving exit Jesus had addressed the parable of the two sons to them. Now he tells them the parable of the wicked tenant farmer.

This parable is all about verse 42, quoting Psalm 118:22, 23:

*"The stone the builders rejected
has become the cornerstone;
the Lord has done this,
and it is marvelous in our eyes."*

Jesus is reminding the Sadducees that God sent prophets to Israel whom they killed. Now He has sent his son, the very stone which the builders rejected. This son would become the cornerstone of everlasting life (Is. 28:16). But due to this rejection the Gospel will transfer to the Gentile world, where the son will be accepted and worshipped. Their faith will produce great fruit (Mt. 21:43).

The Plot Begins 21:45, 46

Not all ancient manuscripts include the 44th verse, but if Jesus said this it helps explain why the religious elite had heard enough. They weren't about to be "crushed" by this upstart! It was time to get rid of the presumptuous blasphemer! Only their fear of the "multitudes" (am ha aretz) had held them back. Nevertheless the seeds of revenge had been sown.

Parable of the Rejected Invitation 22:1–14

This parable has a similar message as that of the wicked farmers. The poignant point: the invited guests reject the king's servants, and in some cases kill them, even as they refuse to attend the wedding banquet. Those who ultimately do attend are the unwashed fringe people, the am ha aretz. But there is a fascinating, and troubling interchange between the king and one of these marginalized folk. It's about wedding clothes.

The rejection by the "washed" led to a frustrated and angry king inviting the "unwashed". The only caveat was the expected wedding clothes that were to be worn by all guests. These surprised, marginalized people had to get busy, clean up, and dress appropriately. But there was one fellow who cynically showed up in his work clothes. He was one of those "thin soil" folk who were more curious than committed. He was in for a bitter reality check.

The "wedding garment" (v.12 KJV) was seen by the rabbis as a symbol of repentance, culminating in righteousness. This parable uses the long serving symbol to teach that those who repent and clothe themselves in the righteousness of Christ are "chosen" for everlasting life (v.14). Those who do not repent will suffer everlasting darkness. A sober message. Very sober.

The Poll Tax Controversy 22:15–22

The Pharisees wanted to "entangle" (KJV) Jesus by forcing him to take a political stand. They assumed he was like the plethora of nationalistic zealots pervading Palestine at that time. They hoped to "trap" him in betraying his suspected secret agenda. They were about to be outwitted.

The malicious plan was to confront Jesus with the issue of paying a poll tax to the Roman occupying forces. To do this they would engage some "Herodians" (hated enemies of the Pharisees) in the encounter. These were partisans of the ruling Herod family. The idea was to put pressure on Jesus from both church and state.

Jesus' response shut them up. He asked for a coin, and whose face was on it. It was Caesar's, of course. So, what's the problem? Pay Caesar what is his. Pay God what is His. Next question? His enemies slink away, their tails between their legs.

Resurrection Controversy 22:23–33

This time it was the Sadducees trying to trip him up. Even though the Pharisees are mentioned more often in Matthew as Jesus' enemies, the most malevolent were the Sadducees. Why? Because they ruled the Temple. They were threatened by Jesus not just theologically (as was the case with the Pharisees) but economically. As Hellenized secularists they had made accommodation with the Romans and were secure in their money-making, both in the temple businesses and in affiliate enterprises. If Jesus were allowed to continue building his base the Sadducees might see their world come crashing down. This is why, later in the Passion story, they were quick to condemn Jesus to death. Caiaphas and all the temple leaders were Sadducees. Their livelihood was on the line.

So one day, in the hearing of the crowd that had gathered around, they tried to trap Jesus on the topic of resurrection. Biblical literalists, the Sadducees did not believe in resurrection because it was not explicitly mentioned in the Pentateuch (the first five books of the Bible). They conveniently ignored Daniel's account of an angelic visitation on the Tigris river in which, among much else, the angel said, "Multitudes who sleep in the dust of the earth will awake: some to everlasting life, others to shame and everlasting contempt. Those who are wise will shine like righteousness, like the stars forever and ever" (Da. 12:2, 3).

In their juvenile hypothetical story about seven brothers married to one woman they tried to make resurrection absurd. The woman's serial marriages to the brothers was predicated on "levirate marriage", a provision Moses had made to protect widows from penury, and to perpetuate a dead husband's lineage (Dt. 25:5, 6). Their punchline, the question they knew would derail Jesus was, "Whose wife will she be in the resurrection?" Jesus makes *them* absurd.

Jesus tells them there is no marriage in heaven because the "power of God" will transform this world's cartoon of reality into a full-blown canvas one day. Love will take on new depth. The heavenly reality will not be anthropomorphized.

And, I imagine Jesus saying, since you've asked, resurrection is a present reality. God has not said, I *was*, but I *am*, the God of Abraham, the God of Isaac, and the God of Jacob. Your fathers are alive. The Sadducees, like the Pharisees, had to melt away, egg on their faces.

The Greatest Commandment 22:34–40

The Pharisees, who generally saw the Sadducees as worldly rivals, were silently delighted that Jesus had "muzzled" (Gk) them (v.34). But they were still on a mission to muzzle Jesus. So they took a theological tack, "Which is the greatest commandment in the Law?"

The rabbis loved to sum up the heart of religion (Aboth 1:1,2; 2:9). They and many other bible teachers after them would often remark on the declension of the Law in scripture.

Moses gave 613 commandments, some relating to moral law, most relating to civil law (365 negative, 248 positive). David reduced them to 11 (Ps. 15:2-5), Isaiah to 6 (Is. 33:15), Micah to 3 (Mi. 6:38), Amos to 2 (Am. 5:4), and Habakkuk to 1 (Ha. 2:4).

Jesus redaction? Love God, love neighbor. With your intellect, emotion, and will. Full stop. All the Law and the Prophets "hang" on these. Love for God is the fulfillment of righteousness, love for neighbor the fulfillment of justice. In this command the essential call of the Prophets is summarized. Do this and you will live (Lk. 10:28). I've written an entire chapter in my book, "*When God Stood Up – A Christian Response to AIDS in Africa*", about righteousness and justice (Harper/Collins publisher). I'll resist the urge to reprint it here. It is a *vital* topic.

Son of David Controversy 22:41–46

Now it was Jesus' turn to ask a question. It wasn't about himself, but about their concept of the person and office of Messiah. He queried the Pharisees who were still ruminating over what he had just said about the greatest commandment. "What do you think about the Messiah? Whose son is he?" Their response was immediate, automatic, "The son of David." "Then why does David call his son "Lord"?" Jesus asks, quoting Psalm 110:1. He saw this psalm as the Lord (YHWH) speaking to David's Lord (ADONAI), the true King, the Anointed One, the Messiah. This meant that "son of David" was about far more than genetics and pedigree – He is David's Lord, Son of God. Indeed Messiah is Lord!

There was an awkward silence. The Pharisees had no further push-back. Indeed they determined to never again ask questions. They couldn't trap him. They had to kill him.

Seven Woes 23:1–39

Before getting to the seven woes Jesus pronounced on the Pharisees, I think it would be good to draw a quick sketch of the Scribes, Pharisees, and Sadducees. You can, of course, get lots of detail by Googling these groups. When you do, remember that the dates given will be "CE" and "BCE", which are abbreviations for "Common Era" and "Before the Common Era" (the pivot point being what Christian historians see as the probable date of Jesus' birth – 4BC).

The Scribes were referred to as "men of understanding" and "just men". They were both literate and educated in the Law of Moses, able to "cipher" ("saphar" Hebrew) the religious writings of the day. Their model was Ezra, a scribe skilled in the Law of Moses (Ez. 7:6) who had returned to Jerusalem when Darius, king of Babylon, signed a decree that the Temple in Jerusalem could be rebuilt. Assiduous in both planning and performance, Ezra was the perfect person to make sure the "DNA" of both the physical, and especially, the spiritual rebuilding effort be pleasing to the Lord. He is described as one who "had devoted himself to the study and observance of the Law of the Lord, and to teaching its decrees and laws in Israel" (Ez. 7:16). So the Scribes became the copyists, editors, and guardians of the integrity of scripture. In Jesus' time they were religious lawyers who mostly tended to alliances with the Pharisees.

For a couple of centuries before Christ a prolonged antipathy had percolated between the temple elite, the Sadducees, and the so-called "lay interpreters" of scripture, the Pharisees. Scribal history had given rise to these lay interpreters. Their designation, Pharisee, was rooted in "parash" (Heb.) which referred to "one who is separate". Over time they seceded from scribal strictures (although they continued in guarded hybridized relationship) even as they also separated themselves from the "am ha aretz" ("people of the Land"). They grew to see themselves as "holy".

Some said the Pharisees "monopolized" the Torah. Their signature became self-righteous formalism.

Handing down their interpretation orally, their authority when challenged was "the Fathers". They built a wall, or a "fence around the Law", the manmade barrier being their intransigent legalism. Some said the Pharisees "monopolized" the Torah. Their signature became self-righteous formalism. They believed in resurrection, angels, and the after-life. They also believed Messiah was coming.

But, even though their raison d'être was religious perfectionism, they too sought political power. Internecine warfare, slaughters, and executions sully their history with the Sadducees. And, like the Sadducees, they made many an appeal to Rome. This is why Rome, almost by default, became the major power broker in Judea.

Like the Pharisees, the Sadducees emerged on the scene somewhere in the 135-105 BC period. Greek rule and cultural presence (called "Hellenism") was at its peak in the region of Asia Minor. The Sadducees were the temple elite, the privileged class of Jerusalem. Both Hellenized and secular, they focused mainly on the Pentateuch in their theology, arguing vehemently against resurrection and the "spiritual" spin of the Pharisees on everything from the afterlife to angels and the end of days. As the priestly caste they controlled the Temple. They owned its commercial enterprises, and legislated punitive sentences on those who opposed their will. This is why they were the ones who sentenced Jesus to death. Legally they had no power to enact their sentences but they were in bed with Rome. Ultimately they prevailed with Pilate, and Jesus died on a Roman cross.

Their Sermon Content is Good, but not Their Practice 23:1–12

Jesus instructs his listeners to respect the "teachers of the Law" (Scribes) and the Pharisees as they preach from "Moses' seat" in the synagogues. The traditional view was that those who taught from the pulpit (modern term for "Moses' seat") were actually endued with a sort of "apostolic succession" from Moses himself as they preached. Jesus affirms the essential context of these sermons and declares that it is applicable to life (v.3a), but the teachers were poor models in terms of their lack of practicing what they preached. There is a subtlety here. The content was good, but the guilt-trip interpretations that these preachers laid on the people were not. Their hermeneutics amounted to a "scold", and even as they inveighed against their congregations, they were, at the same time, not condemning themselves, but preening in public places as pious pilgrims (v.5).

They loved to be called "Father" and "Rabbi" (meaning "my great one" Heb.). Their clothing was ostentatiously religious, and they assumed they would sit in places of honor at public functions. In some ways they were like Jesus' disciples who wanted to sit at his right and left hand when he ascended his messianic throne! Indeed, their religiosity was a caricature of human nature. We all want to be noticed and honored. We like titles – "Doctor, Professor, Reverend, Father, Your Grace, etc.". Jesus says, lose the titles and humble yourselves.

Jesus then goes on to warn the religious leaders about their hypocrisies. But before I comment on them, I need to express this caveat: when we read this litany of woes we should examine ourselves. Not all Pharisees were bad. In general they were like many of us – concerned about loving God and neighbor, trying to "serve" the Lord by doing good, attempting to raise children "in the nurture and admonition of the Lord", with a high view of scripture. Jesus' issue was with leadership. Most Pharisees were not leaders. They were everyday, mostly good people. Perhaps the best-known Pharisees in our Christian "Hall of Fame" would be Nicodemus, Joseph of Arimathea, and St. Paul.

First Woe 23:13[4]

Here Jesus decries the paralyzing suffocation of exclusivity. The Scribes and Pharisees were, in their own view, well-intentioned. They wanted to bring men and women to daily relationship with the Law. But, to do this, they formed narrow silos of faith that excluded intentional and unintentional non-conformists. Again, in Christian history there have often been "closed communion" denominations denying access to the Kingdom other than through adherence to their sub-cultural dogmas. Sectarianism can be both beguiling and delusional.

---

[4]   verse 14 is not in many ancient manuscripts. The KJV includes it. It suggests that the pharisaic leaders were often guilty of leveraging their spiritual superiority to take advantage of the vulnerable.

Second Woe 23:15

To appreciate Jesus' stern rebuke here, we need to remember that the Pharisees saw Gentiles as "children of Hell". They were the unwashed, the "dogs", the offscouring of the earth. So, when they go out into the Gentile world to proselytize they are purportedly attempting to recreate themselves. This, says Jesus, makes the Gentile convert into "twice the child of Hell" they were before.

Jesus is speaking in a culture of proselytism where, for example, years before Christ, John Hyrcannus, the last of the Maccabean priests/kings had offered Idumean Gentiles the alternative of death, exile, or circumcision (conversion to Judaism). These conversions under compulsion produced artificial members of the pharisaic sect who were never truly accepted or trusted as genuine Jews. There was an unwritten law among the Pharisees that no one should trust a proselyte, even to the 24th generation. In that sense they were still, now even more so, a "child of hell".

Third Woe 23:16–22

Oaths were ingrained in the culture of the day. Indeed, some have suggested that the culture was addicted to oaths. Jesus, however, has no time or tolerance for them. He despises the parsing of the relative values of various oaths. He shakes his head at the dullness of the people's reasoning. Essentially he's telling them that the Temple houses the altar, the altar engages the sacrifice, heaven is the location of the Throne, and all lead ultimately to God. It is to him alone that we are accountable. So, let your yes be yes, and your no, no (Mt 5:37). Full stop.

Fourth Woe 23:23,24

Jesus warns against buffering the higher by managing the lower. Tithing of herbs (Dt. 14:22) is no substitute for justice, mercy, and faith. Perfectionism that compulsively strains gnats from one's drink while swallowing camels in the process is rather like trying to pick a bit of sawdust from a friend's eye when you have a cedar log in your own. One can be meticulous about righteousness and unjust at the same time (Mt. 7:3). The Pharisees have lost all sense of proportion.

Perfectionism that compulsively strains gnats from one's drink while swallowing camels in the process is rather like trying to pick a bit of sawdust from a friend's eye when you have a cedar log in your own.

Fifth Woe 23:25, 26

There was a well-known statement that the Lord made to the prophet Samuel as he was recruiting someone to succeed King Saul (1Sa. 16:7b): "Man looketh on the outward appearance, but the Lord looketh on the heart" (KJV). Jesus had little regard for the Pharisees' clean-hands religion. Outward purity means nothing if there is no inner purity. The heart tells the tale.

Sixth Woe 23:27,28

Here we have the outside/inside theme again. The interesting detail, which can be missed, is that the white-washing of graves was not for beauty, but for warning those who were walking in the vicinity. To walk over a grave unintentionally meant spiritual defilement that had to be followed with a rigorous cleansing ritual. This white-washing or "chalking" of graves was refreshed every year before Passover. For a few months, at least, they looked nice. One might forget the decomposed bodies inside.

Seventh Woe 23:29–33

The Jewish view saw a definite generational continuum with regard to righteousness and unrighteousness (Ex. 20:5, 6). Jesus makes it clear that the Pharisees cannot, much as they may wish to, separate themselves from their ancestors' vilification and murder of the prophets. It's very easy, but self-deceiving, to laud the dead, yet the "like father like son" principle applies. Jesus expects the Pharisees will "complete" or "fill up" (KJV) the cup of guilt their fathers held. Hell (yes, Jesus speaks of Hell again and again) awaits.

Threat and Lament 23:34–39

This is 2 Chronicles 36:15,16 all over again. "The Lord, the God of their ancestors, sent word to them through his messengers again and again, because he had pity on his people and on his dwelling place. But they mocked God's messengers, despised his words and scoffed at his prophets until the wrath of the Lord was aroused against his people and there was no remedy." Jesus laments over Jerusalem's hardness of heart, not just because their rejection hurts, but also because Jerusalem itself will ultimately be destroyed. The Roman Titus saw to that in 70AD. In her desolation a remnant will renew its expectation of Messiah's coming. A second "Triumphal Entry" awaits.

THE END OF THE AGE 24:1–26:2

The expectation shared by most of the early followers of Christ was that his return ("parousia") would occur sometime around the events of the Jewish War (culminating in the destruction of Jerusalem and the Temple in 70 AD). But, in this section of Matthew, Jesus teaches that his disciples will have to be on the lookout for a few other markers.

Two things especially stand out: a season of apostasy (24:10-12) and the evangelization of the entire Gentile world (24:14). Then the end will emerge (24:42). Rather than passively waiting around with their eyes on the sky, Jesus' faithful followers are to keep their lamps well oiled (25:4), especially in the care of the marginalized "am ha aretz" (25:31-46). One must not fall into the error of dating the parousia (24:42) because it's unknowable – even Jesus doesn't know (24:36). Any date-setter will be totally wrong. Yet, how may times in history have self-proclaimed "prophets" called their credulous followers to clothe themselves in white and gather on a high mountain to greet the returning Jesus? Let the humble pilgrim beware.

When Will the End Come? 24:1–3

We've got to remember that the Twelve were rustic Galileans. On a casual walk with Jesus past the Temple they comment with tourist-like wonder at its awesome construction. Jesus response? It's all coming down.

Whoa! We hear you Jesus, but don't quite get it. All this talk about death and resurrection… but however it takes place, when will the end come and what sign will we have that you're behind it all? These fishermen wanted to cut to the chase.

Let's take a brief look at the history of this temple. King David had wanted to build a permanent house of the Lord, replacing the tent ("tabernacle") that had contained the Ark of the Covenant for a lengthy period of time stretching back to the wilderness wanderings of Israel. He was unable to do so, however, because, as his son and successor Solomon said, "he could not build a temple for the Name of the Lord his God until the Lord put his enemies under his feet" (1Ki. 5:3). But now, under young Solomon, the Lord had given "rest" from geopolitical adversity, and the king decided to follow through on his father's intention (1Ki. 5:5). You can read about this in 1Kings chapters 5-8, and 2Chronicles chapters 2-7.

On the top of Mount Zion (the historic Mount Moriah of Abraham's day) was the site of a "threshing floor" purchased by David from Araunah the Jebusite (2Sa. 24:16; 2Ch. 3:1). Solomon started the build about 480 years after the Exodus from Egypt. It took several years to build and it stood for 400 years up to the Babylonian Exile (comprising three deportations from 598 – 538 BC).

In 539 BC Cyrus of Persia captured Babylon, overthrowing the Chaldean Empire, incorporating Mesopotamia, Syria, and Palestine into the new Persian Empire. He allowed the exiled Judeans to return to their decimated sand-lot of a city and rebuild the Temple. Zerubbabel was tasked with the project which took about 25 years to complete (Ez. 3). It stood for 500 years. This temple is usually referred to as the "Second Temple" which includes the post-exilic period and the time of Herod with this new (third) temple. Zerubbabel's temple was desecrated and neutralized around 168 BC by Antiochus Epiphanes.

Herod started to build his impressive version of the Temple in 20 BC. He built quickly, not much more than 1½ years, although some ongoing construction lasted 40 years. It was the Temple of Jesus' time. It stood for merely 100 years. As Jesus had predicted it was razed (70AD) by the Romans.

Keep your heads up, and brains in gear.

The Labor Pains 24:4–8

First of all Jesus warns the disciples to avoid being deceived by false end-time prophets who will try to make portents out of the "usual suspects": wars, famines, plagues, and earthquakes. These natural disasters and human conflicts, like the poor, are always with us. Their value is the reminder of creation's vulnerability. At best they should cause us to remember that the history of our planet is limited. In that sense, consider them the beginning of birth pains. Keep your heads up, and brains in gear. Remember that "a day is like a thousand years, and a thousand years are like a day" in heaven (2Pe. 3:8).

Persecution and Apostasy 24:9–14

Long before The End the followers of Christ will be hated to the point where they will be persecuted and killed. The Roman historian Tacitus speaks of Christians as "a class hated for their abominations" (Annals 15:44). Relentless persecution would erode faith and increase the instinct for survival to the point where many would turn away from faith (apostasy) and even betray family members (Mt. 10:21,22). Indeed, the "temptation" Jesus refers to in the Lord's Prayer is the very human tendency to break under torture. Save us from the rack, O Lord! Those who endure will "be saved". Then, once the Gospel has been preached throughout the whole world, to all Gentile nations, "the end will come" (v.14).

Chaos in Judea 24:15–22

Jesus knew that in the decades following his death and resurrection the so-called *"Jewish Wars"* (Josephus) would see many "desolations". Just as Antiochus Epiphanes of Syria had erected a statue of Zeus in the Temple in 168BC (the "desolating sacrilege" spoken of by Daniel (Da. 12:11) so too would others follow (I Maccabees 1:54-64; Josephus, *"Antiquities"* 12). Josephus tells us that the Temple was often turned into a garrison and a fortress by several armies. And, of course, Titus totally razed it in 70 AD. So, there was only one option for those caught up in these chaotic times: Flee! Don't look back.

False Messiahs 24:23–28

False prophets and messiahs will gather many people like vultures around a lifeless carcass. Their interpretation and prognostication (He's out there! He's in here!) will bear no fruit, because they are devoid of truth and life. Don't be deceived. Jesus' coming will surprise everyone.

The Real Parousia 24:29–31

Jesus raises the bar above vain speculations and references Daniel's apocalyptic vision of the end of days, "In my vision at night I looked, and there before me was one like a son of man, coming with the clouds of heaven. He approached the Ancient of Days and was led into his presence. He was given authority, glory and sovereign power; all nations and peoples of every language worshipped him. His dominion is an everlasting dominion that will not pass away, and his Kingdom is one that will never be destroyed" (Da. 7:13, 14). The "sign" the disciples had asked for will be "the Son of Man coming on the clouds of heaven" (v.30). Peter, James, and John had seen the brilliant, blinding heavenly cloud that had accompanied the Father's affirmation of Jesus on the Mount of Transfiguration. This overwhelming light would appear again at Jesus' second coming. No other sign would do.

A Lesson from a Fig Tree 24:32, 33

Nothing profound here – just a fig tree (I wonder if the disciples thought of the poor cursed fig tree?). It's a Spring-time tree. The putting forth of tender shoots is a harbinger of summer, just as the signs of the times anticipate Jesus' return. His coming is inevitable.

Nobody Knows 24:34–36

Nobody knows when all these things will come to pass, with the exception of "the Father". What we *can* know is that the generation who sees the Gospel "preached throughout the whole world" (v.14) will be the generation that experiences The End in its lifetime. No need for speculation. Rather, we must work the harvest fields, for "the night is coming" (Jn. 9:4)

Most Will Be Blind-sided 24:37–41

Life will be going on as usual for most everyone. Work as usual, sleeping, eating, drinking, celebrating life passages, all as usual. There will be no "real time" expectations of The End. But, when Christ comes there will be a division between believer and unbeliever. So… be ready!

Be Ready 24:42–44

There is an ancient rabbinic saying, "Three things come unexpectedly – Messiah, the discovery of a treasure, and a scorpion." Jesus' coming will be utterly unexpected, with no possible speculative warning other than, "Be ready". We are to live everyday with Heaven in our sights.

Good and Bad Servants 24:45–51

The ready/not ready theme continues. Jesus employs a parable of good and bad servants who have been put in charge of their master's household in his absence. The faithful servants will work diligently even though there is no one to check up on them. The unfaithful servants will indulge themselves and fight with one another. The master will return unexpectedly, and the sneaky indolents will be caught in the act. In an age referred to by modern Israelis as "meyode primitivi" (very primitive) the bad guys meet an unhappy end.

There are two applications of this parable, one a space/time and the other a Kingdom of Heaven lesson. In terms of space and time, avoid sinful living just because Jesus' coming seems delayed. In terms of the Kingdom of Heaven, there will be work to do ("ruling" KJV) on the other side. Your work now is preparing you for work then.

The Ten Virgins 25:1–13

This parable needs no explanation. It's enough to recall that five women were ready for the big wedding party, and five weren't. It's the ready/not ready story again. The point: be ready. Preparation for Christ's coming is an indicator of faith. By faith we are already citizens of the Kingdom.

The Bags of Gold 25:14–30

This parable popularized the word "talent", a word we use to this day. In Jesus' time the talent was a fixed amount of silver or gold of considerable value. Usually the parable is seen as a story about three men: the five talent man, the two talent man, and the one talent man. But it's really about the one talent man. The other two are merely foils. It hits the mark because most of Jesus' hearers (and most of us) are one talent people.

Even though everyone is talented, the fact is we are not equally gifted. Nevertheless we are all, like employees, accountable to our employer. God's "absence" provides us room for our talents to be used. In that sense we are "tenant farmers". The farmer risks plague and drought in planting and cultivating seed, which raises the central point of this story: God expects increase. There's no room for neutrality or the maintenance of the status quo. The faithful servant must commit to the risky road less travelled. This parable is about us. How often have we excused ourselves by asking, "What can I do? I'm not capable." Or, "Why did he get so much money and I so little?" Then we blame-shift and impute forces beyond our control for the unfairness of our situation (v.24). And, sooner or later, we become passive and lethargic (v.25). "I'm only one key on the piano." So? What good is a piano with one silent key? As is often the case in human experience we face a choice: life or death? Courage or fear? Risk or regret? Are we willing to take a leap in the dark? No pain, no gain.

The Sheep and the Goats 25:31–46

There is an earth-shaking revelation in this parable that should (and does) upset all self-righteous believers: on Judgement Day many "unbelievers" will be astonished to hear that they have been on the Lord's side all along (vv.37-39). But I digress. Jesus' half-brother James would have said a loud "Amen!" to this teaching (Ja. 1:27; 2:14-16). It is very Jewish. You can't have "genuine religion" without justice for the "least of these". The Kingdom of Heaven is home to those who are both righteous and just. You can't have one without the other.

You can't have "genuine religion" without justice for the "least of these".

The irony is that this very Jewish word from Jesus is directed at Gentiles (v.32a). These are the "unwashed" whom Jewish culture at the time saw as "dogs". Yet, Jewish tradition made a great deal of good works, especially to the poor. What Jesus is telling us is that Heaven puts a premium on the strong caring for the weak, so much so that Jesus himself personifies the marginalized. As you cared for the hungry, thirsty, refugee, naked, sick, and imprisoned, you did it for me, Jesus says. The astonishing fact is that these Gentiles didn't even know Jesus existed! But it would appear they were not unknown to Jesus. Indeed, "God so loved the world" (Jn. 3:16). Eternal reward awaits these unknowingly righteous souls. Eternal punishment awaits those who lived only for themselves (v.46). This teaching should give us all pause. Our cozy religious silos may be no refuge from the omniscient eyes of our Father in heaven.

THE PASSION 26:1–27:66

"Passion" in this context means "suffering". Generally the Passion refers to the last two days of Jesus' life encompassing the Last Supper, Gethsemane, the arrest, trials, crucifixion, death, and burial of Jesus. It has often been called "the greatest story ever told".

The Plot 26:1–5

The Passover ("Hag Pesach" Heb.) occurred on Nisan 15th (Jewish calendar), which can fall anywhere in March or April, depending on the year. The Passover meal ("seder" Heb.) was eaten after sundown on Nisan 14 (technically Nisan 15 in that a day begins at sundown in the Jewish tradition). Because the gospels tell us that Jesus was crucified on a Friday, the following events probably occurred on Wednesday, Nisan 13. Jesus had warned his disciples many times about his impending death (16:21; 17:12; 20:17–19), and now was the time. Much later St. Paul interpreted the meaning of the Passion, "Christ, our Passover lamb, has been sacrificed" (1Co. 5:7). A watershed moment in history was about to take place.

The "chief priests and the elders of the people" (v.3) were strange bedfellows. The chief priests were Sadducees, owners and operators of the temple economy with its subsidiary commercial enterprises. The elders of the people were the Sanhedrin, the 70-member Supreme Jewish Council in Jerusalem. Their authority in executive, legislative, and judiciary functions was sometimes "supreme" and sometimes not so supreme, depending on the whims of the occupying Roman authorities. But the Sadducees and the Sanhedrin (composed mainly of Pharisees) were usually at loggerheads. Their worldview clashed, and they simply didn't like one another. Jesus united them.

They concocted a stealth plot with the mission of secretly arresting Jesus and killing him. The more cautious of this august group wanted to avoid a riot among the tens of thousands of pilgrims who had come up to Jerusalem for Passover, but the events of the next few hours overtook them. A riot would have to serve their purposes.

The Anointing 26:6–13

While the Sadducean Passover plot was being hatched, Jesus and his disciples, seemingly unperturbed, were reclining to eat lunch at the home of Simon the Leper (probably someone Jesus had healed). One of the luncheon guests, an unnamed woman, suddenly approached Jesus with an expensive jar of perfume and proceeded to anoint him with it. To everyone's surprise he made no protest. He was unembarrassed by this overly familiar, if not intimate act. One of the disciples, John, tells us it was Judas (Jn. 12:4-16) objected, calling this shameful display a "waste". It could have been sold and the proceeds given to the poor, he exclaimed. Jesus probably looked this betrayer in the eye and declared that the presence of the poor was a constant but he himself was about to be "wasted" (You always have the poor, you thief! You dip into our alms at will, and you're about to waste me!).

With regard to the poor there's a lesson here. The poor will always be with us, and will always be a significant part of our mission. But any work of justice that is not the corollary of righteousness will be a miscarriage of God's love for the world. Jesus is priority number one. The poor are priority number two. Without the prior commitment to right relationship with God our "good works" are mere philanthropy. Righteousness and justice in concert, however, is pure dynamite.

This woman may have thought she was anointing Jesus in anticipation of his being declared Messiah. Jesus, however, saw her act as preparatory to his burial. As usual, he had a big picture perspective. There was much more at stake than met the eye.

Judas 26:14–16

There are various descriptions of Judas' history. Some say, as "ish keriot" ("man of Kerioth") he was a Judean, others that as "ish sagar" ("man of Sachar") he was a Samaritan. We really don't know. The important question is: Why did he do it? Why the betrayal? Here are seven proposed answers:

1. His enthusiasm for Jesus had cooled.

2. He was disappointed at Jesus' passivity.

3. He thought Jesus to be politically naive (too ready to offend by his teaching, and unwise in his choice of the socially marginalized as friends), a bad choice for national leadership.

4. He had expected Jesus to demonstrate divine power in Jerusalem in a kind of spiritual/political showdown.

5. He had decided Jesus was a false messiah.

6. He was trying to force Jesus' hand.

7. He was simply avaricious (30 pieces of silver (Ze. 11:12) was no small amount – it could purchase a slave).

Maybe he just wanted to save his skin. Like Peter and the other disciples a few hours later, he feared for his life. Matthew doesn't say.

The Last Supper 26:17–30

One of the world's most recognizable murals is "The Last Supper" by Leonardo da Vinci, painted in the latter 15th Century. It's a powerful, evocative artistic interpretation of the Passover seder Jesus celebrated with his disciples. It represents his solemn regard for the Passion. My attempt to "casually comment" seems superficial in light of the worship-ful efforts artists, authors, and theologians have made to depict it over the centuries. It was, and is, truly, one of our world's most memorable moments.

I'm not going to yield to exactitude with regard to Matthew's chronology. I'm just going to relate the general sweep of the story, leaving the parsing of times and dates to others whose interests and abilities are beyond mine.

"On the first day of the Festival of Unleavened Bread" (v.17) ("Hag Pesach" – Passover) technically refers to the day of "preparation". To this day in Israel the preparation "day" for Shabat or any other holy day consists of the day(s) before the actual event. When I lived in Jerusalem, Friday was always my favorite day. My office was right in the heart of the city, a block away from the Prime Minister's residence. At about eleven in the morning the traffic would begin to decline. By two in the afternoon there were hardly any cars or buses wheeling past. Rather, I'd look out the window and see a steady stream of pedestrians walking, challah bread, wine, and flowers in hand. They were on the way to their family homes to celebrate "Kabalat Shabat", a meal welcoming the Sabbath. The holy day began at sundown.

Passover started at sunset on Nisan 14, the beginning of Nisan 15. As I've just stated, the preparation would have occurred during the day. So it was Thursday morning and afternoon when the flurry of activity took place (vv.18,19). The anonymous owner ("a certain man" v.18) of the Passover venue was another of the many followers of Jesus not identified in the narrative. He was expecting the Master.

Without any overt expression of emotion Jesus announced that one of the Twelve would betray him.

At the meal Jesus seemed above the fray. Without any overt expression of emotion Jesus announced that one of the Twelve would betray him. When the disciples asked who it was, Jesus wouldn't say ("The one who has dipped his hand into the bowl with me..." – could mean any of them). But he does say that it would have been better for the unnamed betrayer if he had never been born (v.24). Then he took two of the most common elements of Jewish life – bread and wine – and forever identified them (as they were forever blessed and consumed in countless Passover seders and Kabalat Shabbat meals in the future) as trigger mechanisms for remembering the new covenant for forgiveness of sins that his spilt blood would provide all mankind. He knew he was heading to a cross, but he also knew he would rise again to usher all believers into "the Father's Kingdom" (v.29). Then he led them in singing a hymn, probably a portion of the "Hallel" of Psalm 113–118. Or his choice may have been the so-called "Great Hallel" (Psalm 136).

Jesus Predicts Peter's Denial 26:31–35

Just as they "all" had dipped their hands into "the bowl" (of which there were more than one at any seder) with Jesus, so now they "all will fall away on account" of Jesus (v.31). Only one would betray him, but they all would desert him within a few hours. One would disown him. Betrayal, desertion, disowning – one wonders which was worse. Any leader would think he had failed if his staff were to do the same. No doubt Jesus was, and felt, alone. In a quiet soliloquy he quotes Zechariah 13:7, "I will strike the shepherd, and the sheep of the flock will be scattered". It would be a solitary journey to the cross.

So Jesus knows what is about to take place. He has to respond to Peter's bluster, "Even if all fall away on account of you, I never will," with a sad prediction of a three-fold vehement denial. But, what is truly amazing is that Jesus didn't appear to be taking any of their desertion scenario personally. I'll see you in Galilee, fellows, after I have risen. This simply swept over their heads.

Gethsemane 26:36–46

Over the years I pastored in Jerusalem I often visited the Garden of Gethsemane, situated on the Mount of Olives. Adjacent to the Church of All Nations with its beautiful ancient olive treed garden, is a private garden accessible only through the good graces of a gatekeeper. He knew me and would always produce the key. I could spend as much time in this walled garden as I wished. All alone in peace. And in prayer. I understand why Jesus loved the place.

After singing the Hallel in the Upper Room, Jesus led the disciples down the steep western slopes of the Kidron Valley and then about a third of the way up the Mount of Olives to Gethsemane ("oil press, oil field, oil vat"). Leaving eight of them near the entrance, he took his "Transfiguration Three" – Peter, James and John – deeper into the orchard of olive trees.

Jesus needed companionship and prayer support. Even these "flawed" three were a comfort. At least for a time. Awake for almost twenty-four hours, they succumbed to sleep.

Jesus was "full of heaviness" (v.37 Gk.). Some philologists translate this as "far from home". Both meanings tragically apply. At this point he would have profoundly preferred to be at home with his Father. But, he would have to "tread the winepress" alone (Is. 63:3).

In this crushing aloneness Jesus prayed the ultimate prayer, "Not as I will, but as you will" (v.39). He had a fleeting hope that this "cup" (was he thinking not only of his death, but of the cup of the "blood of covenant"? v.28) would be taken away. At this point his very words in the Sermon on the Mount came into play, "lead us not into temptation" (6:13). The temptation to shirk responsibility, to avoid suffering, to circumvent persecution, even to deny God or family (Mt. 24:10), were all very present. His warning to the disciples, "Watch and pray so that you will not fall into temptation" (v.41) was a warning to himself as well. The flesh tends to resist the risks imposed by the spirit.

Shortly thereafter the temple guards appeared. The sleepy disciples had to rise to their Master's defence.

Jesus Arrested 26:47:56

A large crowd of ruffians arrived with Judas and the temple guards. These pseudo-military guards were armed and uniformed, but the band of "irregulars" had swords, clubs, and any other cudgel they could put their hands on. It was a motley crew. Judas may have already been harboring doubts.

A number of things happened in quick succession. Judas approached Jesus, kissed him, and thereby signaled to the arresting officers whom it was they were seeking. The unruly crowd was milling about. In the heat of the moment one of the Galileans, who should have known better, took a wild swing with a sword, trying to behead one of the high priest's slaves. Jesus stepped in, rebuked the would-be defender, reminded him that he had thousands of angels at his beck and call, and then submitted himself to the officials. He saw this sorry drama as a fulfillment of prophecy. At this point all the disciples, to a man, "deserted him and fled" (v.56). The messianic trajectory looked doomed.

Caiaphas 26:57–68

The kangaroo court met at the palace of Caiaphas, the high priest. The Scribes and Sanhedrin joined the Sadducees, called out of their beds in the early morning darkness of Passover. To meet at such a time and on such a day was unheard of. Oral law proscribed it. Some two-hundred years later Judah the Prince references this particular law in the Mishnah:

> *"In capital cases they hold the trial in the daytime and the verdict must be reached in the day time… an acquittal verdict may be reached on the same day, but a conviction verdict not until the following day. Therefore trials may not be held on the eve of a Sabbath or the eve of a festival" (Sanhedrin 4:1).*

This was the law, but the ruling elite didn't care. They were on a roll. Yes, Judas may have hastened their plan by offering to betray Jesus when he did, but now that they had him they weren't about to let him go. Bring on the false witnesses! We've got to nail him now!

The false witnesses, although many, were weak. Caiaphas, frustrated by these ineffectual liars, finally shouted at the silent Jesus "I charge you under oath by the living God: Tell us, if you are the Messiah, the Son of God" (v.63). Jesus' response evoked relief and outrage at the same time. Caiaphas tore his clothes and pronounced Jesus guilty of blasphemy. In Jewish law blasphemy was cause for stoning, but these officials didn't want to incite a riot among the "am ha aretz". Stoning was a very public spectacle, and Jesus was the "people's king". Besides, the Sadducees, Scribes, and Pharisees didn't want to have innocent blood on their hands. They wanted the Romans to kill him as a pretender to the throne. "He deserves death!" the leaders shouted. But, under Roman law their hands were tied. So, let's take him to Pilate. Maybe we can convince him that Jesus is a threat to the Empire.

...the Sadducees, Scribes, and Pharisees didn't want to have innocent blood on their hands. They wanted the Romans to kill him as a pretender to the throne.

(By the way, there has been a lot of confusion and controversy over the Caiaphas/Annas references in the gospels. Who was high priest? Some feel that the gospels need to be "harmonized". My view is that there is no need for a manufactured harmony. How does one harmonize four sheets of music written in different keys?).

Peter's Denial 26:69–75

Remember Peter's confession of faith at Caesarea Philippi? Remember his prostration in the presence of the Father on the Mount of Transfiguration? Now look at him, *hear* him! Loudly cursing and denying he knows Jesus. It's pathetic. Human, but embarrassing. It took a humble rooster to bring him to his senses.

Jesus Before Pilate 27:1–26

Pilate was not a happy camper at the best of times. Being a procurator of Judea was a Roman punishment. His only perk was living in Caesarea on the beautiful Mediterranean coast. He came to his headquarters in Jerusalem occasionally. His residence there was the Antonia Fortress in the northeast corner of the city. He had a lot to learn in the early days of his rule. Once he brought his troops into Jerusalem without removing Tiberius' picture from their insignia, causing a minor scandal with the Jewish locals. On another occasion he seized temple funds to build an aqueduct. Not smart. He needed cultural sensitivity training. So he was on guard when they brought Jesus to him for judgement.

The tumult had been exacerbated by the sad story that had just occurred. The catalyst to the Jesus fiasco had just created a scene by throwing his betrayal fee onto the temple floor. Then he'd gone out and hanged himself. All this had happened before breakfast. What Pilate wanted was for these raucous religious leaders to go away, and to take their silent prisoner with them. Let me have my coffee in peace. But no, he had a major squabble to adjudicate.

"Are you the King of the Jews?" he asked Jesus. "You have said so," Jesus replied. In Pilate's mind this whole uproar had nothing to do with his procuratorship. The one danger for him was that this "king" might lead an insurgency, which would not go over well in Rome. But this whole debacle had a bad smell. What to do? Then he thought of an out.

There was a true enemy of Rome in his custody. His name was Jesus Barabbas (v.17). It was the custom to give amnesty to one prisoner a year at Passover. Maybe if he gave the people a choice, Jesus of Nazareth or Jesus Barabbas, they might think twice and tell him to keep Barabbas in prison and release what his wife had just called an "innocent man". She had come from a troubled sleep where she had had an upsetting dream about him. To Pilate's dismay the religious leaders incited the mob to call for freedom for Barabbas and crucifixion for Jesus. In a scene worthy of a Shakespearean tragedy he washed his hands in front of everyone declaring his innocence of "this man's blood" (v.24). Then he acquiesced. Regardless of the hand-washing, most of the guilt for Jesus' crucifixion rests on Pilate. Little did he know that his question, "What shall I do with Jesus?" would resonate throughout history. It is still the universal question. What *do* we do with this homeless Galilean?

The Crucifixion 27:27–56

The short-term answer was to crucify him. But first, let the soldiers have their fun. The transfigured Son of God, the healer of thousands, the greatest preacher/teacher of all time, the Holy One of Israel allowed these orc-like brutes to scourge and mock him. The "blood of the Covenant" began to spill on Antonia's pavement stones, the scarlet robe and the crown of thorns bearing witness to humankind's rejection of the Lamb of God. Indeed, Isaiah got it right centuries before when he prophesied, "He was oppressed and afflicted, yet he did not open his mouth; he was led like a lamb to the slaughter, and as a sheep before its shearers is silent, so he did not open his mouth" (Is. 53:7). Then they took him to Calvary.

The Walk to the Cross 27:32

Crucifixion was the act of execution by nailing and/or binding a criminal/victim to a pole or tree set in the ground. Sometimes it was an actual living tree. Rome adopted crucifixion from the Phoenicians and Persians who executed slaves and aliens in this barbarous manner. In Palestine Rome used this method against thieves, insurgents, and seditionists. It was a powerful public spectacle, an effective way to flex its muscles with the Judean rabble.

Essentially it was death by torture. The condemned man was scourged, his back shredded to bloody ribbons. He was stripped (shaming by public nudity), laid on the ground where he was nailed to the crossbeams, ropes securing his upper arms, his legs bent, then nailed by the feet to the pole/tree, and then slammed down into the hole. Thirst, blood loss, exposure, shame, cramped circulation, and slow suffocation as the weight of his suspended body restricted breathing created a perfect storm of suffering. Sometimes his legs had to be broken to hasten suffocation. Nevertheless it usually took hours to die. The Jewish historian Josephus' *"Wars of the Jews"* says there were so many crucifixions during the siege of Jerusalem in 70 AD that there was little room left for crosses or crosses for bodies.

Already weakened by blood loss from his scourging, Jesus was forced to carry the horizontal crossbeam ("patibulum") to Calvary. He was collapsing under its weight. So the soldiers impressed a bystander, Simon of Cyrene, to carry it for him. The entire "via dolorosa" was lined with a mocking, spitting throng. These were the same people who only days earlier had proclaimed "Hosanna!" Plaudits can quickly become taunts.

The Place of the Skull 27:33–44

"Golgotha" ("skull, head" Aramaic) was a hill outside the city wall. It probably was a rock quarry, the site of stoning (lots of ammunition) and crucifixions. It was on a roadway, accessible to the public. The crosses hung the victims at eye level, their nailed feet only inches above the ground. This made it convenient for passersby to gawk, taunt, and spit in the faces of the crucified. It was an irresistible magnet for the mean-spirited, an ideal spot for venting.

> *The entire "via dolorosa" was lined with a mocking, spitting throng. These were the same people who only days earlier had proclaimed "Hosanna!"*

It was a Roman custom to hang a sign or placard around the neck of the poor wretch on the cross, listing the charges against him. This way the mockers could both deride and justify their bile at the same time. In Jesus' case they posted a sign over his head, "King of the Jews". This was both a direct insult to the Jewish leadership, and a warning to any would-be insurgents, "This is what we do to political pretenders." It had double impact. Pilate must have felt very clever in his choice of wording, "A black eye for those sanctimonious priests, and a blow for Rome!"

Jesus' blood was still drying on the hands of the soldiers as they cast lots beneath the cross for his seamless robe. Either the garment was of great value, or the soldiers were poorly paid, or both. None of them would ever have read David's psalm, "They divide my clothes among them and cast lots for my garment" (Ps. 22:18). They were living in the heat of the moment with no regard for history (like most of us). Accountability for my actions? What's that?

At least one of them had a modicum of decency, offering Jesus some wine mixed with an opiate to dull the pain (Ps. 69:21), but he refused it. Then the soldiers stayed by Pilate's order at the foot of the cross to deny access to any delusional disciple determined to take Jesus down before he died.

So the ensuing hours saw myriads of mockers spewing their hatred, including the pathetic insurgents crucified on either side of Jesus. One wonders what it was that so energized these snarling wolves. Perhaps the "Prince of the power of the air" (Ep. 2:2 KJV) was involved, totally focused on the events at Calvary. He had failed in his attempts to derail Jesus (Mt. 4:1-1), but now he was about to kill him. Victory! The rejoicing in Hell was a touch premature, mind you. There was this upcoming issue of an empty grave…

Jesus Dies 27:45–56

Jesus was crucified at the third hour (9 am). The sixth hour is noon, and the ninth is 3 pm. Fear and consternation gripped the onlookers as the sun was darkened from noon to 3pm. Jesus hung dying in the darkness. Suddenly at 3 pm he uttered a loud cry, a direct quote from Psalm 22:1, "My God, my God, why have you forsaken me?" and then he died.

There has been deep debate over why the Father would "forsake" the Son. Logic suggests that God could not forsake himself. The usual comment that God could not bear to look on the imputed sins of mankind also lacks logic. God, right from Adam and Eve to this very day was/is totally aware of, and looks omnisciently, upon the sins of his creatures. The best explanation is that Jesus had been meditating on the messianic Psalm 22 while hanging on the cross. His loud cry was a declaration from Calvary that the Lord was victorious over the Evil One. Indeed, "He has done it!" (Ps. 22:31). Satan and his small-time actors slunk away, the centurion's exclamation, "Truly this was the Son of God!" ringing in their ears.

The Burial 27:57–61

Even though this Friday was the first day of Passover that year (and a "Sabbath" in its own right) it was also the "day of preparation" for the weekly Sabbath which was to begin at sundown. Joseph of Arimathea, a member of the Sanhedrin and a secret follower of Jesus, asked for and received permission from Pilate to bury him in his own newly hand-hewn tomb. It was (and still is) Jewish tradition to bury the dead on the day of their death. And, Moses had proscribed allowing a gibbeted body to remain hanging overnight (Dt. 21:23). So gentle Joseph ritually defiled himself by taking Jesus' dead body down from the cross, wrapping it in yards of spice-packed burial cloths, and laying it in the place where he himself had intended to be entombed one day. While he did this, Mary Magdalene and Mary the mother of James and Joseph watched from a distance in the dusk.

The Tomb Under Guard 27:62–66

The next day was the weekly Sabbath (Saturday). Word got out to the priests and elders that Jesus had been buried in Joseph of Arimathea's tomb (What?! Joseph is one of us! We'll deal with him later.). Unlike the disciples, they had heard loud and clear, that Jesus had said, "After three days I will rise again" (v.63). Afraid that the imposter's followers would effect another fraud by stealing the body and claiming resurrection, they went to Pilate requesting that the tomb would be guarded and sealed. Pilate waved them away, "Do what you want," and they sealed the tomb and placed a company of temple guards to ward away any grave robbers until sundown Sunday. There would be no fraud on their watch!

THE RESURRECTION 28:1–20

St. Paul in 1Corinthians 15 writes a defining essay about resurrection. The key verse is 14, "And if Christ has not been raised, our preaching is useless and so is your faith". Christian faith is rooted in history, in an empty tomb in Jerusalem. This is not the product of some mystic dreamer with no accountability. Rather we're dealing with real time, dust and stone, historical events witnessed and written by flesh and blood, flawed humans. Their accounts don't jibe in the finer points of the narrative, which is a good thing. We'd all dismiss a story that appeared to be the product of committee control.

Paul summarizes his Gospel this way:

1. Christ died for our sins (1Co. 15:3).

2. He was buried (v.4).

3. He was raised (v.4).

4. He appeared to Peter, and then to more than five hundred of the brothers... to James, all the apostles, and last of all to Paul himself (vv. 5-8).

These appearances are critical to the historical record. To this day the word of just one witness, let alone a hundred, can sway the course of justice. Here's a list of recorded witnesses of the risen Christ:

1. Mary Magdalene (Jn. 20:14; Mk. 16:9)

2. Mary Magdalene and the other Mary (Mt. 28:9)

3. Peter (Lk. 24:34; 1Co. 15:5)

4. Cleopas and another disciple (Lk. 24:13 – 35)

5. The eleven (or ten) apostles in Jerusalem (Mk. 16:14; Lk. 24:36: Jn.20:19, 26)

6. Five named disciples and two unnamed in Galilee (Mt. 28:16; Mk.16:15)

7. Five hundred (1Co. 15:6)

8. James (1Co. 15:7)

9. The eleven before the ascension (Mk. 16:19, 20; Lk. 24:50; Ac. 1:3-12)

He is Risen! 28:1–8

It was "Yom Rishon" ("Day the First" Heb.), our Sunday. Jesus had died and was buried on Friday. The guards were posted on the Sabbath, Saturday. So now, Sunday, was the third day. We're not to assume that "three days" meant 72 hours. It just meant Friday, Saturday, Sunday – (Yom Hamishi, Yom Shabat, Yom Rishon). Jesus rose from death on the third day.

> ## *It's as though we're standing on the threshold of another world as we read.*

Matthew's account is parsimonious to say the least. It's a brief kaleidoscope of brilliant events, persons, and impressions: two mourning women, an angel, lightning appearances, trembling, fainting inept guards, the greatest words spoken in history, "He is risen!", and then a word from the risen Christ himself, "Greetings!" It's as though we're standing on the threshold of another world as we read. An old preacher put it this way: "We live in an enclosed valley called Earth, and Easter takes us to a neighboring height to show us a world vaster than we have dreamed" (G. A. Buttrick).

Jesus told the women to have the disciples meet him in the Galilee at an unnamed mountain. There would be no revenge visit to Caiaphas or Pilate, just a peaceful meeting back home in the Galilee he loved. A picnic by the lake would heal the vortex of emotions flooding the hearts of the Twelve.

While the excited women were reporting to the incredulous disciples, the chief priests and their temple guardsmen were in an urgent committee meeting. Their faces still white with fear, the guards were making a report of their own to believing but virulent Pharisees and Sadducees. Here the real "Passover Plot" was hatched. The chief priests ordered their soldiers to lie. Say you fell asleep. The disciples stole the body while you slept. Asleep! OK? Asleep.

Only a vast sum of money would have tempted the soldiers to say they were derelict in their duty. Any other soldier who fell asleep while on watch would be summarily executed. There must have been more than money offered. The soldiers probably asked for relocation costs, and witness protection too. They would spend the rest of their lives in troubled retirement.

The Great Commission 28:16–20

The denouement to the story, like all denouements was brief. A few days walk later the disciples met Jesus at the assigned mountain in the Galilee (my guess is the Mount of Beatitudes). Matthew says they "worshipped him", something they had not done before the resurrection. Astonishingly, some "doubted" even then (v.17). It would have been fascinating to hear these doubters sharing their doubts around the evening campfire.

Jesus ignored the uncertain few, proclaimed his everlasting authority, and sent them out to disciple the Gentile world, with the promise he'd be with them all the way.

THE GOSPEL OF MARK

INTRODUCTION

There are three Marks in the New Testament, one of whom is the "John Mark" of Acts and the "Mark" of Paul's and Peter's letters. Let's look at the references (all in NKJV):

> *"So, when he had considered this he came to the house of Mary, the mother of John whose surname was Mark,"*
>
> —ACTS 12:12

> *"And Barnabas and Saul returned from Jerusalem when they had fulfilled their ministry, and they also took with them John whose surname was Mark."*
>
> —ACTS 12:25

"And when they arrived in Salamis, they preached the work of God in the synagogues of the Jews. They also had John as their assistant."

—ACTS 13:5

"Now when Paul and his party set sail from Paphos, they came to Perga in Pamphylia; and John departing from them, returned to Jerusalem."

—ACTS 13:13

"Now Barnabas was determined to take with them John called Mark. But Paul insisted that they should not take with them the one who had departed from them in Pamphylia, and had not gone with them to the work. Then the contention became so sharp that they parted from one another. And so Barnabas took Mark and sailed to Cyprus…"

—ACTS 15:37-39

"Aristarchus my fellow prisoner greets you, with Mark the cousin of Barnabas (about whom you received instructions: if he comes to you, welcome him), and Jesus who is called Justus. These are the only fellow workers for the kingdom of God who are of the circumcision; they have proved to be a comfort to me."

—COL. 4:10,11

"Only Luke is with me. Get Mark and bring him with you, for he is useful to me for ministry."

—2 TIM. 4:11

"Epaphras, my fellow prisoner in Christ Jesus, greets you, as do Mark, Aristarchus, Demas, Luke, my fellow laborers."

—PHM. 23,24

*"She who is in Babylon, elect together with your greets you;
and so does Mark my son."*

—1 PET. 5:13

Mark had grown up with his mother Mary's house a way station for Jesus and his disciples whenever they were in Jerusalem. As a teenager he had probably sat on the periphery as Jesus, his disciples, and other guests had socialized, discussed weighty matters, eaten, and stayed over in his home. The entire group of Galileans likely knew him by name. He may have been a bit of a "mascot", in that he was so much younger and always "underfoot". As such he may have been seen by some of the Twelve as just a kid, a work in progress. They had no idea of what he would become.

It's believed that Mark's mother was a wealthy widow. Her house had an outer courtyard, a gate, a porch, and a large upper room. Her slave-girl, Rhoda, welcomed guests, and was increasingly busy doing so as the early church began to form. Mary's house was the epicenter of "The Way" as the nascent faith was called. Indeed, when Peter was miraculously freed from prison one night, he went straight to her house (Acts 12:12). He knew he'd find the Christians gathered. Mark, of course, would have watched it all from the sidelines. But he was there.

Several years later it may have been Mark's cousin Barnabas who suggested that Paul hire him as an administrative assistant. There was a need for someone to book ships, lodging, and pay bills as Paul and Barnabas set about their missionary journeys to evangelize the Gentiles of Asia Minor. Apparently he proved "useful" (2Ti. 4:11) with a few hiccups along the way. At one point Paul fired him for some unnamed insubordination/desertion (Acts 15:37-39). But the visionary apostle thought better of him over time, and hired him back. Indeed, Paul eventually called him a "fellow worker" (Cl. 4:10,11).

While Barnabas called Mark "cousin" (which he was), Peter called him "son". This may suggest that Mark had come to faith in Jesus by way of Peter's teaching and mentoring. As a frequent guest at Mark's house, Peter would have had significant opportunity to instruct the young man about "The Way". In the process Peter would have been aware that Mark had been studious and had become skilled in the Greek language. This culminated in what many biblical historians and commentators believe, that Mark became Peter's interpreter, translating his memories of life with Jesus for a Greek readership. This, of course, begs the question: was Peter alive or dead when Mark wrote? We can't be sure. So, whether he wrote as Peter dictated, or whether his writing was a recollection of Peter's recollections, we'll never know. What we do know is that the Gospel of Mark is a very early record of Jesus' life and ministry. Brief and succinct as it is it may have provided the valuable "draft" material Matthew and Luke referenced as they wrote their stories of Christ. The "underfoot" teenager became the "under-girder" of the gospels. In serving Barnabas, Paul, and Peter he became the servant of history, and of all men and women of faith.

JOHN THE BAPTIST AND JESUS 1:1–11

I mentioned in the Introduction that Mark was "succinct" in his account of Jesus' life and ministry. His opening sentence is a case in point. Twelve words with a profound message: Jesus Christ is the Son of God. No preamble. No genealogy. No birth narrative. Indeed he jumps right into the story at the point of what may have been Peter's earliest contact with Jesus: the baptism by John in the Jordan.

First he establishes John's, not Jesus', credentials. He harkens back to prophetic utterances from both Malachi (3:1) and Isaiah (40:3) in describing the wilderness baptizer. To paraphrase, John is a forerunner of Messiah calling Israel to repentance. The opening scene of the drama begins.

Mark unceremoniously calls him "John". No need for introducing him because everyone knew him. He was the most famous of all the street preachers of Judea, so famous that "all the land of Judea and those from Jerusalem, went out to him and were baptized by him in the Jordan River, confessing their sins" (v.5). His message was brief: "Repent, for the Kingdom of Heaven is at hand!"

The concept of baptism was fully consistent with Jewish religious practice. To this day Orthodox Jews ritually immerse themselves in a "mikveh", a specially designed pool of water, in order to cleanse themselves physically and spiritually. There were (and still are) scores of Mikvot (plural) scattered throughout Israel carved out of the living rock. There were/are several usages of mikvot relating to physical purification, but one key usage was to initially purify a new convert to Judaism. Google "mikveh" for a comprehensive treatment of the subject.

Christian baptisms today are conducted one on one by a pastor/ priest with his/her baptismal candidate. In John's day it is likely that several people at a time would walk into the Jordan and immerse themselves at his command. This is what they were used to doing in the mikvot. The only assistance in the act of immersion occurred occasionally when age or affliction required it. There was no cultural dissonance in John's baptisms, but there was a resounding call for spiritual transformation in preparation for the soon expected arrival of Israel's Messiah. This eschatological hope had reached a near fever point because of the much hated Roman occupation. This hope fuelled the massive pilgrimage to the river.

And it *was* massive. Mark tells us, perhaps with a measure of hyperbole, that "all the land of Judea, and those from Jerusalem went out to him and were all baptized..." (1:5). The point of this baptism? Purification (think "mikveh") from sin. Impurity had to flee before the holy Kingdom of Heaven could rush in. Exhale the bad inhale the good. The message was as simple as that.

John's clothing was inelegant to say the least. He had probably heard of how some of the ancient prophets had dressed. Elijah "wore a garment of hair-cloth..." (2 Ki. 1:8) and Zechariah described the typical prophet's attire as "a robe of coarse hair" (Ze. 13:4). John wore camel's hair, turned inward to maximize total discomfort in blazing hot desert temperatures. Hygiene would not have been a value.

A unique feature of John's eschatological message was his prediction that, "There comes One after me who is mightier than I... He will baptize you with the Holy Spirit" (1:7,8). His respect for this coming baptizer is deep. He says he's not even worthy to do a slave's work by stooping down to loose his sandals. A great epic is unfolding here: a "wild man" obsessively baptizing thousands with a call to repentance without which the heavens will not open announces that the hope of the ages is about to enter history's stage. Breathtaking.

Frugal with words, Mark simply records that Jesus, who "came from Nazareth of Galilee", was "baptized by John in the Jordan." Here, the baptizer baptizes the Baptizer. As Jesus submits to John's baptism the voice of the Father in heaven is heard (By whom? Jesus? John? Just one of them? Both? Mark doesn't say.),

"You are my beloved son in whom I am well pleased."

The voice, "Bat Qol" (Heb.) meaning "daughter, or echo, of the voice", combines Ps. 2:7 and Is. 42:1 – "You are my Son… my elect One in whom My soul delights." Psalm 2 is a psalm of accession for a king (Messiah) and Isaiah 42 is a "servant song", a prophecy of the Messiah who executes justice in the service of God and the people. Jesus is to be both King and Servant, righteous and just.

There's something that needs to be said here: this baptism of Jesus by John was *not* theater. Rather, it was a powerful moment of affirmation of John by Jesus, and Jesus by his Father, and the launch of a ministry that would/does change the world. The baby of Bethlehem was now about to become the Savior of mankind.

The Temptation 1:12,13

True to form, the parsimonious Mark describes Jesus' temptation in two brief sentences. No word pictures, no drama, just summary facts.

Notice he records that "the Spirit drove Him into the wilderness" (NKJV). The verb "drove" is "ekballo" (Gk.) meaning "to cast forth, with force." This suggests Jesus was under some form of heavenly compulsion as though his baptism had released an irrevocable divine agenda. He's now a man on a mission.

And what's more, his first "visit" in the wilderness is from Satan himself. No "lower case" demons here but their master himself attempts to deflect Jesus from his course. Mark doesn't record the exchange but merely states that "wild beasts" witnessed it all and then angels "ministered to Him".

Driven by the Spirit, tempted by the Devil and ministered to by angels. What an auspicious beginning to three earth-shaking years of ministry, with a knobby little hill called Calvary as a backdrop! The unfolding story is a gripper.

GALILEE 1:14–9:50

Isaiah called it "Galilee of the Gentiles" (Is. 9:1), modern Israelis call it "the Galil", while in the original Aramaic language Galilee meant "ring" or "circle". Situated at the northern edge of Israel it was almost a nation apart, bustling with trade caravans, rife with tumult and war, culturally and religiously dissonant with the relative piety of Jerusalem in Judea. It was a melting pot, always bubbling it seemed with discordant foreign accents and radical ideas. It was the perfect petri dish for the iconoclastic Jesus of Nazareth who adopted Capernaum, situated in the center of the region, as his hometown and ministry base. "God" had indeed come "out of Nazareth". Now he was about to change the world out of Capernaum.

A major player in this unfolding heavenly visitation was the "Sea of Galilee". Israelis today call it "Kinneret" ("Harp" – Heb.) because it is harp shaped. Over the centuries it has also been named "Gennesar" and "Tabariyeh", and at one brief spell, "Lake Tiberias". Regardless of nomenclature it is not a "sea" but a lake. It is approximately twelve miles long from north to south and six miles east to west. For centuries its clear fresh water has been fished commercially for what is today called "St. Peter's fish" and sardines. Like the "cruse of oil" in Elijah's day, the lake never seems to "run dry". There have always been lots of fish. (Fish farms keep restocking it).

As the epicenter of Galilean commerce the lake was bordered by significant fishing towns and cities. Most prominent of these were Capernaum, Bethsaida, and what are now known as Magdala and Tiberias. Because of the international trade routes above and below the lake, there was a cosmopolitan air to Galilee. It throbbed with life "from the outside".

Jesus' disciples, of course, came from Galilee. Among them were James and John (sons of Zebedee) and Simon and Andrew, who were thought to be part of some sort of commercial fishing consortium. Nathaniel came from Cana, and Philip (along with Simon and Andrew) came from Bethsaida. These men shared a common language, and common cultural values. They were everyday "blue collar" workers, rough and loyal to their hope that the messiah would soon appear to lead them to victory over Rome from Jerusalem.

Jesus' Ministry Begins 1:14,15

In one sentence Mark declares the end of John the Baptist's ministry and the beginning of Jesus' ministry. Once again as readers, we suffer the "whiplash" of sudden edits. There are no transition paragraphs, phrases, or sentences. Mark just shoulders through. Sometimes it's hard to keep up.

The message, like all true prophecy, was like a fist to the jaw.

Jesus picks up where John left off with the same prophetic call, "The time is fulfilled, and the Kingdom of God is at hand." Then he adds "believe in the Gospel" to John's clarion call to "repent". There was no attempt to "win over" the crowd. The message, like all true prophecy, was like a fist to the jaw. It demanded a response. That response of repentance was much more than confession of sin. Confession is emotional; repentance is volitional. Both John and Jesus were preaching a chosen turn in a new direction not just in terms of morality, but in terms of worldview. Open your eyes! Look at what is approaching! Prepare!

Jesus Calls the First Disciples 1:16–20

Disciples were common in Jesus' day. Every rabbi, every zealot, every would-be messiah, had disciples. As soon as a leader/teacher "hung up his shingle" he placed an ad for followers/students. So Jesus' call to "follow me" was consistent with the culture of eschatological expectation that prevailed in occupied Galilee. In more ways than one Jesus was a man of the times. Mind you, Jesus' disciples were seen in two ways: as followers in a crowd and as the inside group called "the Twelve". And there was an even finer distillation: "Peter, James, and John" – "the Three", chosen by Jesus for special moments like the Transfiguration and his agony in Gethsemane. These three saw themselves as elite (see 10:35-41) and suffered the indignation of the other nine as a result. Regardless, all twelve were eventually given special status by Jesus. In Luke 6:12 we read that he selected them from a larger group of disciples and designated them "apostles".

John the Baptist (who also had disciples) lived and baptized in the Roman province of Perea at Bethany. The site of Jesus' temptation is an easy day's walk from there across the Jordan just west of Jericho. It is believed that after his temptation Jesus returned for a time to be with his cousin. While there, Jesus was identified publicly by John as "the Lamb of God" (Jn. 1:29,35). Two of John's disciples were at a location where Jesus was "passing by" when John declared, "Look, the Lamb of God!" We're told that one of the two of John's followers was Andrew, Simon Peter's brother. He and the other unnamed devotee of John's ministry immediately changed allegiance and began to follow Jesus.

Mark gives none of this background information. Rather, he just launches into an almost "bullet point" summary of Jesus' call to Simon, Andrew, James, and John. We know, from John's account (Jn. 1:35-42), that Andrew had already (informally at least) chosen to follow Jesus and he had introduced his brother Simon to him. But, it would seem, as we read Mark, that the call to follow Jesus, with the "cost" of leaving their source of income, did not occur until this moment beside the Sea. The relationship with Jesus was about to be notched up another level.

Simon and Andrew were to become more than acquaintances of this young rabbi. They were being challenged, along with James and John, to become full time partners in a ministry with an unknown future. Jesus' call struck a chord in their souls. All four of them "left their nets and followed him." Mark doesn't tell us of any consult with family and friends. He simply says they dropped everything "at once". The adventure had begun.

Capernaum Becomes Jesus' Base 1:21–28

Jesus had begun walking from John's ministry base in Bethany (in the region of Perea) and now his walk had taken him to the western shore of the Sea of Galilee. Somewhere on the north-western edge of the lake he had encountered and called Simon, Andrew, James, and John. Then as he continued his walk to Capernaum (where Peter had a house) he was accompanied by the four newly-minted disciples. Mark does not record their talk on the way. I wish he had. I also wish he had described Zebedee's consternation at his sons' desertion.

Jesus probably settled into one of Peter and Andrew's guest rooms. Indeed their house probably became his home base in his adopted hometown. When he was on the road he was totally reliant on the hospitality of kind folk ("Foxes have holes, the birds of the air have nests…"), but Capernaum was the one place where he could take to his own room, close the door and be alone.

A few days after his arrival as the sun set over the lake the Sabbath began. Like every other Jew in Capernaum Jesus walked over to the synagogue in the failing light. It was a short walk. I've done it many times over the years. It's about sixteen paces from Peter and Andrew's house.

The ruins of the Capernaum synagogue today are impressive. Constructed of white and yellow limestone it stands, roofless, but elegant in the Galilean sunlight. In the evening its stones glow with a pink/mauve luster. But this synagogue was built over the ruins of the original in the second century AD. The original foundation is still in place. It is built with black basalt rock, gathered and hewn by stonemasons from an ancient overflow of lava from what we now call Mount Hermon in the north. So in Jesus' day the synagogue didn't glow at dusk. Rather it faded into the shadows, the only illumination coming from the lit menorahs shining through the open windows. It was a quiet and holy house of God.

There in the candlelit twilight Jesus sat and taught. What did he teach? Without doubt he would have keyed on the scripture reading for the day from the Torah, the law of Moses (Genesis, Exodus, Leviticus, Numbers, Deuteronomy). Just as today so then: every synagogue everywhere featured the same scripture reading each Sabbath. The common pattern for the rabbi was to either read, or have read (by congregants) the weekly passage and then reference the various rabbinical commentators. These expert interpreters were the "authorities". Jesus, however, quoted no other authority. *He* was the authority. And this blew the worshipers away. "What is this?" They exclaimed. "A new teaching – and with authority!" And his authority on that occasion was underscored by the ease with which he commanded an impure spirit to come out of a troubled congregant. In so doing he catalyzed a scorched cry from the evil spirit, "What do you want with us, Jesus of Nazareth? Have you come to destroy us? I know who you are – the Holy One of God!" This is the first declaration in Mark of who Jesus really was. And it came from the "dark side".

The "dark side" was very clear in its view of Jesus. For the legions of evil spirits Jesus was no mystery. Nor was he a Savior. To them he was a destroyer. They were totally and immediately cowed in his presence. This kind of authority could never have been the product of quoting the learned teachers. As an old theologian put it, Jesus did not dwell "in the prison house of quotation marks" (H.E. Luccock). He was Son of God. And the demons knew it, and trembled. All of Galilee shook as well.

Capernaum at Night 1:29–34

While Jesus and the four disciples were at the Sabbath service darkness descended. In the meantime Peter's mother-in-law who had stayed home, became ill. Jesus returned to the house and immediately healed her. She got up and finished preparation of the Sabbath dinner. Even as they ate they heard a crowd gathering outside in the dusk. Jesus realized he had more work to do this time though he commanded the evil spirits to be silent about who he was. He didn't want or need the hoarse cries of Hell as an advertisement. The mass healings of these night-time supplicants was more than sufficient. It marked the beginning of many thousands of needy people coming to Jesus over the next few years. Indeed, then as now, it is our need that brings us to the Healer. Our soul's cry is for a Savior.

From a Lonely Place to All Galilee 1:35–39

As we see from time to time in the gospels, Jesus needed sleep. But it seems he didn't need a lot of it. He was an early riser, even when he had labored into the night before.

Mark tells us that Jesus got up in the dark and "went off to a solitary place" to pray. This lonely spot may have been somewhere on the mount where he would eventually preach his famous sermon (Mt. 5,6,7). It takes about an hour to climb. Capernaum sits at its foot.

Later, as the morning dawned, Jesus' new disciples found him. "Everyone's looking for you!" they exclaimed. Jesus was unimpressed. Unlike the rest of humanity he wasn't swayed by popularity. Let's get out of here! There's a bigger world out there. Galilee awaits. This was not the only time the disciples would have to change their plans on short notice.

A Strange Encounter with a Leper 1:40–45

I say "strange" because it's only one of three occasions in the Jesus story (the others are in Mt. 9:30; Jn. 11:38) where he "snorted in anger". Depending on the version of scripture the Greek word "embrimaomi" meaning "to be painfully moved; to express indignation against; to rebuke sternly, to charge strictly" can be translated as "charged" (KJV), "strictly warned" (NKJV), "strong warning" (NIV). It seems an uncharacteristic juxtaposition in an encounter that had begun with Jesus' compassion. Mind you, the NIV version says Jesus was "indignant" when the young leper prefaced his request with, "If you are willing". Jesus may have been off-put. Of course he was willing! The needy were to come to him with their need alone, not with conditional phrases and caveats.

Regardless, Jesus reached across the kosher chasm fixed between clean and unclean and touched the man. As far as the Oral Law was concerned Jesus was ritually defiled by the touch, but he didn't seem to care. What he did care about was that he foresaw the young leper's indiscipline in totally ignoring Jesus' stern "snort" about keeping the healing to himself. Mark says the young leper "began to talk freely, spreading the news". Because of this unwanted publicity Jesus sought out "lonely places". The unbridled enthusiasm of the healed had hurtful consequences for the Healer.

A Paralytic and some Scribes 2:1–12

Peter and Andrew's house was now "home" (2:1) for Jesus, and the crowds gathered both inside and outside were threatening the structural integrity of the modest dwelling. Packed shoulder-to-shoulder the eager crowd pressed in on Jesus as he taught, even as they pressed out against the walls. Suddenly they looked up. Somebody was breaking through the roof!

Quickly a hole big enough to lower a young man on a stretcher opened up.

Fishermen owned modest houses. The roofs of these dwellings were a basic construction of saplings laid flat, branches and twigs spread over them, and clay packed down over the layers. The clay would bake in the sun producing a relatively weather-proof protection from the elements. Thieves could easily break through. And so could men of faith concerned about their paralyzed friend. Many in the crowd, even as they watched in amazement at the temerity of the "queue-jumpers", probably wished they had thought of it. Quickly a hole big enough to lower a young man on a stretcher opened up.

CANTELON'S CASUAL COMMENTARY

In the ancient world sickness was seen as the consequence of sin. The greater the sin the more serious the affliction. So this young man's paralysis would be seen as the result of some in-depth transgression. Jesus may or may not have thought in these terms. Mark simply tells us Jesus dealt with his spiritual need first by saying, "Son your sins are forgiven."

The Scribes "were sitting there" in apoplectic fury. "Who can forgive sins but God alone?" They muttered. "This fellow is blaspheming!"

You might wonder why the Scribes would be sitting in front of Jesus when the crowd were all standing in a pushing and shoving mass. They sat because they were deferred to by all as doctors of the Law. The crowd always showed respect for these learned sages. So did Jesus. This is why he evenly asked, "Why are you thinking these things?" Then he went on to demonstrate that both the forgiveness of sins and the healing of paralysis were equally "easy" for the "Son of Man" to accomplish. His authority to do both was his alone. The Scribes slunk away and the crowd "praised God" as the boy walked away. The first faint thunder began to growl in the distant skies. The religious leaders would begin to push back.

Jesus Calls Levi 2:13,14

Jesus was not "politically correct". Mark is about to demonstrate this in 2:13-28. He starts with the calling of Levi (Matthew).

Levi was a publican or tax collector. He sat at his collection booth every weekday in Capernaum. Like all publicans he was despised by the people. Why? Because publicans were fellow Jews who worked for the Romans. The occupiers would offer the various provinces and provincial regions to the highest Jewish bidder. The winner would then employ fellow citizens in the assessment and collection of taxes. They had a quota and made their money (lots of it) by surcharge. So, if the Roman officials wanted 100 shekels per citizen, the contractor would demand 150. His subcontractor (the publican) would then demand and extract 175 from the helpless taxpayer on penalty of imprisonment for non-payment. In this way publicans became very wealthy. And there was nothing the tax-payers could do except vilify and socially isolate the nasty fellow. They are

THE GOSPEL OF MARK

seen as loan sharks, collaborators, unclean dogs. The publican paid the price for his greed. So, the fact that Jesus would call a publican to join his inner circle was no doubt troubling to the citizens of Capernaum. Why would he do this? Didn't he know that a publican's testimony was not allowed in court? That even the poor would not accept alms from such a traitor? That his only friends (if he had any) were fellow social lepers? Well, of course Jesus knew, but he didn't seem to care. This carelessness would be used against him by his enemies.

Jesus Eats with the "Unwashed" 2:15–17

You've probably heard the old adage, "A man is known by the company he keeps." If that is true then Jesus was in trouble. The Scribes and the Pharisees certainly thought so. They pushed back as soon as they saw Jesus partaking in a celebratory meal at the home of Levi, his newest recruit. Eating with the "unwashed" was proscribed by both oral law and tradition. Yet here Jesus was, sitting at table with the only ones who dared associate with the despised publican – adulterers, pimps, other publicans, flatterers, sycophants: all "unwashed". Jesus wasn't intimidated by his "offence", although many years later Peter back-tracked on eating with Gentiles when confronted by Orthodox Jews from Jerusalem (Ga. 2:11-13).

Jesus didn't dispute the issue. He tacitly agreed that these outcasts were "sinners" but then declared that they are exactly his target audience. Doctors care for the sick. So do I. Guilt by association is a canard. Fake news.

To Fast or Not to Fast? 2:18–22

We don't know who the clever ones were that came up with the next objection to Jesus' irreverent style. Mark just says, "some people". Their question put Jesus "between a rock and a hard place", or so they thought, by asking why Jesus' disciples were not like his cousin's disciples, to say nothing of tradition and the Pharisees, in the practice of fasting. Surely Jesus would feel the need to conform to John the Baptists' norms at least. But no. As was his wont, Jesus took it to a higher plane.

The fasting referred to was not the scripturally mandated fast on the Day of Atonement each year. Rather it was the Pharisaic tradition that had evolved where the pious fasted on Mondays and Thursdays each week. John's disciples had obviously adopted this practice while Jesus' had not. The juxtaposition of Levi's feast and the required fast (was it Monday or Thursday?) made Jesus' disciples' indulgence at table all the more apparent. But Jesus' answer to the self-righteous critics was, "Who fasts at a wedding?"

He then went on to engage a metaphor about new and old wineskins. New wine tears and bursts old wineskins. New wine, new wineskins. The Oral Law is an old wineskin. The set ways of the old are already being stressed by the new ways of the Kingdom of God. New wineskins stretch and flex. Old wineskins can't take the pressure. Little wonder the Pharisees were exploding.

A Sabbath Controversy 2:23–28

There is perhaps nothing that separates Jew from Gentile more than the observance of the Sabbath. It stands apart. And it is arguably the most valuable of all Jewish traditions. It is not to be taken lightly by Christians, nor is it to be dismissed as an irrelevance. Personally I grew to love it when I and my family lived in Jerusalem for seven years. I can fully appreciate why Orthodox Jews throughout the centuries have called it, "Queen Shabat". Her entrance every Friday at sundown brings its own special presence: peace, love, family, scripture, ritual, food, and sweet rest. For a survival culture it provides an earthly refuge evoking Psalm 91:1, 2:

> *"He who dwells in the secret place*
> *of the Most High*
> *shall abide under the shadow of the Almighty.*
> *I will say of the Lord*
> *'He is my refuge and my fortress;*
> *My God, in Him I will trust.'" (NKJV)*

As dusk declares the arrival of the "Queen" her shadow envelops the observant Jewish family in "the secret place of the Most High". The Sabbath is living art.

The risk here is in romanticizing it. Or legalizing it. In this passage Jesus teaches us to avoid both polarities. The Sabbath is not about a day. It's about us. "The Sabbath was made for man, not man for the Sabbath" (Mk. 2:27).

In the Hebrew language "shabat" means "cessation, desistance". All physical labor is taboo. It's "a day for quieting the heart". But let's get this straight, according to Jesus it's about the heart not the day. And, if we want to dispute it we should do so with one another, but not with Jesus. He is "Lord of the Sabbath", and he says the Sabbath serves us, we don't serve it.

Another Sabbath Controversy 3:1–6

So, whether it's picking heads of grain (a no-no to legalistic Pharisees) on the Sabbath, or healing a man with a shrivelled hand, Jesus sees the relative worth of the day in terms of doing "good" or "evil". Saving a life on the Sabbath trumps any legalistic proscription of the labor involved. The greater the day, the greater the good.

Jesus' healing of the shrivelled hand raised the bile of the Pharisees to a fever pitch. They became irrationally angry to the point of plotting with their arch enemies the Herodians (the ruling party of Rome) to kill Jesus. He was tying them in knots and they couldn't take it anymore. It escaped them that plotting a death was a very un-Sabbath thing to do.

Jesus the Rock Star 3:7–12

"Rock star", of course, is our culture's description of someone wildly popular. For sure Jesus was that – a celebrity the likes of which the people had never seen before. He drew huge crowds, who walked miles, sometimes days, to get near him. Often they would find him teaching at Kinneret and would crowd in to the point where he was being pushed into the lake (vv.9,10). So he would climb in a small boat, anchor a short distance from shore, and teach from there. Preaching from a ship brings Herman Melville to mind and his words in "Moby Dick" about the power of the pulpit:

> *"Its panelled front was in the likeness of a ship's bluff bows,*
> *and the Holy Bible rested on a project piece of scroll work,*
> *fashioned after a ship's fiddle-headed beak. What could be more*
> *full of meaning? – for the pulpit is ever this earth's foremost part*
> *all the rest comes in its rear, the pulpit leads the world.*
> *From thence it is the God of breezes fair or foul is first invoked for*
> *favorable winds. Yes, the world's a ship on its passage out and*
> *not a voyage complete; and the pulpit is its prow."*
> —MOBY DICK CH 8, HERMAN MELVILLE

So Jesus preached from the prow of his tiny ship, healed the sick, and delivered the spiritually oppressed. And while those who were healed wondered and wept with joy, the impure spirits cried out, "You are the Son of God." But the profound truth from the "gates of Hell" itself swept over the heads of the people. The Kingdom of Heaven had little draw for them. They were living in the here and now.

Jesus Appoints the Twelve 3:13–19

To this point in Mark's narrative he has identified five men called by Jesus to follow him: Peter and Andrew, James and John and Levi (1:16-20; 2:14). On a mountainside ("into the hills") he calls seven more. The full twelve are named: Simon Peter, James and John, Andrew, Philip, Bartholomew, Matthew (Levi), Thomas, James son of Alphaeus, Thaddaeus, Simon the Zealot, and Judas Iscariot. He chooses them with purpose. They are to be sent out to preach and to "drive out demons". Apart from the betrayer, Judas (who committed suicide) they would all suffer death in the pursuit of their high calling. At this point, however they had no idea what awaited them.

Jesus: Beelzebul? Or Crazy? 3:20–34

This passage reminds us of what a precipitous path Jesus was on. It demonstrates the razor's edge dividing "the kingdoms of this world and the kingdom of our God" (Rev. 11:15; quoted in Handel's "Messiah"). Only a hair's breadth comes between those who love Jesus and those who hate him. The Scribes and Jesus' family are a case in point.

The Scribes said, "He's demon possessed" (vv.22,30). Jesus' family said, "He's out of his mind" (v.21). What?!!

The scribal view was that a miracle worker could be in league with Satan. A powerful demon could cast out a lesser. Sooner or later the miracle worker would be carried off by a greater demonic force. In this view Jesus would soon be exposed as an agent of Hell itself.

The family view may have gone something like this: We grew up with him. We never saw any of this ministry (teaching, healing, exorcizing) in his youth and young adulthood. He's got to be crazy. We've had a family conference. We're going to take responsibility for him and put him under care. (Had Mary forgotten the annunciation?)

Jesus' response? To the Scribes he pointed out that Satan can't drive out himself. To his family, "Who are you?" (v.33).

Warning the Scribes that blasphemy against the Holy Spirit was "an eternal sin" (v.29) he then summarily dismissed his "mother and brothers" with a mild rebuke, "Whoever does God's will is my brother and sister and mother" (v.34). Neither the Scribes nor the family liked what they heard. He offended them both. The Scribes walked away angry, the family deeply hurt. And I wonder if Jesus was hurt too? He *was* human after all.... (And, just incase you're wondering what the unpardonable sin is, look at the context. It is unforgivable to attribute the work of the Holy Spirit to Satan.)

Parable of the Sower 4:1–20

Try Googling "Picture of Jesus sowing seeds". You'll get several artistic impressions of the centuries-old practice of broadcasting seed. From time to time on my car trips from Jerusalem through the Jordan Valley to the Upper Galilee I would see a farmer using this method. He'd have a bag of seed hanging (usually) by his left hip, and as he walked he would reach over with his right hand, grab a fistful of seed, and cast it out in a sweeping arc. Over the course of a day he would cover a lot of ground. Uncultivated ground, I might add. Ploughing took place *after* the seeding, not before.

This helps us understand why the sower in Jesus' parable indiscriminately scattered seed on hard, shallow, cluttered, and fertile soils. Subsequent ploughing would blend them all together.

There are as many interpretations of this parable as there are interpreters. But here I'll just make summary characterizations in terms of the anthropomorphized soils' responses:

1. Hard soil – "No way!"

2. Shallow soil – "Very interesting"

3. Cluttered soil – "Too busy"

4. Fertile soil – "Where do I sign?"

The difficult reference to Isaiah 6:9, 10 in the context of "why parables?" stresses a few critical (and troubling, for us) truths. First, there is an "inside-outside" divide between those who have been given "the secret of the Kingdom of God" (v.11) and those who haven't (yet). Second, there has to be an engagement of the mind and will in the appropriation of heavenly truth. The parable both observes and reveals truth for the fertile soul. "'Come now, let us reason together', saith the Lord" (Is. 1:18 KJV). There is no "deep calling unto deep" (Ps. 42:7) unless the human "deep" responds to the depth of God's grace. And third the Lord, who is omniscient, knows the responses of the "soil" even before the seed is cast. His revealed truth is only for the receptive. Unbelievers will not receive it. Unfair? Not if we recognize that the Lord's sovereign choices are predicated on our choices of "yes" and "no". And remember, there's always a "yet" for the slow adapter.

This is a parable about the mystery of God's foreknowledge. It's also about the mystery of an open/closed heart and mind, why some believe and others don't. If you, like me, are still a bit troubled by the seeming unilateral tone of this parable, read on. The next parable helps a lot.

This is a parable about the mystery of God's foreknowledge.

A Lamp on a Stand 4:21–25

Maybe the word "secret" (v.11) troubles us. Sounds exclusive. Or too "gnostic" for our liking. We like to think the Gospel is out in the open for all to see and hear. Exactly! says Jesus. "For whatever is hidden is meant to be disclosed, and whatever is concealed is meant to be brought out into the open" (v.22). The parable of the sower is like "a lamp". It casts light on the proven truth about sowing. The sower must be comprehensive and generous in the arc of his casting. He/she has got to be "big picture" in both expectation of return and scope of vision. Sow little, reap little. Sow big, reap big. Indeed, the wider the arc and the more generous the cast, the more we will reap (v.24). Think big. Think "Kingdom of Heaven". Let its light cast out the darkness. Don't recoil into a fetal position of narrowness.

More Seeds 4:26–34

Jesus continued the seed theme. In these brief parables of the growing seed and the mustard seed he made two elementary but powerful points. Seed grows inexplicably (a true mystery) and its ultimate growth is all out of proportion to its size. These similes (or "similitudes" as the old theologians used to call them) describe the Kingdom. The disciples would be wise to not undersell the Gospel.

Peace! Be Still! 4:35–41

As I write I'm troubled by the recent spate of suicides by celebrities reported on the Internet. These are people rich and famous due to their popularity as movie stars, rock stars, industry stars, You Tube stars, or even "stars" for being stars. They all had the power to collect a crowd. The problem, however, seems to be their inability to collect themselves. Their wealth and fame had trapped them. There was no space for thought, reflection, and rest. No time for healing. It's tough to leave a crowd.

Jesus, of course, had no difficulty collecting a crowd. He was usually swarmed by thronging supplicants and fans. But, he possessed the genius of being able to walk away from a crowd, sail to the other side of Kinneret (v.35), and go up into the hills to pray. He denied the crowds access to his inner self.

A storm suddenly engulfed the boat on this occasion to the point of nearly swamping it. Jesus, asleep in the boat, rested unperturbed. The panicked disciples woke him up, rebuking him for his seeming unconcern for their plight. Jesus ignored their rebuke and rebuked the wind and waves instead, as if some malevolent spirit was behind the turmoil. Then he rebuked the disciples. A lot of rebuking going on!

When Jesus rebuked you, you were rebuked. With the authority that only the Son of God possessed he rebuked evil spirits (Mk 1:25; 9:25), fever (Lk.4:39), the elements (4:39), and even the impulsive Peter (Mk.8:33). His rebukes were strong injunctions in the face of strong adversity like evil, illness, natural forces, and satanic presumption ("Get behind me, Satan!" 8:33). His rebukes were always effective. In this instance "the wind died down and it was completely calm" (v.39).

It's ironic that this "Peace! Be still!" command with its immediate result only increased the disciples' disquiet. Now they were "terrified" (v.41). Who was this man?! Fear of death had been eclipsed by fear of God.

The Gerasene Demoniac 5:1–20

In "*Cantelon's Casual Commentary*" on Matthew I comment fairly exten-
sively on the various points of view re. the location of this story. Suffice
it to say here that some manuscripts of the gospels read "Gerasenes",
others "Gergesenes", and others "Gadarenes". All locales were east of
the Sea of Galilee. Gergesa was closest to the lake and the western edge
provided a cliff-top view of the waters. Nevertheless there is no need for
a dogmatic determination of the location. "Gerasene" will do.

Mark, in his customary brevity, gives no detail as to the time necessary to exit a boat on the eastern shore of the lake and then climb to the
plateau several hundred feet above. Today these are the "Golan Heights".
And "heights" means heights. Mark simply informs us that Jesus got out
of the boat and "a man with an impure spirit came from the tombs to
meet him" (v.2).

In Jesus' day tombs were the preferred dwellings of demons, lepers,
and madmen. They were hallmarks of the world of shadows. People
avoided them. And in the Gentile/pagan world of the Gerasenes they
were seen as the open sores of the underworld. Approach at your peril!

This demoniac had superhuman power. It must have been public
safety concerns that had empowered a group of men to chain and shackle
him. But every time they did so he "tore the chains apart and broke (!)
the irons on his feet" (v.4). What kind of strength can break iron shack-
les?! No one person was "strong enough to subdue him." He was both
a threat by day and a terror by night (v.5). He wandered ceaselessly,
roaring at the skies and mutilating himself. For sure the Gerasenes gave
him wide berth.

So why would this child of Hell come running to Jesus? Why would
he still the malevolent powers within to fall on his knees in respect before
him? Why would he plead "again and again" (v.10) for Jesus to allow him
to stay in the area? Clearly the demon(s) "Legion" knew exactly who Jesus
was – "What do you want with me, Jesus, Son of the Most High God?"
(v.7). Legion was a minor power in the presence of the Almighty. Jesus'
intrusion into Legion's territory only meant one thing to this bit player

in the spiritual world – He had come to destroy him. With pathetic urgency he was calling on Jesus to let him survive.

His desperate fear of destruction led him to beg that Jesus would allow him to "go into" a herd of pigs on the plateau. Jesus gave "permission" (!) and Legion entered the pigs. Little did Legion know that the pigs (perhaps as many as 2000!) would rush "down the steep bank" and drown. Did this mean that Legion "drowned" as well? Mark doesn't say. What he *does* say is that the man was suddenly in his right mind, got dressed, probably in some clothing provided by the disciples, and pled with Jesus to allow him to become a disciple (v.18).

But there was yet more "pleading", this time from the people of the town. They pled with Jesus to leave. In their view (ironically like the Jewish Scribes) Jesus was a "super demon" who would terrorize and dominate them more than Legion had done. Jesus didn't argue. Rather he commanded the former demoniac to be his spokesman with the people, to tell "how much Jesus had done for him" (v.20). Who knew? This former terror became the first Gentile evangelist, travelling to all the ten cities of that region (the "Decapolis") proclaiming the Good News of freedom in Christ. Little wonder "all the people were amazed."

A Dead Girl and a Hemorrhagic Woman 5:21–43

Jesus crossed the lake, back to Capernaum. Before he could disembark a huge crowd rushed to the shore. One of them was desperate, and like the Gerasene demoniac he "fell" at Jesus' feet and "pleaded earnestly" with him that he would come and heal his dying daughter. As one of Capernaum's synagogue "pastors" Jairus would have been well known to Jesus. Indeed, Jesus probably knew Jairus' little girl. "Jesus went with him" (v.24) immediately.

The huge crowd "followed and pressed" around him as he and Jairus walked as quickly as they could to the stricken child. Walking through this milling throng would be similar to trying to make your flight pushing through thousands at an international airport terminal. You make no eye contact, nor do you pay any attention to the assorted elbows and shoulders jostling you about. You just want to get to the gate before the flight departs. This is what is so amazing about "the touch".

Two remarkable aspects of the touch are the anonymous contact itself and the realization by Jesus "that power had gone out from him" (v.30). The woman had been bleeding "for twelve years" and because of this affliction had quite likely been socially marginalized, if not ostracized. She had become like a leper, fearing contact with others because they feared contact with her. The fact that she would break out of her isolation, plunge into the crowd, and intentionally touch Jesus demonstrates her desperation and her faith. She hoped that just a touch of his clothes would heal her.

Many artistic impressions of this story portray the woman kneeling on the ground as she touched "the fringe of his garment" (Mt. 9:20-22 – Google "Touching the fringe of his garment"). If she did so, this was the third time in 24 hours that Jesus responded to a kneeling petition. Nevertheless it was remarkable that Jesus felt her touch. The disciples reacted cynically when he asked, "Who touched my clothes?" but he ignored them. Which brings us to the second remarkable aspect of the touch. Mark tells us he "realized that power had gone out from him" (v.30).

In the Greek language "dunamis" has the nuance of "inherent power", that is, power that exists in the constitution or essential character of something or someone. It by nature represents the thing or the person. Jesus had "inherent power" no doubt. It's assumed in all the accounts of his miraculous ministry. But here we read that Jesus knew that power had been drawn from him, without an act of will on his part. We don't see this anywhere else in Jesus' story. Had this woman taken Jesus by surprise? It's intriguing and mysterious. Yet, Jesus credits the woman's faith for her healing. Her life was changed forever.

This incidental touch happened on the way to Jairus' house. Jesus and Jairus weren't yet there when some well-meaning friends took Jairus aside to relate the sad news that his daughter had died. They suggested he not "bother the teacher anymore" (v.35). Jesus overheard them, told them to "just believe", and then stopped the crowd from advancing any further, taking only the Three with him and Jairus to the house. The home was already surrounded with family friends and neighbors "crying and wailing loudly." Jesus incurred their derision by questioning their raucous mourning and saying, "The child is not dead but asleep." Ignoring the scorn he led Jairus, his wife, and the Three to the little girls' room, took her by the hand, and asked her to get up. She did and walked around to everyone's (but Jesus') astonishment. He then instructed her parents and the Three not to report what had happened. Just let the crowd figure it out for themselves. Remember, this mocking crowd of mourners had already witnessed many of Jesus' miracles in Capernaum. How soon we forget.

No Respect for Jesus 6:1–6

To this point Mark's record has presented Capernaum as the epicenter of Jesus' ministry, with a brief foray into greater Galilee (1:39) and a boat trip across Kinneret (4:35; 5:21). Now he travels to Nazareth, then greater Galilee again (6:6b), Lebanon (Tyre and Sidon 7:24), the Decapolis (7:31), Dalmanutha (8:10), Bethsaida (twice – 6:45; 8:22), the region of Caesarea Philippi (8:27), Mount Hermon (9:2,9), and back to Capernaum (9:33). After these travels he begins the journey to Jerusalem (ch.10).

The Greek word translated "hometown" is "patris". It can also mean "fatherland", but whatever the translation Jesus went to Nazareth. There, on the Sabbath, he went to the synagogue where he taught the scriptures, to the amazement of his own townsfolk. They marvelled at his wisdom, and at the "remarkable miracles" he performed. But their astonishment was mitigated by familiarity ("familiarity breeds contempt"). There was a sneer in the word "carpenter", more than a modicum of social snobbery and jealousy. Who does he think he is? They underscored their hauteur with a rehearsal of the "facts". Isn't he a carpenter? Isn't this Mary's son and the brother of James, Joseph, Judas, and Simon? Aren't his sisters here with us? (v.3). I wonder if the relatives and acquaintances of Napoleon, Jeanne d'Arc, Alexander the Great, and other historical giants suffered the same withering analysis? They had all the facts but they missed Jesus.

This rejection by family, friends, and neighbors universally demonstrates our innate blindness to uncomfortable truth. Our comfortable, familiar "truths" always trump the intruding objective truth. We prefer our old wineskins.

Imagine describing the Mona Lisa in terms of the facts! Nose, eyes, mouth (strangely smiling), hair etc., but missing the genius of da Vinci's artistry. The art of faith often transcends the facts.

Atheism can be marvelous. To believe our world a cosmic accident, our beings nothing but advanced protoplasm, our capacity for love, heroism, moral integrity,nothing but atoms, electrons, and carbon – this is truly something to marvel at. Oh yes, and how does carbon marvel?

One further question. If Jesus' immediate circle were blind, how blind are we?

The First Field Trip 6:7–13

Many monastic orders that emerged in the Middle Ages seem to have taken Jesus' instructions to his disciples before their first ministry trip as a model for all time. These instructions – no bread, no bag, no money, no extra clothes, etc., were entry-level requirements for a kind of "boot camp" training which would prepare the disciples for a mature future ministry leading to martyrdom. They were "training wheels".

The most important provision that they *would* carry with them was spiritual "authority" imparted by Jesus. This would enable the disciples to deliver people from spiritual oppression and heal them from physical affliction. Mark says they "went out" and did exactly that. For sure they discovered soon enough, as their ministry reputation spread, that the "paraphernalia" proscribed by Jesus was indeed unnecessary. All the "stuff" one thinks necessary for adventures can derail the whole enterprise. Less is more.

Herod, Herodias, and John the Baptist 6:14–29

So the disciples are launched on their training mission and Mark gives us a bit of an interlude. He tells us about Herod. When we think of Herod we usually are referring to Herod the Great, the neurotic king who features prominently in the birth narratives of Jesus. But he was only the first of four generations of Herods who dominated Palestine for a century or so, beginning in the 1st century BC.

This original patriarch of the Herodian line was the second child of a major figure in Palestine's Roman history by the name of Antipater. His son Herod ("the Great") married ten women, five of whom were Doris, Mariamne 1st, Mariamne 2nd, Malthace, and Cleopatra. There were several children, one of them being Antipas, born to Malthace. Antipas contested, unsuccessfully, the kingship in 4BC, but he was appointed tetrarch[5] of Galilee and Perea. Like his father he was a builder, founding the city of Tiberias on the western shore of the Sea of Galilee (named after Tiberias, the Roman Emperor). He failed to do due diligence in the choice of the site, however. He built it on an ancient burial ground, rendering the city unclean in the view of Orthodox Jews. So he had to entice Gentiles to inhabit it. He also failed to do due diligence in marrying his divorced half-brother's wife, the infamous Herodias (who also was his niece!). This unfortunate choice gave him no end of trouble with his Jewish subjects, especially John the Baptist who called him out publicly for his sin. Remarkably Herod Antipas both liked and feared John. Herodias hated him (vv.19,20).

Jesus' reputation had been building, indeed exploding, shaking Galilee to its core. Antipas heard about him early on. People tried to explain Jesus' miracle-working power by proclaiming he was a prophet or Elijah or the resurrected John the Baptist. Herod believed the latter, and felt both guilt and fear for he had beheaded John. "Banquo's ghost" prowled the drafty halls of the Macherus fortress.

---

[5]   A "tetrarch" was the ruler of a quarter section of an area. When Herod the Great died (4BC) his domain was divided among his sons. Antipas got Galilee and Perea. A tetrarch was sometimes referred to as a "king", but he was merely a regional governor.

"Banquo's ghost" prowled the drafty halls of the Macherus fortress.

We don't know why Herod had arrested John and imprisoned him in the Macherus dungeon. Maybe he wanted to keep him safe from Herodias' murderous strategems.

Maybe he liked the idea of John's availability whenever he was in the mood for conversation – "he liked to listen to him" (v.20) as a sort of captive household counsellor. The various versions of scripture give us lots of room for thought when reading verse 20. For example:

NIV – "Herod feared John and protected him"
- "When Herod heard John he was greatly puzzled"

KJV – "Herod feared John... and observed him"
- "When he heard him, he did many things"

RSV – "Herod feared John... and kept him safe"
- "When he heard him, he was much perplexed"

The interpretive applications can be many, but the abiding reality in these words is that spiritual and moral truth can throw any of us into confusion and turmoil when it confronts our selfishness. We get angry and defensive. But, we always return to the truth, mostly to turn away from it again. It's hard to close one's mind to the clarion call of what is right even if it's just to remind us why we're so determined to do wrong.

So it's all about wrong – a drunken birthday party, bellicose praises to a dancing girl, a sudden gory beheading, likely revulsion on the part of the revellers, Herod "exceedingly sorry" (KJV), and a sad funeral. Everything went badly wrong.

Five Thousand Fed 6:30–44

The rookie disciples had just returned from their inaugural ministry itineration. They looked, and were exhausted. Jesus encouraged them to take a break in a "desert" place (KJV). They needed a sabbatical.

We all need sabbaticals. Jesus, "the Great Physician", knows the need we have for healing rest. He is the Creator (Jn. 1:3), and has built the need for rest and recreation into us. It's as vital as food and water. Indeed, on our part, stewardship of health and strength is a Christian duty. When we ignore it we eventually bear the consequences. Sometimes our "sudden onset" of illness is nothing more than the inevitable result of our neglect. We blame our age, the environment, our genes, or whatever when the cause of our breakdown may be our own sense of entitlement. We should avoid taking our health for granted.

Just a quick word about the "desert" or "lonely" (RSV) place. Sometimes we avoid solitude. We don't like what happens in that place. When we're apart form the breathless pace we find it hard to breathe. Why? Because the soul breathes a different air than our lungs. Alone with ourselves inevitably means alone with God. And he "searches the heart" (Ps 139:23,24). What He finds can be upsetting. Then again, his presence can fully refresh us. There is a definite upside to solitude. When you're there (often, I hope) breathe deeply.

The disciples didn't need a second invitation. They quickly got into a boat and sailed across the lake to that "lonely place". The problem, however, was that the crowds "saw them going" and ran from all over to the far shore (this would have been a long jog/walk for many perhaps five to ten miles). Even before they landed Jesus and the disciples would have seen the "great throng" (RSV) waiting for them. The whole point of the retreat was ruined. The disciples, no doubt, were irritated, ("send them away" they say later) but Jesus was "moved with compassion" for these "sheep not having a shepherd" (v.34 KJV).

The juxtaposition of "send them away" and "how many loaves?" is profound. I can relate to this. How often in pastoring have I thought, if not said, "send them away"? It reminds me of Father Zasima in Fyodor

Dostoevsky's "Brothers Karamazov" who confesses (to paraphrase) that he loves the masses, it's the individual he can't stand. (The actual quote: "I love Mankind but… the more I love mankind in general, the less I love people in particular… the more I hate people individually, the more ardent becomes my love for humanity as a whole."). Love for mankind can very easily be eclipsed by the demands of that high-maintenance neighbor. We don't see them as "sheep", but as "wolves" (at least for that moment of inconvenience). Needy neighbors can ruin our plans.

"The day was now far spent" (v.35 KJV) and the people were hungry. What to do? Send them away, or feed them? Jesus says the disciples should feed them. They sarcastically respond with, so where are we going to come up with a half year's wages, and the supplier, to feed this huge crowd? Jesus doesn't rise to their tone, but quietly asks, "How many loaves do you have?" (v.38). The disciples maybe hadn't read, or perhaps had forgotten, there was scriptural/historical precedent for what was about to happen (Jesus could have laid a little guilt on them). Both Elijah (1Ki. 17:7-24) and Elisha (2 Ki. 4:42-44) had performed feeding miracles. Jesus was about to do the same.

First, the Elijah story: "Some time later the brook dried up because there had been no rain in the land. Then the word of the Lord came to him: 'Go at once to Zarephath in the region of Sidon and stay there. I have directed a widow there to supply you with food.' So he went to Zarephath. When he came to the town gate, a widow was there gathering sticks. He called to her and asked 'Would you bring me a little water in a jar so I may have a drink?' As she was going to get it, he called, 'And bring me, please, a piece of bread.'

'As surely as the Lord your God lives' she replied, 'I don't have any bread – only a handful of flour in a jar and a little olive oil in a jug. I am gathering a few sticks to take home and make a meal for myself and my son that we may eat it – and die.'

Elijah said to her, 'Don't be afraid. Go home and do as you have said. But first make a small loaf of bread for me from what you have and bring it to me, and then make something for yourself and your son. For this is what the Lord, the God of Israel says: 'The jar of flour will not be used up and the jug of oil will not run dry until the day the Lord sends rain on the land.'

Both Elijah and Elisha had performed feeding miracles. Jesus was about to do the same.

She went away and did as Elijah had told her. So there was food every day for Elijah and for the woman and her family. For the jar of flour was not used up and the jug of oil did not run dry in keeping with the word of the Lord spoken by Elijah."

Then the Elisha story: "A man came from Baal Shalisha, bringing the man of God twenty loaves of barley bread baked from the first ripe grains along with some heads of new grain. 'Give it to the people to eat,' Elisha said.

'How can I set this before a hundred men?', his servant asked. But Elisha answered, 'Give it to the people to eat. For this is what the Lord says, 'They will eat and have some left over.' Then he set it before them, and they ate and had some left over, according to the word of the Lord."

I think the towering question from Mark's account is from Jesus, "How many loaves do you have?" The disciples' answer is indeed our answer. "Never enough." We undersell our giftings, capacities, and our faith. We don't feel adequate to the task. What we forget is that our Father has a genius for multiplication. When we are "weak" then we are "strong" (2Co. 12:9-11). Elijah, Elisha and St. Paul all say, "Amen!" Food miracles are not uncharted territory.

Water-Walker 6:45–56

It would have been twilight by the time Jesus dismissed the crowd and sent the disciples by boat to Bethsaida. Finally alone he "went up a mountainside to pray" (v.46). From his position on the mountain he would easily have seen the lights of Bethsaida a few miles away below and to the right. He also would have seen any light the disciples may have been carrying in the boat, And he would have seen and heard a storm rising from the northeast. The wind began to blow the boat away from the Bethsaida shore southwest toward Tiberias. "He saw the disciples straining at the oars" (v.48). He watched and he prayed. Finally, somewhere between three and six in the early morning he went down to the shore.

Then he stepped out on the water! When Mark tells us that Jesus "meant to pass them by" (v.48 RSV) one wonders if he had assessed their landing point due to the wind and saw that Gennesaret on the northwest shore was their heading. Did he plan to walk there? We don't now. What we do know is that the disciples saw him and cried out in terror. Surely this apparition walking the waves was a malevolent spirit! Jesus called out, "Take courage! It is I. Don't be afraid" (v.50). Then he climbed into the boat and the powerful wind subsided. The KJV says, "they were sore amazed in themselves beyond measure" (v.51). Mark credits this total astonishment to their hardened hearts. This is reminiscent of Isaiah's words centuries before when the Lord described his people as "hearing" without understanding and "seeing" but not perceiving (Is. 6:9b). These men had just seen Jesus feed five thousand with five loaves and two fish! How could they be so blind? Then again how often have people through the ages said "I see it but I don't believe it?" We often guard our subjective "truths" from the objective truth. We want no intrusion from outside to rock our world.

Sure enough, they landed at Gennesaret, a fertile plain between Capernaum and Tiberias. More demanding crowds met Jesus, laying their sick before him. Mark summarizes saying that wherever Jesus went "villages, cities or country" (v.56 RSV) the market places became the venue for miracles. Like the woman with the hemorrhage they were healed by touching the "fringe of his garment".

Can God be Finessed? 7:1–23

These twenty-three verses are full of fascinating content – Pharisees, Scribes, "unkosher" disciples, oral tradition-human rules eclipsing God's commands, attempts to loop-hole Moses' law about the care of parents, dull disciples, what really defiles a person, the role of the heart in good and bad decisions, etc.

The key statement is a pronouncement from Jesus on what makes a person unkosher – "Nothing outside a person can defile them by going into them. Rather it is what comes out of a person that defiles them" (v.15). The issue? Eating without washing one's hands. The Scribes and Pharisees had come all the way from Jerusalem to nit-pick. They asked a question that was a scold (not realizing that Jesus would push back with a scold of his own). "Why don't your disciples live according to the tradition of the elders instead of eating their food with defiled hands?" (v.5) they asked. Jesus' response: "You have a fine way of setting aside the commands of God in order to observe your own traditions!" (v.9). He then gave an example.

He described how the Scribes and Pharisees did an end-run around the Law regarding the care of one's elderly parents. They used an especially greasy loophole. You can avoid caring for your aged parents by designating the amount of money necessary for their care to God instead. It was a "gift" called "Corban" ("devoted to God"). This self-serving rationalization let them off the hook and pleased their self-righteous piety. As if God can be finessed! Do you think God will blink at your self-indulgence while your own parents perish in penury?! Not a chance.

Jesus then turned to the crowd who had witnessed this interchange to make it a teaching moment. He taught them that the outside material world was morally neutral. There is nothing in God's creation that is evil of itself. The defiling influence we should be aware of is our own hearts. Defilement comes from within not without. Evil action is predicated on evil thoughts. There is to be no blame-shifting. We're accountable for "sexual immorality, theft, murder, adultery, greed, malice, deceit, lewdness, envy slander, arrogance and folly" (v.22). If you want to see "unkosher", look in the mirror. And if you want to "honor" the Lord do it with your heart, not your lips (vv.6,7). Touching the fringe of your prayer shawl to the ark of the Torah and then raising it to your lips is no substitute for loving God and neighbor with all your "heart, soul, mind, and strength" (12:30).

The Woman from Tyre 7:24–30

It's so easy to read, "Jesus left that place and went to the vicinity of Tyre." Sounds like he went next door. But the fact is that Tyre is a *long* way from Capernaum. I have driven it over the years when I used to travel from Jerusalem to southern Lebanon to do broadcast ministry. It takes hours in a car. To walk it would take at least two to three days. It's not just the distance, it's the climb. It's a constant, steep grade from the shore of the Sea of Galilee to Tyre and Sidon, comprising thousands of feet of elevation. Even my little Volkswagen was nearly gasping when I finally reached Lebanon. This was no relaxing amble, it was grinding work. Obviously Jesus saw the effort as worth it. He just needed a break. So when he got to Tyre he tried to hide in a house, keeping "his presence secret" (v.24).

Someone leaked the news that the great Healer was in the house. Immediately a Syro-Phoenician woman came knocking at the door. Falling at his feet she begged Jesus to "drive" an impure spirit from her daughter.

Desperation had driven her for she undoubtedly was expecting push-back from this famous Jewish rabbi. She had been called a "gentile dog" many times by Jews. Social stigma had dogged her all her life. So, who was she to ask a favor of a Jew? Especially *this* Jew!

At first reading it seems that Jesus' response was insensitive and harsh. But his words were intentional. He said them for the woman's sake (and *her* racial biases) and for the disciples' sake (who were undoubtedly annoyed by her presumptuous temerity). He threw a well-known cultural/racial adage at her and to his delight she parried (as a Gentile to a Jew) with a clever saying of her own. This repartee was like a knife cutting through long-standing prejudice. It provided a lesson that both Jewish and Gentile onlookers would never forget. God is "no respecter of persons" nor of ethnicity. The woman's daughter was freed from her bondage with both Jew and Gentile marvelling at Jesus' broad worldview and his mastery of the spirit world.

Talking and Hearing 7:31–37

I mentioned last section how far it is from Capernaum on the Sea of Galilee to Tyre and Sidon. In this passage Jesus walks back to the Sea and then continues east, up over the heights and onto the plateau over-looking Capernaum and Tiberias, to a large Gentile region called "the Decapolis".

The Decapolis was a federation of ten Greek cities built by veterans of Alexander the Great's army. Its purpose was for military self-defence; they were "fortress cities". The area of the ten cities was large with Scythopolis (modern Bet Shean) on the west, Damascus on the north and Philadelphia on the south. They were all along or near the major trade routes and military highways. Very welcoming to the rule of Rome, the Decapolis was Gentile in culture but tolerated a Jewish minority.

Mark doesn't specify a city, he simply says "horion" (Greek) which can be translated "borders" or "coasts" (NKJV), or even "region". Jesus had probably entered a small border village where a man with a hearing and speaking impediment (KJV) was brought to him for healing.

Jesus gave no explanation for his use of saliva in this healing (see also Mk. 8:22-26; Jn. 9:11-7). We do know that spit was considered an ancient cure for eye afflictions, but it certainly wasn't seen as the panacea for blindness. It's interesting that Jesus "took him aside" (v.33) as he did the blind man at Bethsaida (8:23). Perhaps the spitting was better done in private. Nevertheless Jesus' fingers in the man's ears, his spit on his tongue, and the Aramaic command "Ephphatha!" ("Be opened") restored both hearing and "plain" speaking to the afflicted man. The onlookers were amazed. Jesus asked them to keep it to themselves. Which, of course, they didn't. Word quickly spread.

Four Thousand Fed 8:1–10

Within a few days news of the wonder-working Jewish healer produced a crowd of four thousand Gentiles following Jesus as he traversed the region. No doubt most of them had need of physical healing, but some were there merely to see the man at work. The novelty of it all had produced a mass enthusiasm with little regard for the necessities of life. This zeal lasted three days, but the crowd was becoming faint from hunger. Jesus saw them flagging in the heat and moved with compassion, acted.

Jesus miraculously multiplied seven loaves and a few small fish into a meal that fed everyone. There were seven baskets of food left over. He then descended the heights back to the lake, got into a boat and sailed its length northwest to Dalmanutha (probably the fishing port of Magdala, half-way between Tiberias and Capernaum). Mark records no words of wonder at what had just occurred. Just another day at the office.

The Tiresome Pharisees 8:11–13

The pesky Pharisees were at it again, this time with a malicious motive: let's reveal Jesus for what he really is, a mere magician. In their view Jesus was indwelt by Beelzebul, and as such was a kind of "super-demon". This power enabled him to do earthly signs but not celestial. Therefore, in asking him to perform "a sign from heaven" they would expose his inability to do so and reduce him to a mere side-show.

Jesus "sighed deeply". He despaired at this "generation's" spiritual blindness, knowing they wouldn't see a sign even if he gave it. But a sign was coming. An empty tomb in Jerusalem would be all the sign the world one day would need. It would be the ultimate pivot-point of history.

The Obtuse Disciples 8:14–21

Once again Jesus and the disciples were on the eastern shore. Ironically at the foot of the Decapolis heights where just a few days ago they had gathered seven baskets of left-over bread from Jesus' miraculous feeding of the four thousand, Mark tells us they "had forgotten to bring bread, except for one loaf." Obviously they were hungry. And just as obviously, in their view, the wonder-working "bread maker" was right there. He could feed them from one loaf. But he had no inclination to do so. He was exasperated at the disciples' dullness. "Do you still not understand?" he asked. Of course I can supply food but I will never perform a miracle for self-gain (remember Satan's temptation to make bread out of stones). We're not about the temporal, we're about the eternal. Instead of grumbling about the lack of food you should be on the alert. Avoid the "yeast" of the Pharisees and Herod. The externalism and spiritual ossification of the Pharisees will kill your spirit. The secular, political expediency of the Herodians will blind you to the coming kingdom. Wake up fellas. We're playing hardball here!

Walking Trees 8:22–26

Jesus' healings were generally done in crowds, which was a touch impersonal. This healing of a blind man in Bethsaida was not. Mark describes Jesus leading the man by the hands as he would a child, to somewhere a bit more private, outside the village. He laid his hands on the man twice after spitting on his eyes. This was no "touching the hem of his garment" event. This was a hands-on healing by increments. The first increment produced seeing "men like trees walking" – like 100/20 vision. The second produced clear vision – 20/20. Why this healing by degrees? Your guess is as good as mine. Maybe Jesus wanted to demonstrate that there was no set pattern, no template, no formula for the work of the Spirit. He will do what He will do.

This was no "touching the hem of his garment" event. This was a hands-on healing by increments.

"Thou Art the Christ" 8:27–30

Once again Mark provides no transition. From Bethsaida to Caesarea Philippi is a very long walk. Recently I drove that route (again – after countless similar drives when I used to commute from Jerusalem to South Lebanon in the 1980's), and it takes just under two hours at the speed limit. It's not only quite a distance, but it also involves a significant uphill climb. Caesarea Philippi is now know as "Banias" and it is situated at the base of foothills leading up to Mount Hermon. In Jesus' time it was a Gentile, Hellenistic city, founded by Herod Philip, one of Herod the Great's sons.

There may have been two purposes for this side-trip – one, a circuitous route to Jerusalem, and two, a bit of a retreat from the pressing Jewish crowds to the relative peace of Gentile territory to both rest and teach his disciples about what was to be known later as "the way of the cross". Jesus was beginning to reveal the stress of his knowing "that the Son of Man must suffer many things" (v.31). The "passion" was just around the corner.

I imagine Jesus and the disciples resting in the shade of trees bordering one of the several streams issuing from the roots of the foothills. It is truly a lush area, idyllic in its pastoral beauty. The question he posed was a very human one – "Who do men say that I am?" He knew that the poor, the oppressed and the sick saw him as comforter, liberator, and healer, but he also knew that he was a polarizing figure. So, what's the word on the street, fellows? What are they saying?

I don't think this question betrayed any insecurity on Jesus' part. Rather, I think the question was intended to test his disciples' sorry perception of whom they were following. This inner circle couldn't figure him out, especially because he was proving to be a big disappointment as a religious nationalist. They kept hoping he'd reveal his "zealot" side. The disciple with the darkest ruminations on this count was Judas. So Peter's confession was a huge shock. It came out of nowhere, "You are the Messiah" (v.29).

This burst of insight from the impulsive Peter proved to be a mere blip lost under duress (his subsequent denial of Jesus), but its truth rings like Big Ben from the Tower of the British Parliament. It has rung with clarion impact down through the ages into our very own time. Jesus was/ is the Christ. Hear the bell tolling…

Peter the Scold 8:31–34

This is a quick but powerful episode in the dynamics of teacher-student relationships between Jesus and his disciples. Peter is in the middle of it.

After Peter's impulsive proclamation that Jesus was Messiah, Jesus shifted the focus from what Peter and the disciples understood "Messiah" meant to what Jesus knew it meant. The disciples saw "Messiah" as national liberator, a king who by force would rout the Romans and rule the earth from Jerusalem. Jesus saw "Messiah" as "Son of Man", a descriptor that transcended the messianic hope of the masses. In Daniel 7:13 and Act 7:56 "Son of Man" has heavenly not earthly, implications. He is not only ruler of space and time, but ruler of all that is in the eternities as well. Jesus referred to himself as Son of Man – an exalted office, with the full understanding that his "equality with God" (Ph. 3:6) meant, ironically, total rejection, humiliation, suffering and death. Unlike his disciples' triumphalist messianic hope Jesus knew that the goal of his earthly kingship was servanthood and the yielding of himself to death as "a ransom for many". He wasn't out to save Palestine, he was about to save all mankind and redeem the universe. So in a prophetic "heads-up" he warned the disciples about what was awaiting him in Jerusalem. Peter didn't like what he was hearing. A "suffering Savior"? No. Can't be. We're expecting a conquering king!

So he took Jesus aside and scolded him. Jesus saw the rest of the disciples listening and pushed back with the strong rebuke, "Get behind me Satan!" Peter's lambast reminded him of the encounter he had had with Satan in the wilderness temptation. The bottom line was to avoid Calvary and choose expedience. Go the way of your consultants and your "better angels". Avoid the pain, keep people happy, short-cut the process. But no. Jesus would not avoid that knobby little hill called Calvary. Satan and Peter's words fell on deaf ears. In the big picture the short-term pain of the cross would mean long-time gain for the universe. But only Jesus could see it. The road of suffering would lead to everlasting life.

The Whole World or Your Soul? 8:34–38

Again there's a chronological gap. Some time has elapsed and now there's a "crowd" pressing in. Jesus gathers them and the disciples to him, and no doubt building on what had transpired earlier, gives a profound teaching.

It's clear that the disciples and the crowds were not on the same page with Jesus in terms of the messianic factor. The people saw through the space/time lens of expedience, Jesus through the everlasting eyes of Heaven. Any disciples Jesus taught will not gain safety, security and national victory via an earthly messiah. Rather it may be only through the crucible of suffering and even martyrdom that a man will save his soul and enter into the eternal presence of the Almighty. And he warns them that if his seemingly unsuccessful messianic track is causing embarrassment and second thoughts, they should know that their shame at his apparent failure will precipitate his being ashamed of them on the Day of the Lord (after which he would rule the heavens *and* the earth). To follow Jesus meant overcoming long held preconceptions about the end of the age, and "denying" oneself in terms of expected personal advantage in the triumphant kingdom to come. One must take up an unencumbered cross of faith and patience predicated on the prayer, "Not my will, but thine be done." I would think there were few "Amens" after this sermon.

The Transfiguration 9:1–8

Jesus' words in 9:1 have caused much discussion among scholars and casual readers alike. The question is, to what is Jesus referring when he speaks of "the Kingdom of God" coming with "power"? The most obvious assumption is that he was looking ahead to the "Day of the Lord" in the end time. Mind you, on one occasion he had referred to the Kingdom as being "in the midst" of the disciples (Lk. 17:20, 21), so it was clear that he didn't think of the Kingdom as necessarily tied to a timeline. I think that what follows clarifies the meaning of his words. Peter, James, and John were about to witness a revelation of the Kingdom at the Transfiguration.

After six days of rest at the foot of Mount Hermon Jesus led the Three up the mountain. It would have taken a few arduous hours to the summit and as they caught their breath, Jesus was suddenly "transfigured" before their eyes. The Greek word for transfigure is "metamorphoo" which means "to change into another form". Jesus' clothes became "dazzling white", a white beyond anything they had seen before. Indeed, they were probably temporarily blinded, shielding their eyes as if they had been looking into the sun. Then, their eyes adjusting to the brilliance, they were amazed to see two other figures standing with Jesus in conversation. They too would have been awash in light. Mark tells us they were Elijah and Moses. Moses, whose face shone on Mount Sinai, had always been seen by Israel as a prototype of the messiah (Dt. 18:15), and Elijah who was transferred from earth to heaven in a fiery chariot (2 Ki. 2:11,12), was seen as the forerunner of the messiah (Ma. 4:5). So there Jesus the Savior stood, bounded by the Law and the Prophets. Such a powerful moment. But there was more power about to be revealed.

Could there be anything more powerful at that moment than the voice of God the Father?

Could there be anything more powerful at that moment than the voice of God the Father? Even as Peter in stricken fear (v.6) croaked out a thoughtless burst of nervous talking about building three shelters (!), the Lord himself spoke out of an ethereal cloud, "This is my son, whom I love, listen to him! (v.7). Matthew 17:6 tells us the voice flattened them to the ground. Then the moment vanished. The shaking Three were now alone with Jesus. Mark records no conversation until they finally began their descent. Maybe they were too scared to talk.

Jesus Speaks About Elijah 9:9-13

For hundreds of years Israel had incubated a belief that a "forerunner" would come to set the house of the Lord in order before the messianic age (Ma. 3:1-5; 4:5, 6). Many identified this person as Elijah. As Jesus and the Three walk down the mountain, they talk about the expected sequence, predicated on the question, "Why do the teachers of the Law say that Elijah must come first?" (v.11). The "teachers of the Law", of course, were the Scribes and rabbis, champions of oral tradition. Jesus, no teacher of reincarnation nor a defender of Oral Law, tells them that "Elijah" had already put in his appearance, preaching repentance leading to the restoration of hearts right before God, in the person of John the Baptist (see Mt. 17:13). But, in one of the most pathos-ridden comments he ever made Jesus sorrows that "they have done to him everything they wished" (v.13) – beheading – and are about to kill Jesus too. However the "Son of Man" would rise from the dead (v.9). The Three looked at each other in confusion, What? What's he getting at? I mean, we just saw Elijah – is that what he means by "Elijah comes first"? We just heard that terrible voice. I'm still shaking. Now he's talking about suffering, rejection and death. Resurrection? What's up with that? This is all too much!

While the disciples asked questions, Jesus' eyes were on the sweep of history. He saw beginning from end. He knew that Israel had failed again and again throughout the centuries to uphold its side of the Covenant. But he also knew that restoration, beginning with the restoration of families (Ma. 4:6), was coming. Elijah had come – "twice"! – the second time in the person of the "forerunner" John the Baptist, who, in the spirit of Elijah, called for repentance. God's covenant with Israel had begun the long journey to renewal which would culminate in Messiah's arrival. The dramatic moment on the top of Mount Hermon would one day (not yet!) be understood by the Three as evidence of how close the heavenly glory was to earth. As the older, wiser Peter would later write, "For we have not followed cunningly devised fables, when we have made known to you the power and coming of our Lord Jesus Christ, but were eyewitnesses of his majesty" (2 Pe. 1:16 KJV). At the Transfiguration,

Peter, James, and John had seen with their own eyes the outskirts of the Kingdom of Heaven with the Law, the Prophets, and the Redeemer of mankind standing at the gate. But for now, they descended to Caesarea Philippi overawed and perplexed.

The Epileptic Boy 9:14–29

On the one hand this is yet another story of the miraculous ministry of Jesus. On the other hand it provides a remarkable portrait of his "humanness". We'll see him angry in chapter 11, but here we see him exasperated. As always, context is important.

Note the juxtaposition of heaven and earth, the Kingdom of God and the underworld of evil, celestial glory and abject human need, the top and the base of the mountain, the shining person of Jesus ("As soon as all the people saw Jesus, they were *overwhelmed with wonder*" – Why? Was he like Moses on Sinai shining with supernatural light? Ex. 34:29, 30) and the helpless look on the faces of the inept Nine. This may have been the most complex setting for any of Jesus' marvelous works.

One of the leading artists of the Italian Renaissance, Raphael (1483-1520), caught this juxtaposition in his famous "Transfiguration" painting (Google it, or better yet, see it for yourself in the Vatican Museum). In it he links the moment of Jesus' glorification with a group of concerned adults looking at a distressed boy. It was the last major work Raphael ever did, still working on it at his death. It's an enduring masterpiece, a work of genius. When you see it in the flesh, like everyone else in the Borghese Gallery, where it is displayed, you stare in silence and in wonder. There is a profound sense of the holy of heaven come down to earth.

The heaven to earth transition may have been at the root of Jesus' exasperation. He and the Three had just "landed" on terra firma at the foot of the mountain when a crowd including the nine disciples who had not witnessed the Transfiguration, rushed to greet him. Mark says "wonder" (v.15) was their chief motivation (I alluded to this already) but there was also a subtext to their enthusiasm. The father of a young boy cries out from the crowd "Teacher, I brought you my son, who is possessed by a spirit that has robbed him of speech..." (v.17). He then describes what look like epilepsy-related symptoms and tells Jesus bluntly that his disciples were powerless in the attempt to "drive out the spirit" (v.18). This is where Jesus expresses exasperation.

"You unbelieving generation… how long shall I stay with you? How long shall I put up with you?" (Do you hear the tone?). These words were directed mainly at the disciples. You can be sure they were all looking down in embarrassment. Then the boy's father made the mistake of saying "if you can do anything take pity on us and help us". Jesus' response is curt, "If you can?" (There's that tone again). He then turned to the boy and rebuked the spirit who came out with a shriek, seemingly killing the lad in the process. The people thought he was dead but Jesus simply took him by the hand and lifted him to his feet. The boy walked away completely healthy while the disciples, in a state of self-doubt asked, "Why couldn't we drive it out?" (v.28). Jesus still exasperated, responded with a blunt, "This kind can come out only by prayer" (some manuscripts include "and fasting"). Mark doesn't tell us how long it took for the culture shock of the human needs on the plain to mitigate the culture of heaven on the mountain.

It probably took some days for the Three to get their feet on the ground, reluctantly at that. Most of us prefer mountaintops.

Who is the Greatest? 9:30–37

It was a long walk back to Capernaum. Their path would have taken them down a gradual descent to the Hula Valley where a shallow marsh-like lake provided a perfect breeding ground for malarial mosquitoes. Then it was a gradual decline to the ridge overlooking the Lower Galilee. This was where the Mount of Beatitudes provided a stunning view of the Sea of Galilee four hundred feet below. Capernaum stood on the northern shore.

You can imagine the scene: Jesus and the Twelve stretched out in a line, sometimes a hundred yards or so from front to back, sometimes in groups of three or four, sometimes talking, sometimes not. And, it would appear, sometimes in heated argument.

What were they arguing about? Why now? Mark tells us they were in an ego-fuelled debate over who was the "greatest". And what precipitated this heat? Could it be that what Jesus had just told them about being killed had raised the predictable question, "Who will be his successor?" Undoubtedly they were all impressed with the tens of thousands who flocked to hear Jesus teach and heal. This was much valued critical mass for a messianic takeover. If Jesus were to die his movement must continue! One of us will have to step forward! As to that other thing, "rising again", who knows what *that* means? We'll deal with that later. For now, the popular base is there, the momentum is great, so who's going to wield the power? Jesus, at the head of this fractious procession may have rolled his eyes at their bickering. Deep down it must have hurt.

Nevertheless, Jesus "held his own counsel" until they got back to his boarding house in Capernaum. There he asked the disciples (even though he knew the answer) what they had been arguing about on the road (v.33). They didn't answer. They were embarrassed.

Later Jesus called them to gather around him and a small child (perhaps one of the disciples' children). This moment provided Jesus with a powerful, poignant response to his disciples' egoistic wrangling. The child represented the least powerful segment of society. So, when he says "Whoever welcomes one of these little children in my name welcomes me [and] ... the one who sent me" (v.37), they were more than embarrassed, but ashamed. What a rebuke to the self-aggrandizing disciples! Jesus, the "powerful" leader all of them foolishly thought they could replace if he died, was assuming the vulnerability and facelessness of a child. You want to lead? You've got to serve. It is the meek "who will inherit the earth" (Mt. 5:5). I wonder if the disciples slunk away in silence?

Jesus' Broad View of Would-be Preachers 9:38–41

In 1Ki. 19:1-18 there is a fascinating story about the prophet Elijah. After an astonishing intervention from Heaven on Mount Carmel (ch.18) he flees for his life from King Ahab's wife Jezebel. His first stop was about one hundred miles south in the desert city of Beersheba. He left his servant there and then walked by himself into the wilderness where, in a fit of pique and/or depression, he sat in the shade of a broom bush and pathetically asked the Lord to take his life. He had been on his way to Mount Horeb (Sinai) but the heat and dehydration were too much for him.

Suddenly, an angel appeared. He had been cooking a meal for the disconsolate prophet while he slept. The angel ordered Elijah to eat and drink before continuing his journey. After forty days and nights of arduous scaling barren quartz mountains and crossing vast, super-heated valleys, he reached the famous mountain. He collapsed onto the floor of a cave and fell asleep. Altogether he had walked almost four hundred miles from Mount Carmel through some of the most challenging topography on earth. He must have been exhausted.

When he woke up he heard the Lord's voice "What are you doing here, Elijah?" Perhaps the inflexion was "What are you *doing* here Elijah?" Or "What are you doing *here*, Elijah?" Whatever the tone, Elijah answered defensively, reminding the Lord of Israel's intransigence then adding mournfully, "I am the only one left, and now they are trying to kill me too." Poor me.

After a violent reminder that the "God of Heaven's Armies" was still in charge (read – tornado, earthquake, and devastating fire) the Lord, in a whisper, asks the question again, "*What* are you doing here Elijah?" And Elijah answers with another bleat of self-pity.

God spends no energy trying to comfort him. Rather, he gives him stern marching orders, basically telling this self-exiled prophet to get on with it. Then, in an ironic "by-the-way", he tells Elijah that he's mistaken. In fact there are seven thousand others in Israel who are a part of Elijah's faithful band. Man up and move on fella. You're not alone.

The Apostle Paul, in Romans 12:3, tells the Roman Christians that they should not "think of [themselves] more highly than [they] ought". This was Elijah's error, and it was also the miscalculation that Jesus' disciples made. They didn't approve of anyone other than Jesus and themselves "driving out demons" in Jesus' name. Whoever was doing this needed to stop, "because he [is] not one of us" (v.38). Jesus answered with broad-stroke maturity "whoever is not against us is with us." But the subtle, finer point was, there are lots of people out there whom I've reserved the right to empower. Don't think you are an exclusive club! Sectarians need not apply.

The "Kingdom" does not rise or fall on our qualifications. Indeed at this point in Jesus' story there was no entry-level prerequisite for ministry other than being "for" Jesus. Any "we're on the inside they're on the outside" labels were trumped by attitude and action. Jesus is teaching his disciples to look for faith even in the most unlikely ("I have not found so great faith no not in Israel" – Mt. 8:10). A takeaway for the Twelve with Jesus is the message we're merely messengers (and it seems there are a few out there we don't know!).

Millstones and Salt 9:42–50

When Jesus refers to "these little ones" (v.42) he is thinking of the "little children" (Mt. 11:25) who are both new and/or weak in faith. He speaks sternly about those who "offend" or "cause to stumble" ("skandalizo" – Gk) any of these baby believers. And of course there is no age limit on those who are newly born to the faith. Someone who is the cause of "feelings of repugnance" in a new believer in Christ would be better off drowned. A millstone "hung around their neck" would do the trick. This of course was an unseemly way to die – especially for a Jew. A proper burial with a marked grave and an honorable memorial was a core value in the Jewish religion and culture. Indeed, the Jewish view was: no grave, no existence. The history of the departed all hinged on that memorial marking the location of what would be seen as sacred bones. To have them scattered in the depths of the sea was unthinkable.

Then Jesus shifts to the topic of "self-stumbling". A "foot" can take you in a sinful direction; a "hand" can steal, hit, and grope; an "eye" can covet and look lustfully – all can cause "stumbling". Jesus engaged hyperbole from time to time, as he does here. He doesn't want a bunch of dismembered, mutilated disciples following him around. But he makes the point that any self-discipline pays off. Hell is real. Jesus *knew* that it exists. Why else die to *save* us?

The reference to fire and salt is hard to follow. Perhaps Jesus was thinking of Leviticus 2:13 – "Season all your grain offerings with salt. Do not leave the salt of the covenant of your God out of your grain offerings; add salt to all your offerings." And Numbers 18:19 – "All the holy offerings [are]... a covenant of salt forever before the Lord for you and for your offspring with you." Each of these references is drawn from a ceremonial context for sure, but the historical symbolism of salt in the Hebrew culture was significant. Salt meant fellowship ("sharing one's salt") with a neighbor over a meal, preservation of food, cleansing and purifying wounds, and even from time to time a medium of exchange. Indeed in the Sermon on the Mount Jesus utilized this time-tested symbolism when he referred to his followers as "the salt of the earth" (Mt. 5:13).

Here, Jesus changes a noun to a verb, "Everyone will be salted with fire" (v.49). The fear of Hell's fire ("Gehenna" – referencing the valley of Hinnom on the southwest valley of Jerusalem, where perpetual fire burned the city's garbage) will indeed "season" the values of the people, causing many to be preserved for God's kingdom. To this end they will not only respect rather than "stumble" their fellow believers, they'll also discipline themselves with regard to "the lust of the flesh, the lust of the eyes and the pride of life" (1Jn. 2:16). It's not just a moral mandate. It's a "covenant of salt" with the Almighty. So, as Jesus wraps up his object lesson about "who is the greatest?" he's instructing his self-aggrandizing disciples to get over it and be children of the Covenant at peace with one another.

JESUS IN JERUSALEM 10:1–15:47

The Worth of Women and Children 10:1–16

Leaving Capernaum, Jesus and his disciples walked south towards Jericho. The Jordan River was the boundary line between Judea and Perea (Trans-Jordan) and the river valley provided the route for travel. Mark doesn't tell us whether Jesus was in Judea or Perea when the Pharisees caught up with him. They were still trying to trap him. This time it was the sticky issue of divorce.

There are a few cultural/historical things to keep in mind as you read about this exchange:

1. The Pharisees were trying to trap Jesus into setting himself up above the Law of Moses.

2. They themselves represented two schools of thought on the issue: the school of Rabbi Shamai (the ultra-conservative) and the school of Rabbi Hillel (the ultra-liberal).

3. Divorce was a man's game – the "wife" was merely chattel.

4. The Pharisees' default, always, was the letter of the Law.

5. Jesus saw institutions as serving people, not people serving institutions.

6. Malachi 2:16 says "For the Lord God of Israel says that He hates divorce" (NKJV).

Divorce in the Greek is "apostasion" which means, "a defection, a standing off, a withdrawal". And, in the Old Testament world it was mostly the man who defected, stood off, and withdrew from the marriage. His wife was powerless, although a concubine (whose woeful status nevertheless included a legal tie to her "master" *was* allowed, under certain conditions, to divorce her man (Ex. 21:7-11). In this passage we read that if an Israelite purely for economic reasons "sells his daughter as a slave" (v.7) she will not be required to serve her master for six years (like a male slave) but shall function as a concubine ("amma" – Heb. "slave, concubine") with all the legal protection that this role provides. In effect she is a substrate of "wife" with menial, domestic and sexual functions under the "covering" of the man of the house. If the buyer of this girl deals "faithlessly with her" (RSV) by refusing to take her in then she is to be "redeemed" (v.8) by another who will pay the purchase price. Then if *this* buyer purchases another concubine/wife he is still obligated to keep the former concubine fed and clothed with her "marital rights" (v.10) respected. If he does not perform these duties she is free to "defect" with no financial penalty. In other words the power of divorce was in her hands. But a wife, wedded by patriarchal negotiation and endowed, did not have this kind of clout. In marrying she became her husband's exclusive property who could cast her aside at will and without redemption. Then, if you can believe this (!), he could force her back at some later date, because she "belonged" to him.

In order to end this abuse of a divorced wife, Moses, the Lawgiver, had insisted that she was to receive a legal document, "a certificate of divorce" (Dt. 24:1), that she could use to deny a former husband from laying claim to her at any point thereafter. This mitigated a woman's mental anguish even as she dealt with the penury that usually followed being "cast out". Moses' "rescue" of divorced wives was reflected centuries later in Jesus' high view of women.

I think we can safely assume that God's hatred of divorce (Ma. 2:16 KJV) reflects his regard for the covenant of marriage and his desire for "godly offspring" (v.15). Divorce fractures families and a waterfall of dislocation cascades into the next generations. The ultimate building block for God's people is the family. Divorce is like a fungus gnawing away at the roots.

Mark doesn't qualify the Pharisees' question as Matthew does. In Matthew the qualifier to the question "Is it lawful for a man to divorce his wife?" is, "for any and every reason" (Mt. 19:3). Mark simply records the blunt questions (offensively posed with a tone no doubt).

The Pharisees wanted to trap Jesus between Shammai's school that provided no room for divorce and Hillel's school that allowed a man to divorce his wife for "any and every reason", which included burning his dinner or his finding a younger, more attractive woman. To side with Shammai meant legalism, to side with Hillel meant social chaos. Jesus sided with neither. Rather, he took a highway above them both.

Jesus acknowledged that Moses had indeed "permitted a man to write a certificate of divorce and send her away" (v.4) but this concession was predicated on "your hearts were hard" (v.5). There was no room for compassion in terms of what this meant for the woman. No regard for certain poverty and shame. So even though Moses' famous certificate provided a bit of relief against her being reclaimed, it did nothing to restore the home, or nurture the motherless children.

Then he takes that high road. God created male and female to become "one flesh". (This term refers to sexual intercourse, but also to the child that is created). It is God, not the officiating rabbi, who joins them together in matrimony (v.9). So who has the authority to separate what the Creator has bound in unity?

Later, in conversation with his disciples Jesus bluntly stated, "Anyone who divorces his wife and marries another woman commits adultery against her (that is against the divorced wife). And if she divorces her husband (commonly done as Greek and Roman influence pervaded the culture of Israel) and marries another man, she commits adultery" (against her former husband – assumed). Adultery was like a home invasion. It broke in and stole the very soul from a duly married couple's household. Marriage was a union. Divorce was a dismemberment.

Jesus, of course, was no legalist. He was not a new chief of the Scribes. He was fully aware that domestic abuse should not be tolerated and that the high ideal of marriage for life was practically impossible for some. Priority number one for any woman was security with love and nurture as companion. Jesus did not promote inflexible codes of conduct. Rather he said, "Come to me, all you who are weary and burdened and I will give you rest. Take my yoke upon you and learn from me, for I am gentle and humble in heart, and you will find rest for your souls. For my yoke is easy and my burden is light" (Mt. 11:28-30).

His "yoke" was characterized by compassion, not legal arguments. He did not bind people. He set them free. Divorce was not the "unpardonable sin". Nor was it to be entered into lightly. Treading on God's sovereignty is risky business.

The ultimate collateral damage of divorce is incurred by children, those "godly offspring". Jesus had a high view of them, as he did of women. Mark may have been intentional, then, in recording the following story. He tells us about Jesus and the little children.

Mark mentions that Jesus and the disciples were "in the house". He doesn't tell us whose it was or where it was. Regardless, a crowd gathered and began to press in with their children hoping Jesus would "place his hands on them" (v.13) in order to bless them. The guard-dog disciples tried to push them back, but Jesus, "indignant" at his disciples and compassionate towards the children, opened his arms and said, "Let the little children come to me." These youngsters were the ones to whom "the Kingdom of God belongs" (v.14). He took each one in his arms and blessed them. I'd love to read the story of what those blessed children became.

The guileless child has the imagination and trust to act on simple belief. Jesus loves me? Great! I'm his.

Just a final comment – Jesus gave another blunt teaching when he said, "anyone who will not receive the Kingdom of God like a little child will *never* (emphasis mine) enter it" (v.15). Adult doubts, skepticism, and second thoughts can sabotage faith. Only those with the childlike capacity to throw oneself into Jesus' arms, as it were, will ever enter into the Lord's eternal presence. The guileless child has the imagination and trust to act on simple belief. Jesus loves me? Great! I'm his.

The Walk Continues 10:17–31

In this passage we're going to see that there is a *cost* to discipleship (vv.17-22), a *snare* in material wealth (vv.23-27), and *heavenly recognition* for those who choose short-term sacrifice (vv.28-31). There's a lot here.

But first, Jesus didn't like being flattered. This man who "ran up to him and fell on his knees before him" (v.17) got off on the wrong foot by addressing Jesus as "Good teacher". Maybe he was just being polite. But Jesus, after rebuking the man, says, "No one is good – except God alone", which is ironic in that Jesus *was/is* the Son of God, so he surely qualified as ultimate good. But the man would not have appreciated that in Jesus' view his referring to Jesus as good was verbal bowing and scraping. It displayed his ignorance of Jesus' true stature. God will not be manipulated.

The man's question, "what must I do to inherit eternal life?" drew a succinct response. Jesus referred him to the commandments, summarizing them by mentioning six. The man was quick to say he'd obeyed them all from childhood. He was "righteous". But was he "just"? Jesus tied the two – righteousness and justice – by challenging the man's "lack" (v.21) of justice. It wasn't enough to obey the Mosaic Law, one had also to obey the call of the scriptures to care for the alien, orphan, and widow. "Go, sell everything you have and give to the poor, and you will have treasure in heaven," Jesus said. The man's face "fell" and he slipped away. Why? Because he was very rich.

In challenging this wealthy man to liquidate assets and give to the poor, Jesus introduced the concept of heavenly "treasure" related to earthly ministry to the needy. Good faith and good works are corollaries, "whoever does not love their brother and sister whom they have seen cannot love God, whom they have not seen," says the "beloved disciple" John (1Jn. 4:20b). "Eternal life" requires both righteousness and justice. You've got to love both God and neighbor. The rich man missed a great adventure.

The disciples, listening in, were "amazed" at this interchange. They were astonished that every human's hunger for riches should disqualify them for salvation. "Who then can be saved?" they asked. To muddy the waters even more, Jesus had just employed a confusing metaphor about a camel going through a needle. This, of course, was hyperbolic imagery. No need to apply some fantastic meaning. Jesus often exaggerated for the sake of emphasis, even using occasional human and common conversational expressions. He was simply making the point that materialism can erode and even obliterate true faith. On the other hand God can redeem any soul who truly repents, whatever the disqualifying sin may be. With him all things are possible (v.27).

Jesus went on to say that those who prioritize Kingdom values will receive great reward in the eternal age to come. But there will be no place for comparison of heavenly assets. All that "Who is the greatest" talk has got to stop. Only God knows who is first and last (v.31). Well, at least James and John weren't listening, as we shall soon see.

The Not-so-Hidden Agenda 10:32–45

Before commenting on James and John and their "chutzpah", I want to address Mark's mention of Jesus "going before them" (v.32 NKJV) on their way to Jerusalem.

It is just a mention but there is a profound mental picture that accompanies "Jesus leading the way". For over two thousand years Jesus has been in the lead. Hundreds of millions have followed over the centuries, "fixing [their] eyes on Jesus, the pioneer and perfecter of faith" (He. 12:2). He blazes trails in the jungle undergrowth of every social, moral, educational, relational, and even political issue. He leads with his eyes firmly fixed on the north star of righteousness and justice, doing his maximum while the foot-dragging disciple (read "you and me") does a lukewarm minimum. Often our negative inertia tries to hold him back, to create a mediocre Jesus in our own image. Fortunately for us, he does not change – he is "the same yesterday, today, and forever" (He. 13:8 NKJV). Those who follow walk in the shadow of a cross.

Perhaps that encroaching shadow created a look on Jesus' face, whether of steely determination or a far away stare of the eyes, that "astonished" the disciples and frightened the hangers-on (v.32). Jesus was on a slow but sure march to his death. And, in the loneliness of that moment he tried once again to give the disciples a heads-up. But, as we'll see in what follows they still didn't get it.

Peter had misread Jesus' first warning about the Passion and was upbraided in no uncertain terms (8:32-33); now the others of the "big

Three" are also rebuked. As well they should. They had the temerity to ask Jesus to "do for us whatever we ask" (v.35).

This kind of open-ended, before-the-fact approach to God is never met with favor. Then to follow with, "Let us sit at your right and the other at your left in your glory", was puerile, self-serving, and presumptuous. It was another body-blow to Jesus in terms of his frustration at his disciples' obtuse religious nationalism. And on a personal level it must have been disappointing. Jesus responded (perhaps with a sigh), "You don't know what you're asking" (v.38). Were James and John ready to be "mocked… spat upon… scourged… killed"? (v.34).

They thought they were. Maybe seeing Jesus in his "glory" (v.37) on Mount Hermon had given them the overwhelming realization of what "Son of Man" really meant. Maybe the Transfiguration had raised the stakes in terms of their own future aggrandizement. But did they really think they had the stature of Elijah and Moses? If they did think they had the "royal jelly" they forgot it a few days later when "they forsook him and fled" (14:50). Indeed, as Jesus himself said in Gethsemane, "the spirit is willing, but the flesh is weak" (14:38).

Jesus knew they eventually would suffer rejection and death (v.39), drinking the "cup" and undergoing the "baptism" of martyrdom, but, at this moment they had no idea. The stars were in their eyes. They wanted Jesus' "glory" to be theirs.

"When the Ten heard about his they became indignant with James and John" (v.41). Nobody likes queue-jumpers, whether it's at the bank, the grocery store, or in traffic. But this went beyond minor irritation. The Ten were angry because they had been out-maneuvered. *They* wanted the key cabinet posts. It was bad enough that James and John were two of the inner circle, the favored "Three". And what about Peter? Had James and John done an end-run around the defacto leader of the Twelve? Each of the disciples coveted preferment. As do we all.

Jesus broke into the squabbling with the sober teaching that leadership in the Kingdom was given through service not lordship. There is no swagger in God's work, just a basin and a towel. Jesus himself would serve mankind by giving his life "as a ransom for many" (v.45).

Blind Bartimaeus 10:46–52

For some reason Bartimaeus has achieved a measure of notoriety. Maybe it's because he was so insistently loud in his calling out to Jesus. Or maybe because this is the last healing Mark records before the Passion. Regardless, he's a memorable figure.

Jesus and the disciples had travelled south from Capernaum via the valley road east of the Jordan River. They crossed over to Jericho where they were joined by a huge crowd. Undoubtedly they stopped for rest and refreshment. Then, as they started walking west, to the edge of the city there suddenly was a commotion – loud, very loud, insistent shouting not from many but from one. Blind Bartimaeus was not going to let this opportunity for healing pass. He made such a racket that the crowd tried to silence him. But he was not about to give up. He kept crying out as vehemently as possible, "Jesus, Son of David, have mercy on me!" Undoubtedly there were many in the crowd who also wanted Jesus' attention but Bartimaeus won the day. Jesus heard him, stopped, and said, "Call him". Bartimaeus jumped to his feet and ran, probably bumping into a few people, and came breathlessly to Jesus.

Mark gives no explanation as to why Jesus asked this enthusiast what he wanted. Sometimes Jesus, for the sake of a teaching moment, asked those he was about to heal what it was they wanted. Simple answer – "I want to see." With that straightforward expression of faith he was healed. Loving every minute he skipped along behind Jesus in total joy. A happy story. No wonder we like good old Bart! He understood what it was to "seize the day" (Carpe Diem!).

The Final Week Begins

Sunday 11:1–11

There were large numbers of people ascending the Judean hills to Jerusalem for Passover. It would have been "bumper to bumper" or "donkey to donkey" traffic. Bethphage was traditionally seen as the official outskirts of the Holy City, the end of a pilgrimage. Near Bethphage, on the south-eastern slope of the Mount of Olives, stood its sister village, Bethany. Mark is not specific, but Jesus and his disciples probably stopped in Bethphage, terminating their pilgrimage, along with many other pilgrims. As they were settling in, Jesus instructed a couple of the disciples to go to Bethany and bring back a colt tied at an unnamed person's door. Undoubtedly the crowds had already identified Jesus the "rock star", and watched in fascination as the disciples prepared the colt for a historic ride. As far as the crowd was concerned this ride would be the "triumphal entry" of the Messiah!

Some of them would have been aware of Zechariah's prophetic cry,

"Rejoice greatly, Daughter Zion!
Shout, Daughter Jerusalem!
See your king comes to you,
righteous and victorious,
Lowly and riding on a donkey,
on a colt the foal of a donkey."

—ZE. 9:9

He also knew the "Hosannas" ("Save now!" Hebrew) would soon morph into "Crucify him!"

Certainly Jesus knew all about these words. So, even as he climbed onto the colt's back he knew he'd be getting the "royal treatment" from the enthusiastic crowd. He also knew the "Hosannas" ("Save now!" Heb.) would soon morph into "Crucify him!" The clip-clop of the donkey's hooves would be eclipsed by hammer blows nailing his hands and feet to a cross.

So he endured the adulation and the presumption, the crowd's agenda – "Rout the Romans! Get on the throne!" was not his agenda. The "ticker tape" ("cloaks and branches") parade ended at the temple courts. There he "looked around at everything", then rode back to Bethany in the dark.

Monday 11:12–19

Jesus was troubled by what he saw at the Temple. He may have been ruminating all night over what he should do. He woke up next morning in "righteous anger", ready for aggressive action. A little fig tree would be his first target (vv.12-14).

Now, before we get too judgemental be aware that "Bethphage" means "house of unripe figs" (Aramaic). The name refers to a species of late-season figs which never appear to be ripe, even when they are edible. Jesus, of course, knew that the figs were in the early stages of formation (spring-time), but muttered at the unfortunate tree anyway. Mark tells us the disciples heard the "sub-voce" curse. The life lesson wouldn't come until the next morning.

The immediate lesson, however, was not verbal. It was brutally physical. Jesus, disgusted with the temple commerce (run by the Sadducees), stormed into the kiosks and stalls packed into the temple courts, overturning the tables of the money changers and the display cases of the merchants. It was chaos – coins, doves, sheep and goats, frightened sales people, and other detritus flying everywhere. Jesus even stopped those trying to escape with as much of their product as they could carry (v.16).

He shouted above the melée, "My house will be called a house of prayer for all nations… you have made it a den of robbers" (v.17). The "chief priests" (controllers of all the money) and the "teachers of the Law" heard this (especially "*My* house" and "*all* nations"). This totally spooked them. Their only option was to hatch a plan to kill him. When the tumultuous day had ended Jesus and his disciples left the city. But the controversy remained.

Tuesday 11:20–13:37–A Lonnnng Day!

Prayer vv. 20–25

Now, back to the unfortunate fig tree. Next morning, "as they went along, they saw the fig tree withered from the roots" (v.20). The bewildered disciples wanted an explanation. Jesus didn't give them one. Instead, he exhorted them to "have faith in God". Then he went on to talk about throwing mountains into the ocean and getting whatever one asks for in prayer. What? I asked for a pony when I was a boy, and didn't get it. Is Jesus Santa Claus?

Here's where solid biblical hermeneutics (interpretative science) can save us from candy-store faith. A fundamental of biblical interpretation is cross-checking various passages that address the same topic or theme. There are many comparative texts. Let's just look at three:

John 14:13 – "And I will do whatever you ask in my name, so that the Father may be glorified in the son."

John 14:14 – "You may ask me for anything in my name and I will do it."

Mark 14:36 – "Abba Father… everything is possible for you. Take this cup from me. Yet not what I will, but what you will".

Notice the caveats (a caveat is "an explanation to prevent misinterpretation; a modifying or cautionary detail to be considered when evaluating interpreting, or doing something" Merriam-Webster Dictionary). There are three:

1. Requests are to be made "in Jesus' name".

2. The answer to the prayer must "glorify the Father" in the Son.

3. Prayer seeks God's will not ours.

With these caveats there is no room for candy-store gluttony. We don't seek self in prayer, we seek God.

Then, there is something else vital to prayer: forgiveness of others. All prayer pivots on a heart free from resentment, bitterness, and unforgiveness (v.25). If our hearts are bound by these spiritual/emotional cancers our prayers will bounce off the ceiling. The Father is deaf to any with an unforgiving spirit. The ultimate prayer? "Not my will but thine be done."

Authority – vv. 27–33

Jesus, fearing no reprisals, walked back to Jerusalem. The religious authorities soon cornered him. They appeared to be "calm" in their approach. Indeed this calmness may have been rooted in guilt. They knew that the commercialization of the Temple was wrong. Jesus' righteous anger the day before mitigated theirs. Nevertheless they tried to make Jesus accountable by questioning his authority as a teacher and Temple-cleanser. He responded to their question with a question: "John's baptism – was it from heaven, or of human origin?" They knew they couldn't answer. If we say "yes" he'll ask why didn't we believe him. If we say "no" the people will rise up. So they answered, "We don't know". And the conversation ended.

Parable 12:1–12

This was one of Jesus' parables that left no room for doubt or misunderstanding. It was an overt offence to the religious leaders. They *fully* understood it (v.12). And most of us who have at least a cursory exposure to the Bible do too. Isaiah 5:7 comes to mind: "The vineyard of the Lord Almighty is the nation of Israel… he looked for justice, but saw bloodshed; for righteousness, but heard cries of distress". Over the centuries God sent "servants" (read "prophets") to warn his people Israel about their spiritual idolatries but they abused and rejected them all. Finally he sent his only son, whom they killed.

"The stone the builders rejected
has become the cornerstone;
the Lord has done this
it is marvelous in our eyes."

— VV. 10,11 – QUOTING Ps.118:22, 23

The fact that Jesus foresaw the intent of the religious leaders' hearts (the quest to kill him) coupled with his apparent dismissing of their Kingdom of Heaven inheritance by saying it would be given to "others" (Gentiles) was more than enough fuel to energize the consequent Passion events. Their rejection and hatred of Jesus had reached the boiling point.

A Trap 12:13–17

I get the sense reading this account that the question posed to Jesus with such flattery and obsequiousness was not ad hoc. I think there may have been several "committee meetings" behind closed doors to develop strategies to trap Jesus. When Mark writes that "they sent some of the Pharisees and Herodians... to catch him in his words" (v.13), it implies premeditation especially in that Pharisees (interpreters of the Mosaic Law) and Herodians (Jewish allies of Rome) were hostile to one another. The senders were the Sadducees and the Scribes, the driving force and "brains" of the emerging plan to kill Jesus. Indeed I wonder if these "pedestrian" Pharisees and appeasing Herodians weren't students, would-be heavyweights in the making. Regardless, they were lackeys, collaborators in the entrapment scheme.

Roman taxes were modest – one denarius per year per person. But for the religious nationalists that denarius symbolized subjection, as did the once yearly sacrifice required to honor Caesar. If these interlocutors had been smart, they would have challenged Jesus about that sacrifice, not about the tax. But they didn't. They figured the poll tax question would suffice.

This was a test of Jesus' perceived zealotry. The assumption was that he was a religious nationalist like his disciples. If Jesus approved the tax he would lose the people, the "am ha aretz". If he disapproved he risked immediate arrest for treason.

Jesus totally amazed them when he answered it's not either/or, it's both/and – Give Caesar what is his, give God what is his. Any other questions? The trap had failed to spring. The Pharisees and Herodians slunk away. But there was more to come.

The Resurrection Questions 12:18–27

This time the real heavyweights, the temple elite, the Sadducees "came to him with a question" (v.18). The question was theological.

They presented a hypothetical serial marriage to Jesus, predicated on Moses' law about "levirate marriage". Here's the passage:

> *"If brothers are living together and one of them dies without a son, his widow must not marry outside the family. Her husband's brother shall take her and marry her and fulfill the duty of a brother-in-law to her. The first son she bears shall carry on the name of the dead brother so that his name will not be blotted out from Israel."*
>
> —DT 25:5,6

Moses then goes on (vv.7-10) to pronounce the disgrace that will be incurred if the brother-in-law "will not build up his brother's family line". Whole family histories in Israel pivoted on this levirate law. Honor and lineage went hand in hand.

The Sadducees' question was not only theological but subcultural. As is often the case with sectarian values, the value in question can take on biblical proportions. In this case the issue was resurrection. They had no issue with the woman being married and widowed seven times, but they thought this to be an excellent hypothesis for upending the Pharisees' belief (and Jesus' too, they assumed) in the after-life. "Whose wife will she be in the resurrection?" they thought to be the most clever of questions.

Jesus turned the question on its head embarrassing the Sadducees in the process. He accused them of biblical illiteracy and of ignorance with regard to the nature and power of God. Simply put, there is no marriage in heaven. Full stop. And, with regard to resurrection Abraham, Isaac, and Jacob are *alive*, not dead. Their bodies have been in the ground for centuries but their spirits are everlastingly engaged with their Creator who "is not the God of the dead but of the living" (v.27). The Father's sovereign power eclipses sub-cultural values and theologies. Sorry fellas, you're quite wrong.

The Greatest Commandment 12:28–34

This is not only the greatest commandment of all time, it is also the ultimate summary of the historic prophetic call to Israel and the world of Gentiles. A focused study of Old Testament prophecy reveals that the essential distillation of God's heart for Israel is that she return to right relationship with Him and right relationship with neighbor. The fulfilment of the vertical is called "righteousness", of the horizontal, "justice". Indeed, "Righteousness and justice are the foundation of your throne" (Ps. 89:14).

The integrity of the upward and the outward is stressed again and again in scripture.

The integrity of the upward and the outward is stressed again and again in scripture. Read what the Apostle John had to say:

> *"Whoever claims to love God yet hates a brother or sister is a liar. For whoever does not love their brother and sister, whom they have seen cannot love God, whom they have not seen. And he has given us this command: Anyone who loves God must also love their brother and sister" (1Jn. 4:20,21).*

234

Love for God and neighbor must go together. Like "love and marriage, and a horse and carriage", you can't have one without the other. Traction in the Kingdom of Heaven depends on that kind of spiritual integrity.

This massive mandate is founded on, "Hear, O Israel: the Lord our God, the Lord is one" (v.29). This is the "great Sh'ma", the cornerstone of Hebrew faith. The proclamation of the unity of God is brilliant light to a polytheistic Gentile world. You can't love stone and wooden idols. Nor can you love a pantheon of Greek and Roman gods. You can only love the One who "loved us first", the One who created us in his image, the God of Abraham, Isaac, and Jacob, and Father of the Christ.

Jesus goes on to say to the inquiring scribe that love for God and neighbor fulfills the demands of righteousness and justice. And how does one love? One loves with "heart, soul, mind and strength" (v.30).

The heart of course is a "feeling" center – the locus of emotions. Soul and mind, in Jewish thinking comprised the intellect (note the Scribe's summary of the two: "understanding" v.33). And the strength of a person is the will. So, Jesus says we love comprehensively: with intellect, emotion, and will. We love with our thinking, our feeling, and our choosing. The stress is on the choosing. We're all monuments to the decisions we have made. Ultimately we *decide* to love.

Note that Jesus was impressed with this young scribe. "You are not far from the kingdom of God," he said. This cordial commendation was a bit of a break from the usual tension. But, there were other religious leaders who shared this young man's openness of heart (read Nicodemus and Joseph of Arimathea). Not everyone was out to vilify Jesus.

Jesus Questions a Messianic Title 12:35–37

After affirming the scribe, Jesus questions a scribal term. "Son of David" was one of the traditional descriptors of Israel's coming messiah. Everyday people used it to describe Jesus, but, apparently it was a misnomer. This is why Jesus points out that David himself referred to the "Son of David" as Lord. If so, how can David's son also be his Lord? The ever-present religious leaders were undoubtedly nonplussed while the crowd were delighted with the repartee.

Warning Against Showing Off 12:38–44

Mark includes an "aside", a departure from the stunning question Jesus had just asked which challenged conventional messianic nomenclature. It has to do with "grandstanding".

"Important seats in the synagogues… places of honor at banquets… lengthy prayers", and public displays of "large amounts" of money thrown into the temple treasury, are all condemned by Jesus. These maudlin performances by the "teachers of the Law" and the "rich" will lead to "severe" punishment, says Jesus. The true standard, he says, is the widow who, "out of her poverty" quietly, anonymously, "put in everything – all she had to live on" (v.44).

Giving "out of wealth" gains no traction with heaven. Even King David knew this when he said to Araunah the Jebusite that he would "not sacrifice to the Lord… burnt offerings that cost [him] nothing" (2Sa. 24:24). God is no restaurant waiter. He will not be tipped.

Jesus' Prediction About the Temple 13:1,2

This is brief but marks a watershed in the story. Jesus and the disciples were referred to as "Nazarenes", from Nazareth. In common parlance this meant they were seen as rough, untutored rustics. "Hillbillies". And, it's true that their world experience was narrow, so narrow that the buildings of the "big city" almost overawed them. The Temple buildings were especially impressive: "What massive stones! What magnificent buildings!" (v.1). Jesus responds, "every one will be thrown down."

This prediction was later misrepresented by false witnesses at Jesus' "trial" before the Sanhedrin, "We heard him say, 'I will destroy this Temple made with human hands and in three days will build another, not made with hands'" (14:57,58). This false testimony led to the high priest's question, "Are you the Messiah, the Son of the Blessed One?" Jesus' answer, "I am" was the final nail. It led to his crucifixion.

And, there was a secondary aspect to this watershed: it catalyzed a question, "Tell us, when will these things happen?" (v.3). Jesus' response is referred to by commentators as "the little apocalypse".

The "Little Apocalypse" 13:3–37

The question posed by Peter, James, John, and Andrew was very human, reasonable, and expected. We all want to know "When?", as in "When will we get there?" Or "When should we expect you?" Or "When will my dream come true?" Much of our lives revolve around "When?" Jesus' response, however, was a warning. Our insistence on an answer to "When?" can induce deception (v.5). Those who demand dates, times, and seasons often create their own. There are as many end-time scenarios out there as there are those presumptuous enough to claim success in figuring everything out. Buyer beware.

There are as many end-time scenarios out there as there are those presumptuous enough to claim success in figuring everything out. Buyer beware.

With that caveat Jesus went on to give a brief overview of the end times. He was not assuming the status of an "oracle"; rather he spoke with the authority of heaven. For sure he "watered it down" for human consumption. But,"be on your guard", he said.

Discernment, not gullibility, is the watchword. Yes, things will heat up – "wars and rumors of wars… earthquakes… famines" – but these will not be the end, rather they will be the "beginning" (v.8). The pivot point will be "the Gospel… first [to] be preached to all nations" (v.10). Everything else, be it family betrayals, wonder-working self-appointed "messiahs", or war zone atrocities, will all be collateral to heaven's core value of evangelizing the nations. So, he calls the disciples to "be on guard… be alert… watch!" There will be an end one day. One should live with a sense of historical and eschatological perspective at all times. The end will come suddenly. Everyone, including the self-styled prophecy experts, will be surprised. Keep your heads up! And keep the Gospel first and foremost in your thinking and in your doing.

Jesus' warning comprises twelve elements. Here they are:

1. False messiahs (v.6)

2. War (v.7)

3. National/international tensions (v.8)

4. Earthquakes and famines (v.8)

5. Persecution (v.9)

6. The Gospel to all nations (v.10). The generation that sees this accomplished will also see the end (v.30).

7. The "desolation sacrilege" (v.14). This was a major expectation of Jewish eschatology based on Dn. 9:27 and Ez. cc.9-10. It was seen as an "abomination" set up by some future conqueror whose image, statues or sacrifices would drive the presence of God from the Temple in Jerusalem.

8. Widespread tribulation (vv.14-20)

9. False hopes (vv.21-23)

10. Celestial convulsions (vv.24, 25)

11. The parousia (second coming of Christ) (v.26)

12. The ingathering of "the elect" (v.27)

He then tells the four disciples that only "the Father" knew when these things would take place. So, there was no use in speculating. Better to keep watch (vv.32-36).

Wednesday 14:1–11

Mark records, "Now the Passover and the Festival of Unleavened Bread were only two days away…" (v.1). Days begin and end at sundown in Israel. So Passover that year started at sundown on Thursday. The paschal lambs were sacrificed before the sun set on that day and then they were eaten at the seder before midnight (Thursday our time, but Friday "morning" their time). So, this was Wednesday – all day – with all day Thursday ahead before Friday "dawned" at sunset. Confusing no? (It took my wife and me months to get used to this when we moved to Jerusalem in 1981).

The chief priests and the Scribes had been huddled in strategy sessions, deciding they had to kill Jesus as soon as the Feast of Unleavened Bread had ended (seven days beginning with Passover). They planned to arrest him immediately. The killing would occur after the throngs of pilgrims (many from Galilee where Jesus was adulated) had gone back to their homes. They were in stealth mode (vv.1,2).

While these religious conspirators were percolating, Jesus was in Bethany on the southeastern slope of the Mount of Olives. He and the disciples were eating at the home of "Simon the Leper" (v.3). It was here that one of the most memorable events in the record of Jesus' life occurred.

It's a story of unmeasured extravagance on the part of an unnamed woman and Jesus' unbridled endorsement of this "waste of perfume" (v.4), even as it dripped from his hair and beard. Many of the dinner guests were "indignant", and scandalized even, by this unwarranted (as they saw it) and tasteless sensual act. For sure some of them thought Jesus should have stopped her in the act of pouring a whole bottle of spikenard over his head. Instead he allowed it. Perhaps some of them wondered, "Are they friends? Intimates?" It certainly seemed out of character. What's more, the perfume "could have been sold for more than a year's wages and the money given to the poor" (v.5). Jesus' response? A blunt, "Leave her alone."

Then he goes on to rebuke his detractors and to commend the woman. There are very few times in the gospels where Jesus appeared to be impressed. The young Scribe (12:28-34) comes to mind, as does the centurion (Mt. 8:5-13), and the widow who gave her all to the Lord (12:41-44). This over-the-top event is a case in point. Jesus was so moved by her "beautiful" act (v.6) that he declared she would be immortalized in history (v.9). Which is more than can be said for most of us.

There is a greater "scandal" than this "beautiful" act. It has to do with the dislocated interpretation many have given over the centuries to Jesus' comment, "The poor you will always have with you, and you can help them any time you want. But you will not always have me" (v.7). It's been used as a rationale for turning a blind eye to preventable poverty, a case for ignoring social justice. This certainly would offend Jesus. His comment, simply paraphrased, would be, "Look. There are beggars at the gates of Jerusalem, even at the gate of Simon's house who are legitimately in need. They're here today. They will be tomorrow, and tomorrow, and next week. I, on the other hand, will be gone. So lighten up." He was *not* establishing a "doctrine of the poor".

And there is one other point, albeit subtle, to be made. There is a case for extravagance from time to time. Those who reduce all personal interactions to a dollar sign not only lack imagination, they lack heart. Many things are priceless – especially acts of unmitigated love.

This subtlety was lost on Judas. In a fit of pique ("all this waste!") he went to the chief priests "to betray Jesus to them" (v.10). They received him with "delight" and offers of money. He played right into their hands. What's more his impulsive resolution forced their hands, too – they would now have to act immediately on their scurrilous scheme.

Thursday 14:12–72

Thursday (as it happened that year) was "the day of preparation" for Passover. There was a lot of work to be done before nightfall. But, like our holiday seasons (Christmas and Easter), people took a running start. Wednesday and Thursday would have been a bit breathless.

240

Before getting into the biblical account of the Passion, let's take a big breath and delve into the history and practice of the Passover:

In Deuteronomy 16:16 Moses instructs that, "Three times a year all your men must appear before the Lord your God at the place he will choose: at the Festival of Unleavened Bread, the Festival of Weeks and the Festival of Tabernacles." (See also Ex. 23:14-17). This provided a base for Israel's liturgical calendar of which Passover (the Festival of Unleavened Bread) was the first. To update your knowledge take some time and read Exodus chapter 12 where the plagues of Egypt culminated in Pharoah's "letting my people go" (7:14 – 11:10). Passover ("Pessach" – Heb.) refers to the death angel "passing over" the Israelite dwellings in Egypt while destroying all Egyptian first-born children and animals. This horrific night precipitated the Exodus.

The first Passover occurred on the eve of the fourteenth day of the first month of the Israelite calendar (Lv. 23:7,8), and has been celebrated at that time every year since. The Feast of Unleavened Bread started the next day and continued for seven days (Lv. 23:7). In Jesus' time as many as 100,000 pilgrims would gather in Jerusalem to take part in these feasts.

Before sundown (at about 3pm) on the 13th (Thursday in Jesus' story) the Passover lamb had to be slaughtered by the Levites at the Temple with the accompanying sacrificial sprinkling of the lamb's blood on the altar. The dressed animal, legs unbroken, head attached, wrapped in its own skin, was returned to the owners who then prepared the Passover meal.

The pilgrims who were unable to bring their own lambs would purchase a "ready made" slaughtered lamb that, in today's terms would have the "kosher" stamp of approval from the temple authorities (this was a big commercial enterprise). They would also rent a room for the meal. The less affluent would celebrate a barbecue-like feast out of doors by their tents. The dressed lamb was spitted on a stick of pomegranate wood, the head and legs folded into the body cavity, then roasted in a portable clay oven over hot coals. The entire sheep had to be eaten. If the group of participants (ten was a minimum) was large, each had to eat a piece of meat at least the size of an olive, while their appetites were satisfied with meat from a sheep not ritually slaughtered. The meal was served on low tables surrounded by cushions for reclining. The people were dressed in white.

If you've never participated in a seder, here's a brief overview of the modern ceremony, as we experienced it in our years in Jerusalem:

1. "Kadesh" – asah kadosh ("make holy"). The oldest male (leader) reads Genesis 1:31 – 2:3 and the family (and friends) say, "I am prepared and ready to fulfil the commandment of drinking the first of four cups of wine." This is followed by the blessing, "Blessed are you, Eternal our God, Ruler of the universe, who creates the fruit of the vine." The participants then drink the wine while leaning to the left.

2. "Urchatz" – wash hands. Cleanliness is a value in Hebrew culture.

3. "Karpas" – dip and eat a vegetable.

4. "Yachatz" – break the middle matzah (unleavened bread). This broken matzah is saved as the "afikoman" (to be hidden and found by the children at the end of the meal). This is a bit of a "treasure hunt" for the kids, perhaps as a way of keeping them involved in a lengthy family ritual.

5. "Magid" – tell the Passover story. This is a lengthy recounting of Israel's affliction under the Egyptians for four hundred years. It comprises stories from Israel's deliverance under Moses, including the Ten Plagues, miraculous intervention by God, songs of joy, and the drinking of the second cup of wine.

6. "Rachtzah" – wash hands and say, "Blessed are you, Eternal our God, Ruler of the universe, who has sanctified us through your commandments and directed us to wash our hands."

7. "Matzi" – bless the matzot saying: "Blessed are You, Eternal our God, Ruler of the universe, who brings forth bread from the earth."

8. "Matzah" – eat the matzah. Break into pieces, sprinkle with salt, distribute to the reclining (and leaning to the left) group.

9. "Maror" – eat the bitter herbs. Another blessing followed by dipping small pieces of bitter herbs into the charoset.

10. "Korech" – eat the "Hillel Sandwich". The leader breaks up the bottom whole matzah and makes "Hillel" sandwiches of matzah and bitter herbs saying, "As a remembrance of the Holy Temple, we do as Hillel did when the Temple still existed. He would combine the Passover offering, matzah and maror in a sandwich fulfilling the Torah's statement: 'With matzot and maror they shall eat it'". The group eats while reclining to the left.

11. "Shulchan Orech" – eat the passover meal.

12. "Tzafun" – eat the afikoman (after the children have run all over the house trying to find it – and they always do).

13. "Barech" – pour the third cup of wine and say grace at the end of the meal. This "grace" is lengthy, both recited and sung. After grace the third cup is drunk. Then the "cup of Elijah" is filled, and the door is opened just in case he may be at the door. The door is closed after Psalm 79: 6,7 and Lamentations 3:66 are read ("Pour out your wrath on the nations that do not acknowledge you, on the kingdoms that do not call on your name; for they have devoured Jacob and devastated his homeland... Pursue them in anger and destroy them from under the heavens of the Lord").

14. "Hallel" – fill the fourth cup and recite the Hallel (Ps. 113-118).

15. "Nirtzah" – pray that it be "pleasing". The meal (and the observance) is done. Conclude with, "Next year in Jerusalem!"

Both kings Hezekiah and Josiah had led national Passover celebrations (2Ch. 30 & 35) as reformers. As Hezekiah saw it, the people of Israel had abandoned the Lord, "Our parents were unfaithful; they did evil in the eyes of the Lord our God and forsook him. They turned their faces away from the Lord's dwelling place and turned their backs on him" (2Ch. 29:6). So, as one of his key reforms, after purifying the Temple (2Ch. 29) he called on Israel to "return to the Lord" (30:6) with the Passover celebration as catalyst to their repentance. It was, as Moses described it, "the Lord's Passover" (Ex. 12:14, 27).

Metaphors can be powerful. As Jesus led the disciples in his "Last Seder" he employed two: matzah as his body, and wine as his blood.

Jesus' Last Seder 14:22–26

Metaphors can be powerful. As Jesus led the disciples in his "Last Seder" he employed two: matzah as his body, and wine as his blood. The immediate impact of the metaphors was not felt. Later, however, the bread and the wine became enduring symbols in the history and life of the Church. To Jesus, this supper was *the* pivot point from the old covenant to the new. A new heaven and a new earth were on the horizon. No doubt the prophet Jeremiah had anticipated this moment:

> *"The days are coming declares the Lord*
> *when I will make a new covenant*
> *with the people of Israel*
> *and with the people of Judah.*
> *It will not be like the covenant*
> *I made with their ancestors*
> *when I took them by the hand*
> *To lead them out of Egypt*
> *because they broke my covenant,*
> *though I was a husband to them,*
> *declares the Lord."*

"This is the covenant I will make
with the people of Israel
after that time," declares the Lord.
"I will put my law in their minds
and write it on their hearts.
I will be their God,
And they will be my people.
No longer will they teach their neighbor,
or say to one another, 'Know the Lord,'
because they will all know me,
from the least of them to the greatest..."

—JER. 31:31-34

They finished the meal with the singing of a hymn, the "Hallel" (Ps.113-118) and then walked down in the darkness to the Kidron Valley and up to the Mount of Olives, one of Jesus' favorite locations for prayer.

The Disciples Don't Know Themselves 14:27–31

Mark, parsimonious with detail, doesn't tell us where this conversation took place. Was it on the walk to Gethsemane? Or in the garden itself? Maybe it was something Mark forgot to record as part of the Last Supper (this could be – for Jesus had received pushback when he said "one of you will betray me" v.18). Nevertheless Jesus bluntly tells them they "will all fall away". He knows they'll desert him. They don't believe him, and Peter, probably both offended and challenged said, "Even if all fall away I will not" (v.29). He even says he'll die with Jesus (v.31). And the others said the same. Obviously they had no idea what awaited. And, in terms of courage they were legends in their own minds. Indeed, as Jesus would observe a bit later, "The spirit is willing, but the flesh is weak" (v.38).

Gethsemane 14:32–42

The word "gethsemane" means "oil press". This was a garden where olives were crushed under the weight of a millstone and the oil extracted. In the Passion narrative Gethsemane was where Christ was "crushed" by the looming weight of mankind's sin and the pending crucible of the cross. In the vortex of eternity meeting time, there in the loneliness of Jesus' agonizing prayer the "Word" became "flesh". The gateway to our salvation was opened with the greatest words ever spoken. "Not my will, but Thine be done." The oil began to flow.

There were eight disciples reclining beneath the olive trees somewhere near the entrance to the garden and three accompanying Jesus into the interior. When they got to Jesus' favorite quiet place, Peter, James, and John threw themselves down to sleep. They had been up all night. Judas had departed from the last seder, and was absent. Jesus was alone about a "stone's throw" (Lk. 22:41) from the weary three, in agony of soul.

The question has often been asked as to how these slumbering disciples could have heard, let alone recalled, the words of Jesus' prayer. It's important to remember that Mark's gospel is a sketch, a summary, of Jesus' life. For sure there was much more unwritten than written. Indeed John, in his gospel says, "Jesus did many other things as well. If every one of them were written down I suppose that even the whole world would not have room for the books that would be written" (Jn. 21:25).

This is why I can imagine Peter dozing, then awaking, dozing some more and waking again as Jesus prayed. Maybe he even walked over to where Jesus had prostrated himself. I see Peter doing this because as stated in the Introduction to this commentary, I mentioned that Peter was the likely eye-witness to much of Mark's narrative. Mark simply recorded what he heard from Peter and added some of his own personal reminiscences as well. His gospel was a collaborative effort.

It is not insignificant that Jesus' words "Watch and pray so that you will not fall into temptation" (v.38) were directed to Peter. Temptation in this instance was not something fleshly, rather, it was something spiritual:

the temptation, when under stress, to desert. This, of course, was something that Jesus had already told Peter (v.30) he would do. As would all the disciples. Judas betrayed Jesus, the eleven deserted him. Willing spirits, weak flesh. Indeed, as my father used to say, "It is ever thus."

Betrayed, Arrested, Abandoned 14:43–50

Suddenly a motley mob of crudely armed men arrived in the darkness. Mark doesn't need to inform us that Judas was "one of the twelve" (v.43), but he's writing with a tone as if to say, "Can you believe this?!" The hastily gathered thugs were probably from the households (servants, etc.) of the high priest and other religious leaders. They were following Judas who had given them instructions. "The one I kiss is the man; arrest him and lead him away under guard" (v.44). The arrest happened quickly but not without incident. One of the disciples (the Apostle John says it was Peter – Jn. 18:10) drew his sword and swung wildly at the head of one of the ruffians. The man ducked and lost an ear.

Jesus submitted to this humiliation with the caveat, "the scriptures must be fulfilled" (v.49) and even as he was led away, the "we'll die for you" disciples abandoned him en masse. Jesus was all alone.

The Kangaroo Court 14:53–65

Jesus was taken in the early morning darkness to a hastily called trial before the high priest, chief priests, and Sanhedrin. This "trial" was an anomaly: in darkness, during the first half of Passover, probably not a full quorum, immediate condemnation, failure to call defence witnesses. The charge (claim to messiahship – not illegal by the way), false witnesses whose testimonies did not agree, in other words – a travesty. But they had him. Finally. And, they were *not* going to let him go even though they had no authority to hold him. Only Pilate had the power to arrest, judge and condemn a prisoner. But the cudgel-bearing gang outside the door and the contemptuous seething cadre of religious leaders within, fed an irrational atmosphere of mob-justice. Nobody but Jesus was thinking straight. Even Peter lost his bearings to his everlasting regret. The verdict was death. These religious sages spat it out, the toxicity of rage clouding their exalted status. They even spat on Jesus, the only one, in silence, to preserve his dignity. It was an ugly scene (v.65). And, as is often the case with ugly scenes, the ugliness and/or the virtue of the parties involved was laid bare. In this sense, the kangaroo court revealed the heart. One wonders who it was on trial and who really was the judge. Jesus' silence evoked Abraham's insight, "Will not the judge of all the earth do right?" (Ge. 18:25). As unjust as these proceedings were there was no doubt in Jesus' mind that the scriptures were being fulfilled (v.49). His Father's will was being done.

Peter's Emotional Breakdown 14:66–72

Peter had fled from Gethsemane with the rest of the disciples (v.50), but somewhere in his flight he had thought better of it and melded into the raucous mob pushing Jesus to the home of the high priest. He sat anonymously (so he thought) in the courtyard, "warming himself" by a bonfire (v.67).

This was the same Peter who had made the declaration at Caesarea Philippi, "Thou art the Christ, the son of the living God" (Mt. 16:16 KJV). The same Peter who had the temerity to rebuke Jesus when he warned the disciples about his impending death (Mt. 16:22; Mk. 8:32). The same Peter who boldly declared, "Even if all fall away, I will not" (Mk. 14:29). Indeed, the very same Peter who had seen Jesus transfigured on Mount Hermon and had been overcome with his glory, and flattened to the ground by the voice of the Father (Mt. 17:6). And now, he's put into a profanity fraught fright by a mere slave girl? Jesus had warned him. Peter had pushed back, "Even if I have to die with you, I will never disown you" (v.31). But now, the instinct for self-preservation trumped all else. He cursed and fulminated even as a rooster crowed, announcing the dawn. It crowed twice. Then Peter realized what he had just done.

There he was, the self-proclaimed
champion in a heap, in the corner,
his garment over his head,
overwhelmed with grief and shame.

He broke down in wracking sobs. Some commentators adopt the meaning of the Greek, "putting his garment over his head." There he was, the self-proclaimed champion in a heap, in the corner, his garment over his head, overwhelmed with grief and shame. At that moment he had no idea that his sorrow would lead to redemption (read about him in the book of Acts). Indeed, tears are often God's starting point in making us new.

Pilate Flummoxed 15:1–5

As the rooster's dawn materialized, the chief priests, elders (Sanhedrin) and Scribes "consulted" (KJV) and then tied Jesus up like a common criminal and delivered him to the Roman authority named Pilate. This pathetic parade of incensed religious leaders had no evidence for Pilate to weigh. They had only the power of a seething mob. If it's surprising to you that a mob, with such anger, could gather so early in the morning, take some time and read the classic "*Wars of the Jews*" by Flavius Josephus. Jerusalem was a boiling pot at that time, the fire stoked not just by Roman occupation, but also by various factions of "zealots" who in their fury were often greater enemies to their fellow Jews than were the occupiers.

Because of the lack of evidence against Jesus, the only possible option for Pilate was to find him guilty of political insurrection. That's why he put a spin (and a denunciation on the religious leaders) by asking, "Are you king of the Jews?" The "charges" were irrelevant. But "king" to a Roman meant "threat", and to the religious elite meant "Messiah" (blasphemy). Jesus gave no reply. Pilate was flummoxed.

Jesus Condemned 15:6–15

The Romans were "masters of the universe" at that time for a reason. Their vast empire from Britain to Egypt and Babylon was the product of a very powerful, disciplined army under military geniuses, with savvy Caesars in charge. But they maintained this mastery by showing grudging respect for regional religious practices, and relative fairness to the subjugated nations. An instance of this diplomatic skill was the "custom" in Jerusalem for the Romans "to release a prisoner whom the people requested" (v.6) at Passover every year. This act was a token of their "largesse". The people's choice this time was either Jesus or Jesus – "Jesus Barabbas" that is (Mt. 27:16).

Mark tells us "the chief priests stirred up the crowd to have Pilate release Barabbas…" (v.11). As I mentioned, the Jerusalem crowds were eminently stirrable at that time. Incitement was easy. Josephus tells us that there were a lot of insurrections, most of them led by zealots like Barabbas. Undoubtedly, Barabbas had become a household name by his incitements, murders, and nationalistic ardor. The crowd shouted for his release from prison. As for Jesus of Nazareth, the "Hosanna!" crowd had morphed into the "Crucify!" crowd. Pilate knew that the religious authorities had illegally arrested Jesus "out of envy" (v.10 KJV), and he knew that the mob was literally mad. He also knew what he *should* do. But he chose expediency. He released Barabbas and "handed [Jesus] over to be crucified" (v.15). He then betrayed his smallness by flogging Jesus to demonstrate that he was in charge. Brutal. The soldiers took him away to have their fun.

Jesus Mocked 15:16–20

The "whole battalion" (v.16 RSV) got involved in the demeaning horseplay. We're talking approximately six hundred men! They all joined in mocking the would-be king, "Hail King of the Jews!" Total humiliation was the goal. Jesus became the personification of all the hated Jews, thus the purple cloak, crown of thorns and the reed (scepter) which they eventually pulled from his hand to beat his crown of thorns into his head, saluting, spitting, and genuflecting. The madness of the mob had infected these usually self-controlled soldiers. They disgraced themselves. Then they led Jesus to Calvary.

Jesus Crucified 15:21–32

We call it "Calvary" because of Luke's translation of "skull" (Lk. 23:33). In other languages of the time "skull" was "cranion" (Greek), "golgolta" (Aramaic), "gulgolet" (Hebrew), and "calvaria" (Latin). But whatever the nomenclature it was the place where the Romans crucified insurrectionists and the Jews stoned adulterers and blasphemers. Situated on the road from the northern Jerusalem gates to Damascus, it was highly visible – a great place for authorities to demonstrate what happened to the unruly. Public shame was almost as punishing as public death.

The site has been romanticized by poets, artists, and preachers as a hill with three crosses on the horizon silhouetted against an ominous sky – "a green hill far away". In contrast imagine a limestone outcropping created by a stone quarry dug out of Mount Moriah. The western face of the quarry is vertical about one hundred feet high and dominated by three cave-like holes, in combination looking like the distorted face of a skull. The base of the hill is relatively flat, providing a lot of jagged stones for throwing. The stoning and the crucifying occurred there – at eye level. One could walk right up to someone hanging on a cross, curse them and spit in their face. It was a cruel place. Today it's the location of East Jerusalem's bus depot.

The cross is undoubtedly history's most recognized symbol – it is the most powerful "logo" ever, even eclipsing the ubiquitous "Coca Cola" signs covering most of the planet. But the stylized crosses hanging around hundreds of millions of necks, and adorning tens of thousands of churches are a far cry from the Roman reality.

There are no extant records of the number of Roman crucifixions. Some historians say thousands, if not tens of thousands. It was their favorite way of dispatching individuals and/or any group, large or small, who had the temerity to oppose Rome. It was "cruel and usual punishment".

Because of their far-flung campaigns they had to improvise with their crosses carrying no "ready-made" supply in their trains of equipment. So, if there were trees in the area, they would rope and/or nail victims to the trunks and branches. If the branches weren't suited to the task, they would create a crude crossbar ("patibulum") and attach it to the tree trunk. If a tree was unavailable, they would erect a post. The idea was to hang the man up, and let him hang in agony for days if necessary, his entire body screaming in pain. If he wasn't dead at a convenient time, break his legs, spear him if needed, then tear him down, throw his body to the side, and get ready for the next day's executions. As to tomorrow's victims there was one caveat: never crucify a Roman citizen. Regardless, there were more than enough foreign enemies to nail to the crosses. Indeed, Josephus records that a few years after Christ during the Jewish Wars the "multitude [of crucifixions] was so great that room was wanting for the crosses and crosses wanting for the bodies" (*"Wars of the Jews"*, Book 5, ch.11).

"And they crucified him" (v.24). Four blunt words, the pivot point of salvation history.

Cyrene was a coastal city in northern Libya. It had a large Jewish community, but its predominant population at the time of Jesus was Roman. Simon, a Cyrenian, was in Jerusalem for Passover. He had just come into the city and happened upon the raucous crowd surrounding Jesus as he stumbled under the weight of the patibulum. One of the Romans spotted Simon and pressed him into service as cross-bearer.

When they got to Calvary the Romans offered Jesus a painkiller. He refused. He chose to "taste death for everyone" (He. 2:9) awake. He would face the shame, the "curse" (Dt. 21:23), the pain and the ugliness with his sensibilities intact. "And they crucified him" (v.24). Four blunt words, the pivot point of salvation history.

252

As he hung on the cross, Jesus was fair game for mockers. He was reviled by head-shaking passersby, by the chief priests and Scribes, and even by the rebels crucified on either side. He truly was, in Isaiah's prophetic words centuries earlier, "despised and rejected by men, a man of sorrows and acquainted with grief" (Is. 53:3). And, to add insult to injury, the soldiers, the stewards of the cross, had a dice game at the foot of it, gambling for a share in Jesus' discarded, blood-stained clothes.

Often, with the most notorious insurrectionists, the Romans would hang a notice around the neck of the victim, outlining the charges against him. In Jesus' case, Pilate affixed a sign above Jesus' head, "The King of the Jews". This wasn't so much a slam against Jesus as it was a mockery of the chief priests' charge, and an ironic declaration of Jesus' place in history. It also protected Pilate in that he could justify his action to the authorities in Rome by this false public declaration of Jesus' seditious intent. Pilate was playing politics, a mean game.

Jesus Dies 15:33–41

Jesus was crucified at nine in the morning. At noon "darkness came over the whole land until three in the afternoon" (v.33). At that point he "cried out in a loud voice", quoting Psalm 22:1: "My God, my God, why have you forsaken me?" and breathed his last. His Father, of course, could not, and would not forsake his Son. But He did allow Jesus to go through the agonies of the cross. Jesus was quoting a messianic psalm written by David that had probably been at the forefront of Jesus' thinking as he hung on that cross for six hours. He might have rehearsed the relevant words,

> "All who see me mock me;
> they hurl insults, shaking their heads.
> 'He trusts in the Lord', they say,
> 'let the Lord rescue him'...
> All my bones are on display,
> people stare and gloat over me.

They divide my clothes along them
and cast lots for my garments..."

—vv. 7,8,17,18

He had prayed in Gethsemane that his Father's will would be done. And it *was* being done. Iron spikes could not frustrate his Father's sovereign plan to rip the curtain in two that separated mankind from his holy presence (v.38). Salvation would no longer be a once-a-year event mediated by priests. It would now be an everyday event mediated by "the Lamb of God who takes away the sin of the world" (Jn. 1:29). At that universe-piercing moment, however, there was only one person who got it: the Roman centurion, standing in front of Jesus as he died (v.30). "Surely this man was the Son of God!" he whispered in wonder. Meanwhile some of Jesus' faithful female disciples watched mutely from a distance (vv.40,41).

Enter Another Joseph 15:42–47

Arimathea was a town about ten miles northeast of Lydda, and about twenty miles east of Joppa (Lydda is modern-day Lod, the location of Israel's international airport, and Joppa is now Jaffa, part of metropolitan Tel Aviv). A prominent member of the Sanhedrin in Arimathea was a man called Joseph. He was rich, good, righteous and apparently someone who secretly admired Jesus.

Joseph was also courageous. It took intestinal fortitude to go to the top and ask Pilate to release Jesus' body to him. Even of greater magnitude was his willingness, as an ultra-Orthodox Jew, to risk social ostracization by ritually defiling himself in touching a dead body. He knew he would be forever suspect and would live on the margins of his Sanhedrin colleagues' religious circle. Touching a dead body was bad enough, but wrapping and entombing *that* dead body – the blasphemer Jesus! – was enough to stigmatize him for life.

Jesus died on "Preparation Day", the Friday ("Yom Shishi") before the Sabbath. Sabbath, of course, began at sundown on Friday, usually around five to five-fifteen pm. This means Jesus died about two to two-and-a-half hours before Yom Shabat began. So while the rest of the Jewish populace prepared for their "Kabalat Shabat" meal (Welcoming the Sabbath), Joseph prepared Jesus' body for burial. He buried him in "a tomb cut out of rock" (v.46) and "Mary Magdalene and Mary the mother of Joseph" watched as he rolled a stone across the entrance. In their eyes it was the final act of closure.

HE IS RISEN! 16:1–8

It may be that Jesus' death just before sunset on Friday precipitated a hasty burial. Perhaps Joseph intended to return twenty-four hours later to complete the wrapping of the body, a critical Jewish tradition and value. The women who had watched Joseph lay Jesus' body in the tomb no doubt saw that he had not been properly prepared. So they came at sundown on Saturday (the end of the Sabbath) to finish the task, by applying spices to mitigate the odor of decomposition. They hoped to get help rolling back the stone.

Imagine their astonishment ("trembling and bewildered" v.8) when in the fading light of the day they encountered an empty tomb with a "young man dressed in a white robe" (v.5) on guard. To these alarmed, speechless women he gave five declarative statements:

1. "He is risen."

2. "He is not here."

3. "Behold the place where they laid him."

4. "Go tell his disciples and Peter…"

5. "There you will see him."

Mark gives no other detail. Indeed, there is a common belief among biblical historians and commentators that the last page of his gospel was lost. The "conclusion" (vv.9-20) is believed to be a second century addition, for it is not included in the earliest manuscripts. So my casual commentary will end here.

But the major takeaway? "HE IS RISEN!

The Gospel of Luke

Introduction

When we refer to the "Four Gospels" we rarely, if ever, think in terms of the third gospel as a two-part work. But it is. The Gospel of Luke was written by "the beloved physician" (Cl. 4:14) Luke, a gentile from Alexandria, to a certain "Theophilus". We don't know specifically who this was, but we do know the title "most excellent" or "excellency" (Ac. 23:26; 26:25) was used to describe the Roman procurator of Judea, as well as high-ranking officials. So Theophilus is named in Luke 1:3 and in Acts 1:1 as the intended reader for Luke's history. It is an extensive two-part treatise comprising one quarter of the New Testament, larger in volume than all of St. Paul's epistles and the book of Hebrews combined. What's more, it is beautifully written, "a master in the art of Greek composition", with Luke "a superb artist with the pen", as some scholars have put it. It's a page-turner for sure.

Others have deemed it "the most beautiful book ever written", which is high praise indeed. Luke's purpose, however, was not style but substance.

He wanted to document the rise of Christianity in Israel (Gospel of Luke) and its spread to the Mediterranean basin and Europe (Book of Acts). With the scrupulous rigor of an historian he attempts to demonstrate the legitimacy of this new faith and its peace-loving, tax-paying, Emperor-respecting nature. Rome should not be threatened by Jesus. He's no insurrectionist. He also wanted to encourage Theophilus and the Roman authorities to be as lenient and protective of Christianity as they were with all religious sects in the Empire. Indeed, he wanted Rome to see Christianity as a world religion (ably demonstrated by the Day of Pentecost in Acts 2), and not merely a Jewish/Gentile mystery cult.

A distinct feature of Luke/Acts is the priority Luke gives to the person and work of the Holy Spirit. In the birth narratives of John the Baptist and Jesus, we see key figures like Zechariah, Mary, and Elizabeth "filled with the Holy Spirit". Simeon, a "righteous and devout" man of God who took the baby Jesus in his arms and blessed him, is described as "moved by the Spirit" who had "revealed to him that he would not die before he had seen the Lord's Messiah". Indeed "the Holy Spirit was on him" (Lk. 2:25-35). When Jesus preaches his first sermon in Nazareth (4:14-21) he quotes Isaiah 61:1,2 as a direct personal reference, "The spirit of the Lord God is upon me." Later, Luke describes Jesus as "full of joy through the Holy Spirit" (10:21), and as he's about to ascend to heaven after his resurrection he orders his disciples "to wait for the gift my Father promised" (Ac. 1:4) and that they would "receive power when the Holy Spirit comes on you" (v.8).

Acts (ch.2) records the fulfillment of that promise, and the Apostle Peter, in the first sermon of the early church, sees the outpouring of the Holy Spirit on the 120 in the "Upper Room" as a fulfillment of the Old Testament prophet Joel's insights (Jl. 2:25-32). Then, as the newly born faith spreads outward from Jerusalem to the world there are several references to the Holy Spirit's empowering.

Of those several here are eight:

1. Peter and John confer the gift of the Spirit on Philip's Samaritan converts (8:15-17).

2. The Holy Spirit is poured out on the Roman centurion Cornelius' household (10:47).

3. Peter (4:8), Stephen (6:8-10), Barnabas (11:24), and Paul (8:17) are each described as "full of" or "filled with" the Holy Spirit.

4. The Spirit "caught up" Philip on the road from Jerusalem to Gaza and dropped him at Azotus (8:39,40).

5. The Holy Spirit impressed the Antiochan church to commission Paul and Barnabas as missionaries (13:2,3).

6. The Holy Spirit endorsed the Jerusalem church council's decision to send out Paul and Barnabas with a key message to the Gentiles who were turning to Jesus (15:22,28).

7. The Holy Spirit forbade Paul and Timothy "to speak the word" in both Asia and Bithynia (16:6).

8. The Holy Spirit appointed the Ephesian elders to be "shepherds" or "guardians of the flock" (20:28).

These are just a few instances where the Holy Spirit is highlighted. In fact there are 74 references in Luke/Acts to the Holy Spirit. But all of these were mere reflections of Jesus' example. "Jesus, full of the Holy Spirit, left the Jordan and was led by the Spirit into the wilderness…" (4:1). There was no doubt – the promised "Comforter" had come (Jn. 14:15-17), and the whole world then, and for centuries to come, would feel his impact on history. Theophilus would be the first of millions of Gentiles to read the exciting story.

Preface 1:1–4

When something is described as "fully established" (v.1) one assumes that the evidence has been collected, cited, and given due process. There are no loose ends.

This is how Luke describes his "account" (NIV), "declaration" (KJV), "narrative" (RSV). It has been fully researched, fairly and rigorously examined, and can be trusted. This priority on accuracy was testament not only to Luke's integrity but to the regard in which he held Theophilus and the earth-shaking story of Jesus. In effect Luke is saying, "Your excellency, you've asked for the story. Here it is. It's an eye-witness story – I interviewed many of them carefully. I've put it together in orderly fashion, and it is the very best I could do. I'm hoping you'll accept it without reservation."

There is a distinct similarity with the preface in the Apostle John's first letter where he says, "That which was from the beginning, which we have heard, which we have seen with our eyes, which we have looked at and our hands have touched – this we proclaim..." (1Jn. 1:1). John would have been one of those eyewitnesses interviewed. Luke was looking to record the facts.

Facts are crucial. An old theologian once wrote, "Some religions can be indifferent to historical fact, and move entirely upon the plane of timeless truth. Christianity cannot. It rests upon the affirmation that a series of events happened, in which God revealed Himself in action, for the salvation of men" (C.H. Dodd, *History and the Gospel*, NY, Scribners 1938, p.15). Mere belief in a mystical Jesus is not enough. Our faith is based on an empty tomb. Yes, there is mystery. But there also is history. Both are vital. "And if Christ is not risen, your faith is futile; you are still in your sins!" (1Co. 15:17 NKJV).

THE ANGEL GABRIEL MAKES TWO ANNOUNCEMENTS 1:5–56

First to Zechariah (1:5–25)

In 1Ch. 24:1-19 we read that the temple priesthood was divided into 24 divisions. The priests served in cyclical intervals throughout the year. Zechariah belonged to "the priestly division of Abijah" (v.5), which was the 8th division (1Ch. 24:10b). Elizabeth, his wife, was also of priestly descent, "of the daughters of Aaron". Luke tells us that Zechariah was serving "In the time of Herod king of Judea", which suggests that the boy babies about to be born (John and Jesus) were born before 4BC, the year Herod died.

Zechariah and Elizabeth are described as "righteous" and "blameless" (v.6). I'm not sure what these descriptors suggest, other than that they were not guilty, in a legalistic sense, of transgressing the 613 laws of Moses. Perhaps Luke is merely reporting that they were upstanding citizens. Regardless of their moral stature, however, they were childless (v.7), due to Elizabeth's barrenness and their "very old" age. Having a baby at their advanced years was out of the question.

Like all priests, Zechariah was called to service in the Temple but not guaranteed of any specific task. The greatest honor was to burn incense (either after the morning or evening sacrifice) in the "Holy Place" right next to the veiled entry to the "Holy of Holies" where only the high priest was allowed once a year on the Day of Atonement. This great privilege and responsibility was determined by a lottery (v.9). It just so happened that this day Zechariah "won the lottery".

So there he was, all alone, his hands trembling (perhaps) with the excitement of the moment, burning incense at the small "altar of incense." And it *was* small – ⁶only one by one "cubits" square and two cubits high. It had four "horns" (one at each corner), and was overlaid with gold. The fragrance symbolized the presence of God. For Zechariah it would be a fearful moment.

That ambient fear was suddenly magnified as "an angel of the Lord appeared to him, standing at the right side of the altar…" (v.11). Dread "fell upon him" (Gk.).

Gabriel (v.19) announced something astonishing – Zechariah and Elizabeth were to have a son! This, of course, was not unique. Manoah's wife, also had an angelic messenger come unannounced to say she would have a son (Jg. 13), and Elizabeth's cousin, the virgin Mary, was about to have a similar experience (Lk. 1:26-38). The birth of Samson,

---

⁶ In ancient times there were three measurement standards for a cubit: the ordinary of approximately 17.6 to 18 inches; the royal of 20.9 inches; the infrequently used 21.6 inches. Most commentators assume that the "Royal" was used in any description of the Temple.

John, and Jesus demonstrated Heaven's hands-on engagement with earth.

It's interesting to factor into theological discussions about when a believer is "indwelt with the Spirit" (at conversion? after?) to read Gabriel's "he will be filled with the Holy Spirit even before he is born" (v.15). With that extra-natal anointing John will one day minister "in the spirit and power of Elijah" (v.17). His ministry will be all about repentance and preparation, both prophet and forerunner. His fiery words will ignite a slumbering nation to the purposes of God. Little wonder he "will be great in the sight of the Lord" (v.15).

Zechariah had prayed for a son over the years but apparently without conviction.

Zechariah had prayed for a son over the years (v.13) but apparently without conviction. This is why he "did not believe" Gabriel's words (v.20). A touch short in patience, Gabriel condemned Zechariah to almost a year of silence, making his priestly role very difficult. In fact, the people were gathered in the temple courtyard to receive the expected blessing from the Holy Place. But, Zechariah came out both late and dumb, correctly interpreted by the people as his having seen a vision (v.22). He had a lot to talk about but couldn't.

Luke doesn't tell us how Zechariah explained (with "signs"? v.22) to Elizabeth what was going on, but somehow they connected. Soon, to their amazement, she was pregnant. Elizabeth went into self-imposed seclusion for the last five months of her pregnancy (v.24). Why she did we don't know. It may have been the norm. Luke doesn't say. She may have feared a miscarriage, and she would not want her friends and neighbors to witness the humiliation that would bring. Childlessness was enough of a "disgrace" (v.25). She couldn't bear the shame of a pregnancy that was not full term. So she hid her swollen belly.

"Hail, thou that art highly favored" 1:26–38

Another angelic announcement occurs in this passage. In the first, Gabriel spoke to the aged priest Zechariah. In the second he speaks to a teenager, Mary. Zechariah and Elizabeth were an old married couple, whereas Mary and Joseph were not married. They were "betrothed", probably from Mary's childhood, but betrothal had the same legal status as marriage. In fact, a young man's engaged intended was often referred to as his "wife". There was no "marriage", however, before sex. So Mary was a virgin. Jewish religious and social norms expected no less.

John was conceived by intercourse between "seniors", whereas Jesus was conceived by the unilateral agency of the Holy Spirit. John was "filled" (v.15) with the Holy Spirit probably at the moment he "leaped" in Elizabeth's womb (at 6 months) upon the greeting from the pregnant Mary (v.41).

As I wrote in the Introduction, Luke/Acts has a strong emphasis on the presence and the work of the Holy Spirit in the history of Jesus' birth, life, death, resurrection, and the spread of Christianity to the world. Here, at the beginning of Luke's account, the Holy Spirit enters the stage. John is "filled" with the Holy Spirit from the womb, and Jesus' conception is effected by the "overshadowing" work of "the power of the Most High" (v.35). That "power" is the Holy Spirit.

As she stood at the cross some 34 years later, Mary (not yet 50 years of age) might have reflected with more than a measure of dismay at the meaning of "highly favored" (v.28). The "favor" of God would mean: running ("with haste" v.39 KJV, RSV) into hiding with the self-secluded Elizabeth in an obscure Judean village, embarrassment before her people in Nazareth, a semi-secret wedding (?), an arduous donkey ride to Bethlehem, birthing her son in a stable, a demanding donkey ride to distant Egypt, humiliating reports of Jesus' ministry and seeming rejection by Jesus ("Who is my mother...? Mt.12:48; "He is out of his mind..." Mk. 3:20,21), her son accused of sedition and blasphemy before a Roman procurator and hung on a cross before a mocking crowd, and years of confusion and disappointment. Perhaps there was a modicum of prescience in her response to Gabriel: "greatly troubled" wondering "what kind of greeting this might be" (v.29).

But, in just a few sentences, Luke describes Mary's response: troubled (v.29), bewildered (v.29b), questioning (v.34), assured (v.37), submitted (v.38a), and obedient (v.38b). No doubt, she's the greatest woman ever to have lived.

Mary Visits Elizabeth 1:39–56

Luke doesn't tell us to which town "in the hill country of Judea" that Mary "hurried", but it has been seen for centuries as Ein Kerem, about three miles west of Jerusalem. It's a beautiful, peaceful village with the prominent church of St. John the Baptist situated at the highest point on the hillside.[7]

The narrative is rather breathless at this point. Mary hurrying, breaking in on the unsuspecting pregnant Elizabeth, the fetus "leaping" in her womb at Mary's excited greeting, and Elizabeth loudly shouting "Blessed! Blessed! Blessed!" (vv.42-45). Blessed is belief! Blessed is faith! Blessed is obedience to God!

In response to her cousin's powerful benediction Mary "sings" a beautiful psalm closely echoing the "Song of Hannah" in 1Sa. 2:1-10. It is called "the Magnificat", one of the most hauntingly exquisite hymns in the praise of God that has ever been sung. This young woman "of low estate" exalts the Lord of history who has cared for "his servant Israel", the hungry, those of "low degree", has humbled the rich and the proud, and has been true to his covenant with Abraham. The song ends. Three months later John is born and Mary heads home to Nazareth.

THE BIRTH OF JOHN 1:57–80

John's birth was enveloped in unusual and unexpected drama. There was the angelic announcement, the "dumbing" of the unbelieving father, the

---

7   My wife and I have a special connection with Ein Kerem – one of our grandsons was born there.

seclusion of the mother, the visit of the pregnant cousin, the surprising news to the village, the circumcision/naming of the child, the sudden "un-dumbing" of Zechariah, and the "fear" that fell "on all their neighbors". Little wonder they asked, "What then will this child be?" The conventional had been eclipsed by the unconventional.

Luke's ongoing theme of supernatural "infilling" continues – "his father Zechariah was filled with the Holy Spirit, and prophesied…" (v.67). With that divine unction Zechariah sings a hymn composed of random quotes of and references to several psalms and prophetic oracles (Ps. 41:13; 111:9; 132:17; 106:10; 105:8,9; Mi. 7:20). The major theme is God's "remembrance" of "his holy covenant" made with Abraham and its fulfillment in a messianic "horn of salvation" from David's "house". A Redeemer is about to enter the stage of Israel's salvation history. The "Son of the Most High" (v.32), will have his "ways" prepared by John, who will be known as "the prophet of the Most High" (v.76). His call will be to a repentance that will "give knowledge of salvation to his people in the forgiveness of their sins" (v.77). Darkness and death will yield to the dawn of peace.

That glorious day, however, would have to wait for a couple of decades. John had to grow from a baby to a man, his development cultivated in rustic settings, producing a strong spiritual/prophetic backbone (v.80). Indeed, he would become "tough as nails".

THE BIRTH OF JESUS 2:1–20

Caesar Augustus, the great-nephew of Julius Caesar, was born Gaius Octavius and was adopted by his great-uncle as son and heir. He ruled the Roman Empire from 27BC to 14AD. Indeed, more than ruler, he was seen by many as the de-facto founder of the Empire. And rightly so, in that he extended Roman dominion throughout the Mediterranean basin to Europe, Britain, and the fringes of Barbarian territories in western Asia. His highway infrastructure is legendary – beautifully built brick roads, with milestones and markers for travellers, so well constructed that many exist in the 21st Century (I have walked some of those brick ways in Britain). The city of Rome itself was literally transformed under Augustus, metamorphosing brick to marble. He was brilliant, wealthy, and seen by Romans as a god. His authority was absolute.

One night, in the shadows of a far corner in one of Rome's occupied provinces, a baby was born. Augustus wouldn't have known about the birth. Why should he? And if he did why would he care? Babies were being born all the time, especially to poor young couples, perhaps under no humbler circumstances than this particular baby. There is nothing much more obscure than a cattle stall and a manger. The gulf fixed between the aroma of animal droppings and the perfumed, marble corridors of palatial Rome was too great to be bridged. Augustus slept in comfort while a young mother wrapped her newborn son in swaddling clothes…

Historians and commentators alike often go to great lengths to explain Luke's reference to Quirinius as governor of Syria at the time. Quirinius was Syrian legate after Herod's death, not before, thus Luke's reference to both John and Jesus being born "in the time of Herod" (1:5) would factor him out. I think we have to cut Luke some slack here – like all historians his default in a grand story is broad brush strokes. His intended reader, Theophilus, would not have been concerned about academic rigor. He had larger interests.

Judea was a Roman province, and as a subjugated people, the population festered under Roman occupation. The pressure to revolt was huge, and there were any number of nationalistic zealots who tried to light the powder keg from time to time. The messianic hope was percolating too. Small groups of zealous religious people were sure Messiah was about to appear. The Essenes, a sectarian religious separatist sect, were gaining momentum, as were small groups meeting for prayer and Torah reading in synagogues all around the country. The atmosphere was ripe for leadership.

So, in an atmosphere charged with resentment at foreign occupation, fanatic religious nationalism, and messianic fervor, a baby was born in Bethlehem. On the one hand it was just another birth. On the other it was earth shaking.

Many scholars, theologians, and commentators find the concept of a virgin birth to be incredible, if not offensive. To mitigate, if not outright deny this perceived insult to reason, there are predictable references to ancient virgin birth myths: eg. A poem found at Ras Shamra in 1933 – "A virgin (bethulah) will give birth"… "Lo, a young woman (almah) bears a son"; unusual birth narratives in the Old Testament: Ishmael (Ge. 16:11), Isaac (17:19), Moses (Ex. 2:2), Samson (Jg. 13:3,5,7), Samuel (1 Sa. 1:20) and a few others. The most controversial is Is. 7:14 – "Therefore the Lord Himself will give you a sign: Behold, the virgin shall conceive and bear a son, and shall call His name Immanuel" (NKJV). The controversy revolves around the word "virgin", which is the translation for two Hebrew words used in the Old Testament. One, "almah", refers to a young, marriageable woman. The other, "betulah", refers to a maid, or maiden. Almah *implies* virgin (premarital sex in Old Testament days was anathema), whereas bethulah specifically connotes total chastity. Thus, according to the detractors of virgin birth, the fact that Isaiah chooses to use "almah" rather than "betulah" leaves the door open at least to the possibility of sexual experience before marriage.

Luke, however, uses the Greek word "parthenos" to denote "virgin". Parthenos is usually employed to translate the Hebrew "betulah". The implication is clear: there was no sex before marriage for Mary. It's important to be aware that the Greeks saw virginity as a core value in their goddesses – their goddess Athena was also called Parthenos (to this day the Athenian temple in Athens is called "the Parthenon"). So the proper use of "parthenos" to describe a young woman was definitive. Theophilus would read it no other way.

The broad strokes of Luke's history, however, had little time for quibbling over technical etymologies. The big picture was clear: before Joseph and Mary slept together she was found to be with child "of the Holy Spirit" (1:18,20). The "overshadowing" ("episkiazo" – Greek) of the "Most High" would catalyze this one-of-a-kind pregnancy. The child to be born would be "holy" and called "Son of God" (1:35). Heaven would touch earth nine months later in a manger. This happened because the "Most High" made it happen. Virgin birth disclaimers, notwithstanding, it's true, or it's not.

Luke tells Theophilus about the census, which required subjugated territories to call the population to their hometowns for registration. These would be male citizens, females were not included. He gives no explanation for Mary's joining Joseph on the arduous trek on the back of a donkey from Nazareth to Bethlehem. Maybe Joseph didn't want her to be alone for the impending birth. Maybe she, like her cousin Elizabeth, had been in seclusion during her pregnancy and Joseph didn't want the birth to create public scandal in Nazareth. Maybe she simply wanted to see Joseph's extended family. Whatever. We can only speculate.

In half a sentence Luke records that Jesus was born (v.7a). Then he says Mary placed the baby in a "manger", a feeding trough for animals (v.7b), and there was no guest-room available (v.7c) hence the stable. The word translated "inn" in some versions is "kataluma" in the Greek. Its primary meaning is "guest-room". This suggests that Joseph probably took Mary to the house of his extended family for shelter, but the home was already full with other family travellers. So they may have resorted to the family stable, a cave over or beside which the house was built. For sure the family members would have made it as clean as possible for the weary couple. There they took up residence with their donkey. The other animals would have kindly made room.

There were other animals too: sheep in the fields being "watched at night" by their shepherd protectors (v.8). They would have been asleep in one of the several caves in that region while the shepherds sat around a campfire under the stars. Suddenly, like a flash of lightening, an angel appeared above them flooding the sky with the brilliant "glory of the Lord" (v.9). The shepherds were struck with terror. I imagine a few of them were flattened to the ground while one or two others fled into the cave to hide among the startled sheep. Dread, terror and sensory overload, as always, accompanies the sudden, overwhelming radiance of God. But the first word from the angel was, "Fear not".

I suppose, from the angel's perspective, there was nothing to fear. But, even as the shepherds were prostrate, hiding, and trembling from the visible shock of the heavens opening, there was more. The thunderous symphony of myriad angels' voices cascaded upon them with ground-shaking praise to God, "Glory to God in the highest, and on earth peace good will toward men"! These humble, illiterate laborers were caught in the vortex of heaven come down to earth. It's a wonder they lived to tell about it. The glory of God is a fearsome thing.

Fortunately the shepherds *did* live. What's more, even as they described to others what it had been like to be caught in that whirlpool of fear and wonder, they were also able to recount the angel's message, "unto you is born this day in the city of David a Savior, which is Christ the Lord…" (v.11).

"Savior" derives from the Hebrew root "to save", or "salvation". "Christ" means "anointed one" or "Messiah". "Lord" means "sovereign". The baby in the manger is all three, says the angel. I need to take some time and examine all three.

The nuance of the Hebrew word "yesha" ("salvation") is that of a "widening of the way" to "deliverance". Salvation is a progressive movement from desperation to safety, from distress to peace. There is always an outside agency in salvation, a champion/hero, a deliverer, a Savior who sweeps into the chaos, and leads the sheep to pasture.

There is always an outside agency
in salvation, a champion/hero, a deliverer,
a Savior who sweeps into the chaos,
and leads the sheep to pasture.

In the Old Testament that champion is the Lord, "the God of our salvation" (Ps. 68:19,20), who saves Israel from real enemies. Indeed, "the battle is the Lord's" (1Sa. 17:47). Yahweh's deliverance is never abstract. Salvation is more than "I got saved!", as an old guy put it to me on one occasion. Saved? From what? By whom? To what end? I'm sure he meant he had accepted Christ "as his Savior", which is a good entry-level decision. But salvation is much more than an initial step of faith.

The pinnacle of salvation history in the Old Testament was God's miraculous deliverance of Israel from Egyptian slavery: "That day the Lord saved Israel from the hands of the Egyptians" (Ex. 14:30). This definite, absolute act of deliverance provided Israel's future national and international signature as "a people saved by the Lord" (Dt. 33:29). What's more, this salvation was a "continuous present" in Israel's ongoing conflicts with other nations: "the Lord your God is he that goes with you, to fight for you against your enemies, to give you the victory" (Dt. 20:4). From victory to victory, from defeat back to victory, Israel learned what it means to grow "from faith to faith" (Ro. 1:17). Salvation is a work in progress.

This progressive work was often presented in the Old Testament as a partnering, tandem effort with judges, "Then the Lord raised up judges, who saved them…" (Jg. 1:16), or with kings, "About this time tomorrow I will send you a man from the land of Benjamin. Anoint him ruler over my people Israel; he will deliver them from the hand of the Philistines" (1Sa. 9:16). These leader/deliverers were anointed and empowered by Yahweh (Ps. 20:6) to defeat Israel's enemies, and in that empowering there was confidence that "nothing can hinder the Lord from saving by many or by few" (1Sa. 14:6). Often the human partner was woefully deficient so the Lord would step in, as always, and the victory would be his (Pr. 21:31).

The dynamic strain of this divine-human interaction produced an awareness on the part of the Old Testament prophets that the ultimate deliverance was " 'Not by might nor by power, but by my Spirit', says the Lord Almighty" (Ze. 4:6)… "Yet I will show love to Judah; and I will save them – not by bow, sword or battle, or by horses and horsemen, but I, the Lord their God, will save them" (Ho. 1:7). Indeed, "Salvation is of the Lord" (Jo. 2:9 KJV), and the gifted partner-judge-king foreshadowed an eschatological Savior who would one day, as the "anointed one", rule the world.

So, even though the shepherds may have been illiterate, they were not unaware of Israel's hope. When the angel said "Savior" they knew exactly what he meant.

"Savior" was then followed by "Christ" ("anointed one") which is Greek ("Christos") for "Messiah" (Heb. "Mashiach"). The messianic hope, as I've already indicated, was a future hope, but in the context of the Roman occupation that expectation had moved from simmer to boil. This overpowering angelic announcement hit the sweet spot of Israel's heart's desire.

Generally in the Old Testament "mashiach" refers to "the Lord's anointed", that is – "king". He was to be a righteous deliverer. Israel's first king, Saul, was exactly that at the beginning of his reign (see 1Sa. 11). He was anointed by the Spirit (1Sa. 11:6) and brought victory to Israel over the Amalekites. He eventually fell from grace and David took his place as partner, or co-regent, with the Lord – "the Lord and his anointed" (Ps. 2:2). It was to David that the Lord, through the prophet Nathan, promised, "Your house and your kingdom will endure forever before me; your throne will be established forever" (1Sa. 7:16). Thus the term "Son of David" became the most common descriptor throughout subsequent centuries for "Messiah".

"Savior" and "Christ" (Messiah) were followed by "Lord" in the angel's announcement. This term is as old as Genesis 1:1. "Elohim" means "God" or "Lord". It is a title of ultimate sovereignty. A word study of "el" (god, God), "eloah" (god, God), and "elohim" (gods, God) is a large undertaking. Let me summarize.

Semitic-speaking peoples in ancient times commonly used the name "El" for a generic god and/or for the God of Israel. In the generic sense "El" could refer to a god, a "mighty" force, or simply "strength". In the Old Testament "El" is often qualified with descriptive words: "The great El" (Je. 32:18), "El doing wonders" (Ps. 77:14), "El of Els" (Dn. 11:36), "El, the God of the spirits of all flesh" (Nu. 16:22; 27:16), "El who sees me" (Ge. 16:13), and on and on…

El is described as faithful, holy, truthful, almighty, heroic, knowledgeable, glorious, eternal, and even jealous. These compound names all describe "the one El" (Ma. 2:10) who is the only "Living El" (Js. 3:10). The El of Israel has no rival. He is Lord.

In "the Song of Moses" (Dt. 32), just before his death on Mount Nebo, he employs the word "eloah" in parallel to "rock" to describe the Lord:

"They abandoned the God who made them
and rejected the Rock their Savior.
They made him jealous with their foreign gods
and angered him with their detestable idols.
They sacrificed to false gods, which are not God -
gods they had not known,
gods that recently appeared,
gods your ancestors did not fear.
You deserted the Rock, who fathered you;
you forgot the God who gave you birth."

—VV.15B,16

"Eloah" is an ancient term. Indeed, the book of Job, the oldest of the books in the Old Testament, utilizes it forty-one times. It is also employed infrequently in other books (Isaiah, Proverbs, Habakkuk, Psalms, 2Chronicles, Nehemiah, Daniel) where the Lord is described variously as a "shield" for those who find refuge in Him, a "terror" for sinners, and the personification of "strength".

The plural form of "Eloah" is "Elohim". It's called "a majestic plural", as in Queen Elizabeth referring to herself as "we". The verbs used with Elohim are consistently singular. On a few occasions the personal "Yahweh" is added to the general Elohim (Ge. 2:4,5; Ex. 34:23; Ps. 68:18). In Israel today God is referred to as "Adonai" ("my Lord") or "Ha Shem" ("the Name").

Many of the Elohim references describe God as Creator ("God, Former of the Earth" Is. 45:18), Sovereign ("God of All the Earth Is. 54:5; "The Lord God of the Heaven and God of the Earth" Ge. 24:3), and Judge ("God Judge in the Earth" Ps. 58:11). But perhaps the most common usage refers to God as "The God of Abraham, the God of Isaac, and the God of Jacob" (Ex. 3:6). Then, there is one obscure Elohim title that I love, "The God of Nearness" – "Elohay Mikarov" – (Je. 23:23). Regardless, this is only a summary. Much more could be said about the "Elohim of Justice, of Certainty, and of Eternity."

The shepherds rushed into Bethlehem to see this wonder for themselves. Luke mentions no house to house search but simply states that they found Jesus and then "spread the word". The people were amazed by the shepherds' report and Bethlehem was soon astir with the story. Mary, on the other hand, exulted in the moment, even as the shepherds' loud, excited praises to God faded in the distance. The "Word" had been "made flesh", and there the hope of the nations lay, asleep in a manger.

THE BABY AND THE BOY 2:21–52

Jesus was circumcised on the eighth day (v.21), and true to Jewish custom was given a name, in this case according to the angel's instructions (1:31). Historically, women were not present at circumcisions (in modern times that practice is not uncommon in ultra-Orthodox Jewish communities) but Luke makes no mention of those present. What followed was the rite(s) of purification for the new mother.

Leviticus 12:1-7 provides the historical/cultural context for Mary's "purification" (v.22). Mothers in Israel were "unclean" for seven days after the birth of a son, and were separated from society for another thirty-three days. After that they were required to offer a purification sacrifice at the Temple. If the baby was female the mother was unclean for two weeks after the birth and was isolated for sixty-six days before her mandatory purification. Her atonement by the priest required a "year-old lamb for a burnt offering and a young pigeon or dove for a sin offering" (v.6). If she was poor she was "to bring two doves or two young pigeons" in order to "be clean" (v.8). Mary and Joseph were poor, so they did the latter (Lk. 2:24).

The story gives no information as to why and how Simeon, an aged priest/prophet, was available for the purification rites, other than he had been "moved by the Holy Spirit" (v.27) to be at the Temple that day. Unlike Zechariah who was obliged to be there at certain times (1:8), Simeon was under no scheduling protocols, other than the Spirit's prompting. Perhaps he was retired. But Luke stresses his spiritual maturity and obedience to the Holy Spirit (vv.25-27). What is more, Simeon had heard from the Lord that he would live to see "the Lord's Christ" (v.26 KJV). Jesus would be "the consolation of Israel" (v.25).

This godly old man gently cradled the eight-day-old baby in his arms and uttered the third great hymn of Luke's gospel, the "Nunc Dimittis" (vv.29-32) – the other two being "The Magnificat" of Mary (1:46-55) and "The Benedictus" of Zechariah (1:68-79). His words resonate to this day:

"Lord, now lettest thou thy servant
depart in peace, according to thy word;
for mine eyes have seen thy salvation
which thou has prepared in the presence
of all peoples, a light for revelation to the Gentiles,
and for glory to thy people Israel."

—vv.29-32 RSV

He looks at the baby in his arms and sees God's "salvation". Perhaps his well studied knowledge of the scriptures washed over him, "The people who walked in darkness have seen a great light… For unto us a child is born, unto us a Son is given…" (Is. 9:2,6), as he joyously declares that this baby is "a light for revelation to the Gentiles". No religious nationalist, Simeon had a broad worldview. "All peoples" would be saved, not Israel only, but Israel would share in the glory because one of their own, Jesus from David's city Bethlehem, had come into the world.

There is a pause as Joseph and Mary marvel at Simeon's song, and then, the ecstasy of the moment behind, he blesses them and utters a foreboding message:

"Behold, this child is set for the fall
and rising of many in Israel,
and for a sign that is spoken against
(and a sword will pierce through your
own soul also), that thoughts out of
many hearts may be revealed."

—vv.34b, 35 RSV

His statement was almost a paraphrase of Isaiah who foresaw the future messiah:

"He will be as a sanctuary,
But a stone of stumbling
and a rock of offence
To both the houses of Israel,
As a trap and a snare to the
inhabitants of Jerusalem.
And many among them shall stumble;
They shall fall and be broken,
Be snared and taken."

—Is. 8:14,15 NKJV

You can visualize Simeon's sorrowing eyes as he declares the future polarizing, saving and damning impact of Mary's son. Perhaps he wept as he warned her about her own eventual heartbreak. He handed the baby back.

Suddenly another elderly prophet, Anna, approached them "at that very moment" (v.38). Luke summarizes in one sentence her interaction with Joseph, Mary, and the baby, "she gave thanks to God, and spoke of him to all who were looking for the redemption of Jerusalem" (v.38). "The redemption of Jerusalem" was parallel to "the consolation of Israel" in messianic terms. Hers was the "micro" view: Jerusalem, Simeon's the "macro": "all nations". Both vital. Jesus will save the world, Jew and Gentile, nation by nation, city by city, one person at a time.

Jesus was no "boy wonder" as many of the Gnostic gospels portray him; rather, he was a mighty oak in the making, the greatest individual the world would ever know, the pivot point of salvation history, the Son of God.

Luke tells Theophilus that Joseph and Mary returned to Nazareth after these purification rites (v.39), and then summarizes Jesus' development over the next twelve years as growth physically, intellectually, socially, and spiritually (vv.40,52). His intellectual and spiritual growth is highlighted in the interesting "in my Father's house" incident (vv.42-49), where Jesus sat "among the teachers" in the Temple, "listening to them and asking them questions." It was evident that "grace" or "favor" ("charis" – Gk.) was upon him and his incremental development was under the careful cultivation of the Father Himself. Jesus was no " boy wonder" as many of the Gnostic gospels portray him; rather, he was a mighty oak in the making, the greatest individual the world would ever know, the pivot point of salvation history, the Son of God.

JOHN THE BAPTIST 3:1–4:13

Like many other writers of history, Luke synchronizes his narrative with the political and religious records of the time. The fifteenth year of Tiberius Caesar would have been somewhere in AD 28-29. This dating stands out in the gospels as unique, but demonstrates Luke's stance as an historian with a view to chronological rigor.

Roman procurators (or "governors") ruled Judea, which was part of the province of Syria, and during Jesus' ministry that governor was

Pontius Pilate (AD 26-36). Galilee was under Herod Antipas, one of the sons of Herod the Great. Another son, Philip, ruled in the north-eastern regions of Palestine, and Lysanias (not a member of the Herod clan) governed Abilene (a region including some of the Lebanese mountains, extending south-east to Damascus). Annas was high priest in Jerusalem from AD 6-15, and his son-in-law Caiaphas succeeded him in AD 18-36. Even though Annas had "retired" he was still a formidable force in legislating religious law. John's ministry took shape under the Annas family's (50-year) religious domination.

John's history revolves around this seminal statement, "the word of God came unto John the son of Zacharias in the wilderness" (v.2). He was no religious or nationalist zealot, rather, like the Old Testament prophets, he "spoke from God". His "wilderness" setting was probably the lower Jordan Valley region north of the Dead Sea. Luke says his message was "a baptism of repentance" (v.3).

To this day, both in Israel and around the Orthodox Jewish world, a cleansing bath, or baptism, is common for all devout believers. The ritual is performed in specially made pools called "mikvot" (plural). I have seen several of these while living in Jerusalem. They are usually small receptacles carved out of the living rock, big and deep enough for an adult to enter and totally immerse oneself. There is a dual stairway providing ingress and egress – enter unclean, exit purified. It's about preparation for worship.

So, the "multitudes" (v.7) who came for baptism were culturally tuned to immersion for cleansing, but were perhaps a bit off-put by John's characterization of them as a "brood of vipers". Their lack of push-back at this offence was evidence of their sense that the "Day of the Lord" was near. Luke describes their anticipation in biblical terms as an eagerness to "see the salvation of God" (vv.4-6, quoting Is. 40:3-5). The Roman occupation had fuelled a long simmering hope that Messiah would come and deliver Israel from the Gentiles. And, if our ritual cleansing will hasten the day then let's get on with it. Let the wild man preach and baptize. We want Messiah now!

Yet, there must have been some resentment at John's radical view of nationalistic privilege. Tracing one's lineage to Abraham wasn't good enough (v.8b). Israelite genes wouldn't cut it if the "fruit" of one's life was unrighteous and unjust (v.8a). Unless concern for the poor (v.11), integrity (vv.12,13), and, even for Gentiles, contentment and honesty (v.14) prevailed, there would be no hope for future peace.

John was quick to dash the hopes of many that *he* was the Messiah (v.16). Indeed, he diminished himself to a status lower than a slave (slaves tied their masters' sandals) and cast the Christ as supernaturally empowered, with a heavenly mandate to separate "wheat" from "chaff" (vv.16,17). Messiah would prove to be a harsh deliverer.

Jesus Baptized 3:21,22

After a brief reference to the tetrarch Herod's antipathy to John and his imprisonment of the wilderness baptizer (vv.19,20), Luke gives an equally brief account of Jesus' baptism. He tells Theophilus that after Jesus was baptized he was praying. During this quiet moment "the heaven opened" (v.21) and a physical descent upon Jesus of the Holy Spirit in the form of a dove was accompanied by "a voice from heaven" saying, "Thou art my beloved Son' in thee I am well pleased" (v.22 KJV). Luke makes no further comment. We don't know if this theophany was seen and heard by Jesus alone, or also by John, or by all the people. So any speculation is simply speculation. Luke moves on.

Jesus' Genealogy 3:23–38

For those trying to impose exactitude on genealogical records there will be frustration here. One cannot harmonize Luke's genealogical record of Jesus' ancestry with Matthew's. Some scholars have suggested that Matthew is concerned with Jesus' royalty, and Luke with Jesus' priest-hood. Nevertheless the emphasis should be on the narrative. When Luke employs the Greek word "hosei" ("about") with reference to Jesus' age at the beginning of his ministry (v.23) it suggest "approximately". Hard to be exact with that word. The key for Luke is the last four words of the genealogy: "the Son of God" (v.38).

Jesus' Temptation 4:1–13

Luke records that Jesus was "tempted by the devil" for forty days in the wilderness. Forty days is a long time, time enough for more than the three temptations that tested Jesus' self-control (vv.3,4), commitment to his calling (vv.5-7), and messianic identity (vv.9-12). Indeed, Jesus was probably tempted in many ways throughout the course of his ministry, even on one occasion by the voice of Peter who was summarily rebuked by Jesus as Satan himself (Mt. 16:23).

During this forty-day testing period, when Satan tempted him, Jesus replied with quotations from scripture (Dt. cc.6-8), even as Satan himself rehearsed the word of God (vv.10,11). The temptations pivoted on the word "if". Satan was attempting to capitalize on any doubts or insecurities Jesus might have had with his incarnate status. Perhaps Satan thought he could push Jesus' "kenosis" (Gk – self-emptying of the independent exercise of his divine attributes – Ph. 2:6-8) to uncertainty about his "nature of a servant". He failed of course. Jesus, "Son of Man" and "Son of God", was not about to be tripped up by any fallen creature, not even by the "prince of the power of the air" (Ep. 2:2 KJV) himself.

JESUS' MINISTRY BEGINS 4:14–5:16

Jesus began his ministry "in the power of the Spirit" (v.14). Luke prioritizes the Holy Spirit. He has just written that Jesus was "full of the Holy Spirit" and was "led by the Spirit" (v.1) in and to his wilderness temptations. In this passage Jesus quotes the prophet Isaiah with a personal application, "The Spirit of the Lord is upon me…" (v.18). The Spirit "anointed" him to preach, proclaim, heal, and liberate the poor, the captive, the blind, and the oppressed (v.18). And this ministry was not just short term but was long term as well – "the acceptable year of the Lord". "Jubilee" (Lv. 25), was about to dawn.

Jesus' listeners in his hometown synagogue (v.16) were prepared to give him the benefit of the doubt (v.22) but were quickly put off by his sudden insult: Gentiles are, and will be, more responsive than Jews to the work of God (vv.24-27). Their anger flashed into violence and they "drove him out of town" and tried to throw him over a cliff (vv.28-30). Jesus simply walked away. Neither Satan nor an unruly nationalistic mob had any power over him. A few years later another mob would "win" only because he let them. "Twelve legions of angels" (Mt. 26:53) were always on call.

Jesus in Capernaum 4:31–5:11

Jesus walked away from Nazareth all the way "down" to Capernaum (about 400 feet below sea level). Nazareth is on a ridge (1400 feet elevation) that the ancient International Highway ("the Way of the Sea") avoided, whereas Capernaum sat right on that major east-west trade route. His rejection by his boyhood home, painful as it may have been, provided a significant catalyst for change and the enlargement of the scope of his ministry. Neither Nazareth nor Capernaum are mentioned in the Old Testament because both were settled after the Old Testament period. But, Nazareth was situated in the territory assigned to Zebulun, and Capernaum sat in Naphtali's allotment (Js. cc.13-19). The prophet Isaiah foresaw the significance of these two regions centuries before Christ:

> *"In the past he humbled the land*
> *of Zebulun and the land of Naphtali,*
> *But in the future he will honor Galilee*
> *of the Gentiles, by the Way of the Sea,*
> *beyond the Jordan."*
>
> —Is. 9:1B

Jesus' move from the backwater of Nazareth to the vital metropolis of Capernaum was critical to the fulfillment of Isaiah's further words in that passage:

> *"The people walking in darkness*
> *have seen a great light;*
> *on those living in the land of deep darkness*

a light has dawned...
For to us a child is born,
to us a son is given..."

—Is. 9:2,6A

Indeed, the territories of Zebulun and Naphtali, the towns and villages along the International Highway (the "Way of the Sea") including the regions of the Decapolis and Perea ("beyond the Jordan"), and all of "Galilee of the Gentiles" saw "a great light". The "zeal of the Lord Almighty" (Is. 9:7d) was at work.

"Preaching in the synagogues..." (v.44) was a core value for Jesus. The first thing he did in Capernaum was preach (v.31). The synagogue was just steps from Peter and Andrew's house, Jesus' likely boarding place. The house would have been typical of the time, a basic rectangular building with a kitchen/eating room, a walled courtyard, an enclosure for a few animals, and two or three small bedrooms, all under a (usually) flat reed and hardened clay tiled roof.

No records exist with regard to the beginnings of the synagogue in Israel's past. Some ancient historians (Philo, Josephus) say the institution can be traced to Moses, yet there are no references to it in the historical books of Judges and Kings. More recent authorities say that the synagogue became a feature of Jewish life during the Babylonian exile when the people of Israel were unable to access the Temple in Jerusalem. Then there is a school of thought that suggests the synagogue took shape during the Persian era under the leadership of Ezra. No one seems to know for sure. What we *do* know is that there was a synagogue in Capernaum, as there were "places" according to Ps. 74:8 "where God was worshipped", scattered throughout "the land". The Capernaum synagogue, it would appear, was one of many in Judea.

An etymological study of the various Aramaic, Hebrew, and Greek names for synagogue is beyond the scope of this "casual" commentary, but one of the first descriptors was the Hebrew "bet am" which means "house of the people". This suggests that the synagogue was used for a number of purposes, civil, political, and spiritual. It certainly was not exclusively a place of worship. Some may even have had small inns attached to accommodate itinerant rabbis and students.

The Capernaum synagogue today is a beautiful sight. Constructed of white limestone blocks and pillars, the ruins stand (built in the 2nd century AD) on an original basalt foundation which some archaeologists think dates back to Jesus' time. Google: "model of Capernaum synagogue" to see a depiction. It was a two-storey building, the upper storey comprised of peripheral balconies where the women sat, the lower for the men. Attached to the lower storey was a partially covered courtyard. And, as is the case today, I expect there were beautiful shade trees surrounding the synagogue, as well as carefully tended gardens. It's a restful place.

His teaching astonished the people, as did his "authority". He taught, healed, and delivered the spiritually oppressed with seamless power, leaving the congregants with wonder.

So Jesus sat and taught on his first (?) visit to the synagogue. His teaching astonished the people, as did his "authority" (v.32). He taught, healed, and delivered the spiritually oppressed with seamless power, leaving the congregants with wonder – "What is this word? For with authority and power he commands the unclean spirits, and they come out" (v.36). There was no wonder on the part of the unclean spirits, however. Their response was terror – "Have you come to destroy us? I know who you are, the Holy One of God" (v.34). Jesus dismissed these petty powers with impunity. He was on to bigger things. So, after healing Peter's mother-in-law of a high fever, then taking a few hours sleep, he announced he was about to "preach good news of the Kingdom of God to the other cities also; for I was sent for this purpose" (v.43). The people implored him to stay (v.42) but he was adamant. The world awaited.

The First Recruits 5:1–11

As he was preparing to launch his itinerary to the "synagogues of Judea" (4:44), the people "pressed upon him to hear the word of God" (5:1a). This was more than insistence, it was physical. Jesus had to escape the huge number of people on the lakeshore by hopping into one of Peter's fishing boats where he sat and taught. There may have been several hundreds of people crowding the beach, intent on his every word. When he finished he suggested to Peter that they go fishing.

Peter agreed, under mild protest, having been fishing all night with no success; but out to the deep water they went. The catch broke the nets! Peter, James, and John (the future "Three") were overwhelmed but their response was unusual: "Go away from [us] Lord; [We] are sinful [men]" (v.8). They interpreted this catch as a miracle, and in the presence of the Miracle Worker they felt unclean. The moment was so powerful it catalyzed a radical, but fearful (10b) decision: to drop their nets and follow Jesus. It was an historic turning point with far-reaching implications.

Jesus Heals a Leper 5:12–16

In Leviticus 13:1-46 Moses describes in detail various afflictions of the skin under the general heading of leprosy. Some of these "defiling skin diseases" were temporary and curable. The priest determined the cure, or lack of a cure. Anyone whom the priest declared an incurable leper was required to isolate him/her self for the rest of their lives. Many chose to live outside the city gates in caves. Anytime a healthy person were to inadvertently approach, the leper was required to put his/her hand over their mouth and cry "Unclean!" It was anathema to touch a leper. Conversely a leper must never approach a healthy person. It was strictly forbidden.

Luke records a story of a leper who broke the rules. He boldly approached Jesus, humbly fell on his face in submission, and asked him for healing. Then Jesus broke the rules. He *touched* him! Anyone witnessing this exchange had never seen its like. They would have been amazed, if not horrified. Luke reports an immediate healing and, for the first of many times to come, Jesus charged the man "to tell no one" but to go to the medical authority, the priest, to receive a certificate of clean health as "a proof to the people" (v.14). Word quickly spread, however, and Jesus had to retreat "to the wilderness" (v.16) to avoid "the great multitudes gathered to hear and to be healed" (v.15). Luke gives no analysis but simply says of Jesus' occasional need for solitude, he "prayed" (v.16).

CONTROVERSIES 5:17–6:11

The "Scribes, and Pharisees" are usually seen as the antagonists in the gospel drama (with a few exceptions like Nicodemas, Joseph of Arimathea, and the Apostle Paul). The Pharisees were a strict religious sect concerned with the interpretation of the Mosaic law and the avoidance of ceremonial uncleanness ("prushim" – Heb. "the separated"). The Scribes ("saphar" – Heb. "cipher") were religious lawyers, the guardians of the Law. Scribes and Pharisees in tandem were formidable and intimidating, not just for their legalistic rigor but also because of their intransigence. In their view the way forward was to look backward. They tended to be humorless and brittle. Rules ruled. In this section Luke records five disputes they had with Jesus.

A Paralytic Healed 5:17–26

The relationship between sin and disease was seen as a given in Jesus' day. The view was: you're sick because you've sinned. There's nothing in the gospel records indicating that Jesus himself believed this, but if the people did then sickness carried a concomitant burden of guilt. This may be why, in this story, Jesus forgives the load of sin before healing the oppression of paralysis. And this led to major push-back from the Scribes and Pharisees.

On this occasion the house Jesus was teaching in was crowded inside and out. Some commentators suggest the house may have been a synagogue because of the presence of Scribes and Pharisees who "had come from every village of Galilee and from Judea and Jerusalem" (v.17). Just these gathered religious leaders might have filled more than one synagogue

Regardless, Luke describes the setting as a house (v.18). The roof, of course, would have been flat, and it could be accessed by an exterior stairway. The swarm of people would have discouraged any late-comer seeking healing, but an ingenious four men thought of a novel way to beat the crowd. They were carrying a friend of theirs on a stretcher, and they decided to take the stairs.

Imagine the scene. Jesus is sitting in the midst of sick, needy, curious, demanding, and pressing supplicants, under the glare of disapproving Scribes and Pharisees. He seems undisturbed by the disturbance, free from the stress of the moment. We don't know if he's dealing with one person at a time as the method of healing. Perhaps people are being healed spontaneously as he speaks. Luke doesn't say. Suddenly a piece of dried mud drops from the ceiling. Then another. And another. Now some dessicated rushes with more mud… then it seems like the ceiling is caving in. A stretcher-sized hole appears and before the people can comprehend what's going on, a young, paralyzed man is lowered "right in front of Jesus" (v.19). Whoa! "Why didn't I think of that!" someone mutters.

Jesus acknowledges the young man but his eyes are fixed on the eager faces staring down through the hole in the roof. Their eyes are full of expectancy. Jesus "saw their faith" (v.20) and was impressed. He turned to the prostrate paralytic and said, "Friend, your sins are forgiven." This immediately set the Scribes and Pharisees off. "Who is this fellow who speaks blasphemy? Who can forgive sins but God alone?" (v.21) they grumbled. They were right. No one can forgive sins but God. That was the point. This is why, in response to this non-verbal attack Jesus referred to himself as "Son of Man" (v.24). This title was never conferred on Jesus by the gospel writers. It is always used as a direct quote from Jesus himself. It may have reverberated in the more than ninety times it is used in the book of Ezekiel referring to God's prophetic messenger. Or it may have reflected the profound implications of Daniel (7:13,14) where "one like a son of man coming with the clouds of heaven" is given by "the Ancient of Days" total "authority, glory and sovereign power" and "an everlasting dominion" and a "kingdom that will never be destroyed". Then, to demonstrate his "authority to forgive sins" he healed the young man and sent him on his way rejoicing (v.25). Unlike the crowd, the Scribes and Pharisees stifled their amazement and gave no praise to God. Something had to be done about this presumptuous upstart.

A Man is known by his Friends? 5:27–32

The citizens of Israel and Judea hated tax-collectors for a few compelling reasons. First, nobody likes to pay taxes. Second, these tax collectors were fellow sons of Abraham who'd been hired as sub-contractors to highly-placed Jews who had won major contracts from the Roman occupiers to collect a certain quota of shekels every tax season. Third, they got a percentage of the money plus whatever surcharges they could force their fellow citizens to pay. And fourth, they had the authority to send delinquents to prison. Little wonder they were persona-non-grata. Tax collectors were seen as scum, right down there with adulterers, drunkards, and prostitutes. The only ones who would associate with them were, in the words of that famous country song, "Friends in Low Places".

Jesus, on the other hand, bore tax collectors no ill will. In fact he called one of them, Levi, to follow him as a disciple (v.27). Then he attended a "great feast" (v.29) put on by Levi in honor of the occasion. Levi's "friends in low places" were many. The Scribes and Pharisees spluttered and fumed at Jesus' indiscriminate behavior but he responded to their pique by saying it's the sick who need a healer; a double 'entendre': there are those who suffer affliction of the body, and there are those who suffer affliction of the soul. Take stock, Scribes. Look in the mirror, Pharisees. You're very ill indeed.

To Fast or Not? 5:33–35

The Scribes and Pharisees fasted twice a week. It was a core value in their piety. Apparently John the Baptist and his disciples fasted (v.33) as well, but Jesus' disciples did not. This lack of rectitude troubled Jesus' detractors. It provided them yet another opportunity to find fault. Jesus had a quick answer: nobody fasts at a wedding! And at the risk of impiety one might infer that no one fasts in heaven – ever.

New Wine Skins 5:36–39

The eating/not eating theme then transitioned to a drinking metaphor. Jesus refers to the common sense practice of storing new wine in new wine skins. New wine expands as it ages, new wine skins stretch to accommodate the fermentation. An old wineskin would simply burst due to lack of elasticity. The application is clear: the Gospel is new wine, the Oral Law of the rabbis is an old wineskin. Little wonder the Scribes and Pharisees couldn't handle Jesus' teaching. Indeed, as they saw it, "the old is good" (v.39). The new was stretching them to the bursting point. Within a few years the religious leaders would burst in an explosion of fury, and deliver the "Son of Man" to the Romans to be crucified.

Two Sabbath Controversies 6:1–11

What were the Pharisees doing following Jesus and his disciples through farmers' fields? You get a mental picture of Jesus walking, a small circle of disciples surrounding and/or following, a larger group of hangers-on in their train, and a bunch of surly Pharisees hurrying after them at a distance, desperate to find fault. Any fault.

This, by the way, was the Sabbath. The Pharisees must have leapt into the entourage at an opportune moment where they didn't transgress the law about "a Sabbath day's journey". The Jewish historian Josephus describes a Sabbath day's journey as approximately 5 to 6 furlongs (a furlong is 606 feet, 2 inches), translating to about 3000 – 3600 feet. When

Joshua was leading the children of Israel across the Jordan he ordered them to follow the lead of the Ark of the Covenant at a distance of "two thousand cubits" (Js. 3:4). This became the traditional view of a Sabbath day's journey (approximately 3000 feet – a cubit is the measurement of a man's arm from the elbow to the end of the middle finger – 1.5 feet on average). For many, however, this was an inconvenience, so the Scribes came up with a plan doubling the allowable distance to 4000 cubits from one's residence. Their solution was to establish one's "home" 2000 cubits away by carrying two meals, before the Sabbath, to a chosen location. At that spot one meal was eaten, and the other stored in a hole or under a rock, thereby creating an official Sabbath "home". Then, one could walk from his weekly residence to his Sabbath residence visiting friends and family on the way, and return having walked 4000 cubits without transgression! Ingenious. Regardless, the enforcers were in the fields, looking to catch Jesus and his disciples in a Sabbath violation. And they did.

"Harvesting and threshing" on the Sabbath were forbidden in a list of 39 Sabbath proscriptions mandated by rabbinic Oral Law. Jesus' disciples were doing what I and a lot of other prairies kids did/do when walking through a ripe grain field, picking some of the heads of grain, rubbing them in their hands, and eating the kernels (v.1). It's a tooth-cruncher for sure.

The Pharisees jumped on this blatant ad hoc harvesting and in a scolding tone demanded, "Why are you doing what is unlawful on the Sabbath?" (v.2). Without skipping a beat Jesus answered their question with one of his own. "Have you never read what David did," in 1Sa. 21:1-6? The subtle suggestion that they are biblically illiterate could have silenced them, but Jesus' reference to David's eating "consecrated bread" shut their mouths for sure. They couldn't acknowledge that human need trumps the letter of the law. "It is ever thus" (as my father used to say) with all legalisms and legalists throughout history. "How we've always done it" takes precedence over what needs to be done. Freedom is too scary.

Luke records no rejoinder by the Pharisees to Jesus' declaration, "The Son of Man is Lord of the Sabbath" (v.5). They doubled back on their Sabbath day's journey to regroup and challenge the upstart rabbi on some future occasion. Perhaps they might catch him in some other Sabbath violation.

"On another Sabbath" Jesus "went into the synagogue and was teaching" (v.6). One of the congregants was a man "whose right hand was shrivelled." True to form the Scribes and Pharisees were there as well, hoping Jesus would offend rabbinic interpretation of the law by healing someone on the day of rest. They were silent, however, still smarting perhaps from the interchange with Jesus in the grain field. So their rancor was non-verbal, but palpable. Jesus knew what they were thinking (v.8). Their malice was exposed by their grudging silence at Jesus' question, "I ask you, is it lawful on the Sabbath to do good or to do harm, to save life or to destroy it?" (v.9 RSV). Whereupon Jesus called on the man to stretch out his hand. Stretching out a hand that heretofore could *not* be stretched was a stretch of faith on the cripple's part. But he did it, and he was healed. There was no need for Jesus to repeat his "Lord of the Sabbath" declaration. His detractors were "filled with fury" (v.11 RSV) and slunk out to hatch a plan (v.11).

> *Stretching out a hand that heretofore could not be stretched was a stretch of faith on the cripple's part. But he did it, and he was healed.*

THE SERMON ON THE PLAIN 6:12–49

The Upper Galilee is very hilly. It's very difficult to find anything other than slopes and valleys. There *is*, however, a level area of a few hundred acres just west of Capernaum on the northwest shore of Kinneret. It is called the plain of Gennesaret and it extends from Tabgha to Magdala.

There is another plain on the northeast shore of the Lake called the plain of Bethsaida. Luke doesn't identify either as the locale for the Sermon, but I think it was either Gennesaret or Bethsaida. The reason it has been referred to traditionally as the "Sermon on the Plain" is to distinguish it from the "Sermon on the Mount". The "Plain" sermon is more succinct and compact than the "Mount", but the essential content is similar. As a preacher myself, I'm very familiar with preaching the same sermon more than once. Yet, even though the content is the same, the style of delivery and the content emphases usually are adaptable to the given time, place, and "congregation". I see no need to attempt to reconcile the "Plain" with the "Mount", as some commentators do. Jesus' message was fluid, not static. It flowed like a river from town to town, working over the souls of men and women with the transforming water of life.

After a night of prayer somewhere on a "mountain" (v.12 KJV) or "hill" (RSV) Luke writes that Jesus called a larger group of disciples to join him, and chose twelve from among them to be "apostles" (v.13). They were Simon (renamed Peter, "the Rock"), Andrew (Peter's brother), James and John (sons of Zebedee), Philip (from Bethsaida), Bartholomew, Matthew, Thomas (the twin), James (son of Alphaeus), Simon (the zealot), Judas (son of James), and Judas (man of Kerioth) (vv.14-16). There is no reference to an "induction ceremony" or to any instructions from Jesus, simply "he came down with them, and stood in the plain…" (v.17 KJV). A huge crowd of needy people were waiting (vv.17b-19).

Then, healing "them all" (v.19) he "lifted up his eyes on his disciples" (v.20) and began to preach. He started with four "beatitudes" followed by four counterpoint "woes". The contrast is stark: poor (v.20b) contrasted to rich (v.24), hungry (v.21) to full (v.25), sad (v.21b) to happy (v.25b), and vilified (v.22) to celebrated (v.26). These polarities are seen in the broader context of "that day" (v.23) which refers to "the Day of the Lord", a future event where Messiah is revealed and the justice of God, reward and punishment, is satisfied. On that day poverty, hunger, sorrow, and alienation will be forever banished even as the rich, full, happy, and socially valued are exposed as empty vessels. The rich will "mourn and weep" (v.25b) even as the afflicted "rejoice" (v.23).

There may have been a few rich people in the crowd. If there were, they might have found Jesus' words a touch harsh. What's wrong with being rich? Why is it bad to be full? Isn't happiness everyone's goal? And certainly, good social standing is a value! All true, but...

There are as many as 2000 references to money in the Bible. Some of those give grim warning about riches. One of the sternest passages on the subject comes from Jesus' half-brother James:

> *"Now listen, you rich people, weep and wail because of the misery that is coming on you. Your wealth has rotted, and moths have eaten your clothes.*
>
> *Your gold and silver are corroded. Their corrosion will testify against you and eat your flesh like fire. You have hoarded wealth in the last days. Look!*
>
> *The wages you failed to pay the workers who mowed your fields are crying out against you. The cries of the harvesters have reached the ears of the Lord Almighty. You have lived on earth in luxury and self-indulgence. You have fattened yourselves in the day of slaughter. You have condemned and murdered the innocent one, who was not opposing you."*
>
> —JA. 5:1-6

Again and again the biblical writers attribute the accumulation of wealth to the exploitation of the poor. Their bent backs bear testimony to injustice. In our day we credit material success to vision and work ethic, but even as we do so, thousands of the poorest of the poor (mainly women) work 12-hour days in the sweatshops of failed states in order for us wealthy westerners to wear the latest ready-made fashions, paying the uber-rich sportswear companies twenty to thirty times the manufacturing cost. Historically, wealth has always had a bad smell. The only way to mitigate the odor is to seek and provide justice for the poor. Jesus took it one step further. The Apostle Paul tells the Corinthian Christians about "the generous act of our Lord Jesus Christ, that though he was rich, yet for your sakes he became poor, so that by his poverty you might become rich" (2Co. 8:9). Rich reward in Heaven is Jesus' gift to the faithful. Then there is his warning to the Church in Laodicea, "you say, 'I am rich, have become wealthy, and have need of nothing' – and do not know that you are wretched, miserable, poor, blind, and naked…" (Re. 3:17 NKJV). Woe indeed.

The "New Wineskin" Laws of Love and Mercy 6:29–45

Jesus then transitions to two of the key elements in the ethics of the Kingdom of Heaven. The first is love. Clearly he is not referring to unsustainable romantic infatuation. Emotions come and go. Rather he is underscoring the volitional commitment that is at the root of all enduring love, and to emphasize the point he calls his listeners to love their enemies. It would have been an impossible command if he had instructed them to "like" their enemies. Like is a feeling. Love is a decision. One can decide to seek the higher good of anyone, including enemies. This action is unconditional, forgiving, and kind. As such it reflects the very nature of the Father (v.35c). You may never like those to whom you show love, but at least you've done the right thing, comprised, as Jesus puts it, of three components: "do good… bless… pray" to and for "those who hate you… those who curse you… those who mistreat you" (vv.27,28). A tall order, followed by something taller still: "Do to others as you would have them do to you" (v.31).

Mercy is gut-level love. We are to actively show forgiveness and generosity to those who physically abuse us (turn the other cheek v.29a), and steal from us (give them more than they stole v.29b). I don't think for a moment that Jesus is saying we should turn a blind eye to sexual assault or wife or child-beating. What he's talking about is the cut and thrust of human dynamics where people are pushing ahead, oblivious to harm done to others. Injury and injustice are the inevitable collateral damage of selfish behavior – Jesus says we should take it in stride and be merciful. It's too easy to push back. Adding fuel to the fire is counterproductive.

The "Golden Rule" is always the best strategy for conflict resolution. The "children of the Most High" (v.35b) know this, and extend grace even to "the ungrateful and wicked" (v.35d).

To Judge or not to Judge? 6:37–45

The operative word in this passage is "blind". Only someone blind to his/her own weaknesses will "judge" and "condemn" (condemnation is usually the goal of judgement). We see behavior on someone's part, we don't like it, it offends us, it's not "right", and we condemn them even as we judge them. In doing so, we self-aggrandize, blind to the possibility that we judge ourselves in judging the other. How do we identify bad behavior in someone else without some awareness of the same tendency in ourselves? But we're blind to our own sins, even as we're blind to the history of the offender we're so quick to condemn. We judge in the dark.

Jesus put it succinctly, "Do not judge, and you will not be judged" (v.37a). We'll not be judged by whom? By the other guy? Or by God himself? Obviously Jesus is referring to divine judgement, which throws our rush to judgement of others into another light. He follows this warning with "Forgive, and you will be forgiven" (v.37c). His point is powerful: If you want to avoid God's judgement don't judge your neighbor, and if you want God's forgiveness you've got to forgive your neighbor. It's a quid pro quo.

The Apostle Paul wrote, "now we see through a glass, darkly..." (1Co. 13:12 KJV), meaning we are essentially blind to the mysteries of life even as we contend for our view of things. He may have been thinking of Jesus' words, "Can the blind lead the blind? Will they not fall into a pit?" (v.39). And a "blind" teacher will have blind students (v.40). At best we have irritated eyes, so how can we see to remove the irritation in "our brother's eye"? (vv.41,42). It's humbling to acknowledge that our neighbor's faults can be trumped by our own. Indeed, our judgements may baldly reveal "What the heart is full of " (v.45). If we can't say something good about our neighbor it's best to say nothing at all.

Two Houses 6:46–49

Jesus concluded his sermon on the plain with three powerful sentences. First of all, calling Jesus "Lord" has meaning only if his words are put into practice. Those who do so lay a deep, immovable foundation for their lives. Those who don't, fall into ruin. Any intermediate or executive authorities, be they leaders or doctrines, may be instructive, but are not foundational. Jesus says we're to start and finish with him. The hymn writer put it well:

> *"My hope is built on nothing less than Jesus' blood*
> *and righteousness… On Christ the solid rock I stand,*
> *all other ground is sinking sand."*
>
> —EDWARD MATE 1834

ADDED DIMENSIONS TO JESUS' MIRACLES 7:1–17

Jesus returned to Capernaum where he was approached by a delegation of Jewish elders with a request from their local Roman centurion. This was unusual but the elders explained their mission by reminding Jesus that this Gentile "loves our nation and has built our synagogue" (v.5). A much loved slave was ill, and the anonymous centurion was asking Jesus to heal him. In his message he expressed his familiarity with delegated authority and humbly believed that Jesus could take authority over his servant's affliction just by saying the word (vv.6b-8). Jesus was impressed. He "said the word" and the man was healed. So, without seeing or touching the sick slave, or conversing in person with the centurion, Jesus responded to "such great faith". Risking raising a few nationalistic hackles he said he hadn't seen the like "even in Israel" (v.9). He was no "respecter of persons" (Ac. 10:34,35 KJV) but he certainly was a respecter of faith.

Luke then records Jesus' miracle of raising a dead man to life in Nain. As the crow flies Nain is about twenty miles from Capernaum. It would have been an arduous walk. He and his disciples may have overnighted at the

294

foot of Mount Tabor. A "great crowd" (v.11 RSV) accompanied Jesus and the Twelve as they approached the town, where they encountered another large crowd about to exit the gate. This was a funeral procession. A much loved (it would appear from the size of the crowd) widow had just lost her only son. His bier was being carried to the graveyard outside the town walls. Jesus "saw" (v.13) the grieving widow and was immediately moved with compassion. He walked to the bier and, eschewing ritual defilement, touched it and said, "Young man, I say to you, arise" (v.14). The young man immediately sat up and began to talk. The two crowds became one in their "fear" (v.16) at what they had just witnessed. They glorified God in wonder, proclaiming "God hath visited his people!" (v.16c KJV). They credited Jesus with being "a great prophet", the category "great" suggesting he was of equal stature to Israel's mighty men of God who had raised the dead in the past (Elijah and Elisha – 1Ki. 17:17-24; 2Ki. 4:17-22, 32-37). Little wonder Jesus' fame spread (v.17). His miracles were multi-dimensional.

JESUS AND JOHN THE BAPTIST 7:18–35

What follows is a cautionary tale, an illustration of how a political/ religious agenda can eclipse a powerful revelation from heaven itself.

Luke's narrative of Jesus' baptism by John (3:21,22) is very brief, but profound. The profundity lies in the report that "heaven was opened and the Holy Spirit descended" on Jesus "in bodily form like a dove" and "a voice came from heaven: 'You are my Son, whom I love; with you I am well pleased'." This was classic theophany. And, with respectful regard to those who interpret otherwise, what if John both saw the dove and heard the voice of God? "Bodily form" and "voice" seem to imply an audience. If, indeed, John bore witness it then helps explain his later conundrum when his disciples brought a report about Jesus' ministry (v.19).

John had expected a warrior messiah. It's likely that he had inter-preted the dove and the voice as confirmation that the "Deliverer" had come. Like his Essene counterparts (Google: "Essenes") John believed that the "Day of the Lord" was about to dawn; thus, his baptisms of repentance were intentionally designed to prepare a purified people for that event. The "King" was at the door. Soon a throne would be established in Jerusalem, the Roman occupiers would be routed and Messiah would rule the world. But John's disciples' report of Jesus' ministry disturbed him. In fact he began to think he'd got it wrong. This is why he sent a loaded question to Jesus, "Are you he who is to come, or shall we look for another?" (v.19 RSV). The glorious theophany at the Jordan had been cast into a dark shadow of eschatological doubt and disappointment.

Jesus' response to John? Your concept of messiah is skewed. He sent John's messengers back with a veiled rebuke, referencing Is. 35:5,6; 61:1. To this list of messianic qualifications Jesus added "lepers are cleansed" and "the dead are raised up" (v.22). Then he added a personal note of his own disappointment, "Blessed is he who takes no offence at me" (v.23 RSV). They *were* cousins afterall. Jesus expected more of his friend.

John was not a politically correct
servant of the status quo, not easily swayed,
not self-serving. Rather, he was a prophet
of the Elijah-Elisha school,
a fist-in-the-jaw kind of preacher,
the greatest spokesman of all time.

Jesus then turned from this in camera discussion to the Twelve and the public. He raised his voice above the crowd noise and began to praise John, the wilderness prophet who, at that point, had a longer ministry track-record and greater fame than Jesus himself. John was not a politically correct servant of the status quo, not easily swayed (v.24), not self-serving (v.25). Rather, he was a prophet of the Elijah-Elisha school, a fist-in-the-jaw kind of preacher, the greatest spokesman of all time (v.2-8). He was the forerunner to the coming of Messiah and the inauguration of a "Kingdom of Heaven" era that would culminate in the Day of the Lord. As such he was the personification of Malachi's prophecy: "I will send my messenger, who will prepare the way before me" (Ma. 3:1).

John marked a tipping point in the history of God's dealings with mankind. As such he represented the last of the great biblical prophets, even as he announced the new era of grace. Thus, even as the greatest of the past, he was the least in terms of God's voice in the present (v.28). It would not be John, but Jesus, who would declare, "He who has seen me has seen the Father" (Jn. 14:9). Nevertheless, Jesus, God incarnate, humbly saw himself as a servant ready to obediently die that humankind could be saved from his Father's wrath at sin (Ph. 2:6,8). But it was John who prepared the way of the cross.

Jesus then capped off his defence of John with a scathing rebuke of the religious establishment (vv.31-35). He compared these unbelievers to children playing make-believe with the game of "weddings and funerals". They played "weddings" with music and dancing, but John wouldn't sing or dance – therefore he was a demoniac (v.33). Then they played "funerals" with weeping and wailing but Jesus wouldn't mourn – therefore he was a carouser (v.34). These were foolish children. The "children of wisdom" were the "am ha aretz", the everyday people, the tax collectors and sinners (v.35). They were "new wineskins" whose lives would expand with the transforming new wine of grace.

The Prostitute and the Pharisee 7:36–50

Why would a righteous Pharisee invite a notorious "glutton and a drunkard, a friend of tax collectors and sinners" (v.34) to his house for dinner? Obviously he was intrigued, and maybe he was an "undecided voter", ready to cut Jesus some slack. Then again maybe Simon (the Pharisee's name) liked living on the edge. Luke doesn't say. Jesus was seen entering the house and word spread. Were sparks going to fly?

Both the KJV and the RSV translations say, "And behold…" (v.37), which in the Greek means, "Look! See! Lo!", an expression of surprise and amazement. In the context it's more like, "can you believe this?!" Not only was Jesus' arrival at Simon's house shocking to the onlookers, but now *she* had arrived! What was a prostitute ("a woman of the city" – street walker) there for? Luke's sources may have suggested that tongues were wagging. This dinner was shaping up to be a gathering like that at Levi's house (5:27-32).

For Simon's dinner guests the meal turned into a bit of a scandal. The "woman of the city" walked into the room, stood by Jesus' feet (people reclined to eat), then bent down wetting them with copious tears, wiping them with her hair (!), kissing (!!) and anointing them with ointment from "an alabaster box" (vv.37-39). Everyone rushed to judgement, with Simon making the decision that Jesus was no prophet – "If this man were a prophet, he would have known who and what sort of woman this is who is touching him," he said to himself (v.39). Jesus, knowing what Simon and the others were thinking, answered with a parable about a moneylender and two insolvent debtors (vv.41-43).

The story had a simple point: those who love much have been forgiven much. The woman's over-the-top behavior (vv.44-46) indicated her profound sorrow for her life choices and her overwhelming hope for God's forgiveness. When Jesus said, "Your sins are forgiven" (v.48), there was no theological conflict in her mind – of course he can forgive me, he is Son of God. Simon, on the other hand, and the other dinner guests, still dwelt in the wasteland of oral tradition, "Who is this, who even forgives sins?" (v.49 RSV). They resisted the new wine, conflicted, while the woman left the room "in peace" (v.50), no longer "a woman of the city" but now a woman of the Kingdom.

THE TRAVELLING TEACHER AND MIRACLE WORKER 8:1–56

The Itineration Begins 8:1–3

Luke had a high view of the women who accompanied Jesus and the Twelve. They are prominent in his gospel. A case in point is his highlighting three of them as Jesus begins his itineration "from one town and village to another" (v.1). He mentions Mary Magdalene, who had been delivered of serious oppression (v.2), Joanna, the distinguished wife of a senior official in Herod's court, and the historically obscure Susanna. Apparently all three were significant financial supporters of the itinerant band (v.3b).

Mary Magdalene figures largely in all four gospel accounts, especially in the events surrounding Jesus' resurrection. She was a Galilean from Magdala, a wealthy fishing and trading center. Anytime Jesus walked south from Capernaum along the western shore of the sea he would have gone right through the town. There is no mention of when Jesus first met her, no support for the view that she was a prostitute, nor is she to be identified as the woman in chapter 7. She wasn't Mary of Bethany either. She was present at Jesus' crucifixion, came to anoint his body after his death, reported the empty tomb and the angelic message to the Eleven, and, most importantly, was the first to personally encounter Jesus after his resurrection. She was a major player.

The Parable of the Sower 8:4–18

When commenting on the Sermon on the Plain I made the point that preachers (including me) often preach the same material from time to time, not only to their church congregations, but to other audiences when guest-speaking somewhere. Luke tells Theophilus that "from town after town…" (v.4) Jesus told the same parable. It's one of the best known: the parable of the sower.

Many times in the 1980's on my journeys from Jerusalem to the Upper Galilee I saw sowers sowing seed. They would have a bag slung over their shoulder hanging (usually) on their left hip. As they walked the fields they would reach with their right hand over to the bag of seed, gather a handful and sling it out in an arc. Occasionally I'd see a farmer doing this in the early morning as I drove to our radio station in Southern Lebanon, and he'd still be at it in the early evening on my return down the Jordan Valley. What intrigued me the first time I saw it was their broadcasting of the seed on the fields *before* ploughing. This way they could plough the seed *into* the ground.

The parable is not about seed. Rather it's about soil. The implied question is, what kind of soil are we? Hardened (path)? Superficial (rocky)? Distracted (thorns)? Fertile (depth)? The key component is depth, which is exactly what Jesus is getting at when he explains the purpose of parables in response to his disciples' dull-headedness (v.9). Heaven's truth is not for the merely curious, whose depth goes no farther than the senses (shallow seeing and hearing v.10b). Depth of "soil" is depth of soul, and it is critical when "Deep calls unto deep" (Ps. 42:7). So as God's voice speaks, "Be careful how you listen" (v.18). Think deeply about what you're hearing. And remember God sometimes speaks "in a still small voice" (1Ki. 19:11-13 KJV).

Jesus' Extended Family 8:19–21

Luke chose to ignore the troubling detail that Mark includes re: Jesus' view of his family. In the Mark passage (Mk. 3:20-34) we read that Jesus' nuclear family (mother, brothers, sisters) had come in a group to Capernaum to "take charge" of him because they thought him to be "out of his mind" (Mk. 3:21). Jesus must have been hurt. After all he was human. There may have been a bit of pique in his voice as he responded, "My mother and brothers are those who hear God's word and put it into practice" (v.21). "Hear" and "do". Full stop.

Jesus Stills a Storm 8:22–25

The Sea of Galilee is a relatively small lake sitting in a basin about four hundred feet below sea level. It is surrounded in the west, north and east by great heights while its southern shore leads out to the Jordan Valley. The climate is sub-tropical, unbearably hot in the summer. And, the winds which sweep down from the elevated sides of the basin can be fiercely sudden, embroiling the lake in unpredictable bursts of weather. I remember standing on the shore watching the spray from three and four foot waves blowing sideways in a gale. As a local fisherman from Tiberius once said, "this lake has a temper."

Its temper was certainly evident on this occasion. While Jesus slept in the boat the storm struck with such violence that the disciples, seasoned fishermen with years of experience on the lake, panicked. "We are perishing!" they exclaimed as they woke Jesus. He rebuked them, "Where is your faith?" And then, rebuked the wind. The sudden calm produced a fear deeper than that of the storm. "Who is this?" They whispered to one another, marvelling. They had no idea.

Jesus Restores a Demoniac 8:26–39

It's a bit difficult to ascertain where this story took place. Depending on the extant manuscripts we read "Gerasenes, Gadarenes, Gergesenes", all referring to residents of one of the ten cities of the Decapolis (Gentile territory) east or southeast of the Sea of Galilee. So we have three: Gerasa, or Gadera, or Gergesa. Luke refers to the location both as a "region" (vv.26,37) and a "town" (vv.27,34) and, in one instance, "countryside" (v.34). The one town that appears to meet the criteria of "across the lake" (v.26) with "hillside" (v.32) and "a steep bank" (v.33) is Gergesa, located on what we now know as the "Golan Heights" on the eastern shore of the lake. Jesus "stepped ashore" (v.27) and the incident took place. He did not have to walk several miles, as he would have done, if the town had been Gerasa (approximately 20 miles east of the Jordan river) or Gadera (down at the southern tip of the lake). Mind you, after the stilling of the storm, the boat could have sailed the length of the lake and landed near Gadera, but there was no "steep bank" there last time I drove by...

Regardless, the event that took place was one of the most significant in Jesus' early ministry. For two reasons: one, because he was proclaimed "Son of the Most High God" (v.28) by demons no less! (see also 4:34, 41); and two, because the very first person sent out by Jesus as an evangelist to the Gentile world was the newly delivered demoniac himself! (v.39). It was highly unusual for Jesus to encourage anyone he healed to make it public. His instruction was normally "Tell no one." He resisted the pressure to declare his messianic role prematurely. With Gentiles, who had no messianic expectations, he knew they'd have no end-time fervour proclaiming that the king had come. So, Mr. Ex-demoniac, go out and tell your story. The Decapolis needs the Gospel.

Jesus' power and divinity (v.28), a demon(s) whose name (v.30) is "Legion" (Latin for an army division of about six thousand), a fearful negotiation (v.31) on Legion's part that Jesus not send him (them) into the "abyss" (bottomless pit of the dead), permission to enter a herd of pigs who then "rush down the steep bank into the lake" (vv.32,33), the people of the region shocked by the sight of a now clothed ex-demoniac sitting at the feet of his deliverer, and overcome with fear at the demonstration of such power to the point of asking the miracle-worker to leave (vv.35-37), a demoniac turned evangelist (v.39)… the pace of it leaves you breathless.

As he read this account, Theophilus may have wondered, "Why did the people ask Jesus to leave? Why were they so afraid?" Perhaps the answer lay in what Luke wrote a few pages later where he recorded the response of some people to Jesus' power over demons (11:14-26). They credited it to his being a sort of super-demon, "By Beelzebul, the prince of demons, he is driving out demons" (11:15). In other words, a hierarchy of demonic personalities was assumed, and Jesus was one of the senior powers. He was to be dreaded and avoided! The gentile Gergesenes, likewise, feared that they were in the presence of great evil, so they asked Jesus to go away, and stay away. Much to their relief Jesus left (v.37c). The former demoniac, on the other hand, was loath to see him depart (v.38). You can be sure the disciples had a lot to talk about on the return sailing to Capernaum, not the least being the question, "Why is it that demons fear him because they see him as divine, while the people fear him because they think he is demonic?" In the course of a day the Twelve had experienced both an elemental and a theological storm. Maybe the only one at peace was Jesus. Perhaps he slept through the second storm too.

A Dying Girl and a Bleeding Woman 8:40–56

The crowd in Gergesa had rejected Jesus, the crowd on the shore at Capernaum welcomed him warmly, "they were all waiting for him" (v.40 RSV). One of them was a synagogue leader by the name of Jairus who would have been well known to Jesus. Just as the demoniac had done (v.28) he "fell down at Jesus' feet" (v.41 KJV), the ultimate sign of supplication and submission. His "only daughter, about twelve years of age… was dying" (v.42 RSV). She too was probably well known to Jesus. So, with the people almost crushing him (v.42) he started walking to Jairus' house. A woman who had probably marginalized herself for twelve years (because of chronic bleeding) timidly approached him in the anonymity of the crowd and touched "the border of his garment" (v.44 KJV). She was seeking healing and she got it, immediately. In all the elbows, knees, and shoulders jostling Jesus this touch was unique. "Who touched me?" he asked, "I know that power has gone out from me" (vv.45,46). The woman, trembling, "fell at his feet", admitted that she was the one and told him she had been instantly healed from her pernicious condition. Jesus gently responded, "Daughter, your faith has healed you. Go in peace" (v.48). Just touching Jesus wasn't the way to healing. If it were, everyone in that oppressive crowd would have been healed. What's more it would have reduced Jesus' ministry to some sort of tactile ritual, a sort of magic. No, it wasn't the touch that did it. It was the touch of faith.

At that moment a messenger came to Jairus saying, "Your daughter is dead; do not trouble the Teacher anymore" (v.49). Jesus overhead and assured Jairus that if he "believed" all would be well (v.50). And, to the consternation of the crowd of family members, neighbors, and professional wailers, Jesus announced that the girl was just asleep (v.52). The crowd of admirers suddenly became a crowd of mockers. Unperturbed, Jesus went into her room, taking with him her parents and Peter, John, and James (v.51), and simply took the girl's lifeless hand and told her to get up. Which she did, to her parents' astonishment. Jesus gave two commands: get her something to eat, and keep this to yourselves. How?

How are we to keep this to ourselves? Maybe he means we're to say publicly that Jesus was right – she was only sleeping. We can do that. But we *know* she was dead! Keeping that secret is going to be tough.

JESUS AND THE TWELVE 9:1–62

The First Training Mission 9:1–6

Jesus called the Twelve together and invested them with "power and authority over all demons and to cure diseases" (9:1 RSV). This was pretty heady stuff for this rough-hewn group. There was more than a risk of egos out of control. To mitigate and balance the spiritual pride potential, Jesus insisted they carry no material security in terms of luggage, money, food, and extra clothing. They were to be totally dependent on charity (vv.3,4). They were not to spend any time or effort trying to be listened to and cared for (v.5). It was to be a baptism of risk, vulnerability, and dusty faith. Luke doesn't say how it went.

Herod Perplexed 9:7–9

In the Greek the English word "perplexed" means "to be utterly at a loss". This was the case with the tetrarch Herod. He had beheaded the wild prophet (v.9) to stop the masses of people flooding down to the Jordan for baptism, and in so doing nipped major insurrection in the bud (or so he thought?). The beheading met another need – to silence his wife, who hated John. But, just as he was feeling relief from these concerns, Jesus appeared on the scene and the stress factor rose precipitously. This cousin of John was doing far more than baptizing; he was healing the sick, raising the dead, stilling storms, drawing huge crowds. What really scared Herod was the rumour that Jesus was John raised from the dead (v.7). His guilt and superstitious fears threw him into turmoil. Luke says he, "sought to see…" Jesus. Perhaps a face-to-face with this prophet from Capernaum would bring some peace. But if Jesus was John redivivus what would Herod do? Apologize?

A Free Meal for 5000 9:10–17

After the Twelve returned from their training mission Jesus led them a mile or so east of Capernaum to Bethsaida. This town was (and is still – in ruins) located on the north-eastern edge of the Lower Galilee on the bank of the Upper Jordan River. It was the hometown of Philip, Andrew, and Peter, but never embraced the Gospel (10:13) even though these native sons comprised fully one quarter of the Twelve. It was a fishing town with water access to Kinneret via the river.

A crowd soon followed. Jesus welcomed them and spent the afternoon teaching and healing (v.11). The westering sun signalled the end of the day. The Twelve were concerned that this huge crowd (5000 men and how many uncounted women and children?) might have to spend the night with neither food nor shelter (v.12). So they asked Jesus to dismiss the crowd to local towns and villages to buy food and find lodging (or else return to their homes in the dark). Jesus said, "You give them something to eat."

I can imagine the disciples' consternation. What? You want *us* to feed these thousands? You've got to be kidding! All we've got is "five loaves of bread and two fish" (v.13), (barley bread and smoked or pickled fish was typical food, especially for the poor). Jesus didn't argue. He instructed them to have the crowd sit in orderly groups of fifty, then he took the humble lunch, looked to heaven, gave thanks, and began breaking the bread. Like "the cruse of oil unfailing" (1Ki. 17:7-16) the food in Jesus' hands was inexhaustible. The Twelve had more than enough to feed everyone (v.17a). In fact, each of them gathered a basket of left-overs (v.17b). I would like to have heard the conversations of the people as they walked home through the night. This had been a meal they would never forget.

The Great Confession 9:18–26

Luke transitions to a conversation Jesus had with the Twelve during a time of private prayer. He doesn't say where this took place. Nor does he say what Jesus was thinking. Jesus asking, "Who do the people say that I am?" seems a bit unusual. Was he being uncharacteristically introspective? Surely he already knew what people were saying. Was he looking for affirmation? Or was this question an intentional lead-in to, "Who do you say that I am?" Maybe it was time for the over-stimulated disciples to focus in. Time to see beyond and behind the miraculous work of their Master to heaven's master-plan. Maybe it was time to start playing hardball.

Maybe it was time for the over-stimulated disciples to focus in. Time to see beyond and behind the miraculous work of their Master to heaven's master-plan.

Peter blurted, "The Christ of God" (v.20 KJV). He said it, not as a rational conclusion to thought – indeed he didn't appreciate what he was saying. But his confession was the bullseye of heaven's plan. It was a supra-rational declaration from God the Father in the mouth of this impulsive fisherman. Jesus captured its timeless genius by saying, "Blessed are you, Simon son of Jonah, for this was not revealed to you by flesh and blood, but by my Father in heaven" (Mt. 16:17).

Now for the hardball: Jesus told them (in camera) that he, "the Son of Man" (a messianic title), was about to undergo major adversity. In sum, the seventy members of Jerusalem's Sanhedrin (elders, chief priests, and the teachers of the Law) would reject and kill him. But, he would be resurrected on the third day (v.22). A trying path of pain and sorrow lay ahead. So if any of the Twelve wanted to opt out of this upcoming suffering, now was the time. If they chose to stay it would mean self-denial and the weight of a cross bending their backs and souls every day till the end. This living death, ironically, would save their lives (v.24). The cost would be worth it (v.25). But there would be times when they would second-guess themselves (v.26). Staying the course would be rewarded with Messiah coming "in his glory and in the glory of the Father and of the holy angels."

The Transfiguration 9:27–36

I chose to start my commentary on the Transfiguration with verse 27. This statement from Jesus, "Truly I tell you, some who are standing here will not taste death before they see the Kingdom of God," has caused concern and controversy for many over the years. The assumption has been that seeing the Kingdom of God meant being alive for the Day of the Lord at the end of days. Thus, Jesus' statement doesn't jibe. But, if he is referring to the Transfiguration as the revealed Kingdom then three of the Twelve, Peter, James, and John, would see it "about eight days later" (v.28). And, of course, this is exactly what happened.

The Bible doesn't name the mountain of Transfiguration, but historically there have been two options identified. One is Mount Tabor, five miles east of Nazareth, and the other is Mount Hermon, the peak of which is about five miles north-northeast of Caesarea Philippi. Tabor dominates the eastern horizon of the Jezreel Valley in Lower Galilee and is a modest nineteen hundred feet in elevation. Nevertheless the view of the Jezreel from the summit is stunning. I've often felt like I was in an airplane when standing at the top. Hermon lifts its majestic head over the northern tip of the Golan Heights, so high at more than nine thousand feet it makes those heights seem like mere hills. Its summit stands on the border between Syria and Lebanon and has been controlled by Israel since the Six Day War in 1967. On cloudy days the summit disappears, on sunny days I have seen it from as far south as Tiberias. My sense is that Hermon is the Mount of Transfiguration, not just because of its height, but more because of its proximity to Caesarea Philippi (read Mt. 16:13-17:8).

Five pivotal words provide the infrastructure for the world-changing story of Jesus: Annunciation, Incarnation, Transfiguration, Resurrection, and Ascension. All five are charged with the high voltage of the super-natural. And all five give insight into the meaning of "kinosis", the "self-emptying" of Jesus as Paul describes it in Ph. 2:5-8.

"Have this mind among yourselves,
which you have in Christ Jesus, who,
though he was in the form of God, did
not count equality with God a thing
to be grasped, but emptied himself,
taking the form of a servant, being
born in the likeness of men. And being
found in human form he humbled
himself and became obedient unto
death, even death on a cross." (RSV)

Peter, James, and John got a glimpse of this on Mt. Hermon. "They saw his glory…" (v.32), and must have wondered, on later reflection, at how much Jesus had given up.

In a brief eleven sentences Luke describes the moment when Heaven touched earth. He tells Theophilus that Jesus took the Three "up onto a mountain to pray" (v.28). While praying Jesus was transformed – a "flash of lightning" brightness is about as bright as it gets. This heavenly apparel (v.29b) was a match for the "glorious splendor" of Moses and Elijah who suddenly appeared, "talking with Jesus" about "his departure" (vv.30,31). The Three, who had a tendency to sleep when praying at night (see Mt. 26:40-45) awoke to this stunning scene, and Peter, never at a loss for unpremeditated outbursts, suggested they build three "shelters" on the spot, one for Jesus, one for Moses, and one for Elijah (v.33). Luke makes a parenthetic aside, "He didn't know what he was saying." Just then a cloud envelops them and they hear God's voice, "This is my son, whom I have chosen; listen to him" (v.35). Luke records no reaction on the part of the Three, just silence.

Back on the Ground 9:37–43

Raphael's masterpiece, "The Transfiguration", which hangs in the Vatican museum, captures what happened next. For hundreds of years it was considered the most famous painting in the world. More recently Leonardo da Vinci's "Mona Lisa" holds that title.

In the upper half of the painting Raphael portrays Jesus, Moses, and Elijah hovering above the sleeping Three. In the lower half he portrays a spiritually possessed boy and his protective father surrounded by a crowd. Heavenly glory and the earthly desperation of humanity are juxtaposed. Jesus and the Three "came down from the mountain" (v.37).

Two things stand out as Jesus rebukes "the unclean spirit" and "heals the boy" (v.42): the fact that the disciples (who had recently been invested with the "power and authority to drive out *all* demons" – emphasis added) in v.1 could not exorcize this one (v.40); and the other is the reaction of the people who "were astonished at the majesty of God" (v.43 RSV). The Greek word for "majesty" (megaleiotes) denotes "splendor, magnificence". One wonders at this word in the mouths of the "am ha aretz", the everyday people. Was some of the transfiguration glory still evident? Somehow, in this miracle, they saw more than a miracle, they saw the glory of God.

Before moving on, there is one more aspect of the story that demands comment. It is Jesus' exasperated slamming of the disciples, "O faithless and perverse generation, how long am I to be with you and bear with you?" (v.41a RSV). This outburst was in response to the boy's father's report, "I begged your disciples to drive it out, but they could not" (v.40). As just pointed out, the disciples had been empowered by Jesus on their first "training mission" (vv.1-6) to heal and deliver "people everywhere" (v.6). Apparently they were successful because they returned with a good report (v.10). Now, within days, they were inept, disempowered ("perverse" – Gk. – "distorted, twisted, turned aside, corrupted") by what? Luke doesn't say. Hubris perhaps? Pride has a way of dimming the eyes to the glory of God.

Who's the Greatest? 9:43b–50

Hubris indeed. It not only blinded them to who Jesus was, it darkened their understanding (v.45). Jesus tried to warn them about his impending death (v.44) but all they heard was "There's going to be a change in leadership." They were impressed with the crowds, the notoriety, and the few successful healings and deliverances they'd accomplished. They liked the popularity. So, Jesus is going? You'd expect sadness. Instead they got into an argument about who would be heir-apparent (v.46). Jesus pushed back gently. He called a young child to his side, referring to children as "the least" in direct contrast to "the greatest". I think we can assume the disciples got the point. The Kingdom of Heaven is about strength in weakness (2Co. 12:9,10). To lead we've got to serve.

There was still a lingering hubris after this powerful lesson, however. The disciple John tells Jesus that a stranger had been casting out demons in Jesus' name but the disciples had stopped him "because he does not follow us" (v.49). Notice the plural pronoun. Shouldn't the offence have been, "because he does not follow *you*"?

Samaritan Resistance 9:51–56

This is just a short anecdote revealing strong religious/cultural bias. Jesus was on his way to Jerusalem, so he sent a few "messengers" ahead to a Samaritan village to make food and lodging preparations as he would be passing through in a day or two. The Samaritans refused to allow him passage. Why? "Because his face was set toward Jerusalem" (v.53 RSV). They assumed he was going to worship at the Temple in Jerusalem, which in their view was a direct insult. Didn't Jesus know that Samaritans believed that Mount Gerazim, in Samaria, was *the* holy hill, not Zion? If we host him in our village it will be seen as an endorsement of Jewish heresy. He's obviously a false prophet!

James and John, the "sons of thunder" (Mk. 3:17), were so incensed at this rejection that they presumptuously insisted that they "call fire down from heaven to destroy them" (v.54). Jesus told them to keep quiet.

He was a Savior, not a destroyer. So they moved on. But the impetuous brothers may have muttered with another dollop of hubris, Elijah did it (2Ki. 1:9-16), why not us?

So You Think You Want to Follow Jesus? 9:57–62

I ride a motorcycle, and have done so for most of my life. One of the primary rules for staying upright is "Look ahead. If you look down, you go down." It's rather like ploughing a furrow with a tractor or even (as in history) a horse. To keep a straight furrow you've got to look ahead. If you look down, or to the right or left, the plough follows your eyes. Both motorcycle and tractor trace your line of sight.

This essentially is what Jesus said to a few enthusiasts who declared their intention to follow him. Discipleship meant 100 percent focus on the Kingdom of Heaven. Any distraction, be it filial responsibilities, security concerns, or relationship bonds, could see a deviation from the course. Before making such a commitment, count the cost.

Jesus Sends Out Seventy More 10:1–24

Luke writes that Jesus sent out seventy "others" to "every town and place where he was about to go" (v.1). In one sense they were to make preparations for his arrival (like the "messengers" to Samaria – 9:52), but in another way they were to "heal the sick" (v.9) like the Twelve (9:1-6). Nevertheless, it is clear that Jesus was strategic about his itinerary. He was also intentional and deliberate about his team's cost, energy, and time efficiency (vv.5-12). The seventy were to make no effort to minister to any town that resisted their presence (as the Samaritan village had done in 9:51-43). This was strictly business.

Jesus knew that some towns would reject these advance agents. Perhaps this was one reason why he sent them out "two by two". Indeed, he likened these resistant population centers to "wolves" and the seventy to "lambs" (v.3). And, this theme of rejection resonated in his own home region – Chorazin, Bethsaida, and Capernaum – along the northern shore of the Sea of Galilee. They had all had first-hand exposure to Jesus' teaching and healing, yet they had not repented of their sin. This, of course, was the ultimate rejection, for Jesus, like his cousin John, was all about the Kingdom of Heaven and the vital role of repentance for entry. Jesus' response to this intransigence? "Thou shalt be thrust down to hell" (v.15 KJV). Perhaps Capernaum, like the ancient king of Babylon, Nebuchadnezzar, had proudly declared, "I will ascend into heaven" (Is. 14:13-15), but the very opposite would be the case (v.15).

Luke jumps ahead to the return of seventy very excited messengers, reporting, "Lord, even the demons submit to us in your name" (v.17). Well, good for you, "I saw Satan fall like lightning from heaven", so don't get too full of yourselves, just "rejoice that your names are written in heaven" (vv.18-20). Time and again Jesus was the adult in his interaction with his followers whom he charitably called "babes" (v.21).

Jesus then turned to his "Father, Lord of heaven and earth" to thank him for revealing himself and "hidden" things to the unlearned, intellectually humble, everyday people. Jesus was pleased to see children loving their heavenly Father *before* they knew him (much like we do as children, loving our parents before really knowing them). And, turning to the Twelve he reminded them of how blessed they were to "hear" and "see" with supra-rational ears and eyes (vv.23,24). This was a "full of joy through the Holy Spirit" moment (v.21) for Jesus.

The Great Commandment 10:25–28

The culture of the Scribes and the Pharisees revolved around the Mosaic Law. The rabbis had identified 365 "thou shalt nots" and 248 "thou shalts" for a grand total of 613 commandments. The Scribes were the lawyers, the Pharisees the interpreters. They were scrupulous in their work and demanding in their insistence that the people toe the mark. Those who didn't conform did so at their peril. Thus, Jesus was on their radar constantly. Like obsessive-compulsive curmudgeons they followed him relentlessly, pushing back against his "new wine" teaching. Jesus was a thorn in their side, even as they were in his.

Just another instance of push-back occurred one day with a Scribe (lawyer) "testing" Jesus with a leading question, "What must I do to inherit eternal life?" (v.25). Jesus responded by asking the Scribe to answer the question himself, knowing that the well worn, time-proven, orthodox Jewish truth would emerge.

The scribe blended two scriptures in summarizing the Law – Dt. 6:4,5 and Le. 19:18 – "Hear, O Israel: the Lord our God, the Lord is one. Love the Lord your God with all your heart and with all your soul and with all your strength... love your neighbor as yourself." Jesus was impressed and affirmed the Scribe. Jesus *was* Jewish after all, and in his famous Sermon on the Mount he stated clearly, "Do not think that I have come to abolish the Law or the Prophets; I have not come to abolish them but to fulfill them" (Mt. 5:17). As was evident at the Transfiguration, Moses and Elijah were his friends.

The default of the rabbis was to save oneself by regulation. Love, on the other hand, was less restrictive but more demanding, and risky too. Love will not be codified.

The challenge to Israel had always been the question: Is it "either-or" or "both-and"? Either Moses or Elijah, or both Moses and Elijah? Moses was more accessible through "rules" but Elijah (the Prophets) was a bit more elusive. Why? Because the essential distillation of the prophets' message to Israel (built, by the way on the Deuteronomy and Leviticus passages) was that of righteousness and justice. Their call challenged Israel to fulfill the demands of relationship with God (love on the vertical plane – righteousness) and the demands of relationship with neighbor (love on the horizontal plane – justice). Rules provide answers in the raw whereas love requires a measure of finesse and flexibility. The default of the rabbis was to save oneself by regulation. Love, on the other hand, was less restrictive but more demanding, and risky too. Love will not be codified.

The Good Samaritan 10:29–37

There's no need to rehearse this parable – it is the most famous of all (the parable of The Prodigal Son is #2). It teaches us that love is indiscriminate and is often catalyzed by compassion (vv.33,37). If we can help our neighbor in his need we fulfill the call of justice. I am my neighbor and he is me.

Nevertheless it's good to be apprised of the huge racial and cultural gap there was between Jew and Samaritan in Jesus' day.

The city of Samaria was built by Omri, king of Israel, in 870 BC (1Ki. 16:24). It became Israel's capital. In 722 BC it was besieged and taken after three years by the king of Assyria, Shalmaneser (2Ki. 17:1-6). He quickly deported about thirty thousand Israelites to Assyria, repopulating Samaria with Gentiles from Cutha, Babylon, Hamath, and other foreign nations. These foreigners adopted a syncretistic form of the Israelite religion. So, the Jewish view was that at best Samaritans were half-breeds and their religion a heresy.

On the other hand the Samaritans held that the Assyrian deportation in 722 was merely partial. They said that many Israelites stayed in Samaria and, what's more, the exiles returned after fifty-five years. They claimed to be descendants of these Israelites. But, and this a big "but", they believed that Moses had designated their Mount Gerazim as the chosen place for the worship of God (De. 27:12). In their view the Temple in Jerusalem was bogus. Both Jew and Samaritan saw the other as inferior. There was no love lost between them. So, when Jesus told the inquiring Scribe about a "good" Samaritan, the crowd of listeners would have uttered more than a few sub-voce epithets.

There are about 400 Samaritans in Israel today. They still conduct the Passover on Mount Gerazim every Spring. My wife and I attended one of those ceremonies a few years ago. Here's my memory of it, in the text of a sermon I preached at a prominent pastor's funeral:

Back in 1983 the Israeli Ministry of Tourism invited Kathy and me to attend the Samaritan Passover on Mount Gerazim near Nablus, Israel. This Passover ceremony has been celebrated throughout the aeons of time – it is the most authentic insight into Old Testament sacrificial practices that exists today. We were honored to be invited to this closed ritual, intrigued at what we might experience.

It was a cold and windy late afternoon on Mount Gerazim. The wind was blowing with such force that many of the Samaritans and invited guests leaned into the blast, their faces covered with scarves against the cold, as they walked up to the sacrificial site on a small table of land at the top of the mountain.

Set on the rocky soil was a small enclosure. Gathered within were the last remaining Samaritans on earth – 400 strong. Next to the enclosure were twelve deep pits with blazing fires in each. As we guests gathered around the enclosure, we saw, to our wonder, that each Samaritan family had a lamb. And such lambs! Perfectly groomed. As spotless and pristine as if they had just been fashioned by their Creator. And – each lamb had beautiful red roses woven into its wool. It was a breath-taking sight.

The lamb nearest to us was so close that I shyly reached over the short fence and stroked its wool. The Samaritan father, holding it on a leash of multi-colored braided cord, looked at me and smiled. In broken English he said, "Welcome to our day of salvation!"

Each of the Samaritan families with their lambs stood silently in the enclosure. They were waiting for the sun to set. It was already descending over the Jezreel Valley to the north. We could see Mount Tabor, the mount of transfiguration (?) on the horizon, and between us and Tabor we could see the distant town of Nazareth in the fading light. In two minutes the sun would set.

Just then, two burly, young Samaritan men left the enclosure and walked over to a small white hut standing about 50 meters away. They knocked on the door, and out came a stooped old man, clothed in white, his long white beard and hair blowing in the wind. This was the Samaritan high priest. The young men half carried him over to a large rock that stood on the edge of the mountain top. They lifted him up onto the rock, and then joined him there.

Like Aaron and Hur holding up Moses' arms during the battle with the Amalekites (Ex. 17:12-14), they held the high priest's arms to heaven. He stood silent until the sun disappeared over the horizon. Then in a quavery voice, barely audible over the rushing wind, he intoned a prayer. Every eye was on him.

When he had finished, the young men carried him back to his little hut. As they did so, we turned our heads back to the enclosure. To our shock every lamb lay dead on the ground, their blood already soaking into the earth. Not a sound had been made. No protest – just silent death.

Then, there appeared to be a small commotion in the midst of the 400 Samaritans. Suddenly the two young men who had lifted the priest onto the rock, lifted a baby, clothed like the priest, in flowing white. They lifted him high – up above the crowd. As they did so the Samaritans broke out in spontaneous prayerful song, and, as the young men turned in our direction we were stunned and amazed to see lamb's blood smeared on the baby's forehead.

The deep meaning of this struck us immediately. Here was symbolized new beginnings, salvation, new birth. Innocence had trumped sinfulness. The nation of Samaritans was born again!

Later, the mystery of the twelve blazing pits was made clear. Each lamb was butchered and roasted in those pits. Every last morsel had to be eaten before midnight. And, in the early starlit morning, the Samaritans descended Gerazim, washed clean by the blood of the Lamb.

That Good Part 10:38–42

Luke records a short anecdote about hospitality for Jesus and the Twelve in an unnamed village on their itineration route. The two sisters who were hosting the travelling group were Mary and Martha (vv.38,39). Martha "was distracted with much serving" (v.40), probably wanting to honor Jesus (and herself) with a multi-course dinner. Mary, on the other hand, just wanted to hear Jesus' teaching (v.39). To Martha's complaint that Mary was neglecting the serving responsibilities Jesus simply said, "Mary hath chosen that good part" (v.42 KJV), and kindly commented that a one-course dinner would have been enough (v.42a). Sometimes less is more.

How to Pray 11:1–13

On one occasion the disciples saw Jesus at prayer (as he was wont to do) and one of them asked him to teach them to pray. Jesus responded with a short prayer (vv.2b-4) and a brief methodology (vv.5-13).
The prayer itself has six core values:

1. Address God as "Father".

2. Hallow his name ("Ha Shem" – Heb.).

3. God's Kingdom has priority.

4. Our daily needs are important.

5. Forgiveness is the pivot point of relationship with both God and neighbor.

6. Protection from persecution is vital so that we are not tempted to deny our faith.

The "method" in prayer:

1. Be persistent (v.8).

2. State the need ("ask" (v.9a).

3. Look for a solution ("seek") (v.9b).

4. Be proactive ("knock") (v.9c).

Interestingly, Jesus has an insight into the foundational exchange in prayer: the "Holy Spirit" (v.13b). The unnamed disciple who made the request for a prayer lesson may have been surprised to hear Jesus imply that the ultimate goal of prayer is the supernatural infusion of the presence of God himself. All real needs are met when the Holy Spirit indwells the seeking heart.

The Finger of God 11:14–28

In this passage we see Jesus' total domination of the spirit world. The people are astonished and intimidated by his power over demons. Not knowing who Jesus really is, their only explanation for his ease in exorcism is that he is working for the "prince of demons", Satan himself. In this sense they're seeing him as a mega-demon, a "superhero" of hell. What they didn't know was that power over demons was merely entry-level. Jesus was no super-demon. Indeed, he expelled evil spirits by "the finger of God" (v.20). The manifestation of the Kingdom of Heaven had just begun. But he cautioned the people not to take the world of evil lightly. If so they would be victimized in multiple ways (vv.24-26). Better to "hear the word of God, and obey it" (v.28).

The Sign of Jonah 11:29–32

Before making any comment let me refer you to Exodus 27:7 where the grumpy Israelites petulantly ask, "Is the Lord among us or not?" This after the miraculous crossing of the Red Sea, the amazing provision of manna and quail in the wilderness, and water from the rock at Meribah! Israel's history of quarrelling, grumbling, and complaining in the face of signs and wonders demonstrates that the miraculous has a shelf life. Little wonder Jesus taught in the parable of the rich man and Lazarus that "they will not be convinced even if someone rises from the dead" (Lk. 16:31).

A "sign" in both the Old Testament and the New Testament can/ could mean a number of things. Rather than write an essay on the range of options, suffice it to say that a sign was essentially revelatory in nature. It was an indicator of the supernatural. It was an "uncovering" of the heavenlies. It staggered and stopped (at least temporarily) the mouths of believers and unbelievers alike. But then, its impact slowly faded in time.

Jesus ground his teeth at the "wicked generation" asking for a sign (v.29). He then baldly declared that he was a "sign" to "this generation" even as Jonah had been a sign to Nineveh (v.30). What was Jonah's sign? His appearance? Miraculous works? Personality? No, it was his call to repentance. (And, there's no indication they were impressed with his great fish adventure!). Nineveh repented but "this generation" won't. The lesser signs of Jonah and Solomon (vv.31,32) convinced a heathen city-state and a world famous queen (Queen of Sheba) of the Kingdom of Heaven's repentance requirement; thus, Jesus says these Gentiles will condemn this generation of Israelites for their unbelief. Stern stuff.

Clear Vision 11:33–36

The sign theme continues. Here, Jesus is a "lamp". He shines in a dark place and transforms hopelessness into brightness. Then, to mix metaphors, he calls the eye "the lamp of the body" (v.34). The message is clear. The key is to "seek first the kingdom of God and his righteousness" (Mt. 6:33) with eyes made bright by faith. As the Apostle Paul put it, "he has rescued us from the dominion of darkness and brought us into the kingdom of the Son he loves, in whom we have redemption, the forgiveness of sins" (Cl. 1:13,14).

Jesus Eats with His Enemies 11:37–54

Apparently Jesus didn't take opposition personally. He had the mature perspective that allowed him to accept an invitation to dinner at the home of one of his adversaries (v.37). The evening didn't start well.

319

Jesus "reclined at the table" before washing his hands. The Pharisee was offended. But Jesus had only got started.

He launched into three "woes" against the Pharisees and followed with three more against the Scribes who were reclining at table with him. But before these indictments Jesus clarified the meaning of kosher. You want clean hands? Try being "generous to the poor", then "everything will be clean for you" (v.41). Kosher is not about the outside, it's about the inside.

Jesus' most damning accusation regarded the pharisaical legalism scrupulous in tithing without regard for "justice" (love of neighbor) and "the love of God" (righteousness). Both should be core values (v.42). Then he faulted their arrogance and ostentation in their entitlements – "the most important seats in the synagogues and respectful greetings in the marketplaces" (v.43). But the most cutting was his accusation that they were "unmarked graves" (v.44). Jewish graves were whitewashed to warn casual pedestrians not to step on them. If they did they were immediately ritually unclean (un-kosher). Jesus was saying that mere physical contact with a Pharisee had the same effect. Whoa! The chutzpah of the man! It's amazing they didn't throw him out on the spot.

But he wasn't finished. He turned to the Scribes, "you experts in the Law", and accused them with loading people "down with burdens they can hardly carry" without any sense of their moral responsibility to help (v.46). The controlling wall they had built around the Law was a heavier burden than the Law itself. Indeed, Jesus saw their assiduous building of tombs for "prophets and apostles" (v.49) as disingenuous and deceptive. Like the Pharisees' obsession with kosher, the scribal obsession with legalities had entombed the people in ignorance (v.52), and Jesus warned the Scribes they would be held responsible (vv.47-52). Little wonder the dinner guests aborted the meal and went outside in a fury (vv.53,45).

GETTING IT RIGHT 12:1–18:30

The Fear of God 12:1–12

An assumption many readers of the gospels make is that the narrative is linear. This is almost never the case. A good example is the present chapter. It is a compilation of teachings with very little cohesion, other than they come from Jesus, who taught in various contexts. This, of course, does not mitigate their value. Nor does it diminish Luke's arrangement of material. He was a thorough researcher.

Luke tells Theophilus that on one occasion an "innumerable multitude" (v.1 KJV) had gathered to hear Jesus. In Greek the word is "myrias" which can refer to "ten thousand" or "a myriad, numberless host". In the book of Acts myriad is "five ten-thousands" (Ac. 19:19). This was a *big* crowd. So big, in fact, the people were "trampling on one another".

What follows is a bit like watching a tennis match. We look to the left, Jesus is addressing the disciples (v.1b-12); look to the right, and he's talking to the crowd (vv.13-21); to the left, the disciples (vv.22-53); then back to the crowd (vv.54-59). It's a touch dizzying. If you don't necessarily read it as a chronological account, it's less demanding. But how demanding was it for Jesus? How does one focus on twelve with a trampling mob of 50,000 demanding people (eg. v.13) milling about? Talk about multi-tasking!

Even though the crowd was pressing, Jesus managed a huddle with his disciples. Luke doesn't say how the topic came up, but records Jesus warning the Twelve about the "leaven" or "yeast" (hypocrisy) of the Pharisees. This metaphor usually had bad connotations. Hypocrites conceal their private thoughts, words, and actions, but the day when darkness will yield to daylight is coming (vv.2,3). "Be sure your sin will find you out" (Nu. 32:23 KJV). We may, or may not, be found out by our neighbors, but we certainly will be found out by God. And He's the one to fear. He has the final say about heaven and hell (vv.4,5). Understand that your life is of inestimable worth (v.7). So if you accept that nothing is hidden from God, go public with your faith in him (v.8), and God will go "angelic" (v.8) with you. And remember, no one can sin against the Holy Spirit and be forgiven (v.10). To blaspheme is to kill one's own soul. When you're under pressure and persecution from the authorities, affirm the Holy Spirit and the Holy Spirit will affirm you (v.11). He's got your back (v.12).

So if you accept that nothing is hidden from God, go public with your faith in him, and God will go "angelic" with you.

The Insecurity of Wealth 12:13–21

This passage needs very little comment. "Eat, drink, be merry" (v.19) is tactical foolishness. "Rich toward God" (v.21) is strategic wisdom. Our ultimate security is in God's hands. He says, "Fool!" (v.20), to anyone who believes and acts otherwise. Heaven's values are counter-cultural.

Materialism and Anxiety 12:22–34

In contrast to the rich fool, "consider the ravens" [who] neither sow nor reap… neither have storehouse nor barn…" (v.24). Birds are never idle, nor do they worry about material needs, "God feeds them" (v.24). What's more, birds don't covet – indeed, covetousness is usually at the root of anxiety. Lilies, grass, and ravens all freely benefit from God's provision. So should we. Better to "seek his kingdom" (v.31), and the other stuff will follow. And the material goods we seek should be worth the effort. Our "treasure" reveals our values (v.34).

The Parousia 12:35–48

What follows is a bit obscure, but gains a touch of clarity if read in the light of 17:20-37. The "coming ("parousia" – Gk.) of the Kingdom of

God" (17:20) and "the days of the Son of Man" (v.22b), seem to be on Jesus' mind as he instructs his disciples about watchfulness. They needed to know that there was more to the Kingdom than signs, wonders, and profound teaching. History was certainly being made, but there was an eschatological process at work. God had a plan that would reach far beyond "the end of days". That new age was coming, and Jesus would usher it in. This would be his "second coming", when all things in heaven and on earth would be brought to completion.

Jesus had a profound sense of the urgency, the imminence, of the end of days. Unlike his disciples (and us) his vision was not shrouded by a space/time filter. Whether the new age was twenty minutes away, or twenty millennia for that matter, mankind and the world were on the razor's edge of eternity. One had to stay alert.

Each of the three parables (the waiting servants vv.35-38; the householder and the thief vv.39,40; the faithful and unfaithful servants vv.41-46) stresses the shortness of time and the need to be on watch. All Christ-followers are to be unencumbered (v.35), ready (v.40), and faithful (v.42). And, to the extent they have been warned, they will be held accountable (vv.47,48). This is serious business. Jesus is coming soon.

Jesus – Not "Meek and Mild" 12:49–53

Jesus knew he was a polarizing figure. His words and works would divide nations and families. By his own admission he came "to cast fire upon the earth" (v.49a RSV). His death ("baptism" v.50) would divide the saved from the damned (no political correctness here!). But, as already stated in vv.47,48, judgement would be relative to knowledge. You can be sure the disciples were struck to the heart. Am I in or out?

Jesus Rebukes the Multitude 12:54–59

While Jesus had been warning the disciples about the parousia, the 50,000 or so had continued to mill about and trample one another (v.1). Jesus turned his attention back to them, and (I surmise) to the one who had presumptuously demanded that he adjudicate a family dispute (v.13). He accused the crowd of watching the weather rather than the signs of the times, and bluntly told the cheeky interlocutor to work out the domestic conflict on his own, or else settle with his disgruntled brother before the case was brought to court. Jesus had had enough.

Pilate – A Nasty Man 13:1–5

Book 18 of Josephus' *"Antiquities of the Jews"* draws a very unattractive picture of the Roman procurator, Pilate. He was quick, even eager, to slaughter Jews and Samaritans when provoked. He had probably been assigned to the politically fractious sandbox of Palestine as a demotion. He was bitter about it, and his resentment showed. And, according to this interchange (v.1), he had apparently slaughtered some Galilean Jews in the Temple as they were making their blood sacrifices. Animal and Jewish blood had "mingled". Once again Pilate was guilty of an abomination.

Luke doesn't say why "some present" felt it necessary to inform Jesus of Pilate's cruelty. Regardless, Jesus makes no comment other than to warn them that death awaits everyone, whether by natural causes, a procurator's wrath, or an unfortunate accident (v.4). Before we die we must deal with our broken relationship with the Father. The only way is to "repent" (vv.3,5). Pilate should be first in line.

The Parable of the Fig Tree 13:6–9

This parable has blunt force: just as we all must repent personally, the nation of Israel must also repent. The time is short before it is "cut down".

A Crippled Woman Healed on the Sabbath 13:10–17

If it's right to "loose" animals from their stalls on the Sabbath to water them, is it not more than right to "loose" a "daughter of Abraham" from eighteen years of affliction? Jesus' detractors, once again, were "put to shame" (v.17), but the crowd loved it.

The Parable of the Mustard Seed 13:18,19

One recalls Zechariah's words when reading this parable: "For who hath despised the day of small things?" (Ze. 4:10 KJV). Jesus had just begun to introduce the Kingdom of Heaven. He and the Twelve were very small compared to the world's history and empires. Yet, like the small mustard seed, the Kingdom would one day grow to eclipse the kingdoms of the world. Indeed, all peoples and nations would one day "[nest] in its branches" (v.19).

Mustard Seeds Grow, Leaven Swells 13:20,21

This parable makes the same point. A little bit of leaven (like a tiny mustard seed) has an impact far beyond its size. It swells. So, too, the Kingdom will swell.

Entitlement and the Kingdom 13:22–30

Very few of us in the West have a "kingdom view" of anything. We live in, and our forefathers fought for, a democracy. Universal suffrage has forever reduced monarchy to mere formalism. So there is a disconnect when we read about "the Kingdom". Thus, I will digress for a few pages and give you a brief overview of the biblical concept of the "Kingdom of God/Heaven".

Luke records that "Jesus went through the towns and villages teaching as he made his way to Jerusalem" (v.22). The people came to him not just for healing, but were intrigued by his teaching. Why? Because he taught them about the Kingdom of Heaven, a subject very near and dear to their cultural/religious tradition. Jesus had a way of making this time-worn belief come alive. Indeed, it was the central theme for his teaching.

There are several references in the Old Testament to the Kingdom. Here are just a few examples:

"Your throne, O God, will last forever and ever,
a sceptre of justice will be the sceptre of your kingdom."

—Ps. 45:6

"Your kingdom is an everlasting kingdom,
and your dominion endures through all generations."

—Ps. 145:13

"I will set him over my house and my kingdom forever."

—1 Ch. 17:14

"Deliverers will go up on Mount Zion
to govern the mountains of Esau.
And the kingdom will be the Lord's."

—Ob. 21

"Yours, Lord, is the kingdom;
you are exalted as head over all."

—1 Ch. 29:11b

"In the time of those kings, the God of heaven will
set up a kingdom that will never be destroyed…"

—Da. 2:44

These, and many other references, all picture a sovereign on a throne administering kingly rule over heaven and earth. This is what the crowds were visualizing as Jesus taught. But the fascination was his three-dimensional view of the Kingdom as ruling not just the heavens and the earth, but the individual soul as well. Heaven knew each of them by name. But, even more radical was Jesus' view of the Kingdom as universal – even Gentiles were included!

Generally, with some exceptions, Israel saw "the God of Abraham, Isaac, and Jacob" as a local deity. "The Land" ("ha Eretz" – Heb.) was his territory. Other nations had their own lands and gods (Chemosh in Moab, Milcom in Ammon, for example – 1Ki. 11:33). If the land prospered it meant that its god was both happy and powerful. If it suffered famine, drought, or defeat in war, its god was either weak or absent. The god's reputation was at stake. This is why the Lord in Ezekiel 36 declares he will restore the fortunes of Israel not for their sake, but "for the sake of my holy name, which you have profaned among the nations…" (v.22 et al). This is also why the Syrian leper, Naaman, after being healed in Israel, asked permission to take a few loads of earth back to Syria in order to erect a shrine where he could worship the god of the Israelite soil – the God of Abraham, Isaac, and Jacob (2Ki. 5:17). He also asked the "man of god" for permission to give lip-service to Syria's local deity, Rimmon, which was graciously allowed by the far-seeing Elisha. Later prophets were to be even more progressive.

A lengthy study must be done to appreciate how the prophetic message about God's nature, sovereignty, and expectations progressed. Over time the later prophets began to present God as not merely the sovereign of Israel, but as the champion of righteousness and justice in the world. Yes, he was there to meet Israel's needs, but he was also there to rebuke and punish them for unrighteous and unjust behavior. He was not only sovereign king, He was also holy judge – not just of Israel, but the world. Nevertheless the general population ignored the prophets, even killing them on many occasions, preferring the local deity to the universal king of righteousness and justice. They were religious nationalists. The prophet Isaiah's words were lost to them, "I am the Lord, and there is no other, beside me there is no God" (Is. 45:5). They wanted a king on his throne in Jerusalem, a messiah who would establish a kingdom, *now*. Let the other gods bow to him. Let Israel rule! Thus the cry at Jesus' "triumphal entry": "Hosanna" – "Save now!" (Heb.).

So Jesus had to re-educate the people. The Kingdom was not to be a nationalistic powerplay. Rather, it was to have a present day "small beginning" and grow to a size that would encompass the world and beyond. All nations, and all individuals, be they Jewish or Gentile, were to be judged at the end of days. The Kingdom would see many refused and many welcomed. The key to entry was not national entitlement but personal repentance. This was both intriguing and baffling to the people. Sometimes they thought they understood him. Jesus knew they did not. The events of the crucifixion ("crucify him!") and resurrection ("he is risen!") proved him right. The Kingdom was, and is, a conundrum. For sure it is not a democracy. But make no mistake, it is coming. Jesus' warning is timeless, "the time is fulfilled, and the kingdom of God is at hand; repent, and believe the Gospel" (Mk. 1:15 KJV). "Thy kingdom come" is the daily prayer that spans the ages and stretches to the eternities.

The Great Hope 13:31–35

Not all Pharisees were unfriendly to Jesus (Nicodemus and Joseph of Arimathea come to mind), so we needn't look at this warning from some of them as disingenuous. They told Jesus to flee because "Herod wants to kill you" (v.31). After all, he had killed John the Baptist, why not Jesus? Jesus' answer was bold: he didn't fear demons and wasn't intimidated by diseases, so Herod was a minor threat – he had more important work to do in Jerusalem.

That important work was to be the watershed of salvation history. He was to die for the sins of humankind in Jerusalem. The thought of his impending death in that holy city brought on a lament (v.34). Jerusalem had a history of stoning and killing those sent by God to call the people back to righteousness and justice. It would happen again, not at the hand of an insignificant despot, but by the Lord's own children. Their "house", that is the Temple ("God's house"), had been forsaken by its occupant (v.35). The Father had left, and his son was about to be sacrificed on a criminal's cross. But there was hope, a hope beyond the comprehension of the Pharisees, and even the disciples:

Jesus would come again. He would come "in the name of the Lord" (v.35). Luke would record the angelic announcement in his second book to Theophilus, "This same Jesus, who has been taken from you into heaven, will come back…" (Ac. 1:11). Jesus is coming again! This is "The hope of the Church".

Guess Who's Coming to Dinner! 14:1–24

While Jesus sat/reclined at dinner as guest of a prominent Pharisee, a fascinating mix of healing and discussion took place. The healing had to do with a man suffering from what several versions call "dropsy" (edema – swelling due to water retention). He must've been a man of influence to have been included in this "by invitation only" dinner with the radical Galilean rabbi, in spite of his condition. But he was there and Jesus healed him, even though it was the Sabbath. He "sent him on his way" (v.4b) probably due to the man's sudden need to show himself to his family and friends. Regardless, Jesus perceived the non-verbal push-back from the host and guests for "working" a healing on the Sabbath. So, he asked them a piercing question about their own Sabbath behavior (vv.5,6) and then told two parables about distraction, hubris, entitlement, and the Kingdom of Heaven. The room was silent.

One of the guests broke the silence with a well-known beatitude (v.15) but Jesus was unimpressed with the condescending bromide. He bluntly made three points, all directed at those sharing the meal:

1. You'll miss out on the feast of the Kingdom because of your busyness (v.18).

2. The poor, the crippled, the lame, and the blind (v.13) whom you see as "sinners" will feast at the banquet while you will be rejected.

3. Spiritual pride (v.11) and your sense of national entitlement (vv.23,24) will nullify entry to the Kingdom. The Gentiles, those who live outside the city on the roads and in the laneways, will take your place. Luke gives no account of Jesus wearing out his welcome, but I expect he was invited to leave (if not to jump off a cliff! 4:29).

The Cost of Discipleship 14:25–35

Luke stresses the fact that "great multitudes" of people (v.25) followed Jesus as he walked from town to town. They were, like all crowds, a complex of mixed motives, personal agendas, and religious/political ideals. They ran the gamut from the child-like innocent to the flaming revolutionary firebrand. Each saw Jesus through the lens of their own needs and expectations. Many were simply too keen in their desire to follow him. Their enthusiasm was eviscerating. They were drawing out Jesus' lifeblood even before he gave it willingly on Calvary. He had to prune the tree.

Imagine the pruning effect of the word "hate"! It polarized the crowd even as it polarizes us today – "If anyone comes to me and does not hate his own father and mother and wife and children and brothers and sisters, yes, and even his own life, he cannot be my disciple" (v.26 RSV). Many probably slunk away, shocked and disappointed by what they'd heard. They may not have understood, or appreciated, Jesus' predisposition to hyperbole at key moments in his ministry.

Imagine the pruning effect
of the word "hate"! It polarized
the crowd even as it polarizes us today.

For instance, "And if your right hand causes you to sin, cut if off and cast it from you; for it is more profitable for you that one of your members perish, than for your whole body to be cast into hell" (Mt. 5:30 NKJV). Did Jesus want a bunch of dismembered disciples following him around? Of course not. But he was exaggerating for the sake of emphasizing that adultery was forbidden for the child of God.

On another occasion he was very terse with the crowd who were pressing in on him, hoping for another free meal (Jn. 6:26). Jesus stopped them in their tracks with, "Most assuredly, I say to you, unless you eat the flesh of the Son of Man and drink His blood, you have no life in you" (Jn. 6:53). He went on to describe his flesh and blood as "the bread which came down from heaven" (v.58 NKJV), but the words had had his intended effect: "From that time many of his disciples went back and walked with him no more" (v.66). Jesus knew how to thin out a crowd.

Jesus' use of the word "hate" may not have been as hyperbolic as it was nuanced. Luke, who wrote in Greek, would have known these nuances. One need not be a Greek scholar to do the research and discover at least three uses of "to hate" in scripture:

"And you will be hated by all for My name's sake."
—Mt. 10:22 NKJV

"Blessed are you when men hate you,
And when they exclude you,
And revile you, and cast out
Your name as evil."

—Lk. 6:22

"But I say to you who hear: Love your enemies, do
good to those who hate you, bless those who curse
you, and pray for those who spitefully use you."

—Lk. 6:27

These are but a few examples of "hate" as unjustifiable malice. This kind of hatred actively shuns (Lk. 6:22b), slanders ("reproach" v.22c), and publicly imputes evil (v.22d) on its object. It "prays against" ("curse" – Gk.) and "falsely accuses" ("spitefully uses") the one it vilifies. It sees its object as worthy of death.

Then there is "hate" as virtue, as in an aversion to evil. Both St. Paul and the anonymous author of the book of Hebrews captured this nuance:

"We know that the Law is spiritual; but I am unspiritual,
sold as a slave to sin. I do not understand what I do.
For what I want to do I do not do, but what I hate I do."
—Ro. 7:14,15

"You have loved righteousness and hated wickedness…"
—He. 1:9

St. James' brother Jude caught this nuance too:

"Be merciful to those who doubt; save others by snatching
them from the fire; to others show mercy, mixed with fear
– hating even the clothing stained by corrupted flesh."
—Ju. 22

Later, in the apocalyptic book of Revelation Jesus commended the Ephesian church for hating "the practices of the Nicolaitans" (early Christian heresy) which "I also hate" (Re. 2:6).

A third use of "to hate" is in the context of relative preferences:

"No one can serve two masters. Either you will hate the one
and love the other, or you will be devoted to the one and
despise the other. You cannot serve both God and money."
—Mt. 6:24

This is where our present passage rests. Jesus is referring to the preference of God over anything or anyone else. Some commentators refer to this act of preferment as "renunciation". But this should not be misunderstood. Jesus often affirmed the family, blessed children, and even provided for the security of his widowed mother from the cross (Jn. 19:25-27). He loved his mother, but he also "so loved the world" (Jn. 3:16). So his life's calling required an alignment of core values. We must do the same.

He went on to talk about carrying a cross. Jesus carried his long before his ultimate crucifixion. It was the cross of self-denial, the cross of obedience to the Father, the cross of accountability, the cross of self-discipline, the cross of being misrepresented and misunderstood, the cross of suffering, the cross of loneliness…

Why did he carry it? Was it because he had a destiny? Was it because he knew that destiny required dedication and discipline? Was it because he was living for something bigger than his own needs?

To carry a cross you've got to have a world view. You've got to live for the big picture. A self-absorbed life won't do. But it costs to live beyond one's self-interest. Sometimes it hurts to see the need of your neighbors and minister to them lovingly. In the light of eternity, however, the cost is short-term. It's a wise investment, requiring thought (vv.28-33), and acceptance of the sober truth that the Kingdom doesn't come cheap. "So we fix our eyes not on what is seen, but on what is unseen, since what is seen is temporary, but what is unseen is eternal" (2Co. 4:18).

Salt is Salty (or it's not) 14:34, 35

Followers of Jesus who do not prioritize righteousness (love for God) and justice (love for neighbor) lack both the zest and the preserving quality of salt. A true disciple is both enthusiastic and compassionate. He/she is energized by vision for the future Kingdom and by compassion for the neediest (Ja. 1:27). That kingdom mentality sees them ordering their lives with spiritual and moral rectitude, "Seeking first the kingdom and its righteousness [justice]." They keep their edge.

Jesus stresses that saltiness is a matter of choice. If we choose not to hear we will be "thrown out" (v.34a). So, open your ears and pay the price (v.34b).

God's Love for Losers 15:1–32

The chapter begins with the Scribes and Pharisees at it again, accusing Jesus of socializing with low life – "tax collectors and sinners" (read "prostitutes"). They were over-reacting and misrepresenting the situation, but they just couldn't countenance a "rabbi" mingling with the marginalized. Jesus saw it otherwise. These lost souls were exactly why he had come.

Parable of the Lost Sheep 15:1–7

Today in North America an entire city of millions of people can be brought to attention by an "amber alert", a call via all media outlets for citizens to be on the lookout for one lost or abducted child. We respond viscerally and actively because there is within us a reflex to rescue the helpless. Regardless of our station in life, or our spiritual/moral condition, the "image of God" within us reaches out to a lost child. That image is but a pale reflection of our Creator's heart for lost men, women, and children throughout history. He actively seeks to find the lost. That's why He sent his Son. "For God so loved the world…" (Jn. 3:16). The following three parables capture God's love for lost souls, starting with the iconic parable of the lost sheep.

Maybe the key point in this parable is not the "lostness" of the sheep but its value as a sheep. Its worth is the same in the fold as it is when wandering the wilderness.

Parable of the Lost Coin 15:8–10

Again, there is a central point. Value is value, whether lost or found. The coin, in this case, is lost in the house, whereas the sheep was lost outside the fold. Whether the woman was intent on spending it, or saving it, Jesus doesn't say. But she wanted to find it, so she sought it, found it, and included her neighbors in the celebration. When the lost is found, Jesus says, there is rejoicing even in heaven (vv.7,10). There is a pivot point, however. More of that in the next parable.

Parable of the Lost Son 15:11–32

Maybe this should be called "the parable of the lost sons", because there are two in the story, one lost outside the house, the other inside. The younger son was self-absorbed in his pursuit of pleasure, the older son in his self-righteousness. Both were in need of redemption. One repented (v.21), the other did not (vv.29,30). What intrigues me is how the older brother assumed that his younger brother had "devoured" the father's wealth "with harlots". He may have made this assumption because that was his own fantasy. The father, like the shepherd, and the woman, actively sought out the lost, suggesting that our "search for God" may be a response to his search for us. "No one can come to me unless the Father who sent me draws them" (Jn. 6:44). But that "coming" pivots on repentance (vv.7,10,21). Jesus constantly stressed that repentance was the key to entry into the Kingdom of God. It's a non-negotiable. *Everyone* needs to repent. "There is no one righteous, not even one; there is no one who understands; there is no one who seeks God. All have turned away, they have together become worthless; there is no one who does good, not even one" (Ro. 3:10-12). And, just a reminder: confession is not repentance. Confession says, "I did it"; repentance says, "I'll never do it again." Confession is a burst of relief. Repentance is a stone-cold act of resolve: "I will arise and go to my father" (v.18). Our capacity to make decisions is a vital aspect of our worth. God respects it.

The Street-Smart Manager 16:1–9

This parable can be off-putting at first reading. Jesus seems to be applauding dishonesty. Some have used it as an excuse to defend their own shrewdness. But there is a subtlety here that's easy to miss. As was the case with all his parables, Jesus told this one with the Kingdom in view.

No one, let alone Jesus, would see "cooking the books" (vv.5-7) as virtuous. The unjust steward was in damage control, looking out for himself, planning ahead. When his chicanery was revealed, his master commended his foresight not his dishonesty. Jesus is doing the same, with a twist.

The twist is this: how about helpful citizens of the Kingdom of God acting with foresight? All good ends are built on well thought-out means. How about the "means of unrighteous mammon"? (v.9 RSV). With that money you can "make friends" of the poor, and they will repay with prayers of gratitude that will see you "receive[d]… into… eternal habitations" (v.9b) – this was how the religious tradition of Jesus' day saw the "quid pro quo" of charitable acts. In other words, think in terms of eternal reward when planning for the future. As the old adage says, "Only one life, 'twill soon be past, only what's done for Christ will last."

"Unrighteous Mammon" and True Riches 16:10–12

"Unrighteous mammon" (vv.9,11) was a common term in religious Jewish culture. All money, however acquired, was seen as tainted in some way. But the taint could turn to fragrant aroma if used in righteous endeavors.

Jesus calls his followers to be faithful in their management and disbursal of money, with a view to their earthly investments producing "true riches" (v.11). Ultimately one's only treasure is banked in the Kingdom of Heaven.

God and Money Don't Mix 16:13–15

"You cannot serve God and mammon" (v.13 RSV) is not an imperative. It's merely a statement of fact, like "oil and water don't mix". Money, of course, is not the issue. The *love* of it is the issue. If you love it it's difficult to love God at the same time. And if you love God you won't love money. You'll use it, certainly, but you won't love it. The two loves are mutually exclusive.

Apparently some Pharisees overheard this teaching, and were offended because they "loved money" (v.14). So they "sneered" at Jesus, mocking his naive counter-cultural values. They saw their wealth as a reward for righteousness. Jesus saw it as a snare (v.15). Indeed, he called their spiritualized materialism "detestable". Hearing this, you can be sure the Pharisees felt their contempt justified.

Three Random Sayings 16:16–18

The first of these three unrelated sayings (v.16) refers to the tumult of the times re: "the Kingdom of God". As I've already discussed in this commentary (see 13:22-30) there were more than a few interpretations, religious and cultural, fuelling the simmering frustrations and expectations of the people in Jesus' day. This volatile atmosphere had been brought near to the boiling point by the catalytic influence of John the Baptist.

John was the pivot point between "the law and the prophets" and "the Kingdom of God". Jesus' high view of John's role in salvation history made him unique among scores of end-time zealots who had tried (and were still trying) unsuccessfully to rout the Romans and force the Kingdom into existence. So their "preaching" of the Kingdom was rife with violent talk and action. Jesus, of course, was not endorsing this zealous culture of violence, but was merely observing the painful false labor of a nation attempting to induce a premature eschatological delivery.

The second saying (v.17) may reflect the reckless view of some that Jesus' teaching abrogated the Law of Moses, releasing all kinds of sinful mayhem as "sinners and tax collectors" trampled roughshod over the traditions of the elders. Jesus made sure to stifle this misrepresentation. In his view the scribal "stroke of a pen" in the rigorous copying of the text of the Law was as inviolable as the very creation itself.

As a stand-alone the third saying (v.18) is indeed unrelated to the other two – but, the concept of inviolability may tie this one to the second. Jesus bluntly states that marriage between a husband and wife is inviolable. There are no mitigating factors in the Law. And he takes no time on this occasion to talk about "sexual immorality" (Mt. 19:9), or irreconcilable differences (implied in Mt. 19:8) that often surface in domestic life. He stands with the Law. Period.

Unbelief brings its own blindness.
He who will not see will not see.

The Rich Man and Lazarus 16:19–31

This parable needs no theological reflection. Nor is it necessary to discuss the ancient Jewish concepts of "sheol" or "hades", "hell" or "gehenna". Suffice it to say that for most of Israel's history there was belief in an afterlife. Jesus simply employs common imagery to make a profound point: the religious elite will not be convinced of the Gospel, even by Jesus' resurrection. Unbelief brings its own blindness. He who will not see will not see.

On Millstones, Forgiveness, and Faith 17:1–10

When Jesus referred to "these little ones" (v.2) he sometimes meant children (Mt. 18:1-5; Mk. 10:13-16) and sometimes those who were newly born to the Kingdom. Any child, whether chronologically or spiritually, will offend, requiring understanding and forgiveness, even if it's seven times a day (v.4). We are to forgive, not because we're weak enablers, but because "little ones" are citizens of the Kingdom both now and in the future.

The disciples recognized that this posture of forgiveness required both maturity and faith. So they humbly asked Jesus to "increase our faith!" (v.5). Perhaps the aspect of millstones sinking them into the sea added to their ardor – thus the exclamation point. Assimilating Jesus' teaching was serious stuff.

Jesus responded with matter-of-fact bluntness. The increase of faith starts with duty (v.10). The disciples were servants, not lords, in the Kingdom. As servants they were expected to do as they were told (v.9). There may have been some muttering. They preferred to see faith as philosophy and theology, not action.

The Grateful Samaritan 17:11–19

This anecdote stresses one point: God doesn't ask for much, but gratitude is one of Heaven's core values. Ten lepers are healed simply by following Jesus' command to go and show themselves to the local health officials (the priests). They are healed on the way. Nine of them (all Jews) continue to the priests, but one (a Samaritan) in total joy turns back and loudly thanks Jesus, throwing himself at Jesus' feet in a paroxysm of gratitude.

Why only this one? Why the foreigner? Could it be that as the ten walked to the priests, the Samaritan held back, perhaps in doubt as to the priests' willingness to assess the health of a Gentile? The nine continuing in a group, the Samaritan following at a distance, feeling very much the outsider? Suddenly feeling strength in his diseased feet, health in his ravaged hands? Turning back from the distant nine and running to Jesus, overcome with astonishment and excitement?

Who knows how it happened? But it did happen. And once again, it was the outsider who praised God, while the insiders carried on spiritually numb, blind to the Kingdom. The Pharisees certainly got the message. They'd had enough of this Kingdom talk.

When will the Kingdom Come? 17:20–37

Their patience thin, their sense of offence palpable, the Pharisees said something like, "Ok. Ok. Enough. Let's cut to the chase. When *is* the Kingdom going to come?" This was just as much a "demand" (v.20 KJV) as it was a question. They *wanted* the Kingdom to come. Indeed they had been anticipating the Day of the Lord for at least four centuries during what is called the "inter-testamental period". But their expectation of its final coming was predicated on portents: natural disasters, cosmic chaos (moon into blood), and universal warfare. These would be the "signs" signalling the end of days. And so they were on the lookout. But Jesus threw a wrench into their eschatology, "The Kingdom of God is not coming with signs to be observed…" (v.20 RSV). He jolted them with "behold, the Kingdom of God is within you" (v.21 KJV).

The conventional response by commentators is that Jesus could not have been addressing Pharisees with this last statement. But why not? The Pharisees like all human beings, were created by God in his "image" (Ge. 1:27). Everyone has his stamp on their soul. Pharisees were not bogeymen. There were some very good ones, like Nicodemus, Joseph of Arimathea, and the Apostle Paul. In his "Areopagus address" in Athens Paul told a crowd of animists and idolaters that "in him [they] move and have [their] being", and that "We are his offspring" (Ac. 17:28). Being made in the image of God means there is a homing instinct for heaven in both the righteous and the unrighteous, the Pharisee and the "sinner". It's like the "smoking flax" or the "bruised reed" (Is. 42:3), and intuitive (albeit faint) knowledge and expectation of the Kingdom to come. God seeks to redeem, not destroy. The when? And where? (v.37) is up to him. So live like the Kingdom is coming today (vv.22-37). Better yet, live like it's here right now "in the midst of you" (v.21 RSV).

Prayer: A Petition, a Boast, or a Plea? 18:1–14

Although the Lord may welcome a simple heart-to-heart conversation, he usually hears one-sided requests. In these three examples via parable Jesus affirms two.

The widow (vv.2-8) is persistent. So much so the "unjust judge" (v.6) grants her petition just to get her out of his hair. In fact, his concern, "she will wear me out" (v.5 RSV), means literally, "lest she come at last and beat me" ("lest she blacken my eye"). She must have been a formidable woman!

The despised tax collector (v.10) was so stricken with his burden of sin that he "would not even lift up his eyes to heaven", but "beat his breast, saying, 'God be merciful to me a sinner!'" (v.13 RSV). His prayer was a desperate plea for forgiveness. This was a prayer that saw him "justified" before God.

The proud Pharisee, on the other hand, took stock of his righteous acts (vv.11,12) and congratulated himself before God. His spiritual narcissism got him nowhere (v.14). In Jesus' view faithful persistence and humility are the companions of a broken and a contrite heart" (Ps. 51:17). These the Lord "will not despise".

I wonder if the Lord sometimes "despises" agenda-driven prayers? I wonder how often the "prayers of the saints" are purely love-driven in worship? This *is* a love story after all. Prayer is about relationship.

Jesus' Love for Infants 18:15–17

In this brief account we see Jesus rebuking his "handlers" for mishandling children. In the Greek the word is "infants". Mothers were bringing their babes in arms to Jesus for his blessing. The disciples saw this as a distraction and an annoyance. Jesus saw it differently. An adult has many material, philosophical, religious, and residual guilt concerns to overcome when approaching the Lord. A child, on the other hand, is bathed in innocence. That uncritical, simple trust is prerequisite to entering the Kingdom. It belongs to those of a "childlike spirit".

The Rich, Young Ruler 18:18–30

The Kingdom talk continued, this time in the form of a sincere question from a wealthy young synagogue governor. He got off on the wrong foot, however, by calling Jesus "good" (v.18). Jesus' response was a subtle double entendre: essentially he was saying, "Don't flatter me, and only God is good". In other words, "If you really knew who I am you'd prostrate yourself before me." No one should have the temerity to flatter God.

The question was, "What must I do to inherit eternal life?" He wanted to know the entry requirements for the Kingdom of God. He had been faithful to the core values of the moral law (the Ten Commandments – vv.20,21) but he was still "lacking" (v.22) something.

That lack was the product of misplaced loyalty. He loved his money (v.23), and, as Jesus had made clear (16:13), the love of God was to trump all other loves. So, Jesus' challenge to the young man's true love saw him sadly slink away. Watching him leave, Jesus exclaimed at the almost insurmountable barrier that "riches" build between this world and the next. His listeners, like all human beings, had a high regard for material security. In a reflex of guilt they asked, "Then who can be saved?" (v.26 RSV). Jesus answered that God could make it happen (v.27).

Peter jumped in, perhaps rationalizing his own love of money, by blurting that the Twelve had bankrupted themselves to follow him (v.28). Jesus kindly reminded him that he'd be more than compensated "in the world to come" (v.30 KJV). God is in debt to no one, other than to those who are "kind to the poor" (Pr. 19:17a). These compassionate ones he not only pays back, but rewards (19:17b).

THE JOURNEY TO JERUSALEM CONTINUES 18:31–19:48

Jesus and his disciples had probably been following the eastern shore of the Jordan River as they travelled towards Jerusalem. The road through Samaria from Capernaum was a shorter distance, but arduous because of the terrain. This route through Perea was fairly level, but once Jericho had been reached, the ascent to Jerusalem was difficult. I have driven it many times with my little car nearly breathing its last as we crest the hill in Bethany.

Somewhere near Jericho Jesus and the Twelve were talking, and for the third time (9:22,24) he gave them a heads-up about what would happen to him in Jerusalem. They didn't get it (18:31-34).

As they came into the city a blind beggar, aware of Jesus' arrival by the noise of the crowd, called out loudly for attention. "Jesus, Son of David, have mercy on me!" (v.38). Jesus responded with an unexpected question: "What do you want me to do for you?" (v.41). Obviously the question was intended for the crowd. The blind beggar gave the predictable answer, and Jesus healed him. There was great rejoicing and praise to God on the part of everyone (vv.42,43). Luke doesn't say if the messianic title used by the beggar, "Son of David", was given any thought by the crowd. But for some who followed Jesus and the Twelve up to Jerusalem, it may have fuelled more than a few "Hosannas" a few days later.

In all the fuss, rejoicing, and pushing and shoving, those in the crowd may not have noticed a short man up a tree. Perhaps one observant person shouted and pointed, "Look! Up there! Zacchaeus the tax collector!" Jesus looked up and called Zacchaeus down with the stunning announcement that he wanted to stay that night at his house. The people were shocked, "He has gone to be the guest of a sinner" (v.7). Tax collectors were persona non grata, the scum of the earth in the people's view. They were amazed, and troubled, that the "Son of David" would associate with such a man.

Zacchaeus, without preamble, made his own announcement, "Look, Lord! Here and now I give half of my possessions to the poor, and if I have cheated anybody out of anything, I will pay back four-times the amount" (v.8). He was the poster-boy for repentance.

Both John the Baptist and Jesus preached repentance as key to entry into the Kingdom of God. In response to this tax collector's repentance Jesus declared him "saved" (v.9). And he took the opportunity to remind those gathered at Zacchaeus' house that salvation of the lost was his first priority (v.10).

A Warning Parable to the Risk-Averse 19:11–27

This is a fairly lengthy parable with a brief but poignant application. It's a story Jesus told predicated on the people's mistaken expectation that the Kingdom of God was about to appear (v.11). It teaches a blunt lesson: the king will arrive in his own time. The people's political/religious agenda is irrelevant. So, they should invest their lives productively. Anyone fearful of failure will ultimately lose.

The Triumphal Entry 19:28–48

Time and again in the gospels there is reference to the fulfillment of Old Testament prophecy in the life and teachings of Jesus. This passage is a case in point. There are several Old Testament references that provide a prophetic/historical context for what has been termed "the triumphal entry". Here they are, in no particular order:

"Rejoice greatly, O daughter of Zion; shout,
O daughter of Jerusalem: behold, thy king
cometh unto thee: he is just, and having
salvation; lowly, and riding upon an ass,
and upon a colt the foal of an ass."

—ZE. 9:9 KJV

"Blessed is he who comes in the name of the Lord..."

—PS. 118:26

[8] *"Then the man of God began to weep.*
'Why is my Lord weeping?' asked Hazael.
'Because I know the harm you will do
to the Israelites,' he answered. 'You will
set fire to their fortified places, kill their
young men with the sword, dash their little
children to the ground, and rip open their
pregnant women.'"

—2KI. 8:11B,12

[9] *"Woe to Ariel, to Ariel, the city where*
David dwelt... Yet I will distress Ariel,
and there shall be heaviness and sorrow...
I will camp against thee round about,
and will lay siege against thee with a
mount, and I will raise forts against thee.
And thou shalt be brought down, and thy
speech shall be low out of the dust..."

—Is. 29:1-4 KJV

---

[8] For the Jewish historian Josephus' perspective, Google Josephus *"Wars of the Jews"* Book 5
[9] For the Jewish historian Josephus' perspective, Google Josephus *"Wars of the Jews"* Book 5

"Even them will I bring to my holy mountain,
and make them joyful in my house of prayer...
for my house shall be called an house of prayer
for all people."

—Is. 56:7

"Is this house, which is called by
my name, become a den of robbers
in your eyes?"

—Je. 7:11

"For the zeal of thine house hath
eaten me up..."

—Ps. 69:9

In Luke's account we find a mélange of prophetic (Isaiah, Jeremiah, Zechariah, Psalms) and historical (Kings) material that blends with at least two agendas (Jesus' and the people's), incorporating a parade, an unexpected purging of the Temple, a lament over Jerusalem, and the initiation of a plot to kill Jesus. If you read the above passages you'll see "the triumphal entry" in three dimensions (past, present, future).

A few quotes from the narrative are intriguing: "The Lord has need of it" (v.31); "Blessed is the king who comes in the name of the Lord!" (v.38a); "Teacher, rebuke your disciples!" (v.39); "If they keep quiet, the stones will cry out" (v.40); "The days will come upon you when your enemies will build an embankment against you and encircle you and hem you in on every side. They will dash you to the ground... because you did not recognize the time of God's coming to you! (vv.43,44); "My house will be a house of prayer, but you have made it 'a den of robbers'" (v.46).

In v.31 Jesus refers to himself as "Lord". In v.38a the people call him "King". In v.39 the Pharisees call him "Teacher". In v.40 Jesus states that the natural world ("stones") is ready to recognize and endorse his kingship. In vv.43,44 his prophetic lament over Jerusalem foreshadows the siege of Jerusalem in 70 AD by Titus. And, in v.46 he stresses the significance of the Temple as the touchstone of interaction between heaven and earth.

But, most intriguing in my view, is the reason he gives for Jerusalem's future demolition under the Romans: "because you did not recognize the time of God's coming to you." Jesus had a high (indeed the highest) view of himself. He was God's "visitation" (Gk.). Little wonder the Sanhedrin wanted to kill him (v.47). In rejecting him, as they would in just a few days, the people would be rejecting God himself. But at this point "all the people hung upon his words" (v.48). Indeed, all history hangs on his words.

Most intriguing is the reason he gives for Jerusalem's future demolition under the Romans: "because you did not recognize the time of God's coming to you."

THE SANHEDRIN TRIES TO SILENCE JESUS 20:1–47

The Sanhedrin was a council of seventy men comprised mainly of chief priests (Sadducees), Scribes, and elders (Pharisees). It governed civil society with legislative, executive, and judiciary authority. Its judgements were like those of a supreme court. It was sometimes referred to as the "beit din gadol" (Heb.) which means "great house of justice". And, for those who saw it as the ultimate arbiter of social/religious law it was called "knesset ha gadolah" meaning "the great synagogue". Thus, only Jews of Israelite descent were members of this august body. Two of those members figured prominently in the life (and death) of Jesus: Nicodemus and Joseph of Arimathea, both good men.

The Sanhedrin was the ultimate Jewish authority in Roman-occupied Jerusalem. This may have been at the root of their question to Jesus, "Tell us by what authority you do these things, or who it is that gave you this authority" (v.2 RSV). Undoubtedly they were still reeling over Jesus' cleansing of the Temple a few days previously. They knew in their hearts that the Sadducean commercialization of God's house was wrong, but as has always been the case in human history, it's all about money.

The question related not only to civil but also to religious authority. The Sanhedrin were empowered to both keep the peace and maintain the traditions of the elders (Oral Law). In their eyes Jesus was a threat to both. So they were trying to trap him, either in terms of some insurrection so that they could charge him before the Roman procurator (Pilate) or, failing that, they hoped to ensnare him in some heresy or blasphemy to undermine his authority with the people. Jesus answered this question with a question of his own (v.3).

Jesus was not being "Socratic" as much as "rabbinical" with this question-for-a-question technique. To this day (and I speak from personal exposure to rabbinical schools – "yeshivot" – in my years in Jerusalem) it is a common teaching/learning approach. A rabbinical student never learns alone. He/she must have a "foil", another student, who argues the other side of an interpretive truth with the expectation that clarity will emerge out of this dynamic tension. In the Jewish cultural/spiritual world belief is communal. Indeed one cannot even pray in a synagogue service if a "minyan" (ten men) is not present. In Jesus' time the "traditions of the elders" was that communal orthodoxy. So, as far as the Sanhedrin was concerned, Jesus was dangerously offside.

Nevertheless, he asked them about that other out-of-the-box threat, his own cousin John the Baptist. Was he from man, or from God? This trapped his interlocutors. If they answered "from heaven" they knew Jesus would ask, "Why didn't you believe him?" And if they said, from men, "the people will stone us" (vv.5,6). It was a lose-lose situation. So they kept silent. As did Jesus, and he moved on, telling this deputation a troubling story.

A Disturbing Parable 20:9–19

There's no need for us to interpret this parable of the wicked tenants. The delegation from the Sanhedrin made an immediate application. Luke says, "they knew he had spoken this parable against them" (v.19). Offended, and afraid, they sought for a way "to arrest him immediately". Fuelling their urgency was the troubling shadow of Isaiah's prophetic warning adding weight to Jesus' parable:

> *"I will sing for the one I love*
> *a song about his vineyard:*
> *My loved one had a vineyard*
> *on a fertile hillside.*
> *He dug it up and cleared it of stones*
> *and planted it with the choicest vines.*
> *He built a watchtower in it*
> *and cut out a winepress as well.*
> *Then he looked for a crop of good grapes,*
> *but it yielded only bad fruit.*
> *Now you dwellers in Jerusalem and people of Judah,*
> *judge between me and my vineyard.*
> *What more could have been done for my vineyard*
> *than I have done for it?*
> *When I looked for good grapes,*
> *Why did it yield only bad?*
> *Now I will tell you*
> *What I am going to do to my vineyard:*
> *I will take away its hedge,*
> *and it will be destroyed;*
> *I will break down its wall,*
> *and it will be destroyed;*
> *I will break down its wall,*
> *and it will be trampled.*
> *I will make it a wasteland,*

neither pruned nor cultivated,
and briars and thorns will grow there.
I will command the clouds
not to rain on it!
The vineyard of the Lord Almighty
is the nation of Israel,
and the people of Judah
are the vines he delighted in.
And he looked for justice, but saw bloodshed;
for righteousness, but heard cries of distress."

—Is. 5:1-7

They were also more than aware of Isaiah's, Daniel's, and the psalmist's warnings (Is. 8:14; Da. 2:34; Ps. 118:22) of what would happen to those who thwarted God's purposes for mankind. The prospect of being "broken... crushed... ground into powder" by gentle Jesus, meek and mild, was galling. So they fulminated and plotted. Neutralizing him became their obsession.

Jesus Won't be Cornered 20:21–26

So "the teachers of the law and the chief priests" (v.19) sent "spies who pretended to be sincere" (v.20) with what they thought was a clever question. After flattering Jesus, publicly (vv.21,26), they asked whether it was "right" to pay the annual poll tax levied by Rome on every Judean male. This was a loaded question: if he said yes, then he would alienate all the fervent nationalists (including the Twelve) among his myriad followers; if no, then he could be arrested for treason. Jesus' answer was succinct: God's property is his, the Emperor's is his. Pay both their due. His interrogators had no come-back.

A Resurrection Controversy 20:27–40

Just a reminder: the Pharisees (and the Scribes who were mostly from the pharisaic school of thought) believed in resurrection; the Sadducees

349

did not. The Pharisees were the "conservatives", the Sadducees were the "liberals".

These liberals came to Jesus with what they thought was a clever question based on a very complicated scenario. The first of seven brothers married but died before fathering a son. So, according to Moses' law of "levirate marriage" (Dt. 25:5,6), the second brother, the third, the fourth, and so on all died in turn after marrying this most unfortunate widow. Then she herself died. Question: "in the resurrection whose wife of them is she?" (vv.28-33 KJV).

To give them their due, the Sadducees accepted the first five books of the Bible (the Pentateuch) only. There is no mention of the life to come, or of resurrection in those books. So their question had a legitimate theological justification. With this hypothetical challenge to Jesus they were trying to illustrate the obscurity of resurrection, and to trap Jesus in, at least, a non-Sadduceean heresy.

Jesus was quick to declare that marriage has no relevance in heaven, where there is no death and no need of procreation. Those who will one day inhabit heaven will be "those who are considered worthy" (v.35), a view consistent with the pharisaic belief in a "resurrection of the just" (14:14). Moses may not have written about resurrection but he implied it when he recounted the voice of God from the burning bush, "I am the God of your father, the God of Abraham, the God of Isaac and the God of Jacob" (Ex. 3:6). God is God of the living, so the Sadducees' patriarchs were still alive. Once again Jesus' questioners slunk away, mute. The Scribes, on the other hand, who had heard this exchange, and who believed in resurrection, actually complimented Jesus, "Well said, teacher!" (v.39). Jesus must have been shocked.

A Parting Shot from Jesus 20:41–44

As the Sadducees retreated Jesus sent an unexpected question their way, "Why is it said that the Messiah is the Son of David?" (v.41). Maybe a few of them understood what Jesus was getting at. They had not questioned him about resurrection out of theological interest. No, they had questioned him publicly in order to undermine his public credibility. They were trying to chip away at his massive popularity with the people, those very ones who triumphantly were hailing him, "Son of David", a code for "Messiah". The Sadducees, mistakenly, thought Jesus was accepting this designation. "Son of David" was loaded with political ramifications. It was an earthly term for "insurrectionist".

Jesus dealt a blow to this inference. "Son of David" could not mean "Messiah". Did the Sadducees not know the Psalms? David himself had referred to the Messiah as "Lord" (Ps. 110:1). So how could he at the same time "be his son?" (vv.42-44). In other words Jesus was saying, "Don't saddle me with a political agenda." Yes, Jesus was Messiah, but not on their terms.

Watch Out for Those Guys! 20:45–47

Jesus turned from the Sanhedrin delegation to address the Twelve and the crowd who'd listened in. He focused his scathing comments on the Scribes.

"Beware of the Scribes", was his blunt warning. These purported "holy men", tasked with the vital ministry of defending the Mosaic Law, were scoundrels, exploiting the weakest link of society (widows), parading around in their "long robes", preening and praying publicly. They were in for "greater damnation" (v.47 KJV) in the world to come. Heaven doesn't look kindly on show-offs. Spiritual pride combined with social injustice is a sure formula for "greater condemnation" (RSV).

A Widow's Copper Coins 21:1–4

Jesus "looked up" (v.1) from the crowd who had gathered around him in "the temple courts" (20:1) and saw some of his Sadduceean, Scribal, and Pharisaic critics "putting their gifts into the temple treasury" (21:1). The temple tithes and taxes were collected at thirteen trumpet-shaped boxes located in the women's court. The giving protocol required the giver to verbally announce both the amount and the purpose of the gift. To be sure, Jesus' detractors, pompous and wealthy, made loud public declarations of their largesse. One poor widow, however, anonymously slipped her two little copper coins into the trumpet, and melted humbly into the crowd. Jesus was impressed.

It was the quality, not the quantity of the gift that stirred Jesus to say, "this poor widow has put in more than all of them" (v.3). These pathetic little "mites" (KJV) – "all she had to live on" (v.4) – were diamond-like in Jesus' view, whereas gifts "out of the abundance" of the deep-pocketed rich were like chunks of coal. Gifts that cost the giver nothing are not gifts at all. God is no waiter. Give your tips to someone who is.

A Picture of What is to Come 21:5–38

To appreciate this passage one should begin with the last two verses: "Each day Jesus was teaching at the Temple, and each evening he went out to spend the night on the hill called the Mount of Olives, and all the people came early in the morning to hear him at the temple" (vv.37,38). These teaching sessions at the Temple and Jesus' nights spent in Bethany on the south-western slopes of the Mount of Olives were Passover-related and short-term. Thousands of pilgrims (perhaps as many as one hundred thousand) came up to Jerusalem for the three mandated annual festivals (Passover, Pentecost, Tabernacles). There was a carnival atmosphere in the city. And everyone wanted to be there for Passover, the "Super Bowl" of festivals. So everything that Jesus did and taught at this time was done in a milling crowd.

One morning some of the crowd who had assembled at the Temple to hear Jesus were remarking (like tourists) on the beautiful stonework. Jesus interrupted with a grim word, "the days will come when there shall not be left here one stone upon another that will not be thrown down" (v.6 RSV). Really? they thought. Then out loud, "Teacher, when will these things happen?" And, being a "signs and portents" religious culture they asked, "What will be the sign that they are about to take place?" (v.7).

Any student of history will be quick to reference Josephus ("*Wars of the Jews*" 6:4,5) and remark about the total destruction of Jerusalem by Titus in 70AD. In a relatively short period of time Jesus' words came true. But there is more in Jesus' words that applies above and beyond

70AD. That's why it's important to read this passage as "broad brush", big picture strokes of color – some strokes short-term, some long-term. Jesus was not writing a systematic treatise about the end of days. Rather, he was painting an "impressionist" work that could only be appreciated by stepping back a bit, viewing it with eyes of the soul.

In that this is not a treatise I won't comment on it as a treatise. Instead I'll look at the painting from a few paces back and comment on what I see/hear Jesus saying:

1. Keep your head clear (v.8,9).

2. There will be geopolitical upheavals (v.10).

3. There will be natural disasters (v.11).

4. There will be persecution of Christians resulting in family fracture, martyrdom, social rejection (vv.12-17).

5. Jerusalem will be destroyed by Gentile forces (vv.20-24).

6. Universal traumas will culminate in the coming of "the Son of Man" (vv.25-28).

7. The generation that sees "the times of the Gentiles... fulfilled" (v.24 – compare Mk. 13:10) in concert with these shaken "heavenly bodies" (v.26) will see the coming of the Lord (vv.27-32).

There is a mix of elements in this dissertation, some short-term local, some long-term universal. But the overall message is, "lift up your heads, because your redemption is drawing near" (v.28). The faithful are to live their lives in a spirit of expectation. The heavenlies are sprouting leaves (v.30). Jesus is coming soon. This is the "parousia", the historic "hope of the Church".

The Last Supper 22:1–23

The identification of the Passover with the Feast of Unleavened Bread was a natural cultural blend. Passover, a one day event, began at sundown on Nisan 14 and ended at sundown on Nisan 15 (Thursday sundown to

Friday sundown). Thursday was "the day of preparation" when everything was set in order for the feast, including the slaying and roasting of the paschal lamb. But the Feast of Unleavened Bread ran for seven days, starting with Passover (Le. 23:5,6). No "hametz" (leaven – Heb.) was allowed in any dwelling for that week. To this day in Israel Orthodox Jewish families purge their homes of leaven before the Feast, and commercial food stores shroud any of their aisles which feature breads, biscuits, or confections that are made with yeast. "Matzah" (unleavened bread) rules.

After Peter and John had overseen the venue and preparatory details for the Passover seder (vv.8-13), Jesus and the others joined together just before sunset ("When the hour came…" v14a) to eat the meal. Leonardo da Vinci's 15th century mural of "The Last Supper" is one of the world's most famous paintings, but it gives a misleading impression of how people ate together in Jesus' day. They didn't sit but "reclined at the table" (v.14b). This meant that the table was approximately eighteen inches off the floor, and it was surrounded by cushions for comfort on the incline. And, one ate with one's hands (as does much of our world to this day – eg. India, Sri Lanka, Ethiopia).

There has been a lot of polarizing parsing of Jesus' few words about the bread and the wine. But what is going on here? Luke records a traditional seder which would have had various Passover-specific items on the menu including bread (matzah) and wine. The seder liturgy is similar to the weekly "Kabbalat Shabbat" ("Welcoming the Sabbath") ceremony that occurs in observant Jewish homes every week on "erev Shabat" ("Sabbath eve"). The oldest male at the table blesses the wine and distributes it to all those gathered for the meal. Then he breaks and blesses the bread, passing it to all. Jesus attached a significant meaning to this ritual by declaring the poured wine and broken matzah to be trigger mechanisms for memory. He didn't want to be forgotten (v.19b). This meant that every time his followers broke the bread and poured the wine, not only at Passover but also every week at Kabbalat Shabat, they would pause in remembrance of the "lamb who was slain". The Twelve were "founding members" of a "new covenant" of grace (v.20). But they would have been perplexed by trans-substantiation/con-substantiation disputes that would later divide the Church (trans-substantiation: the bread and wine are mystically transformed into the actual body and blood of Jesus; con-substantiation: Jesus accompanies the bread and wine). They, of course, had no control over what future centuries of Church leaders would create from this poignant historic seder.

Another element of poignancy was the brief reference to betrayal. When Jesus said, "the hand of him who is going to betray me is with mine on the table" (v.21), all the disciples (including Judas) would have quickly removed their hands. From their perspective he could have meant any of them. They looked at each other with suspicion (v.23).

Who's the Greatest? 22:24–30

This was not the first time the disciples' egos rose to the surface (see Mk. 9:34 and Lk. 9:46). The ongoing contest to be alpha male betrayed their total lack of understanding with regard to the person and purpose of Jesus. They were locked into a nationalistic concept of the end of days. They fully expected to be the triumphant Messiah's cabinet who would rout the Romans and rule the world from Jerusalem.

The ongoing contest to be alpha male betrayed their total lack of understanding with regard to the person and purpose of Jesus. They fully expected to be the triumphant Messiah's cabinet who would rout the Romans and rule the world from Jerusalem.

Jesus had already told them that "the one who is least among you all" would be "the greatest" (9:48). But they obviously weren't listening.

355

Their hunger for power trumped this counter-intuitive and counter-cultural servanthood that Jesus was talking about. How could a leader be "one who serves"? (v.27).

Nevertheless Jesus looked beyond this obtuseness and affirmed them for their three years of discipleship (v.28), and declared something that they again would misunderstand. When he said, "I confer on you a kingdom…" (v.29a), they could think only in terms of temporal rule. The concept of the "Kingdom of Heaven" was, even yet, beyond them. They would have resonated to "Kingdom… thrones… judging the twelve tribes of Israel" (v.30), but their betrayal (Judas), denial (Peter), and desertion (the Ten) just a few hours later revealed their self-serving agendas. They weren't about to back a "loser". However, the subsequent resurrection (ch.24), ascension (Ac. 1) and Day of Pentecost events (Ac. 2) would transform them from cowards into champions. Their destiny was not to rule the world, but to transform it with the "good news" (Gospel) of the Christ.

"Simon, Simon" 22:31–34

Luke's summary of the conversation does not include what must have been a reactive bluster from Peter. Whatever it was, Jesus gave a kind rebuke, "Simon, Simon…" (v.31). I say "kind" because Jesus included "all of you", not just the defensive Peter, as targets of Satan's wiles. But he knew that Peter would be traumatized a few hours later when he realized what he had done in disowning his friend. A sleeping rooster was soon to crow (v.34).

Two Swords? 22:35–38

Yes, the disciples had two swords and they used at least one of them shortly thereafter on the Mount of Olives (vv.49,50). Jesus encouraged them to buy swords if they didn't have one by selling their cloaks. Protection from enemies would take priority, at least for awhile, over protection from the elements.

Jesus quoted Isaiah 53:12 where the "suffering servant" is seen by the populace as one of "the transgressors" (v.37). The disciples would be among those transgressors. The people would crucify Jesus. What would they do to the disciples? Indeed, all but John suffered martyrs' deaths. There's no historical record of them using swords in personal protection, but apparently Jesus wanted them prepared for any eventuality with "purse... bag" and "sword" (v.36).

Maybe his mentioning swords was an accommodation on his part to the disciples' sense of vulnerability. We don't know. But he ended the seder conversation with, "Enough!" Time to get on with it.

THE PASSION 22:39–23:49

Betrayed by one of his own, arrested by thugs, and mocked by the high priest's guards, Jesus resolutely practised what he had prayed, "Father... not my will but yours be done" (v.42). The drama unfolded quickly: Jesus at prayer, disciples asleep, a crowd of ruffians with Judas in the lead, a swinging sword, a near miss, a severed ear, a healing, pushing and pulling Jesus down through the Kidron Valley and up to the house of the high priest, Peter's fear of arrest and his denial of Jesus, mockery, beating, insult. It's a gripping read.

Two powerful things stand out as I read. One is something Jesus said, the other something he did. To the arresting "officers of the temple guard" (v.52) he said, "This is your hour – when darkness reigns" (v.53). And to Peter his message was non-verbal: he "turned and looked straight at Peter" (v.61).

The betrayal, arrest, and mockery of Jesus all took place under the cover of darkness. The Apostle John, writing about a conversation Jesus had with one of the Sanhedrin members, Nicodemus, records Jesus saying, "And this is the condemnation, that light is come into the world, and men loved darkness rather than light, because their deeds were evil" (Jn. 3:19 KJV). Luke doesn't name any of "the Council of Elders" (v.66 – read "Sanhedrin") and not all were there (it *was* Passover after all).

It's very unlikely Nicodemus was there, although we see him playing a prominent role in Jesus' burial after his crucifixion (Jn. 19:38-42). But, the point is: men love to do their evil deeds in the dark. We forget that "light is come into the world" and nothing is hidden from the Lord. One thinks of C. S. Lewis' classic children's books, *The Narnia Chronicles*. In "The Last Battle" one of the closing scenes has the disgruntled, disbelieving dwarfs insisting on staying in the darkness of a false prophet's shed while the light of Narnia, and the freedom it brings, is just on the other side of the door. "The dwarfs is for the dwarfs," they grumble. Leave us alone. We prefer the dark.

As for Peter, we can relate. All of us can remember a moment when we were "found out" and that parent, teacher, loved sibling, or friend said nothing, but looked at us with eyes full of disappointment and hurt. It's crushing. It certainly crushed Peter, "he went outside and wept bitterly" (v.62). The look said, "You say you don't know me, but I know you." Indeed, Jesus looked right into the darkness of Peter's soul. What else to do but weep bitter tears?

The upside is that Peter's profound shame led to repentance, for later in the story he fulfilled Jesus' prophetic insight, "When you have turned back [read "repentance"], strengthen your brothers" (v.32b). He stood tall on the Day of Pentecost (Ac. 2) as he preached the powerful first sermon of the early church.

Great sorrow and mental/spiritual distress leading to repentance has often been the catalyst for great hearts to magnify the Lord. One of Scotland's most famous sons, the much loved blind poet-preacher Dr. George Matheson, in a private moment of intense anguish composed a hymn that was published in "The Scottish Hymnal" in 1885. He wrote that "it was composed with great rapidity: it seemed to me that its construction occupied only a few minutes, and I felt myself rather in the position of one who was being dictated to. It was the quickest piece of work I have ever done." [10] *"Oh Love That Will Not Let Me Go"*.

---

[10] Google "O Love", or "O Love That Will Not Let Me Go" – You Tube

THE GOSPEL OF LUKE

"O Love that will not let me go,
I rest my weary soul in Thee:
I give Thee back the life I owe,
That in Thine ocean depths its flow
May richer, fuller be.

O Light that followest all my way,
I yield my flickering torch to Thee:
My heart restores its borrowed ray,
That in Thy sunshine's blaze its day
May brighter, fairer be.

O joy that seekest me through pain,
I cannot close my heart to Thee:
I trace the Rainbow through the rain,
And feel the promise is not vain
That morn shall tearless be.

O Cross that liftest up my head,
I dare not ask to fly from Thee:
I lay in dust life's glory dead,
And from the ground there blossoms red
Life that shall endless be."

Jesus Condemned 22:66–23:25

It was still dark as Jesus was arraigned before a hastily convened, ad hoc "trial" by "the elders of the people and the chief priests and the scribes..." (v.66 KJV). This was the Sanhedrin. There may not have been a quorum in that it required getting people out of bed. Some may have scrambled in late.

They wanted to catch Jesus in a blasphemy. Their question was double-edged, "If you are the Messiah tell us" (v.67), and "Are you then the Son of God?" (v.70). If Jesus answered "yes" he would be accused of insurrection against Rome ("Messiah" being "king of the Jews"), and the ultimate blasphemy – claiming divinity. Jesus was in a lose/lose situation. So he refused to answer. "You say that I am," was all he said. But this was enough for a kangaroo court. They hauled him off to Pilate who lived at the Antonia fortress.

The Roman procurator may have been rubbing the sleep from his eyes, grumbling at being rousted from his bed, as the raucous crowd accompanying the Sanhedrin roared their approval at the Sanhedrin's charges against Jesus. Their accusation, of course, had nothing to do with blasphemy. Rather, they focused on Jesus' threat to the rule of Rome: destabilizing the nation (v.2a), forbidding his followers to pay taxes to Rome (a lie – v.2b), claiming kingship in direct defiance of the Emperor (v.2c), and teaching insurrection (v.5). They were adamant, "urgent" even (v.5), or as the KJV puts it, "fierce".

Pilate found their charges specious (v.4) but was under extreme pressure. He saw an opportunity to opt out when Jesus' accusers shouted, "He stirs up the people all over Judea by his teaching. He started in Galilee and has come all the way here" (v.5). The key word, to Pilate's relief, was "Galilee". This was the tetrarch Herod Antipas' jurisdiction, and he was in Jerusalem at that moment (v.7b). So Pilate quickly, and happily, sent Jesus across the city to the tetrarch's apartment at the Herodian citadel.

Unlike Pilate, Herod Antipas was "glad" ("exceeding glad" KJV) to see Jesus. He had wanted to meet him for some time. He wanted to see a magic show (v.8). He tried to get Jesus to talk, but the only talking was coming from his accusers who were "vehemently accusing him" (v.10). Jesus' silence vexed him, so his blandishments morphed to contempt and mockery (v.11a). He gave "a gorgeous robe" (KJV) to his soldiers to place on Jesus' shoulders and sent him back to Pilate. At that moment, and Luke doesn't say why, the two rivals, Herod Antipas and Pilate, "became friends" (v.12 RSV). Maybe they both resonated to the irony of the royal vestments.

Pilate tried three times to convince the leaders and the mob that Jesus was not guilty of their changes, "But they were urgent, demanding with loud cries that he should be crucified" (v.23 RSV). They insisted that Pilate release a man slated for crucifixion and kill Jesus in his place. "Crucify, crucify him!" They shouted. Pilate caved and sent Jesus to Calvary.

Jesus Crucified 23:26–49

In the Mosaic Law there were several prescriptions for dealing with crimes and misdemeanors. One of the more cruel punishments was to stone the miscreant to death and then hang his body on a tree or pole as a public warning to those who might be considering breaking the law (Dt. 21:23). It was a horrible thing to be hung from a tree. The Israelites detested it. Indeed, the Apostle Paul, a Pharisee, wrote, (quoting Deuteronomy) "Cursed is everyone that hangeth on a tree" (Ga. 3:13). So the cross became a huge issue for the Jews of Jesus' day. How could someone cursed by God be the Messiah?

The Greeks, Romans, Egyptians, Persians, and Babylonians all employed crucifixion for crimes such as cowardice in war, theft, piracy, sedition and other violent acts like assassination. Alexander the Great is reported to have crucified two thousand Syrians after the fall of Tyre. And, as we see in this text, the Romans utilized this horrific form of tortuous death for insurrectionists, murderers, and violent criminals during their occupation of Palestine.

A brief description of crucifixion is in order, but it won't be pretty. The Romans scourged the victim before crucifying him. This loss of blood would hasten death. The victim was required to carry the crossbeam to the place of execution. He was then roped to the cross, sometimes nailed, and left hanging to die a thousand deaths over the next few days. Heat, thirst, jagged swelling wounds, inflammation, aching tendons and joints, and exposed nerves were excruciating. Often there were throbbing headaches. And for those whose deaths were protracted, tetanus could convulse the torn body till at last the heart failed and the victim died. Sometimes the Roman soldiers, out of pity, would shorten the victim's misery with the thrust of a sword or spear. Or, more out of cruelty than compassion, they would break the victim's legs, causing the body to

361

collapse forward, compressing the chest and lungs, causing death by asphyxiation.

Apparently Jesus was already weak as he tried to carry the cross to Calvary. So the soldiers "seized one Simon of Cyrene" (v.26 RSV) and forced him to carry it behind Jesus. Little is known of Simon. Cyrene was a city on the North African coast of the Mediterranean with a significant Jewish population. Luke mentions this Libyan city three times in his second volume (Ac. 2:10; 6:9; 13:1). It may be that Simon was in Jerusalem as a Passover pilgrim. Nevertheless he's the only person in history to literally carry the cross of Christ. This act elevated him to heroic, if not saintly status in the view of Christians throughout the succeeding centuries.

The narrow streets of Jerusalem do not handle a crowd well. I've been caught several times over the years in both festive and mournful crowds of thousands. The streets are jammed. You stand shoulder to shoulder, back to front, shuffling along at a snail's pace, with either shouts of joy or wailings of sorrow splitting your ear drums. It can be a touch scary. You're caught, and you have no control. Escape is nearly impossible. So, as I read Luke's account of the "great multitude" and ululating of the women lamenting Jesus' plight (v.27), I can identify. You can be sure it was chaotic.

At one point Jesus stopped and spoke to the wailing women, warning them that a day would come when they would prefer death by earthquake or landslide (v.30) to the intense suffering that would come upon them. His crucifixion would be a watershed. Right now Jerusalem was relatively "green" but once "dry" she would burn in a great conflagration of divine wrath (v.31). A few decades later his words would come tragically true. (Google: Josephus, *"Wars of the Jews"* Book 6)

There are two Calvary's today. Both are marked by hundreds of thousands of pilgrims who visit Jerusalem each year. The "oldest" is within the Church of the Holy Sepulchre, the "younger" is adjacent to a garden outside the Damascus gate. One was "discovered" by St. Helena, the mother of the Roman Emperor Constantine in the 4th Century, the other by British General C. G. Gordon in the late 19th

Century. Centuries of pilgrimages bear witness to the tradition that St. Helena got it right, whereas the Garden Tomb advocates' only claim is that Gordon's Calvary is an "excellent visual aid". (Google: "Church of the Holy Sepulchre" and "Gordon's Calvary pictures"). Personally, I've spent hours in each, and I love them both. Neither, by the way, may be the actual site, although most archaeological study suggests St. Helena *may* have been on the right track.

They were strategically placed by the Romans on a major road(s) leading from the city to other major cities. The point was maximum visibility for maximum impact.

Both sites were/are "outside the gate" (He. 13:12). This underlies the fact that execution sites were never within the city proper. They were strategically placed by the Romans on a major road(s) leading from the city to other major cities. The point was maximum visibility for maximum impact.

These execution grounds were used by both Romans and Jews. The Romans crucified their victims, the Jews stoned theirs. Insurrectionists and criminals were crucified, blasphemers, adulterers, and heretics were stoned. The public stood by during these executions (see Acts 7:54 – 8:1), the victims of stoning bleeding to death at their feet, the victims of crucifixion at eye-level. Brutal.

Depending on the written language the site of Jesus' crucifixion was "Calvaria" (Latin), "Kranion (Greek), or "Golgotha" (Hebrew), all meaning "skull". Sometimes it's referred to as "Skull Hill". Luke, summarizing as usual, gives no descriptive detail. He simply states, "there they crucified him" (v.33 KJV, RSV). Even as he was being hung on the cross he prayed for his enemies. The soldiers weren't listening. They were too keen casting dice to get their hands on that "gorgeous robe" that Herod had draped over Jesus' shoulders.

The gawkers gawked and the mockers mocked. Even one of the two criminals crucified on either side of Jesus sneered at him. And, there was powerful non-verbal abuse in the form of the notice affixed above his head in Latin, Greek, and Hebrew: "This is The King of The Jews". Pilate wanted to cover his back by representing Jesus as an insurrection-ist, a would-be king. He also wanted to give an in-your-face insult to the religious leaders who had insisted on Jesus' death by announcing to the world (thus the three languages) that Jesus *was* the Messiah. Then, irony of ironies, the very first person to enter Paradise with the crucified Lord was a repentant criminal! (v.43). His entry must have made the angels sing! The number one trophy of grace! Here he is! As the heavens rejoiced they made preparation for all those who would follow until the dawning of the Day of the Lord.

Darkness descended on Jerusalem from noon until three in the afternoon. Then, with a loud voice Jesus cried, "Father, into your hands I commend my spirit" and "breathed his last" (v.46). At that moment the curtain separating the Holy of Holies from the rest of the Temple was torn in two. Only a remarkable power could have done that. The curtain (veil) was richly and heavily woven (perhaps as thick as six inches), decorated with cherubim on blue, scarlet, and purple twined linen (Ex. 26:31; 36:35; 2Ch. 3:14). It hung from four pillars of acacia (Ex. 26:32) and provided a veritable impassible barrier both symboli-cally, and physically. It was a formidable reminder of the inaccessibility and holiness of the God of Abraham, Isaac, and Jacob. Whereas the high priest entered past the veil only once a year to make atonement for the people in the Holy of Holies, now God was accessible at all times to all the people. Jesus' death split open the barrier between heaven and earth. The only one to appreciate the significance of the moment was the Roman centurion (v.47). The gawkers slunk away, while some of the faithful watched from a distance (v.49). The body of the Christ hung in the darkness, alone.

Jesus is Buried 23:50–56

Enter Joseph of Arimathea. Even though he lived about ten miles north of Lydda (modern day Lod) he was a member of the Sanhedrin. *But* (and this is a big "but") he "had not consented to their purpose and deed" (v.51) when the Sanhedrin had called for Jesus' death. He was a devout Jew "looking for the Kingdom of God" (RSV). Whereas he had till now been a secret believer he risked his reputation, his place on the council, and his physical/spiritual purity (because touching a dead body meant ritual defilement) to take Jesus' body down from the cross, prepare him, and carry him to his own "rock-hewn tomb" (v.53 RSV) to bury him before sundown. What is more, he did this work as an Orthodox Jew, work of any kind forbidden on the Sabbath (the Passover was a special Sabbath, even though, in this case, it was also preparation day for the weekly Sabbath that would start a few hours later that day at sundown – v.54).

As Joseph did this courageous, loving work, Luke records that the believing Galilean women (vv.49,55) were watching. He says they "prepared spices and perfumes" (v.55) with the intent to return to Joseph's tomb after the Sabbath to finish what had been a hurried preparation of Jesus' body. Their shock, grief, and disappointment would not mitigate their love.

He Has Risen! 24:1–12

The women may have slept poorly that night as keen as they were to get to the tomb at first light. Their spices were intended to lessen odor during the four days of customary visitation by friends and relatives to the burial site of the recently buried. But, when they got to the tomb they were surprised to see that the stone used to cover the entrance had been "rolled away" (v.2). They cautiously went into the tomb to discover that Jesus' body was not there. They were "perplexed" (v.4 KJV). Suddenly two angels appeared, and as the women prostrated themselves in fear, the angels asked, "Why do you look for the living among the dead?" Before the women could gather themselves to answer, the angels made the greatest announcement in history: "He has risen!" They then reminded the women that Jesus had given them a heads-up about resurrection back in the Galilee (vv.6,7). The women remembered, and those words were without doubt on their breathless lips as they walked/ran back to tell the Eleven what had transpired. Their astonishing news, however, was quickly dismissed as "nonsense" (v.11). The only one of the Eleven to give credence to the report was Peter. His wings had been clipped on the Thursday night previous. Now his repentant heart took flight as he "ran to the tomb" (v.12).

On the Road to Emmaus 24:13–35

In his second volume (Acts 1:3) Luke writes that Jesus made many post-resurrection appearances over the next forty days. One of the first has captured the imagination of all readers, especially theologians and artists (!) (Google "Road to Emmaus"). He relates that "two of them", meaning two of "all the rest" of the disciples to whom the women reported Jesus' absent body at the tomb (v.9), decided that very day to walk back to their homes in Emmaus. One of them was named "Cleopas" (v.18).

As they walked they were discussing what had just happened. They were not rejoicing (yet) at the news about the empty tomb. They were confused, disappointed, and sad (vv.14-17). Their downcast spirits betrayed their sudden loss of hope that Jesus had been the Messiah: "we had hoped that he was the one who was going to redeem Israel" (v.21). But now he was dead. Or was he? (vv.19-24).

Suddenly Jesus joined them. Luke records no surprise on their part, perhaps because they had been walking with "faces downcast" (v.17) and may have assumed he had simply overtaken them on the road. Nevertheless, they didn't recognize him – "their eyes were holden", (KJV), which means in the Greek that they were being kept from recognizing him by some supernatural agency. He both questioned and rebuked them (vv.17,19, 25, 26) and then "explained to them what was said in all the scriptures concerning himself" (v.27). He intrigued them, to the point that they invited him to dinner (vv.28,29).

Jesus, over the meal, "took bread, gave thanks" and "broke it" (v.30). At that moment the eyes of the two disciples were no longer "holden".

They recognized him, and even as their hearts raced Jesus disappeared. They were so amazed they got up, and even though it was dark, walked all the way back to Jerusalem to tell the assembled disciples what had just happened. There was no push-back this time. The Eleven reported, "It is true! The Lord has risen and has appeared to Simon" (v.34). You can be sure they talked well into the night.

Some time in the early hours of the next morning, Jesus shocked them by suddenly appearing in the room.

Jesus in Jerusalem 24:36–49

Some time in the early hours of the next morning, Jesus shocked them by suddenly appearing in the room. They were so frightened, thinking he was a ghost, that his greeting, "Peace be with you" was lost. He comforted them and showed them his hands and feet that had been wounded, evidence (remarkably) that his now glorified body still bore a scar or two (vv.38-40). Then he asked for something to eat!

As he ate he did what he had done a few hours earlier with Cleopas and his friend, "he opened their minds so they could understand the Scriptures" (v.45). Then he mandated them as witness-bearers, and told them to stay in Jerusalem until "my Father" clothed them "with power from on high" (vv.46-49).

Jesus Ascends 24:50–53

A few weeks later, Jesus ascended to heaven. He tells Theophilus more about it in the first chapter of his second volume (Acts 1). To be continued...

THE BOOK OF ACTS

INTRODUCTION

There have been many critiques and spins over the years by theologians that cast the two volume work "Luke/Acts" into various degrees of light. It is not the purpose of this "Casual Commentary" to explore any of these. However there are common threads that emerge in the study of these disparate interpretations:

1. Luke is writing a history.

2. He sees the work of the Holy Spirit in the founding and organizing of the early church.

3. He affirms the Christian faith as universally applicable (that is, for Gentile as well as Jew).

4. He aims to convince the Roman authorities that Christianity is no threat to the Empire.

CANTELON'S CASUAL COMMENTARY

For the Christian Church the Gentile Luke is as vital an historian as Josephus is in his *"Antiquities of the Jews"*. Both men have given us critical narratives, without which we would be in the dark. There are no parallel histories to either work. Both put a Jewish story into a world-wide setting. We owe them a huge debt.

The Apostle Paul had a very high view of Luke. He accompanied Paul on some of his itinerations and kept a diary or travel log (thus the "we" passages in 16:10-17; 20:5-16; 21:1-18; 27:1-28:16). Paul refers to him as "the beloved physician" (Cl. 4:14), the faithful friend (Pm. 24; 2Ti. 4:11) and co-worker. Paul found him in Antioch, the city where Christianity was launched into the Gentile world.

He may have been a slave at one point but had been given the opportunity to train in medicine. He was fluent in Greek and Aramaic, was rigorous in research, and was an effective writer. Indeed, "Luke/Acts" is the largest historical narrative in the New Testament. His work spans the gulf between the story *of* Jesus and the story *about* Jesus. For Christians throughout the ages he is the "beloved" bridge-builder.

FROM JERUSALEM TO ANTIOCH AND BEYOND 1:1–12:25

Jesus Ascends 1:1–11

In Volume One of Luke/Acts the author tells Theophilus the story *of* Jesus. This second volume is *about* Jesus, specifically the presence and work of the resurrected Christ in the Church and in the world. In Acts, Luke records the spread of "The Way" (as early Christianity was called) from Jerusalem to Antioch, from Palestine to Asia Minor and Europe. He transparently describes the emergence of a Jewish/Gentile faith delivered through the agonizing birth pains of an exclusive sect of Galilean fishermen who became "apostles" but didn't even recognize the infant Church at first. Indeed, until the first Church council (Ac. 15) some of them had seen it as an illegitimate hybrid. Like all births, the breakout of Christianity was fraught and messy. The final "push" was the Ascension.

370

The first volume had ended with a cursory account of Jesus' ascension (Lk. 24:51). In the second Luke provides critical detail.

It's fascinating to read that Jesus gave "instructions through the Holy Spirit to the apostles he had chosen" (v.2). In the Introduction it was mentioned that the Holy Spirit is a constant theme in Acts. Even Jesus is represented as teaching "through" the Spirit. In Luke's day there was no developed doctrine of the Trinity. The concept itself, and the interaction between the members of the Godhead, was left for Church Fathers, councils, and theologians to sort out in later centuries. For Luke's purposes, however, he introduced Jesus' reliance on the Holy Spirit as foundational to the gifting, baptism, and evangelizing that was about to create and sustain the nascent Church.

The "convincing proofs" (v.3) of the resurrection were absolutely vital to kick-start the new era of the Spirit. These proofs were entailed in appearances Jesus made to his disciples over the course of forty days. Paul, the "least of the apostles" (1Co. 15:9), would later stress the appearances of the resurrected Jesus as the only evidence to prove the validity of Christianity (1Co. 15: 3-18). And, to speak "about the Kingdom of God" (Ac. 1:3) with any authority at all, demanded resurrection. Otherwise the purported Son of God was still in the ground, another failed messiah.

Luke gives no specific location as to where Jesus and the disciples were "assembled together" (v.4 KJV). The Greek word used ("synalizo") can mean "being assembled together", or "eating salt together", or "lodging together", or even "bivouacking together" ("camping with them in the open"). The military term "bivouac" engages the imagination.

According to Volume One (Lk. 21:37) Jesus and the disciples spent their nights the week previous to the crucifixion "on the hill called the Mount of Olives". Maybe the disciples were camping again, and Jesus showed up at the campsite. It certainly jibes with Luke's reference to "the vicinity of Bethany" (Lk. 24:50) as the general area where the ascension occurred. Then again, Bethany, on the eastern slope of the Mount of Olives, was the home of Mary, Martha, and Lazarus. Maybe the Eleven were visiting there. Luke leaves us guessing. (Alas, speculation and conjecture are the companions of all interpreters of historical texts).

So, whether they were being served a meal by Martha, or they were gathered around a campfire, Jesus gave them a command: "Do not leave Jerusalem, but wait for the gift my Father promised, which you have heard me speak about (see Lk. 24:49). For John baptized with water, but in a few days you will be baptized with the Holy Spirit" (vv.4,5). John the Baptist had baptized with water, a ritual known to Jews as immersion in a "mikvah". It was a departure from the norm, however, in that he did it in a river. But he had referred to a coming baptism by Jesus that would be "with the Holy Spirit and fire" (Lk. 3:16). No one knew what John had meant, nor did the disciples on this occasion. This Holy Spirit talk went over their heads. They wanted to hear something else: "Lord, are you at this time going to restore the kingdom to Israel?" (v.6). At this point the resurrection had yet to alter their hope for a national theocracy. The "Kingdom of God" in their view meant "Kingdom of Israel". They totally misunderstood the "promise" (v.4). They intently "gathered around him" (v.6) for his answer.

Jesus' mandate would require a teeth-clenching, gut-wrenching leap into the religious/cultural dark.

Jesus firmly responded, "It is not for you to know the times or dates the Father has set by his own authority" (v.7). In other words, "None of your business!" But there *was* something they needed to know: "You will receive power when the Holy Spirit comes on you." This power, endued by the Holy Spirit's baptism would equip them for worldwide (not just Jerusalem-wide, or Judea-wide) witness to the resurrection. The "ends of the earth" meant "gentile", and "Samaria" meant "half-breed". Yikes! Were these Galileans ready for this? Jesus' mandate would require a teeth-clenching, gut-wrenching leap into the religious/cultural dark. What they would learn, however, was that the Holy Spirit would light the way. A "light to the Gentiles" would take on new meaning.

Luke's description of the ascension is a declarative statement, "After he said this, he was taken up before their very eyes, and a cloud hid him from their sight" (v.9). There is no adverbial or adjectival embellishment. But the word "cloud" has great significance.

The book of Daniel, in the Old Testament, is a fascinating read. It is a mix of historical narrative, mysterious visions, and apocalyptic content. In one of his visions Daniel sees "One like a son of man, coming with the clouds of heaven" (7:13a). The "Ancient of Days" would give him "an everlasting dominion" and "all nations and peoples of every language" would worship him (vv.13b,14). Most rabbinic and theological interpreters read this as a reference to the future Messiah. I see it that way too, but for my present purposes it's the "clouds" that interest me.

During the exodus from Egypt "the Lord went ahead of them in a pillar of cloud" (Ex. 13:21a). Later at Mount Sinai the cloud was both an evidence of the overshadowing presence of God and a means of shielding Moses and Israel from direct contact lest they die ("you cannot see my face, for no one may see me and live" (Ex. 33:20). Centuries later King Solomon said, "The Lord has said that he would dwell in a dark cloud" (1Ki. 8:12).

The cloud imagery was utilized by the angel Gabriel when he announced to Mary that she would bear a son, "the power of the Most High will overshadow you" (Lk. 1:35), and three of the Gospel writers wrote about the cloud that appeared and covered Peter, James, and John at the transfiguration: "a bright cloud covered them... a cloud appeared and covered them..." (Mt. 17:5; Mk. 9:7; Lk. 9:34). Ezekiel referred to the cloud as "the glory of the Lord" (Ez. 1:28). The rabbis equated the "glory of God" with the "name of God" and called it "the Shekinah".

"Shekinah" (shacen" – Heb) means "to dwell" or "that which dwells". The rabbis used it to describe the nearness of God to his people as he put his "name" ("Ha Shem" – Heb.) in a special place. Moses instructed the Israelites "to seek the place the Lord your God will choose... to put his Name there for his dwelling" (Dt. 12:5). Some of those "places" were the ark of the covenant (Nu. 10:35, 36; 1Sa. 4:3c), a cloud and a pillar of fire (Ex. 13:21), various sanctuaries: Shechem (Ge. 12: 6,7), Beersheba (Ge. 21:33), Bethel (Ge. 28:16-19), Peniel (Ge. 32:30), Shiloh

CANTELON'S CASUAL COMMENTARY

(Jg. 18:31), and, of course, the Tabernacle, then the Temple in Jerusalem, "the city where God has placed his name" (2Ch. 6:6).

In the Christmas story Luke records that "the glory of the Lord shone around" the terrified shepherds at the angelic announcement of Jesus' birth (Lk. 2:9). At the Transfiguration the Three "saw his glory" (Lk. 9:32) with a much matured Peter reflecting years later, "He received honor and glory from God the Father when the voice came to him from the Majestic Glory, 'This is my son, whom I love; with him I am well-pleased' " (2 Pe. 1:17). So, whether it was the Old Covenant with "the cherubim of the Glory overshadowing" the Ark (He. 9:5) or the New Covenant where "The Son is the radiance of God's glory" (He. 1:3), the ultimate view of Jesus was expressed by James – "our Lord Jesus Christ, the Lord of glory…" (Ja. 2:1 NKJV). So, as the cloud descended, then ascended, taking Jesus with it, the disciples knew this was no raincloud. It was the "presence", the "glory", the "Name", the Father himself. It was no surprise to suddenly see "two men dressed in white" (angel clothes) standing beside them. Heaven was touching earth at that moment. Their promise that Jesus would "come back" became the "hope of the Church" ("parousia" – Gk.).

A New Apostle vv. 12–16

Rabbinic law mandated that an observant Jew could not walk more than two thousand "cubits" on the Sabbath day. This distance (approximately three thousand feet) was based on the story of Joshua leading the children of Israel across the Jordan river (Js. 3:4). The Ark of the Covenant was to go first, and the people were to follow at an interval. A "Sabbath day's journey" became common currency when determining distance in general. It could apply to any day of the week.

Down the mount the disciples walked, across the Kidron Valley, and up to the city – "a Sabbath day's walk" (v.12) – to the upstairs room in John Mark's mother's home. This would be known in history as the "Upper Room", the place where John the Baptist's words came to life, "He will baptize you with the Holy Spirit and fire" (Lk. 3:16), the birthplace of the Church.

Sometime later ("In those days…" v.15) a large group of believers joined the Eleven (v.11) in that room. Altogether there were one hundred and twenty men and women (vv.14,15). It was both a prayer and a business meeting. The point of the business was to nominate two men, one of whom would be chosen by lot to replace Judas Iscariot as one of the Twelve.

In his preamble to the choice Peter applied David's words (Ps. 109:8) to Judas which "the Holy Spirit spoke long ago…" (v.16). Judas, as treasurer, had played an integral role in the day to day administration of Jesus' ministry. In their travels with Jesus they had learned that love for God required love for neighbor, both worship and work. There had to be some management of itineration details, stewarding of donations, paying of bills, etc. Judas had carried a lot of that responsibility. But somewhere along the way he had become deceitful ("adikia" –Gk.– "injustice, wrong, iniquity, falsehood, deceitfulness") and had accumulated enough money (through skimming? Jn. 12: 5,6) to buy a field (v.18). This was not the money he had been given for his betrayal of Jesus (Mt. 27:5). That field had become the "Field of Blood" (v.19) when Judas, in remorse, had hung himself after throwing the "thirty pieces of silver" at the feet of the priests in the Temple. Apparently he had hung there for days (weeks?) until either the rope broke, or worse, his decomposed body fell to the ground.

The qualifications for the new apostle were straightforward: he must have been with Jesus from the start of his ministry, and was a witness to the resurrection. This meant that the choice would most likely be limited to the seventy-two (Lk. 10). Justus and Matthias were nominated. The people prayed (v.24) and Matthias was chosen by lot.

The Church is Born 2:1–47

The Day of Pentecost 2:1–13

In Leviticus Moses relayed the Lord's instructions with regard to "my appointed festivals" (23:1). These festivals included the Passover and the Festival of Unleavened Bread (vv. 4-8), the Festival of Weeks (vv.15-22), the Festival of Trumpets (vv.23-25), the Day of Atonement (vv.26-32), and the Festival of Tabernacles (vv. 33-44). Passover (Unleavened Bread), Weeks, and Tabernacles were the three annual agrarian festivals that required every Israelite male to attend the Temple (Ex. 34:22,23).

Passover began "at twilight on the fourteenth day of the first month" and Unleavened Bread began the next day (Le. 23:5,6). From the fifteenth to the twenty-first of that month ("Nisan" is the first month of the religious year and the seventh month of the civil year) there was to be no yeast in Israel's homes.

When my family and I lived in Jerusalem I used to walk from our home on Mount Scopus (next to the Mount of Olives) to my office in Rehavia (central Jerusalem). The ultra-orthodox community of Mea Shearim ("one hundred gates") was on my route. Year after year I was always fascinated by what took place the week before Passover. Rabbinic tradition over centuries has escalated the proscription of yeast to annual general housecleaning. Large kettles appear at the main intersections of Mea Shearim where they are filled with water, set over bonfires (or gas-powered flame) to boil, and the dishes and cutlery of each home are placed in them for cleansing. This happens while their homes are thoroughly purged of anything bearing yeast (bread, crackers, cereals, cakes, etc.). The local food stores (usually small corner grocery stalls called "makolet") throw out (or store off site) and/or burn much of their yeast-bearing product. What they can't purge they cover with plastic or cloth shrouding over the shelves. Many of the larger groceterias in West Jerusalem do the same. During this time the Jewish genius of cooking/baking with unleavened "matzah" emerges. Many times our family were entertained in our neighbors' homes with coffee and matzah-based cakes and cookies. For that week of "Unleavened Bread" the banishment of yeast is universal in Orthodox Jerusalem. A rising cake in a Jewish oven is forbidden.

Fifty days (seven weeks) after that first day of Unleavened Bread is the Festival of Weeks (or "Pentecost" – "pentekoste" – Gk. "fifty"). This was the joyful day when Israel celebrated the first (of two) wheat harvests. At the Temple two loaves of leavened, salted bread were presented ("waved") to the Lord in gratitude. Regardless of the day of the week, it was a Sabbath.

The same congregation that had witnessed the selection of Matthias was gathered again in the Upper Room (although there are some commentators who suggest that the apostles were the only ones in the room – Luke not specific). Undoubtedly, as was their wont, they were in prayer. Suddenly the sound of a violent wind "filled all the house where they were sitting" (v.2 KJV) and "tongues… of fire" rested on each one gathered. John the Baptist's words were fulfilled (Lk. 3:16). Then "they were all filled with the Holy Spirit and began to speak in other tongues, as the Spirit gave them utterance" (v.4 RSV).

This was no reprise of the Tower of Babel (Ge. 11:1-9 – "babal" – Heb. "to confuse"); rather, the tongues were understood by the various ethnic and racial visitors in Jerusalem (v.6). What they heard spoken in their own languages was the unifying message of "the mighty works of God" (vv.5-11). They were "amazed and perplexed", but some were cynical (vv.12,13). The significance of these tongues, however, was not the supernatural aspect, but the Spirit-led breakthrough of the message of heaven to the whole world. The Gospel of the risen Christ would now spread from Jerusalem to the far corners off the earth.

The First Sermon of the Church 2:14–36

Peter rose to speak. Perhaps there was a balcony enabling him to address the crowd gathered at the amazing sound emanating from the room above. It seemed that most of the nations (vv.8-11) to which these pilgrims had been dispersed were represented. They were indeed "Men of Israel" (v.22) but they were visitors interspersed with "Men of Judea and all who dwell in Jerusalem" (v.14). Regardless, this was the happening place that day.

It was a one point sermon: Jesus is "both Lord and Messiah" (v.36b). The proof of this claim: the resurrection (v.24). Jesus has been "raised… exalted to the right hand of God" and has "received from the Father the promised Holy Spirit" and has "poured" it out on these believers (v.33). The imagery of "pouring" is powerfully expressed by the prophet Joel (vv.16-24). The ancestral prophets of Israel were right. The train has left the station.

The people were moved (3000 of them!), not only by the message, but by Peter's authority as "a witness to the resurrection" (v.32). This, of course, was what the baptism in the Holy Spirit was about (1:8). The resurrection was, is, and always will be the pivot point of faith. The empty tomb in Jerusalem is history's silent witness that Jesus is "both Lord and Messiah".

A Terrific Beginning 2:37–41

Peter's sermon led to a question and answer session. The listeners, "cut to the heart", wanted to know what they should do (v.37). Peter answered with three verbs: "Repent… be baptized… receive."

Repent for your obtuse rejection of Jesus as Messiah and your subsequent crucifying of the Savior. Publicly demonstrate that repentance by baptism. Receive "the gift of the Holy Spirit" (v.38). All three actions were to be predicated on "the name of Jesus Christ". He was central.

A Brief Look at Baptism

Luke reports that 3000 people in Peter's audience responded positively to "repent, be baptized, receive" (v.41). The amazing thing is that these thousands "were baptized". Luke doesn't say how, or where. There are scores of "mikvot" (rock-hewn pools of water for ritual and proselyte immersions) throughout Jerusalem. I have seen many over the years. But these would have been overwhelmed by huge lineups if all 3000 had been baptized that day. It is probably the case that they were baptized over the course of several days. By precedent baptism became the entry-level signature of Christianity, following both Jewish religious/cultural practice and John the Baptist's end-time call to the nations (Jesus himself appeared to have delegated baptism to his disciples, although there is a hint he may have baptized – Jn. 3:22 – but then John says no, he didn't – Jn. 4:2).

In its most basic etymological meaning, baptism is the use of water for spiritual/religious purification. In both historic and modern Orthodox

Judaism there is a direct link to "mikvot" ("mikvah" – Heb. "collection", as in collection of water). Devout Jews (men) would immerse themselves up to seven times in a mikvah before worshipping in the Temple. Women would immerse themselves each month after menstruation. In the Talmud two of the nine norms of repentance are "wash and make yourselves clean..." (Is. 1:16). The other seven are, "Take your evil deed out of my sight", "stop doing wrong", "learn to do right", "seek justice", "defend the oppressed", "take up the cause of the fatherless", "plead the case of the widow" (Is. 1:16-17). Ezekiel described God's purifying Israel as both physical and spiritual: "I will sprinkle clean water on you, and you will be clean; I will cleanse you from all your impurities and from all your idols. I will give you a new heart and put a new spirit in you; I will remove from you your heart of stone and give you a heart of flesh" (Ez. 36:25, 26). He captured the essential significance of Christian baptism centuries later where "old things" were "passing away" and "all things" were "becoming new" (2Co. 5:17).

In what has become known as "the Great Commission" (Mt. 28:19, 20), Jesus mandated the disciples to evangelize "all nations" and to baptize them "in the name of the Father and of the Son and of the Holy Spirit." As they obeyed this order they developed over time a multi-faceted appreciation for the genius of baptism. It was described as vital in:

1. Remission of sins (Ac. 22:16; He. 10:22).

2. Regeneration, new birth (Tt. 3:4-6).

3. Union with Christ (Ga. 3:27; Ro. 6:3-6).

4. Becoming a child of God (Ga. 3:26, 27).

5. Bestowal of the Holy Spirit (1Co. 12:13).

6. Becoming a member of the Church (Ac. 2:41).

7. Salvation (Mk. 16:16).

Unfortunately, various church traditions over the centuries became polarized by "baptismal formulas". Questions like "When is one saved?"

and "Is the Holy Spirit conferred at, before, or after water baptism?" reduced the significance of baptism to mere theological parsing. Any and all of these divides are clearly eclipsed by the blunt, inarguable statement, "Whoever believeth that Jesus is the Christ is begotten of God" (1Jn.5:1 KJV). There are no other qualifiers.

As to core values, personal moral decisions, even liturgical preferences, the liberating fact is that we are works in progress – "everything is *becoming* new." We are *growing* "in the grace and knowledge of our Lord Jesus Christ" (2Pe. 3:18) and *growing* "from faith to faith" (Ro. 1:17). We are in *dynamic* not static relationship with the Lord. It is an *adventure*.

So, baptism is entry-level, the beginning step of a faith journey. It has great social value: public witness; great moral value: a new start; and great spiritual value: "I believe, repent, obey."

Church history teaches us that the Early Church was definitely a work in progress.

Core Values of the Early Church 2:42-47

I don't hear it much anymore, but as a "PK" (Preacher's Kid") growing up in church, I remember well-meaning people setting up the early church as the ultimate ideal ("We want to be like the early church"). They weren't knowingly saying they wanted to be Jewish, attending synagogue, adhering to kosher laws, discriminating against Gentiles, etc., but they were romanticizing the early church, making it into a "feel-good" fantasy, not a "warts-and-all" hybrid of roughhewn Galileans and squeaky clean Jewish legalists. Church history teaches us that the early church was *definitely* a work in progress. Nevertheless its core values emerged very quickly.

Luke identifies seven core values:

1. Apostles' Teaching v.42a

There was no "catechism" as yet (nor would there be for a century or two) but there were the Jewish scriptures (our "Old Testament"). The history of God's dealings with a generally recalcitrant Israel, but especially his delivering them from Egypt, revealing his will to Moses via the Ten Commandments, and his providing for them during forty years of wilderness wanderings, was rich in life lessons and instructive theology. The strong words of the prophets, the poetry of the Psalms, and the otherworldly visions of Ezekiel and Daniel were fuel for the soul. Then, the recollection of Jesus' life and ministry, built on the Law and the Prophets, gave the apostles more than enough content for teaching the new believers in depth.

2. Fellowship v.42b

For us humans fellowship is a no-brainer. We need each other. Social interaction is vital for balanced living. And, when it comes to worldview we have a need to share, discuss, fine-tune, and celebrate it with others. This was certainly the case with the 3000 newly-minted believers. Because Peter had positioned Jesus as central to everything, Jesus became the rallying point for community. Their fellowship revolved around the celebration of the risen Christ. Indeed, the Apostle Paul referred to it as "the fellowship of his Son" (1Co. 1:9).

3. Breaking of Bread v.42c

The expression "breaking of bread" occurs in both Luke (24:30; 24:35) and Acts (20:7-11; 27:35). It generally refers to eating together as in an "agape meal", but sometimes describes a "eucharistic" ("thanksgiving") celebration of the broken body of the Lord. They broke bread in their homes (v.46b) as adjunct to their daily meetings in the temple courts (v.46a). So there was a blending of the social with the liturgical. In either case they "remembered the Lord" with expectation of the Parousia.

4. Prayer v.42d

Prayer was a constant in both fellowship and the breaking of bread. And, of course, it was foremost in temple gatherings. The prayers were extemporaneous at times, but heavily weighted in the Jewish practice of reading and reciting the Psalms as petition and praise. You see this blend everyday at the Western Wall in Jerusalem. The critical mass of prayers are read from the Psalms but individual requests are written on pieces of paper, shoved into the cracks between the stones, and verbalized by supplicants either bobbing their heads in silent petition or resting their heads on their arms as they lean against the sacred stones. The early Christians were all Jews, and to be Jewish is inseparable from prayer.

5. Fear of God v.43

The story of Ananias and Sapphira (Ac. 5) provides context for this sudden intrusion of "fear" into the mix of values. It became clear to the new church that one did not trifle with the Almighty. The miraculous (v.43b) was both encouraging and concerning – this was not magic, it was the outworking of the presence of a holy God. One must walk carefully in his sight. He was the God of Abraham, Isaac, and Jacob, not some Johnny-come-lately lightweight deity. So curb your enthusiasm, fine-tune your soul, and defer to the Holy Spirit.

6. Social Justice vv.44,45

These early believers saw themselves as a threatened minority. They had seen with their own eyes (maybe some had even participated) what the religious leaders and the people of Jerusalem had done to Jesus. They were now his followers not because of rational argument but of the miraculous done in his name by the apostles in the still astonishing reality of the resurrection. They were charting a new course rife with present and future persecution. So every believer mattered. They had to be valued and protected. And, the best protection, as the world of nature knows, is for the threatened species to band, flock, or herd together, and turn to face the foe.

So they cared for one another. If that meant sharing, they shared (v.44). If it meant liquidating assets, they liquidated (v.45). They were in this together, and they would live or die together. The poorest among them got priority.

7. Corporate Worship vv.46,47

The Temple was their worship venue of choice. As faithful, daily attendees, they modelled consistent Jewish piety. They were anything but secularized. They were seen and known as devout and full of constant praise to God. They were exemplary, so much so, that they enjoyed "the favor of all the people". What's more their numbers grew every day.

The Jerusalem Church 3:1–5:42

A Healing Miracle 3:1–10

This healing was notable for a few reasons. First of all it was the initial post-resurrection miraculous intervention by any of the disciples. They had seen Jesus perform signs and wonders, and had experienced some of his power themselves in their "boot camp" itineration (Lk. 9:1-10; 10:1-24), but this was a miracle of a different order.

It was done "in the name of Jesus Christ of Nazareth" (v.6), and as such was "arms length" from the work of Jesus in the flesh. It signified that spiritual authority had been bestowed on the Twelve. It also revealed the power of "the Name".

In the Old Testament "the Name" is identified with "the God of Abraham, Isaac, and Jacob." The very pronouncement of God's name is to invoke his presence. And God himself often refers to the honor or dishonor attributed to his name by the piety/impiety of Israel. What's more, Jerusalem is referred to as the "holy city" because God has chosen to place his name there (Google "A Place for God's Name"). Indeed, the honor of "the Name" trumps all else, including the honor or dishonor of God's Chosen People (Read Ezekiel 36 with vv.21,22,32 in focus).

So, in light of the resurrection and ascension of Jesus, the apostles finally saw that he was who he said he was. He truly was both "Son of Man" and "Son of God". To invoke his name was to invoke the very power of heaven itself. Luke records several instances (Ac. 2:38; 3:16, 4:12, 30; 5:41; 9:14; 16:18; 19:13). Mind you, I don't think it was lost on the Twelve that Jesus had healed by his own "authority" (Mk. 1:27). Their power was merely executive. No room for them to "think of themselves more highly than they ought to think" (Ro. 12:3).

The healing of the lame beggar at the "Beautiful Gate" set all Jerusalem abuzz. It caught the attention of the Sanhedrin too. Peter and John were about to be jailed.

Peter's Second Sermon 3:11–16

Luke writes that this "walking, and leaping, and praising God" (v.9) beggar "clung to Peter and John" (v.11 RSV) as the "astounded" people ran to the scene. Peter saw the swelling crowd as an excellent opportunity for a second sermon.

He pulled no punches. As an Israelite himself he called the "Men of Israel" gathered before him to account for their treatment of Jesus. Even though Pilate, the Roman procurator, could find no fault in Jesus, this crowd had loudly pressured him into releasing "a murderer" in exchange for "the Author of Life" (v.15 RSV). This designation (also rendered "Prince" or "Captain" in Greek) meant that Jesus, unlike all humanity, was not created. Rather, he had life without beginning or ending. "In him was life, and that life was the light of all mankind" (Jn. 1:4). "Through him all things were made…" (Jn. 1:3). He was/is none other than God.

Peter then declared that the Twelve had witnessed the resurrected Christ (v.15b), and as bonafide apostles they now had the authority to heal "in the name of Jesus" (v.16).

This beggar was the first fruits of the dawning of the Church. He acknowledged both the crowd's and the Sanhedrin's ignorance (v.17) in their transgression against the Christ ("the Messiah"), but stated they should have known better if they had heeded "the mouth of the prophets" (v.18). Their only option was to repent in order to "obtain relief" ("refreshing" – Gk.) from their weight of sin and participate in God's ultimate restoration of all things, as the prophets had foretold (vv.20,21).

His concluding words were powerful in that he reminded these "fellow Israelites" (v.17) of their historical and religious link to Moses, Samuel, Abraham, the prophets, and "the covenant which God gave to your fathers" (vv.22-25). Jesus was "the prophet from your brethren" (v.22 RSV) that Moses had spoken of (Dt. 18:15), and the one whom "Samuel and those who came afterwards" had "proclaimed" (v.24). The covenant God had made with Abraham was intended to cast Israel as the catalytic light to the Gentiles. Jesus, as the personification of God's people, would save the world, beginning with Israel herself (vv.25,26). The "suffering servant" (see Is. 52:13–53:12) was at work.

The Sanhedrin Stonewalled 4:1–22

Luke reports that at least two thousand in the crowd responded to Peter's sermon with repentance (v.4) – this number, added to the three thousand who responded at Pentecost amounted to five thousand. The public support for the new Jewish sect was threatening and disturbing to "the priests and the captain of the temple guard and the Sadducees" (v.1). They were the ones who had bribed the guards at Jesus' tomb to lie about the resurrection. They weren't about to tolerate anyone "proclaiming in Jesus the resurrection of the dead" (v.2). So they threw Peter and John into jail (v.3), to stand trial before the Sanhedrin the next day. Jesus' warning to his disciples, "they will deliver you up to councils" (Mk. 13:9), was about to run its first test case.

The hearing went poorly for the Sanhedrin. They tried to put Peter and John on the defensive – "By what power or what name did you do this?" – but got an in-your-face mini sermon from Peter instead (vv.8-12). They were outmatched. How could they prevail against the Holy Spirit (v.8a), the healed beggar standing right there! (v.14), the "name of Jesus Christ of Nazareth" (v.10), a scathing quote from their own

385

scriptures (v.11 – Ps. 118:22), and "a notable sign" (v.16) that "everyone in Jerusalem" knew about? They slapped Peter and John's wrists and let them go (vv.18-21). The exuberant beggar, no doubt, led the way, dancing and leaping all the while.

Life in the Spirit 4:23–5:16

As stated in the Introduction, Luke saw the Holy Spirit as critical in both the founding and organizing of the early church. His entire history is predicated on heaven touching earth with supernatural power. The present passage bears this out, pivoting on 4:31 – "After they prayed, the place where they were meeting was shaken. And they were all filled with the Holy Spirit and spoke the word of God boldly." But it's very interesting to note that communal life in these early days was not marked by unhealthy spiritual phenomenology. Rather, communal prayer, social justice, integrity, and steady evangelism comprised the signature of faith.

After their release, Peter and John hastened to the Upper Room to tell the assembled believers what had just happened. You can be sure their friends listened with rapt attention. There was a lot of drama happening. And a lot of prayer too. Luke says, "they raised their voices together in prayer to God" (v.24). This means loud. But the volume was tempered by substance. Their prayer was a précis of salvation history (vv.24b-30), with this petition: "enable your servants to speak your word with great boldness" and "to heal and perform signs and wonders through the name of your holy servant Jesus." They weren't about "to hide their lamp under a bushel" (Mt. 5:15).

Their prayer for boldness answered (v.31), the early believers "continued to testify to the resurrection of the Lord Jesus" (v.33) not only verbally, but in committed social action. These five thousand or so newly-minted disciples would certainly have reflected the demographic and socio-economic realities of the general populace – young and old, male and female, rich and poor alike. The issue of poverty became job one, not so much by intentional planning, but by "god's grace… powerfully at work in them all." The outpouring of the Holy Spirit was also an outpouring of grace from the Father. Not only were spiritual needs met, but physical/material needs as well. These powerfully spirit-infilled believers suddenly were aware of the plight of others. They began to sell extraneous properties and gave the money to the apostles to distribute to the poor (vv.32-35). Even Barnabas joined in (v.36).

This highly idealistic nascent Church was, of course, very fragile. The virulent opposition of the established religious authorities combined with the naiveté of the baby Christians created a perfect storm of vulnerability. The Church was in the cross-hairs. The last thing they needed was internal strife or scandal. Integrity was vital. This is why the Ananias and Sapphira incident (5:1-10) is included in the story. The "great fear" that "seized the whole Church" (v.11) brought a sombre balance to the excitement of those formative days. Nevertheless, the evangelistic impetus prevailed as "more and more men and women believed in the Lord and were added to their number" (v.14). The Church was becoming an unstoppable force.

More Persecution 5:17–42

The Sadducees controlled the Temple. They had the power of performing sacrifices, overseeing festivals, managing and profiting from its economy, and impacting catalytically the religious culture of Jerusalem. They were movers and shakers. Even the Sanhedrin was at their beck and call. And they didn't like the apostles. They had just gotten rid of the big threat, Jesus of Nazareth, and now his disciples were claiming he'd risen from the dead. What's more, they were performing miracles! How could they tolerate a bunch of little Christs running around? Their problems had multiplied by a factor of twelve. And, Luke reports, they were fuelled not just by hate but by "jealousy" (v.17). So they arrested the apostles and put them in jail.

Prison bars were no barrier to "an angel of the Lord" (v.19). Miraculously freeing the apostles "at night", the angel instructed them to go back to the Temple (the epicenter of Sadducean influence) and "tell the people all about this new life" (v.20). This life ("zoe" – Gk.) was

CANTELON'S CASUAL COMMENTARY

no mere lifestyle. It was a radical worldview: life rooted in the Incarnate Son himself, fully one with the Father, eternal holiness, righteousness, and justice. At dawn the apostles walked to the Temple and began to teach the crowd of early risers.

As you read Luke's account you see a very frustrated Sadducean elite, "filled with jealousy" (v.17) and "at a loss" (v.24) trying to control a group of preachers who were already under someone else's control (the Holy Spirit), adamantly refusing anyone's orders but God's – "We must obey God rather than human beings!" (v.29). They wanted to kill them, now! (v.33).

One cooler head prevailed. "A Pharisee named Gamaliel", a member of the Sanhedrin, made a persuasive speech (vv.35-40), convincing the high priest to "Leave these men alone! Let them go!" (v.38). Reluctantly relenting, the authorities "had them flogged" (v.40) and sent them on their way with bloodied backs. Instead of bemoaning their injuries and the injustice of it all, the apostles rejoiced "because they had been counted worthy of suffering disgrace for the Name" (v.41). How do you stop champions like that? You don't. Luke says "they never stopped teaching and proclaiming the good news that Jesus is the Messiah" (v.42). And the beat goes on to this very day.

The "Light to the Gentiles" Begins to Shine 6:1–8:40

The First Deacon Board 6:1–7

Many of the thousands who came to faith in Christ during those halcyon days were secular, or "Hellenistic" Jews. They had adopted the culture and language of Greece. "Alexander the Great" in conquering much of the then-known world in the 4th Century BC left a huge imprint on the defeated nations. Colonization, Greek language and resettlement, created a Hellenistic civilization. The impact on Palestine was a case in point. Jerusalem, Judea, and Samaria all bore the effects of Greek culture. Many Jews became Jewish in name only, easily adapting as Hellenists to the quasi-secular Roman culture of Jesus' day.

Jerusalem, Judea, and Samaria
all bore the effects of Greek culture.
Many Jews became Jewish in name only,
easily adapting as Hellenists to the
quasi-secular Roman culture of Jesus' day.

The "daily distribution" of food (v.1) to the poorest of the new believers very quickly became a bone of contention because the Hellenistic Jewish/Christian widows thought the Hebrew Jewish/Christian widows were being given priority. This highly commendable social justice effort was an administrative headache which the apostles quickly passed on to an appointed group of seven trusted men (vv.2-4). Everyone was pleased with this arrangement. So the apostles continued to "stay in their lane" with prayer and teaching the word of God, and the number of disciples in Jerusalem increased rapidly (v.7).

Interestingly, Luke records that "a large number of priests became obedient to the faith" (v.7b). The KJV says, "a great company of the priests...". The word "company" is "ochlos" in the Greek and has a fascinating nuance. This "disorganized throng" (Gk.) was ad hoc. There was no intentional strategy on the part of the apostles to convince the priestly class about Jesus. These Sadducean leaders, highly influenced by their disbelief in resurrection and suspicious of Jesus' messianic signature, were convinced by what? Signs and wonders? Eloquence on the part of the apostles? Or by the Holy Spirit? Jesus had said, "No one can come to me unless the Father who sent me draws him..." (Jn. 6:44). Luke being Luke would have said (or written) a loud Amen!

The First Martyr 6:8–8:3

One of the seven deacons was Stephen, known as Saint Stephen throughout Christian history – for good reason. He was not only the first martyr of the Christian Church, but he was also the first great defender of the faith. His defence of Christianity before the Sanhedrin precipitated his death (somewhere around 36 or 37AD). He was probably a Hellenistic Jew in that he belonged to "the Synagogue of the Freedmen", men from Cyrene, Alexandria, Cilicia and Asia (v.9), and as such had a broader, more liberal background than the Galilean and Judean disciples of Jesus. It is believed he may have been one of "the Seventy" who accompanied Jesus and "the Twelve" throughout most of Jesus' ministry. As you read his defence before the Sanhedrin (7:1-53) it is clear that he had not shared the religious nationalism of the Twelve. He was a "big picture" follower of Christ. And, without doubt, he was the most distinguished of "the Seven". Indeed, in some ways he "out-apostled" the apostles.

Unlike his history of Paul, Luke says nothing about the genesis of Stephen's powerful ministry capacities (v.8b). He simply states that he was "full of God's grace and power" without the benefit of a "Damascus road experience". This supernatural empowering marked his teaching as well, so much so that his detractors couldn't "stand up against" his wisdom (v.10). So they conspired against him, persuading the synagogue to slander him by saying they had witnessed his "blasphemous words against Moses and against God" (v.11). Blasphemy always created a public outcry, and in the ensuing imbroglio they seized Stephen and forced him to stand before the Sanhedrin. Through false testimony they added to their charges against him. Not only was he a blasphemer, but he was also calling for the destruction of the Temple (vv.13,14), which resonated with the charges that had been brought against Jesus himself (Mk. 14:58). But they were somewhat daunted initially because like Jesus, whose face was "changed" at the Transfiguration (Lk. 9:29), and Moses who "was not aware that his face was radiant" (Ex. 34:35), Stephen's "face was like the face of an angel" (v.15). Little wonder the entire Sanhedrin's eyes "were fastened" (Gk.) upon him. Surely his celestial countenance gave them pause.

The high priest, no doubt knowing that the charges against Stephen had been brought by liars, asked, "Are these charges true?" Both Moses and the Temple were sacrosanct. In response Stephen addressed both concerns as he rehearsed salvation history.

Here's a summary of the main arguments of his address:

1. God had unilaterally revealed himself to Abraham, long before Moses. No single person but many (Abraham, Isaac, Jacob, Joseph, and Moses) had experienced God's self-manifestation. Moses himself had acknowledged this when he prophesied, "The Lord your God will raise up for you a prophet like me from among you…" (Dt. 18:15). This meant that Moses' law was incomplete. Another would come to whom Israel must "listen". What was more, God "tabernacled" with Israel in a tent during their forty years wandering in the wilderness after God's miraculous intervention in freeing them from four hundred years of slavery in Egypt. Then, under Solomon, the tent became a temple. But Solomon himself had said, "But will God really dwell on earth? The heavens, even the highest heaven, cannot contain you. How much less this temple I have built!" (1Ki. 8:27). So, both Moses and the Temple were transitory. "The God of glory" was dynamic, not static, as were his prophets. The "habiru" (crossers over) were wanderers, with a "wandering" Presence accompanying them. The Almighty always pushed back against stultifying institutionalism. Even a throne in Jerusalem would not contain him (all religious nationalists take note!).

2. This latter-day loyalty to Moses was an aberration. Israel's long history had been one of resistance to and rejection of Moses' law, "our ancestors refused to obey him. Instead they rejected him and in their hearts turned back to Egypt" (v.39). They killed the prophets, chose spiritual uncircumcision (v.31), and were deaf to the Holy Spirit. The "Righteous One" (v.52) had been their latest conquest.

The Sanhedrin responded with mob fury, "gnashing their teeth at him" (v.54), "covering their ears and yelling at the top of their voices" (v.57), "rushing at him" and dragging him "out of the city", and stoning him. The first to throw stones were the false witnesses who "laid their coats at the feet of a young man named Saul" (v.58). Stephen died incrementally, stone by stone. With labored breath he prayed like his Master,

"Lord, do not hold this sin against them" (v.70). As he breathed his last Saul smiled approvingly, but as an educated Pharisee he must have been troubled by Stephen's impeccable arguments from the scriptures. Soon Saul of Tarsus would be Paul the Apostle.

The Gospel to Samaria and Ethiopia 8:1–40

Stephen's death catalyzed "a great persecution" of the Jerusalem Church, and a scattering of the apostles. In the short term this was major adversity, but in the long term it was the beginning of reaching the world with the Gospel. Saul was instrumental in the Jerusalem persecution. Luke says he "began to destroy the Church" (v.2), arresting believers in their houses and dragging them off to prison. When you resist you're dragged. When you're dragged you're humiliated. When you're imprisoned it seems that hope is lost. The injustice kills your spirit. But Saul rejoiced at his success in this holy war.

One of the "scattered" apostles, Philip, had great ministry impact in a major Samaritan city. One of his first converts was a famous sorcerer named Simon whom the people called "the Great Power of God" (v.10). This caused quite a stir, to the point that Samaria "accepted the word of God" (v.14). Peter and John were sent by the Jerusalem council to build on Philip's success. They laid hands on the newly baptized believers and "they received the Holy Spirit" (v.17). Simon naively wanted in on the action but was severely rebuked by Peter (vv.19-24). In fear he quickly asked for prayer! In the meantime the Gospel momentum grew in this Jewish/Gentile region.

Another of Philip's converts was the finance minister of the Ethiopian court (v.27). After a religious pilgrimage to Jerusalem he was reading the Book of Isaiah. Philip, led by "an angel of the Lord" (v.26), intercepted the man's chariot and explained the passage he was reading (Is. 53: 7,8). The man believed and immediately requested baptism. So Philip baptized him in a convenient roadside stream. The man returned to Ethiopia full of joy, and probably became his country's first Christian evangelist. The message of the Church was becoming universal.

Saul's Conversion 9:1–19

The "young man named Saul" (7:58) was a Hellenist Jew from the great university city of Tarsus, the capital of Cilicia which was at that time part of the Roman province of Syria. It was a liberal city where philosophers, poets, writers, and physicians created an elite culture of learning. Its university was its heart, its Roman-born students world citizens, its influence widespread. Indeed, it was "no ordinary city" (21:39). Saul was proud to call Tarsus his home and was a true Greco-Roman patriot. He represented in his person the conjunction of Hebraism and Hellenism, truly a man of the world.

Saul was born a Pharisee (23:6) and his Pharisee father sent him to Jerusalem to study with Rabbi Gamaliel (22:3) who was the grandson of the towering Rabbi Hillel. So his education was liberal in contrast to the competing conservative school of the equally famous Rabbi Shammai. But, even though Saul had the broader worldview of Gamaliel, he was not a secular skeptic as were the Sadducees. He believed in the resurrection of the dead (23:6), and as the Apostle Paul, he adapted many Pharisaic doctrines in writing and preaching a nascent Christian theology. He knew the Aramaic language as well as Greek and Latin, and his eloquence drew the respect of his Jewish audience (22:2) when he later defended his hope in Christ. He was well educated, well rounded, a force. But, before his conversion he was a force for evil, not for good, "breathing out threatenings and slaughter against the disciples of the Lord" (v.1 KJV).

After the killing of Stephen, Saul was on a roll. Hyped with adrenalin and activist hostility he applied to the high priest to provide him letters of introduction to the synagogues of Damascus. He wanted to hunt down followers of "The Way" (v.2), arrest them, and take them to trial in Jerusalem were he would happily vote in the Sanhedrin for the death penalty (v.26:10). He had no idea that he was about to be arrested himself – by Jesus no less!

Luke, of course, was not an eye-witness to Saul's conversion. As an historian he relied on "primary research" (interviewing eye-witnesses and/or the principals themselves) but, as the apostle's travelling companion during the third missionary journey he had the advantage of personal experience in much of Paul's biography. He doesn't say whether or not he personally heard Paul's accounts of his conversion before the Jerusalem mob (ch.22) or before Agrippa (ch.26). Perhaps this accounts for the slight differences of detail in each. Nevertheless, there is no doubt that Saul experienced the most dramatic and world-changing conversion in the history of the Church.

Saul travelled with an entourage. He needed several strong men to muscle Christians out of their homes and workplaces, shackle them, and herd them to Jerusalem for trial. These were the eye-witnesses (or should I say "ear-witnesses"? v.7) to the instantaneous surrender of their anti-Christian champion to the very One he was persecuting. The sudden flash of light and the thundering voice threw them in fear to the ground (v.7; 26:13,14). Saul, blinded by the light, had to be led by the others into Damascus. As he stumbled along the shock of the encounter must have resonated with overwhelming power. He had just met the "Lord… Jesus" (v.5), in all his resurrected glory, a meeting both traumatic and transformative. Jesus' most virulent enemy had become his "chosen instrument to proclaim my name to the Gentiles…" (v.15). After three days without food or water Saul was ministered to by a disciple named Ananias. He was heard and "filled with the Holy Spirit" (v.17). He was now ready to preach.

What Happened Next 9:20–31

Sometimes there is "a great gulf fixed" between biography and autobiography. Generally the discrepancies lie at the feet of the biographer who tends to use a broad brush and seamlessly blend the colors. On the other hand one tends to provide the finer points with attention to detail when writing one's own story. This helps one (at least!) when reading through Luke's historical lens in the light of Paul's personal recollections in Galatians 1:15–2:1. Here's the Galatian account:

"But when God, who set me apart from my mother's womb and called me by his grace, was pleased to reveal his Son in me so that I might preach him among the Gentiles, my immediate response was not to consult any human being. I did not go up to Jerusalem to see those who were apostles before I was, but I went to Arabia. Later I returned to Damascus.

Then after three years, I went up to Jerusalem to get acquainted with Cephas and stayed with him fifteen days. I saw none of the other apostles – only James, the Lord's brother. I assure you before God that what I am writing you is no lie.

Then I went to Syria and Cilicia. I was personally unknown to the churches of Judea that are in Christ. They only heard the report: 'The man who formerly persecuted us is now preaching the faith he once tried to destroy.' And they praised God because of me. "Then after fourteen years, I went up again to Jerusalem…"

After the drama of his conversion Paul (Saul) says he sought solace (and time for reflection?) in the deserts of Arabia, whereas Luke says, "straightway he preached Christ in the synagogues…" (v.20 KJV). Then Paul says he went up to Jerusalem "after three years", but Luke has him secretly escaping Damascus "when many days had passed" (v.23-25) and going up to Jerusalem. Luke then says that Saul "attempted to join the disciples", but because they feared and didn't believe him to be a true disciple (v.26) Barnabas "took him" under his wing and endorsed his legitimacy (v.27). But in Galatians Paul says his only contacts in Jerusalem were Peter and James, the Lord's brother.

These are representative of occasional bumps on the road of recording history. The *huge* point, however, is this: Saul "proclaimed Jesus, saying, 'He is the Son of God'" (v.20 RSV). Both biography and autobiography have Saul "preaching the faith…" even while his former Hellenist allies "were seeking to kill him" (v.29 RSV). The Holy Spirit made sure that the main focus was the risen Lord.

THE GOSPEL TO THE GENTILES 9:32–11:30

It all started with Peter. It would appear that he had become an itinerant, travelling "here and there among them all" (v.32 RSV). Stephen's martyrdom had scattered the Jerusalem believers, so they were a dispersed flock in need of episcopal oversight. Peter became the prominent pastor. In his travels he "came down also to the saints, that lived in Lydda" (modern day Lod). In both Lydda and nearby Joppa (modern day Jaffa – part of Tel Aviv) Peter performed miracles of the "signs and wonders" type that were expected of true apostles (healing a paralytic – vv.33-35, and raising someone from the dead – vv.36-43), and his reputation spread throughout the coastal region (v.42).

Cornelius and Peter 10:1–48

Peter was a rustic Galilean provincial, Cornelius an Italian man of the world; Peter a Jew, Cornelius a Gentile. Neither would have crossed the path of the other. They lived in separate worlds. But they were drawn together by a world above them both.

As a Roman centurion of the Italian Cohort, Cornelius would have been a prominent player in the military and social life of Caesarea, capital of the Roman province of Judea. He was a man of influence. Interestingly, Luke says he was also a man of prayer, with a heart for the poor (v.2).

Cornelius was a "God-fearer", a term used to describe a Gentile who believed that the "God of Abraham, Isaac, and Jacob" was the true God, and who had some sort of loose affiliation with the synagogue. He was not a proselyte but an adherent to the Jewish faith. He would have received no push-back from the liberal Roman culture. Rather, moderate syncretism was tolerated, if not encouraged. Cornelius' piety, however, was a cut above, so much so that it drew the attention of heaven itself (v.4). The Lord sent an angel to him with a message that ultimately would change the world.

"In a vision an angel of God" instructed Cornelius to "send men to Joppa" to find Peter who was staying at the seaside home of Simon the tanner (vv.3-6). Cornelius chose two servants and one of his men, "a devout soldier" (a fellow God-fearer), to go to Joppa. They were made aware of his heavenly visitation (v.8) and were spiritually tuned to their task.

I have often driven the highway between Joppa (Jaffa) and Caesarea. It takes about an hour. Walking, however, could take upwards of a day. While Cornelius' men were walking, Peter was on the flat rooftop of Simon's house praying. "He fell into a trance" (v.10) and "the Spirit" (v.19) gave him a profound vision with instructions to follow Cornelius' men to Caesarea. The vision? Anything, including un-kosher animals, that "God has made clean", are kosher (vv.11-15). The application? Peter would find out once he got to Caesarea.

The vision? Anything,
including un-kosher animals,
that "God has made clean", are kosher.
The application? Peter would find
out once he got to Caesarea.

Two days later Peter and his entourage (v.23) arrived at Cornelius' house. He was quick to remind the prostrating centurion that he was just a man (v.26). When they entered the house there was a huge number of people waiting for him. With little regard for protocol Peter bluntly reminded them that it was forbidden for a Jew to "visit" (read "eat") with Gentiles, but the Lord had shown him (in the Joppa vision) that kosher law was not observed in heaven. "So why did you send for me?" he asked.

Cornelius recounted the vision and instructions he had received from the angel. As he listened, Peter no doubt resonated with the emerging sense that something cataclysmic was taking place. Was he the first Jew to realize that "God does not show favoritism but accepts from every nation the one who fears him and does what is right"? (vv.34,35).

And was Cornelius the first Gentile to invite a Jew to tell him and his family "everything the Lord has commanded you"? (v.33). The vast gulf fixed between Jew and Gentile was about to be spanned, with Christ both bridge-builder and Bridge.

Peter summarized the Gospel for Cornelius' household, stressing, as always, Jesus' resurrection (vv.34-43). To the astonishment of the Jewish believers who had accompanied Peter, the Holy Spirit "came on all" the assembled Gentiles (v.44), evidenced by extemporaneous glossolalia (v.46). Peter immediately ordered that these new believers be baptized. The nascent Church had broken through the walls of Jerusalem and was now on the threshold of "the uttermost parts of the earth" (1:8).

Growing Pains 11:1–30

The Church had to grow. So did Peter. So did Saul (Paul). And growing, of course, is never easy.

Before the Church could grow numerically, it had to grow spiritually, which meant that the cultural and theological core values of Jewish sectarianism had to yield to Hellenistic globalism. The "uttermost parts" demanded a broad worldview. Circumcision of the body had to give way to circumcision of the soul. For a time "the circumcision party" of the early church pushed back.

When word spread to Jerusalem about Peter's visit to Cornelius, the legalists of the early church (later known in Church history as "Ebionites") were quick to criticize (vv.1-3). They levelled the same accusation against Peter that had been made against Jesus himself – "You ate with Gentiles!" (see Lk.15:2; 19:7). This was a cultural bridge too far. It was seen as both defilement and endorsement of sin. A devout Jew would never countenance such apostasy.

Peter explained his actions by crediting "the Spirit" who told him "to have no hesitation about going" to Cornelius' (v.12). He appealed to the witness of the "six brothers" (v.12) who had also seen "the Holy Spirit come on them as he had come on us at the beginning" (v.15). He had had to not only acknowledge the profound message of the Joppa vision, but he had also been forced by what he had experienced in Caesarea to understand that the "same gift he gave to us" (v.17) was now universal. He could not let any lingering sectarianism on his part "stand in God's way". His world was now far larger than both the Upper Galilee and the Upper Room.

To their credit the Jewish believers in Jerusalem raised "no further objections" and "praised God" that He had "granted repentance that leads to life" (v.8) to the uncircumcised. But, from time to time, in the early years at least, their praises may have stuck in their throats. Even Peter relapsed on occasion (Ga. 2:11-14).

The Church in Antioch 11:19–30

As stated earlier, Stephen's martyrdom had precipitated a major dispersion of believers to the Mediterranean basin and parts of Asia and Europe. Luke reports that some of them became evangelists, mainly to fellow Jews (v.19). "But there were some of them, men of Cyprus and Cyrene, who on coming to Antioch spoke to the Greeks also, preaching the Lord Jesus" (v.20). Preaching to Gentiles by unnamed preachers provided a seed-bed for the eventual full-court press of the Apostle Paul.

Church officials in Jerusalem heard about these ad-hoc preachers, and, predictably, were nervous about the unchecked spread of the Gospel. They were Jews afterall, with a mindset that was conditioned by centuries of adherence to oral tradition. They may have moved cautiously beyond this man-made "fence around the Law", but they valued discipline. So they "sent Barnabas to Antioch" to check out the burgeoning community of Gentile believers.

Luke wrote that Barnabas was one of the first new followers of Christ who contributed the proceeds of a property sale to the welfare of needy believers (4:36). His birth name was Joseph, "a Levite from Cyprus", but the apostles called him "Barnabas" ("son of encouragement") because of his uplifting preaching. He was cousin of John Mark.

After encouraging the Antiochan believers Barnabas travelled to Tarsus, trying to find Saul. When he found him he convinced him to accompany him back to Antioch to teach "great numbers of people" (v.26). The two taught for an entire year, no doubt contributing by way of their focus on Christ to the moniker "Christian", which was first used to describe these Syrian disciples. Barnabas and Saul became a formidable team, both as preachers of the Gospel and champions of the poor (vv.29, 30).

Herod Persecutes the Church 12:1–25

King Herod Agrippa I was the grandson of the infamous Herod the Great (Lk. 1:5). Raised in Rome, he was a boyhood friend of the young Caligula. Upon his accession to Roman Emperor, Caligula promoted Agrippa to the rank of Tetrarch over his great-uncle Philip's former territories (Lk. 3:1); and after Claudius succeeded Caligula, Agrippa was given Judea and Samaria as well. All this occurred while he still lived in Rome. He soon moved to Judea, keen to ingratiate himself to his new Jewish subjects. One of his first decisions was to persecute the Church. He started by executing James, the son of Zebedee, which "met with approval" by those keen to rid Jerusalem of the gadfly apostles (vv.1-3).

He then arrested Peter, intending to make a public display after "the days of unleavened bread" (v.3 KJV). Passover was celebrated on Nisan 14, and the "days" followed from the fourteenth to the twenty-first. While Peter was guarded in prison by sixteen soldiers, "earnest prayer for him was made to God by the Church" (v.5).

Luke doesn't suggest what the goal of the "earnest prayer" was, but he does say that John Mark's mother's servant Rhoda was summarily "dissed" by the prayer warriors when she announced that Peter was at the door (v.5). Apparently none of them had prayed that an angel would free him from prison. Peter quickly recounted his miraculous deliverance, ordered them to "tell James" (Jesus' brother), and left "for another place" (v.17). The believers probably slept little that night. The soldiers paid with their lives (vv.18, 19).

After the commotion died down, Agrippa left Jerusalem for his permanent palace in Caesarea. To settle a dispute with "the people of Tyre and Sidon" he called for a public assembly where he made a speech, dressed in a mail-like robe covered in brilliant silver sequins that nearly blinded the crowd with the reflection of the sun (Josephus, *"Antiquities"* 19:8:2). Overwhelmed with this combination of regal oratory and heavenly light the flattering Caesareans cried, "This is the voice of a god, not of a man" (v.22). Agrippa revelled in the adulation (God was not pleased) and five days later died, aged fifty-four. The "word of God", however, "spread and flourished" (v.24).

THE TRAVELS OF PAUL – ANTIOCH TO ROME 13:1–28:31

The First Mission 13:1–14:28

Barnabas and Saul were "sent off" (v.3) to the Gentile world by the Church in Antioch. Luke describes their mission as "the work to which [God]… called them" (v.2). There was no training in Christian theology, because at that time there was no Christian theology. "The word of God" (v.5) was their teaching context, the synagogues were their venue, and the resurrection of Jesus was the key component in a radical new message to both Jew and Gentile. Pauline theology grew incrementally, on the move, with its roots deep in the soil of the Jewish scriptures and time alone (3 years) in the deserts of Arabia.

Their first move was to Cyprus, "sent on their way by the Holy Spirit" (v.4). Their visit must have taken a few weeks as they travelled "the whole island" from Salamis on the northeast coast to Paphos on the southwest coast. No account of the stops along the way are given, other than an interesting encounter with a sorcerer and a believing pro-consul. Luke makes clear, however, that Saul ("also called Paul") was "filled with the Holy Spirit" right from the beginning. This mission was not merely informational, it was transformational – let any opponent of the Holy Spirit beware! "Elymas" (vv.8-11) might have given a muted "Amen".

There is no need to reproduce maps tracing Paul's missionary journeys – they are readily available on Google. So, "From Paphos, Paul and his companions sailed to Perga in Pamphylia…" means something in terms of geographical context to anyone who employs the handy internet search engine. From the seaport of Attalia (adjacent to Perga) they set out on a road trip that led first through the mountains to Pisidian Antioch. And, as was his wont, Paul attended the synagogue on the Sabbath. Synagogal liturgy was universal in the Jewish world – public reading of the Law and the Prophets, prayer (with recitation of the "Sh'ma"), followed by preaching and/or teaching. Visiting rabbis were often invited to give "a word of exhortation" to the people (v.15). Paul was invited to do so. In vv.16-41 we read his first recorded sermon.

Paul was at the synagogue, not only because he was a devout Pharisee, but also because his calling was to preach Jesus "to the Jew first and also to the Greek" (Ro. 1:16). So he began by reminding the Jewish congregants that "God chose our fathers" and made them into a nation at the Passover when he "led them out" of Egypt after four hundred years of slavery. This was followed by forty years of high maintenance wandering in the wilderness. After that generation of murmurers and complainers had passed, the Lord led the younger generation into Canaan, destroying seven nations of indigenous people in the process (v.19a). For the next 450 years they were led by "judges" who, in the main, gave "meyode primitivi" ("very primitive" – Heb.) leadership to an ever-increasing, idolatrous people. Then came "Samuel the prophet" (v.20) whose clarion word to the Israelites was, "If you are returning to the Lord with all your hearts, then rid yourselves of the foreign gods and the Ashtoreths and commit yourselves to the Lord and serve him only…" (1Sa. 7:3). Samuel had been God's choice to lead Israel, but the people wanted to make their own choice – they wanted a king, like the nations around them. The Lord reluctantly gave them Saul, who reigned for 40 years. He then removed Saul, replacing him with David, "a man after my own heart" (v.22). It was David who would be the spiritual progenitor of the messianic line.

Paul then shifted from his précis of Israel's history to "this man's descendants" (v.23), referring to the ultimate inheritor of David's line, "the savior Jesus". John the Baptist, the last of the historic prophets, announced his arrival.

The baptizer needed no introduction, even here in Galatia. His reputation had spread far and wide. Indeed, many had thought him to be the Messiah. John, however, had disabused the people of that notion. In his first volume Luke had recorded, "The people were waiting expectantly and were all wondering in their hearts if John might possibly be the Messiah. John answered them all, 'I baptize you with water. But one who is more powerful than I will come, the straps of whose sandals I am not worthy to untie. He will baptize you with the Holy Spirit and fire.'" (Lk. 3:15,16).

"All the people of Israel" (v.24) heard John's announcement, but "the people of Jerusalem and their rulers did not recognize Jesus" (v.27), even though they read about their ultimate rejection of him in "the words of the prophets" every Sabbath in the synagogue. (The congregants in Pisidian Antioch would have to scramble later, checking out "the words of the prophets". No one could match the erudition of this highly educated scholar/historian apostle). But, just as John's reputation had spread, so too had the messianic expectation of devout Jews. No doubt Paul was tapping into that anticipation. This may be why "the people invited them to speak further about these things on the next Sabbath" (v.42).

"These things" centered around Paul's singular thesis: "God raised [Jesus] from the dead" (v.30). This was the Gospel, "the Good News": "What God promised our ancestors he has fulfilled for us, their children, by raising up Jesus" (vv.32,33). Forgiveness of sins, indeed *freedom* from sin, not possible "to obtain under the law of Moses" (v.39), was now offered to all, both Jew and Gentile, who would put their faith in "the holy one".

Paul ended his sermon with a warning "heads-up" from Habakkuk 1:5. Don't let your "wonder" lead to scoffing. If you do so, you will perish. Hear and believe. Many of the audience, Jew and God-fearing Gentiles alike, wanted to hear more. Next Sabbath they'd flock to the synagogue to hear part two of Paul's world-shaking sermon.

The Gospel to the Gentiles vv.44–52

Not all the Jews were convinced. In fact, as a huge crowd gathered next Sabbath, Jewish protesters "heaped abuse on him" (v.45). Paul and Barnabas were not intimidated. Rather, they pushed back.

"It was necessary that the word of God should be spoken first to you", they said (v.6a RSV). In other words, the Jews were to be given first right of refusal. After all, they were the ones God had ordered to "be a light to the Gentiles" (v.47a). But, irony of ironies, the "holy one" they had rejected, one of their own, had through resurrection become that light. Now, because of their narrow, religious nationalistic view of messiah, they would be eclipsed by the universal love of God. The Gentiles would accept the risen Christ. Paul and Barnabas would focus on them (v.46b). Little did these two know that "the ends of the earth" (Is. 49:6) would be their parish. It began that day as "the word of the Lord spread through the whole region" (v.49), good news happily embraced by the Gentiles (v.48). Their hearts resonated to the call of the Holy Spirit (v.48b). Paul and Barnabas' opponents, however, forced them out of town (vv.50-52).

A Rocky Start 14:1–20

Leaving the Pisidian believers "filled with joy and the Holy Spirit" (13:52), Paul and Barnabas headed southeast to Iconium, one of the major cities in the Roman province of Galatia. And they "went as usual into the Jewish synagogue" (v.1). But, as usual, major opposition arose even as "a great number of Jews and Greeks believed". Paul and Barnabas hung in, assisted by the grace of God empowering them with the performance of "signs and wonders" (v.3). Their adversaries, undeterred, hatched a plot to kill them. They heard about it and fled further south to the cities of Lystra and Derbe. Ironically, adversity added strength to their already considerable visionary energy. It pushed them on.

In Lystra, at Paul's command,
a man crippled from birth was healed.
The people were blown away with
amazement, loudly shouting,
"the gods have come down to us
in human form!" They immediately
declared Barnabas "Zeus",
and Paul "Hermes".

In Lystra, at Paul's command, a man crippled from birth was healed. The people were blown away with amazement, loudly shouting, "the gods have come down to us in human form!" They immediately declared Barnabas "Zeus", and Paul "Hermes". There was a temple to Zeus in the city whose priest, overawed by the miracle and peoples' acclaim, "brought oxen and garlands to the gates and wanted to offer sacrifice with the people" (v.13). Paul and Barnabas were mortified by this adulation and shouted over the throng that they were as human as anyone else. Paul called on them to "turn from these vanities unto the living God" (v.15 KJV). He made no appeal to Jewish history or to the Gospel – these heathens had no knowledge of the God of Abraham, Isaac, and Jacob. They were marketplace pagans. But they *did* have regard for things above. So Paul challenged them to embrace the creator of "the heavens and the earth and the sea and everything in them" (v.15). Their heathen ways were excusable in that God "in the past" had tolerated the ignorance of the nations. Yet he had always been available to anyone who saw him in the "rain", the "crops", the "food", and the "joy" of life (vv.16,17). With this reminder of God revealed in nature he barely managed to "restrain the people" (v.18 RSV). In all this uproar some of Paul's enemies from Antioch and Iconium suddenly showed up, "won" the fickle crowd over, and proceeded to stone him. They left him for dead, but the indefatigable apostle "got up and went back into the city" (v.20). He was formidable.

Return to Antioch vv. 21–28

Moving on to Derbe, Paul and Barnabas had great success. Then they retraced their steps through Lystra, Iconium, and Pisidian Antioch, affirming and exhorting the believers, and setting up leaders to oversee pastoring and governance of the new congregations. Then, back through Perga and Attalia, they set sail to Antioch, with a report of the great work God had begun among the Gentiles.

Why the Tumult?

One might wonder why the Gospel met with such virulent opposition in Galatia. The reason was that the Gospel offended both the monotheistic Oral Law of Judaism and the polytheistic worldview of the Gentiles. The "God of Abraham, Isaac, and Jacob" and the "Jupiter and Hercules" pantheon were both placed under stress by this new message of the resurrected Christ. Paul had to convince the Jews that "the Christ" ("the anointed one") fulfilled the Law, and the Gentiles that there was only one God whose Son had come to save the world from spiritual death. His appeal to history (the life, death, and resurrection of Jesus as fulfillment of the Law and Prophets) and his demonstration of present-day Holy Spirit empowerment (signs and wonders) in combination with his relentless faithfulness to the "heavenly vision" provided a foundation of faith which has stood immoveable to this day.

The Jerusalem Council 15:1–35

This tumult in Galatia was symptomatic of broiling debate elsewhere, especially in Jerusalem. For sure, Peter's experience with Cornelius and his household in Caesarea a decade or so earlier had been initially accepted by the Jerusalem Church leadership. But long-term religious and social values die hard. A Pharisaic Christian sect (known by historians as "Judaizers") had slowly been gaining strength. They believed salvation was impossible for Gentiles unless they converted to Judaism first, with the mandatory requirement of circumcision. In fact they eventually sent a delegation to the Gentile Church in Antioch declaring their conversion to Christ bogus. Salvation was for Jews only (v.1). Paul and Barnabas "had no small dissension and disputation with them" (v.2) to the point that the Antiochan leadership sent them to Jerusalem to settle the matter. On their way they visited new congregations in Lebanon and Samaria, probably overnighting with hospitable believers. It was a long walk from Antioch to Jerusalem through difficult terrain and merciless heat. It was nice to have a break with friends along the way. They needed some casual conversation too. The Church Council they were about to attend would not only be the first in history, but it would be very intense, with anything but friendly banter.

Paul and Barnabas were formally welcomed by the leadership ("apostles and elders"), and even as they sat down, "the party of the Pharisees stood up and said, 'The Gentiles must be circumcised and required to keep the Law of Moses'" (v.5). The battle lines were drawn – conservative versus liberal, old versus new.

Luke's summary of the event, and of the speeches, touches the salient points, but does little in describing the adversarial atmosphere. A major dispute was brewing, the resolution of which would impact heaven and earth for centuries to come. Would there be a breakthrough or a shipwreck? Peter and James came to the rescue.

Again, Luke doesn't give Peter's speech verbatim, but the main points are clear:

1. God made the decision to include the Gentiles (v.7).

2. God focuses on the heart (v.8a).

3. God gave his Holy Spirit to the Gentiles (v.8b).

4. God does not discriminate racially (v.9).

5. It is God who purifies the heart (v.9b).

6. The Jews can't keep the Law, so why insist that the Gentiles do? (v.10).

7. Salvation comes through grace (v.11).

This quieted the Council, but they became totally "silent" (v.12) as Paul and Barnabas reported on "the signs and wonders" God had done among the Gentiles. When they had finished it was James' turn to speak.

James began by referring to something not included in Luke's summary of Peter's speech where God "first" visited the Gentiles (Abraham in Mesopotamia?) to create "a people for his name" (v.14). This, of course, predated Peter's visit to Cornelius. The subtle, but powerful point: we were *all* Gentiles! Indeed, the Hebrews ("hibiru" – "crossers over" – Heb.) were not a nation until after the Passover in Egypt. The term "Jew" didn't apply till centuries later after the split of the Kingdom into Israel (in the north) and Judea (in the south) during the disastrous reign of Solomon's son Rehoboam. The prophets had foreseen a renewal of "David's fallen tent" (v.16) in which "the Gentiles who bear my name" (v.17) would participate. This is a mystery "known unto God… from the beginning of the world" (v.18 KJV), far beyond the agenda of this Council. So all the "Jewishness" these Gentile believers needed was to adhere to the [11]Noahide Law (eat no food offered to idols, nor meat that hasn't been properly bled, and be sexually chaste – as the Lord instructed Noah in Genesis 9).

Obedience to these simple commands, in combination with attendance at synagogue every Sabbath would suffice (v.21). No more of this controversy please – we are the Gentiles, and the Gentiles are us.

The Council accepted James' decision (he was, after all, Jesus' brother, and the most prominent of the early church leaders). They sent Paul, Barnabas, Silas ("Silvanus" – a Hellenized Jew), and Judas Barabbas (a Hebrew Jew) to the Church in Antioch with a letter apologizing for "subverting" their souls" (v.24 KJV) and calling on them to follow the Noahide Law (v.29). This was well received (v.31). So peace prevailed and a period of encouragement through preaching and teaching ensued

---

[11] These laws were sifted by the rabbis over centuries. Google "Noahide Laws". James mentions 3 of 7.

(v.35). The shipwreck had been averted. The world was about to be changed forever.

Paul's Mission to Europe 16:1–18:17

The tendency to "disputation" did not die right away. The corporate dissension may have been mitigated, but there were still relational stresses. Case in point was the division between Paul and Barnabas over John Mark (15:36-41). There may have been a deeper issue than Mark's "desertion" during the first missionary journey (15:38). It may have been a residual strain resulting form the occasion in Antioch where both Peter and Barnabas had been "carried away" by the intimidating demands of "the circumcision party" (Ga. 2:11-13). Paul may have seen Barnabas as divided in his loyalties. Barnabas is not referenced again in Acts. He and John Mark went to Cyprus, Paul and Silas to Europe.

Human nature being what it is, we should not be surprised that Paul himself wavered in the matter of circumcision, for no sooner did he arrive in Lystra than he had Timothy circumcised (vv.1-3). Timothy was a young man with great leadership potential whose mother was Jewish and father was Greek[12]. To avoid further dispute with the Jews Paul did the expedient thing (I wonder if he may have been slightly embarrassed...). He did what he did because he wanted to mentor the young man. And he may have wanted to protect this youthful recruit from harassment. Whatever, Timothy proved to be worth the effort. He became a faithful and gifted intern. His learning curve, however, would be steep.

So Paul, Silas, Timothy and a select group (including Luke – note the "we" passages vv.10-17) set out to visit and encourage the churches in "the region of Phrygia and Galatia" (v.6). Lystra, Iconium, and Pisidian Antioch were undoubtedly key visits on the way. Luke records

---

[12] To this day in Israel, if your mother is Jewish you're Jewish, but you're expected to be circumcised.

that the Holy Spirit kept them from preaching the word in the Roman province of Asia (sometimes referred to as "Asia Minor", modern day Turkey). When they had travelled north to the border of Mysia (probably at the city of Dorylaeum) they were stymied again as the Holy Spirit forbade them journey further into Bithynia. So they turned west and risked "danger from rivers, danger from robbers... danger in the wilderness" (2Co. 11:26) through miles and miles of infrequently travelled territory. The port city of Troas was their destination. While there Paul had a vision in the night calling him to Europe – "Come over to Macedonia and help us" (v.9). They quickly found a ship heading for the island of Samothrace. They were on their way to Philippi (vv.11,12).

Macedonia 16:11–17:15

Luke calls Philippi "the leading city of that district of Macedonia", which may have rankled the citizens of Amphipolis and Thessalonica (the capital), but accurately describes a city that had patterned itself after Rome. It was a city with attitude.

Where does one start when attempting to plant a church in a Roman military colony? A strategic planning session? Advice from veteran church planters? A church growth seminar? All of the above? Or none of the above? How about connecting with a devout group of "God fearing" women who have a weekly prayer meeting down by the river? This is exactly what Paul and Silas did (vv.13-15). It wasn't the usual synagogue stop but apparently "riverside" was a familiar euphemism used by Philo and Josephus when referring to a place of prayer. In that traditional synagogue services were for men only, with the women segregated behind screens or sitting in an upper balcony (which is still the case in Orthodox Jewish synagogues in Jerusalem[13]), it may be that this riverside prayer gathering was a female phenomenon.

---

[13]   If there was a synagogue in Philippi it would have been very small in that the city was a Roman military colony

A prominent merchant dealing in purple Thyatiran dye named Lydia "opened her heart" to the Gospel. She and "her household" were Paul's first European converts.

Paul and Silas in Prison 16:16–24

A week or two later Paul and Silas were making their way back "to the place of prayer" when they had yet another encounter with sorcery (see 8:9; 13:6). This time it was "a slave girl who had a spirit of divination" (v.16 RSV). She "brought her owners much gain by soothsaying". Ironically, as happened occasionally in the ministry of Jesus, the very denizens of Hell became vociferous promoters of the Kingdom – "These men are servants of the Most High God, who proclaim to you the way of salvation", she shouted, again and again, day after day, till Paul was fed up with the annoyance. He commanded the spirit to come out of her and suddenly she couldn't "divine" anymore. Her owners were furious, so much so that they banded together (with some chosen ruffians no doubt) and "dragged" Paul and Silas back into town to face an agitated mob and some compliant "authorities" (v.19).

It was common practice for magistrates to hear cases in "the market place" (the "agora", meaning "place of judgement"). The essential accusation was Paul and Silas' "Jewishness" (v.20). Luke and Timothy were not arrested maybe because they were seen as Gentiles. Nevertheless, the crowd had become so intensely hostile that the intimidated authorities had them "severely beaten" with "rods" (vv.22,23), then they were thrown into prison, their wrists chained and their feet in stocks to guarantee no escape. Luke doesn't say what the magistrates planned to do with them. Perhaps they would keep them imprisoned until they could make the case before Rome that Paul and Silas were "anti-emperor", preaching a Gospel that promoted "another king" (17:7). Then again, maybe they would simply release them next day and run them out of town (vv.35,36).

A miraculous deliverance was about to occur, but before that earthquake something just as remarkable took place: two recently flogged men, their backs shredded and bleeding, *singing* praise to God! If ever

411

there was an example of the total empowering and indwelling of the Holy Spirit in Paul and Silas' lives this was it. The other prisoners listened in the darkness and were amazed.

Then, in the blackness of the night, the earth began to violently shake. The prisoners must have been terrified as bits of cement caulking fell on their heads and the cracking of the walls and floor shook their wounded bodies (all the prisoners had been flogged no doubt). Then, to their astonishment "everyone's chains came loose" (v.26). The jailor, sleeping somewhere adjacent to the prison, woke up, saw the prison's doors open, and in a rush of fear drew his sword to kill himself (knowing his life was forfeit if even one prisoner escaped – see 12:19). "But Paul cried with a loud voice, 'Do not harm yourself, for we are all here.'" The distraught jailor rushed in, some torches lighting the way, and saw that Paul had spoken the truth. He cast himself at the feet of Paul and Silas, as they stood there, shackle-less, and uttered a timeless cry, "What must I do to be saved?" Paul's reply was his theology in ten words, "Believe in the Lord Jesus, and you will be saved" (v.31). Later, the jailor himself washed and anointed their wounds, and was (with this household) baptized before the morning light. And, as has historically been the case with all new believers, "he rejoiced with all his household that he had believed in God" (v.34). God's salvation and joy go hand-in-hand.

Apparently Paul, Silas, and the other prisoners (!) voluntarily went back into the damaged prison, for why else would the jailor later ask them to "come out" (v.36b RSV) on order of the magistrates? No way, said Paul, they've broken the law by beating uncondemned Roman citizens and have thrown us into prison. Now they want us to go quietly? No way. "Let them come themselves and take us out" (v.37). These petty officials, shaking in their boots, came to the prison, abjectly apologized (perhaps with financial compensation?), and politely asked Paul and his entourage to leave Philippi. Paul and Silas graciously left, dropping into Lydia's on the way out of town.

By the way, I was in Philippi a few years ago, taping a Bible teaching series for television. The prison is still there – essentially carved out of a limestone hill. I was amazed at how small and innocuous it is. It's very easy not to notice it at all. But heaven noticed it all those years ago. It stands, a silent reminder of the sovereignty of the Lord and his care for his servants.

Thessalonica 17:1–9

Luke may have stayed on at Philippi (perhaps his skills as a physician were needed) because the "we" is replaced by a "they" in v.1. The "we" reoccurs in ch.20. Regardless, Paul, Silas, Timothy, and some others took the well-established Roman military road, the "Via Egnatia", through Amphipolis and Apollonia to Thessalonica, a city of major importance. Its prominence subsisted for centuries both before and after Christ.

The narrative is brief, recounting a three week "reasoning from the scriptures" in the synagogue, success in persuading "some Jews" and "a large number of God-fearing Greeks" that Jesus was the Messiah, and a subsequent riot. It was Philippi all over again, with the exception of imprisonment. Paul's host, Jason, however, had to post bond to avoid jail.

The brevity of the account should not be misunderstood. Paul spent much time in Thessalonica. In 1Th. 2:9 Paul reminds the Thessalonian Church of his "toil and hardship" working "night and day" at his tent-making so as not "to be a burden to anyone". In 2Th. 3:7-13 he presents his own example of a faithful work ethic. And, from time to time the Philippian believers financially subsidized Paul as he had need (Ph. 4:16). His labors were not in vain. He planted a sustainable church. Indeed, for centuries Thessalonica continued as a pillar city for Christianity. In fact it became known as "the Orthodox City", a beacon of light right up there with Jerusalem and Antioch. But lighting that beacon took its toll. Luke gives us no time frame, but eventually Paul's opposition became ugly.

Berea vv.10–15

Jason and "the believers" spirited Paul, Silas, and Timothy out of Thessalonica under cover of darkness. Wanting no repeat of the Philippian flogging they "sent" them to Berea. It was a small, but ancient city whose history went back to the 4th Century BC. Luke records that the Berean Jews were "of more noble character" than the "lewd fellows of the baser sort" who had "assaulted the house of Jason" in Thessalonica (v.5 KJV). Paul, as was his wont, headed straight for the synagogue. In any strange city a synagogue was like home to him. After all, he was a Pharisee, and there was no better place to reason the truths of heaven than a Jewish house of worship.

He met with great success, evangelizing many Jews, Greeks, and (again – see v.4b) "a number of prominent Greek women" (v.12). For someone who in later centuries was vilified by some theologians for a purportedly low view of women it would appear from Luke's record that Paul had great impact in seeing women come to faith. Obviously he had their respect, and they had his.

But, Paul's Thessalonian enemies caught up with him in Berea and began "stirring up and inciting the crowds" (v.13 RSV). Through some subterfuge the Berean believers "sent Paul off on his way to sea" and after sailing the eastern coasts of Macedonia he was met (probably at the port of Piraeus) and escorted to Athens. Silas and Timothy stayed behind.

Athens vv.16–34

Athens was a liberal city, intellectual, philosophical, inclusive, and religious. Its cerebral culture permeated everything. At the time it had only minor political clout and had little influence on the commerce of the Mediterranean basin, but it did have a famous university and was seen by some as the pinnacle of discursive philosophy. The citizens were almost obsessive about debate, especially the discussion of new ideas. As such they were very keen to engage anyone who had a new slant on the meaning of life, or speculation about the deities above and below. They were metaphysical junkies.

When Paul arrived in Athens he began to "reason in the synagogue with both Jews and God-fearing Greeks, as well as in the marketplace day by day…" (v.17). His reasoning skill led to city-wide notoriety to the point that "a group of Epicurean and Stoic philosophers began to debate with him" (v.18)[14]. He intrigued them with his advocacy of "foreign gods" – "Jesus and the resurrection" – "Jesus and Anastasio" (Gk) which some may have mistaken to be the names of a god and goddess. They weren't necessarily taking Paul seriously (calling him a "babbler" – "seed picker") but they were hungry for anything new (vv.19-21).

Paul's "Areopagus Address" was given on Mars Hill, just a stone's throw northwest of the Acropolis. I've been there twice – once with my family and another time with a television crew when I had the privilege of reading and analyzing Acts 17 on camera. Sitting on a boulder at the top of the hill I was able to enjoy the view of both the Acropolis, over my left shoulder, and the Agora (marketplace) below on the right. Mars Hill is not imposing, but it is commanding in its prominence.

Luke, of course, gives a mere summary of Paul's discourse. You can be sure that he spoke for a long time. Indeed his voracious audience would have expected a lengthy oration. He may have started on the wrong foot by criticizing his hearers from being "too superstitious" (v.22 KJV), and "ignorant" (v.23). Why? Because they had erected an altar "To an Unknown God". But any offence they may have felt was quickly mitigated by Paul's delicious offer, "him declare I unto you". They all leaned forward in anticipation.

There is no need for much comment on Paul's presentation. It reads well and you, dear reader, are intelligent. Just let me summarize the summary bit by bit:

vv.21,23 – You overly religious Athenians are trying to cover all the bases by erecting an altar to an unknown god.

vv.24,25 – The god you're ignorantly acknowledging is the God who made the worlds, both the heavens and the earth, and He cannot be reduced to a statue or altar or temple.

v.26 – He is the sovereign God of history.

v.27 – We are essentially spiritual beings and any attempt through philosophy or idolatry to find him is evidence of our need for him and of his proximity to us.

---

[14]   Google "Epicurean" and "Stoic"

v.28 – Mankind cannot function apart from him. Your poets have said as much. We bear his DNA.

v.29 – We who are spiritual must not think that God, who is spirit, can be made to indwell our man-made idols.

v.30 – Idolatry is ignorance, but God has "winked" at it. But now, because of what's happened in Jerusalem there is no more winking. You've got to repent.

v.31 – Why? Because judgement is coming, with the resurrected Christ as judge.

There was a mixed reaction. Some "sneered" and others wanted to hear more. Paul simply left.

He had little success in Athens, although one of his converts was "Dionysius the Areopagite" (v.34), a member of the Upper Council of Athens. To be a member one had to be above sixty years of age and fill a high governmental office. This Dionysius is traditionally believed to have become the first bishop of Athens, eventually dying a martyr's death.

A Year and a Half in Corinth 18:1–17

Paul must have been a touch discouraged (maybe humiliated) by his mediocre impact in Athens. Obviously he was upset – in 1Co. 2:3 he wrote, "I came to you in weakness with great fear and trembling" – so much so that the Lord had to speak to him in a vision saying, 'Do not be afraid; keep on speaking, do not be silent. For I am with you...' (vv.9,10). He may have thought that he had been too cerebral in Athens, falling into the intellectual sub-culture too easily, too reliant on his formidable reasoning skills.

Compared to any self-styled philosophers and thinkers in Athens Paul was a giant. He may have felt he had overwhelmed the people on Mars Hill. Perhaps he'd been a bit of a bully, "thinking of himself more highly than he ought to think" (Ro. 12:3b). Whatever the case, he determined as he reflected on Athens, that when he got to Corinth he would avoid any academic trappings, any "eloquence or human wisdom", and "know nothing... except Jesus Christ and him crucified" (1Co. 2:1,2).

From now on he would "stay in his lane". (Nevertheless there would be no future "letter to the Athenians" as there would be letters to the Romans, the Thessalonians, the Philippians, Galatians, etc.). Even the mighty apostle was a work in progress.

So he arrived in Corinth a bit beat up, both emotionally and physically (how long would it take for a flogged back to heal?). He was probably psychologically fatigued as well, having suffered tumult and riot in Thessalonica and Berea, an undercover escape to Athens, only to endure mockery and rejection. Little wonder he chose to "lie low" with his new tent-making friends, Aquila and Priscilla, and just make a living for a while. Mind you, he still "reasoned" at the synagogue every Sabbath, but there's no record of marketplace debate (vv.1-4). He needed to recover.

Silas and Timothy, who had stayed behind in Berea, finally joined up with Paul in Corinth. This lifted his spirits, and he put manual labor aside to focus exclusively on preaching. Jesus as Messiah was his message (v.5).

The fact that the Jews suddenly became "abusive" (v.6) suggests that all the previous synagogue teaching by Paul had been sourced in the Jewish scriptures dealing with the messianic hope in general. It was one thing, for example, to expound on the "servant" in Isaiah 53, it was another to say this servant was Jesus. They pushed back with such hostility that Paul remonstrated, "Your blood be upon your own heads!" From now on "I will go to the Gentiles." Shaking his clothes in protest he turned his back on these stiff-necked people and started his own congregation right next door to the synagogue in a private home. As modern Israelis would put it, Paul showed remarkable "chutzpah". Ironically the synagogue president, Crispus, became one of Paul's first congregants (vv.7,8).

Paul, who chose not to personally baptize his converts, made an exception for Crispus, and a few other prominent Corinthians (1Co. 1:13-17). He admired courage. And he was courageous himself, faithfully exposing the scriptures for the next eighteen months even as he was continually facing persecution. It was a comfort to know via a vision that he was not alone – not only was the Lord with him, but so were "many people in this city" (vv.9,10). Maybe the newly appointed "proconsul of Achaia" was one of those "many people". He became Paul's great defender (vv.12-16).

Gallio was proconsul, or governor, of Achaia, which included all of Greece south of Macedonia. He was brother to the famous philosopher Seneca, tutor of Nero. Seneca and many other prominent leaders praised Gallio for his kindness and generous spirit. He was a true Roman statesman. He was no pushover, however. A Jewish "insurrection" (v.12 KJV) didn't faze him a bit. They wanted him to punish Paul for promoting a new religion "contrary to the law" (of Rome). The fact was that Christianity was seen by the Romans as a Jewish sect; but it *was* Jewish, and Judaism was recognized as a legitimate ethnicity/religion by Roman law. These insurrectionists were claiming that Christianity was not Jewish and was therefore illegal. Gallio would have none of it. He saw an agenda behind this spurious charge. Basically he said, Get these guys out of here! And his soldiers "drove them off" (v.16). The crowd then vented their anger on the new president of the synagogue named Sosthenes. They may have heard a rumour that he was following in the footsteps of his predecessor, Crispus, who had come to faith in Christ. They beat him up. (Was this the Sosthenes of 1Co. 1:1?). Gallio was unmoved, while Paul moved on (vv.18-23).

On the Road Again vv.18–23

In six short sentences Luke provides a transition from Corinth to Antioch, setting the stage for what has become known as Paul's "Third Missionary Journey". Cenchreae is the western port of Corinth (there is an eastern port as well – Corinth is situated on an isthmus). There Paul cut his hair "because of a vow he had taken" (v.18). This vow required he attend the Temple in Jerusalem for one of the three annual feast days (probably Pentecost – the "Feast of Weeks" – fifty days after Passover). Acts like this remind the reader of just how Jewish Paul was. He was a Pharisee educated for years in Jerusalem by the great rabbi Gamaliel.

Synagogues were his venue of choice. The Temple was his spiritual home. The Jew Jesus was his Messiah, and his life (Ph. 1:21).

Paul was a Pharisee educated for years in Jerusalem by the great rabbi Gamaliel. Synagogues were his venue of choice. The Temple was his spiritual home. The Jew Jesus was his Messiah, and his life.

Aquila and Priscilla accompanied Paul by ship to Ephesus, where they remained. Paul, on the other hand, stayed a few days and then departed by ship for Caesarea, a long and dangerous sail. He arrived safely, travelled up to Jerusalem, fulfilled his vow, and then went north to Antioch. From there, "he travelled from place to place throughout the region of Galatia and Phrygia" (v.23). He was now free to evangelize Asia on an "ad hoc" journey.

A Brief Digression vv. 24–28

Apollos, a Jew from Alexandria, is a minor player in terms of Luke's narrative about Paul, but historically played a much larger role in the early churches. Some biblical historians even suggest that he was the author of the anonymously written book of Hebrews. Nevertheless Luke takes a moment to acquaint Theophilus with this influential preacher.

While Paul was in Antioch, about to launch his third missionary itineration, Apollos arrived in Ephesus (approximately 53 or 54 AD). His powerful intellect honed by an Alexandrian education had equipped him in eloquence and knowledge. He was "mighty in the scriptures" (v.24

KJV), "fervent in spirit" and an "accurate" teacher about Jesus. Like Paul, he spoke "boldly" in the Ephesian synagogue , but unlike Paul there is no record of tumultuous pushback from his hearers. Perhaps that was due to the fact that at that point "he knew only the baptism of John" (v.25 RSV), which meant that he had yet to experience the specifically Christian indwelling of the Holy Spirit that accompanied baptism into the name of Jesus. So, until Aquila and Priscilla "explained to him the way of God more adequately" (v.26) his message was about repentance and preparation for the coming of the Messiah. On his next preaching stop (Corinth – vv.27,28) he was then able to prove "from the scriptures that Jesus was the Messiah."

Indeed, Apollos was able with his likely education in the contemporary school of the Jewish philosopher Philo to go beyond the entry level required of Paul (as trailblazer) and provide "strong meat" to the hungry new believers in Corinth. He was more than able to "water" what Paul had "planted" (1Co. 3:1-9). He was effective and impressive, so much so that many of the Corinthian believers thought he had eclipsed Paul, Peter, and even Jesus! They became factional – "I follow Apollos" (1Co. 1:10-12). Paul saw this as immature and dangerous, but blamed the people, not Apollos. Later in his letter to Titus Paul encouraged him to look to the needs of Apollos in his itineration ministry to the churches (Tt. 3:13). There is the possibility that Apollos delivered this letter. He was truly one of Paul's valued "co-workers in God's service" (1Co. 3:9).

Back in Ephesus 19:1–41

Sometimes when reading Luke there is a blur of events as he quickly summarizes (which all historians do). Here we have a case in point – "Paul took the road through the interior and arrived at Ephesus" (v.1). Like a movie that instantly shifts from scene to scene Luke shifts from Antioch to Ephesus ignoring the lengthy journey (Antioch to Tarsus, to Derbe, on to Lystra, Iconium and Pisidian Antioch, to Colossae, Laodicea, and Heirapolis, on to Ephesus) through mountains, river valleys, and endless empty roadways. This, as my Israeli friends would put it, was quite a "shlep".

When he got to that huge city Paul found twelve "disciples" who, like Apollos before them, had not yet heard that John the Baptist's ministry had been fulfilled in Jesus (vv.1-7). So, they were immediately baptized in the name of Jesus, and after Paul "placed his hands on them" they experienced their own "Day of Pentecost" infilling of the Holy Spirit. This was an early indication of the huge teaching task ahead for the likes of Paul, Timothy, Apollos and other key builders of the early church. And, as Luke continually stresses explicitly and implicitly, the presence and work of the Holy Spirit was critical to sustainable growth.

Two Years of Grinding it Out vv.8–20

Paul was in synch with the culture of Asia and Greece in terms of the common custom of itinerating philosophers, sophists, rhetoricians, and lecturers attracting live audiences of eager, bored citizens "having itching ears". Indeed, when one of the synagogues began to resist Paul he "left them" and set up his own venue in a rented lecture hall owned by a "Tyrannus". Paul would then be seen as just another travelling speaker and not a "setter forth of strange gods". He taught for a relatively peaceful two years, occasionally setting out to other parts of Asia (Colossae, Laodicea, Hierapolis Cl. 2:1; 4:13) where he was so successful in planting churches that Luke says, "all the Jews and Greeks who lived in the province of Asia heard the word of the Lord" (v.10). It may be that he sowed the seeds of the seven churches in Revelation during this time in Ephesus.

His ministry was underscored by the miraculous. He didn't promote or teach about personal items of clothing having supernatural powers, but he allowed his "handkerchiefs" and work "aprons" to be distributed as wonder-working relics. But, for those who mistook these things as magical, or tried to invoke Jesus' name as a cure-all, there was a bitter lesson to be learned. Luke records this (humorous) life-lesson in vv.13-16. This incident frightened other occultists to the point that they burned their relics and enchantments and submitted to "the word of the Lord" (v.20). They also learned that Jesus' name was no incantation, rather it was to be "held in high honor" (v.17).

Future Plans vv. 21,22

As always, Paul the Pharisee had a homing instinct for Jerusalem. He planned to go back, but first he wanted to go to Macedonia (Philippi and Thessalonica) and Achaia (Corinth). The Corinthian Church was in special need of attention due to both moral and doctrinal aberrations that had arisen there (1Co. 5:9). As for Jerusalem, apart from his love of the city, he wanted to deliver financial aid to the Church from his Gentile congregations (1Co. 16:1). Lastly he had wanted to visit Rome for some time (Ro. 1:13; 15:23). He sent Timothy and Erastus on ahead to Corinth to collect the Jerusalem offering (v.22 – see 1Co. 16:1-10).

The Riot in Ephesus vv. 23–41

The juxtaposition of new believers burning their books of magic (v.19) and the uproar of the silversmiths makes for entertaining reading. The tumult was incited by a prominent businessman named Demetrius who saw Paul's message as a severe threat to profits. He accused Paul of leading Ephesus "and in practically the whole province of Asia" to believe that "gods made by human hands are no gods at all" (v.26). He tried to connect this loss of business in silver idols of Artemis (Diana) with the diminution and discrediting of the goddess herself. Her "divine majesty" was at stake (v.27), to say nothing of his bottom line (always a powerful argument to combine religion with money). The crowd of craftsmen was easily transformed into a furious, shouting mob, yelling, "Great is Artemis of the Ephesians!" They grabbed Paul's assistants, Gaius and Aristarchus, and dragged them to the great amphitheatre. It is huge. When our television cameramen were setting up on the stage, I climbed up to the top seats, a few years ago, and looked with amazement at 5000 other seats and imagined it full of screaming people calling for Paul's head. The acoustics, by the way, are amazing. I could hear every word the camera and audio crew were saying as they prepared for taping. (The space between the front row of seats and the stage could easily accommodate another 1000 people standing.) This riot was about to explode in violence.

The unruly mob saw Paul and his followers as Jewish, making no distinction between Jews and "people of The Way" (Christians). So any Jew in Ephesus was also under threat. This is why the Jews in the crowd desperately shoved an obviously well-known and respected Jew by the name of Alexander to the front to disavow any connection between them and these Pauline heretics. But his Jewishness was all the angry crowd would acknowledge – and in their mind Jews were anti-idol. So, down with all enemies of Artemis!

Fortunately a cooler head prevailed. The "town clerk" appealed to the rule of law and calmed them down. If Demetrius and his craftsmen wanted to press charges the courts would handle it. The multi-breasted Artemis would prevail. The crowd, many of whom still didn't know why they were there (v.32), dispersed.

An Ambush Foiled and a Long-winded Sermon 20:1–12

As often happened, adversity drove Paul onward. The "uproar" in Ephesus was enough to see him acting on his plan to get to Jerusalem via Macedonia and Achaia (a rather circuitous route). After Corinth the plan was to sail for Caesarea, then overland up to Jerusalem, but as often is the case "the best laid plans of mice and men… gang aft a-gley" (Robbie Burns).

Luke covers Paul's travels through Macedonia in one sentence, "When he had gone through these parts and had given them much encouragement, he came to Greece" (v.2). The "these parts" probably included Philippi, Apollonia, Thessalonica, and Berea – all of whom had congregations of believers. When he got to Corinth he stayed three months. While there it is likely that he wrote the Epistle to the Romans.

Just as he was arranging for a ship to take him from the port of Cenchreae to Syria he found out there was an ambush awaiting him (v.3b). So he quickly decided to go overland, back through Macedonia, and redeemed the added effort by recruiting representatives of each church who would accompany him to Jerusalem carrying the offerings that had been collected for the impoverished Church there (v.4). When Paul and this entourage of elders reached Philippi, the group went ahead to Troas. Paul joined them a few days later after celebrating Passover with the Philippian Church (vv.5,6).

On "the first day of the week" in Troas, Paul and the group ("we" means Luke was also there) got together for a communion service. "Yom Rishon" ("Day the First" – Heb.) began at sundown after "Yom Shabat" ("Day the Seventh"). So the service began in fading sunlight on what to us would be Saturday evening. After the meal Paul began to speak. Paul "talked on and on" (v.9) until midnight (v.7). A young man named Eutychus sat on a window ledge as Paul droned on. Predictably he fell asleep and dropped three storeys to the ground. The people rushed down and picked him up dead. Paul followed, "threw himself on the young man and put his arms around him" (recalling actions by both Elijah (1Ki. 17:21) and Elisha (2Ki. 4:34, 35) and announced that the boy was alive. Then back upstairs where the lonnnng talk continued until daybreak. Eutychus wisely went home.

Paul Says Goodbye to the Ephesian Elders vv.13–38

After the all-nighter Paul and his entourage set out – the group by ship, Paul on foot. He would walk to the port of Assos (Luke doesn't say why). From there they enjoyed "a coasting voyage", stopping at a different harbour each night. Leaving Mitylene, capital of Lesbos, they overnighted at Chios, Samos, and Miletus, a seaport about forty miles south of Ephesus. Paul sent messengers from Miletus to the elders of the Ephesian church asking them to come meet with him. It would have taken a day for the message to reach them, and another day to dutifully walk to Paul's lodgings. When they arrived, Paul gave them final instructions.

In 1Co. 9:22 Paul states that he was "all things to all men" for the purpose of leading them to Christ. This relational flexibility extended to his homiletical skills. He could, and did, speak effectively to educated Jews, uneducated Gentiles, and intellectual philosophers. He was able to adapt his message to his audience. This address to the Ephesian elders is a case in point. Here he combines a defence of his ministry methods with a heartfelt call for these elders to "keep watch over yoursevles and all the flock of which the Holy Spirit has made you overseers" (v.28a). He knows that in his absence "savage wolves will come in among you and will not spare the flock" (v.29). He warns them "with tears" (v.31). He wept not for himself (v.24) but for the precious souls who were objects of "the task the Lord Jesus" gave him to "testify to the good news of God's grace" (v.24). Indeed, they are inestimably valuable trophies of grace.

From Miletus to Jerusalem 21:1–26

Luke describes the farewell with the Ephesian elders as "a tearing away" ("apospao" – Gk.), or to use an old English term, "reft away". In the vernacular, "it tore our hearts to leave them". But leave them they did, and sailed to the island of Cos. Then they hopped from Cos to Rhodes and Patara. They passed the southern coast of Cyprus and landed in the port of Tyre in Phoenicia (Lebanon) which was in the greater Roman region of Syria. A seven day stay with the Tyrinian believers was followed by a brief stop to visit the Christians in Ptolemais, then they went on to Caesarea. There they stayed with "Philip the evangelist, one of the seven" (v.8 – see 6:1-7), who had managed, with all the time he spent away from home (ch.8), to father four daughters who later became prophets (v.9).

Several days later a Judean prophet named Agabus came down to Caesarea with a warning for Paul about trouble that would occur in Jerusalem. In spite of this colorful message and the weeping and pleading of both his entourage and Philip's household, Paul could not be dissuaded from his resolve to go up to Zion. When they arrived they were billeted with a Cyprian believer named Mnason who had a home in the city.

They were warmly welcomed by "the brothers and sisters" (v.17), and the next day met with James and the elders of the Jerusalem Church. There is no mention of any of the Twelve present, but "James the Just" (Jesus' brother) was the undisputed leader.

Paul's Uncharacteristic Acquiescence vv.16–26

Paul brought his report to James and the Jerusalem Church leadership. He had ministered in Antioch, Galatia, Phrygia, Asia, Macedonia, Achaia, Miletus, Tyre, Ptolemais, Caesarea – all significant Gentile regions and cities. Churches had been planted, signs and wonders performed, great persecutions overcome, *and* a large offering received for the impoverished Jewish believers in Jerusalem. The response to this report was enthusiastic. However...

James immediately reminded Paul that "thousands" of Jews had come up to Jerusalem for Pentecost, many of them believers who had retained their orthodoxy – "zealous for the Law" (v.20). When they heard that Paul was in town they would be scandalized. In their view he was a Jewish heretic who had taken the message of grace too far. The Law of Moses, the core value of circumcision, and the cultural values attending oral tradition were all under threat. So, "what shall we do?" (vv.20-22). If something proactive isn't done there may be a tumult, and the integrity of the Church will be brought into question.

So James presented a proactive, preemptive plan. He asked Paul to publicly join four new believers who had made a vow (probably a Nazarite vow) and would be offering the appropriate sacrifice at the Temple (two lambs, a ram, some oil and flour – Nu. 6:13-21). He should pay for these offerings. What's more he too should shave his head (as he did last visit) and go through a purification ritual (probably seven immersions in a "mikvah"). The Noahide Law would suffice for Gentiles (v.28) but Paul, you're no Gentile! Surprisingly, the Paul who had pushed back against the "Judaizers" in Antioch, and had opposed Peter and split with Barnabas over the gulf fixed between Law and Grace, yielded. Was he "older and wiser"? Tired? Losing his grip? Luke doesn't say. But he does report that the fix didn't last.

Paul Violently Attacked vv. 27–39

The local Jews had been mollified by Paul's public piety but there were Asian Jews who had travelled to Jerusalem for Pentecost who recognized him and "stirred up the whole crowd", accusing him of teaching "everyone everywhere against our people and our Law and this place [Temple] by bringing in Greeks to defile this holy place" (vv.27,28). Trophimus, an Ephesian Gentile had accompanied Paul to Jerusalem but there is no record of his entering the Temple. Nevertheless, a huge mob furiously dragged Paul from the Temple and tried to kill him. As they were beating him (they would have stoned him if they had been outside the city) the Roman commander, alerted to the uproar, arrived on the scene with a company of soldiers. This intimidated the rioters and the beating stopped. Amazingly Paul asked to speak to the people (vv.37-39). When the commander was satisfied that Paul was not an Egyptian terrorist, but a Jew from Tarsus, he acceded to the request.

Nevertheless, a huge mob furiously dragged Paul from the Temple and tried to kill him.

Paul Addresses the Mob 21:40–22:21

Paul "motioned with his hand" requesting silence. No doubt his personal authority combined with a Hebrew/Aramaic dialect contributed to the "quiet" that ensued (21:40 – 22:2). Like Stephen (7:2) he began by showing respect, "Brothers and fathers…" (v.1). Defending himself against the charges shouted in the temple precincts (v.21:28) he gave a succinct summary of his Jewish pedigree:

1. I'm Jewish.

2. My hometown is the formidable city of Tarsus.

3. I was brought up right here, in Jerusalem.

4. I have an ivy-league education – my mentor/teacher was the famed rabbi Gamaliel.

5. I am an expert in Oral Law.

6. I have a zeal for God.

7. I was a religious activist.

8. I was a brutally effective persecutor of early Christians.

9. I was well-known to and endorsed by the high priest and the Sanhedrin as a defender of Judaism.

10. I was given authority to track down, arrest, and bring back Jewish Christians who had fled to other countries (vv.1-5). With brutal violence I oversaw their scourging, imprisonment, and even their deaths.

Paul was fully aware that there was no one in that crowd who could match his credentials. Many of those who heard him may have wished they could be just like him. But in his case there was this "but" – why had the ultimate Jewish champion gone off the rails? Paul answered that unspoken question by recounting his Damascus Road conversion.

On the Damascus Road vv. 5–22

Paul was about to tell a story that was over twenty years old. Some of the details he gives to this virulent mob he does not give to King Agrippa in ch.26, and vice-versa. He wasn't reading from a manuscript. He was retelling the details of a story as they came to mind. The main point: I met Jesus and I've been forever changed.

He had been given authority by the "brethren" (v.5b – read "high priest and Sanhedrin") to track down followers of "The Way", arrest and bring them "bound" back to Jerusalem for punishment. "About noon" (a personal reflection not mentioned in 9:3, but in ch.26 it was "mid-day") a "great light", eclipsing the noonday sun in brightness, knocked him to the ground. Prostrate and blind he heard a voice asking, "Why do you persecute me?" (v.7). Not "Why are you persecuting The Way?" Paul was persecuting Jesus himself. In the blinding light his question was both reflex and wonder: "Who are you Lord?" Intuitively he knew this was an epiphany (his entourage, on the other hand, saw the light – and weren't blinded! – but didn't understand the voice). He then asked what he had to do, and the Lord told him to go to Damascus for further instructions about "all that you have been assigned to do" (v.10 – see 26:16-18). He had been overcome with a "glory" (v.11 KJV) that would become his sustaining hope (2Co. 3:7-18). It was the glory of a new covenant, the glory of grace. This was uncharted territory for a Pharisee.

It took three days to recover his equilibrium (9:9), but it wasn't until Ananias, "a devout observer of the Law" (v.12) came to visit, that he regained his sight (v.13). The transformation that had begun with a blast of sound and light was now fine-tuned by Ananias' prophetic insight: "The God of our ancestors has chosen you to know his will and to see the Righteous One and to hear words from his mouth. You will be his witness to all people of what you have seen and heard" (vv.14,15). Led by the hand into Damascus (v.11) he was now to be led by the Spirit to the world.

As he spoke to the seething mass before him in the temple court-yard Paul was not giving a chronological history. The crowd didn't care (although later scholars would parse and prune) that his written account in Galatians 1:18-20 would be at variance with this powerful speech. Paul was giving an "epiphanal" account, recalling those moments when heaven intersected with his life, an all too human life, that to his shame, had seen him zealously persecuting the Church (v.19). His lowest moment had been his complicity in the death of Stephen twenty-five years before (v.20). But then came the earth and history-shaking call: "I will send you far away to the Gentiles." This reignited the wrath of the mob.

Religious/cultural history is a powerful thing. It's unlikely that there were many theologians in this garment-stripping, dust-throwing, red-faced, spitting crowd of rioters. Few of them, if any, could define "heresy". But all of them could define "blasphemy". To claim that the God of Abraham, Isaac and Jacob was behind a call to bring Gentiles into the fold of Judaism was too much. Gentiles were "the unwashed", the enemy, the offscouring of the earth! They would be ruled *by*, not rule *with*, the Jews in the messianic kingdom. Paul must die! "He's not fit to live!" (v.22).

While the crowd was "shouting and throwing off their cloaks and flinging dust into the air" the Roman commander showed up with a centurion and his troops. They arrested (and saved!) Paul, taking him to the barracks where he would undergo interrogation and flogging (vv.23,24). This was common practice, especially when forcing a slave to confess. As he was being stretched out for the flogging, Paul asked a question that struck fear to the heart of the centurion, "Is it legal for you to flog a Roman citizen who hasn't even been found guilty?" Roman law was explicit re: the rights of its citizens. Due process was a core value. Both centurion and commander backed off. Paul was returned to the barracks.

Paul Brought Before the Sanhedrin 22:30–23:11

The Sanhedrin, composed of Pharisees and Sadducees, didn't like being ordered around by the Romans, but in this case they readily complied when Claudius Lysias (23:26) commanded them to assemble. He wanted to know what was going on. He had Paul "stand before them" (v.30).

Paul, unlike Jesus who "opened not his mouth" when before the Sanhedrin, lashed out at the high priest who ordered his mouth to be struck. In fact, when he referred to his status as a Pharisee, and then divided the court (Pharisee vs. Sadducee) by claiming he was on trial because of his belief (as a Pharisee) in resurrection he himself later claimed (24:21) that he "shouted". Both Paul and the Sanhedrin were on edge. Such a fury ensured that Lysius had his soldiers wrest Paul by force from some of the overheated judges before they tore him to pieces! The only safe place for him was the barracks. So back he went. To his great relief and encouragement, in a vision he received a word from the Lord telling him his ministry would continue, all the way to Rome.

A Conspiracy and a Transfer vv.12–35

That night, while Paul was hearing from heaven, a group of over forty men made a vow to fast until they had killed him. The plan was to have the Sanhedrin request Paul's presence the next day for further inquiry into his case. Their co-conspirators in this shady business were men who should have known and acted better, "the chief priests and the elders" (v.14). In that there is no mention of the "scribes", who would be Pharisees, it's possible that this plot was presented to Sadducees only. After all, they had rioted the day before in the Sanhedrin against both Paul *and* the Pharisees. And, they had the most to lose in terms of any turmoil in Jerusalem in that they controlled the temple economy. Regardless, they agreed.

Paul's nephew (son of his sister) heard about it. It may have been that his mother was married within the high priestly class and he overheard the plot discussed. We don't know. But, he went to the barracks and told Paul, who told the centurion, who told Lysias. The fact that Lysias "took the young man by the hand" (v.19) suggests he may have not yet reached his teens. He told the boy to maintain secrecy. It could be Lysias wanted to take full credit for saving Paul from this menace. It would look good on his resumé. He quickly ordered two of his centurions, who oversaw one hundred soldiers each, along with seventy horsemen and two hundred "spearmen" to get ready to leave for Caesarea by nine o'clock that night. He fully intended to get his obviously very important prisoner to the Governor on the coast. While the 470 soldiers got their horses, weapons, and kit together, Lysias quickly wrote a letter which the soldiers would give to Governor Felix. It stated the reason for bringing Paul to him, and it made him look like the responsible authority Rome expected him to be. Besides, a "papyrus trail" often led to a promotion.

This remarkably large escort left a few hours later with Paul in the midst on a horse. They travelled about forty miles northeast to [15]Antipatris, a Roman military relay station. The next day the infantry returned

---

[15]   Named after Antipater, procurator of Judea under Julius Caesar, and father of Herod the Great.

CANTELON'S CASUAL COMMENTARY

to Jerusalem and the cavalry accompanied Paul the remaining twenty five miles to Caesarea. They handed Lysias' letter and Paul over to Felix who put Paul under guard in Herod's palace. Once again adversity pushed Paul forward. This time he would be on his way, slowly but surely to Rome.

Paul in Caesarea 24:1–26:32

Before Felix 24:1–27

Paul would spend the next two years in casual confinement in Caesarea. While there he underwent "examinations" or trials before three powerful men: Felix, Festus, and Agrippa 2nd. There is no need to duplicate what a good Bible dictionary or Google can do in terms of giving you, the reader, historical background on these men. I will just give a cursory treatment to their stories as we follow Paul's story through chapters 24-26.

Much, if not most, of our extra-biblical information about historical figures of that time relies on the Jewish/Roman historian Josephus and the Roman Tacitus (Google them). Both of these men have a dim view of Antonius Felix. They describe him as avaricious, lustful, cruel, and corrupt; but, as the Sanhedrin's lawyer Tertullus smoothly put it, "We have enjoyed a long period of peace under you…" (v.2). He even credits Felix for instituting "reforms". Judea was almost impossible to govern. Apparently Felix's draconian style worked, at least in the short term (being married to the Jewish princess Drusilla helped). In the long term, however, he was removed from Caesarea by the Emperor, and banished.

Five days after Paul had been escorted by Lysias' seventy horsemen to Caesarea, the high priest Ananias and some of the elders from the Sanhedrin came down from Jerusalem to meet with Felix and present their charges against Paul. Their lawyer Tertullus began with flattery (vv.2-4) but then cut to the chase: two charges, one indictable by Roman law, the other of no interest to Felix. The possibly indictable offence was insurrection, "a ringleader of the Nazarene sect" (v.5b), but the other, "tried to desecrate the Temple" (v.5c) was irrelevant. Tertullus' employers all chimed in, asserting "that these things were true" (v.9).

Felix, who had read the letter from Lysias and already had a jaundiced view of the volatile Jewish leaders, said nothing but "motioned" for Paul to speak (v.10). His defence was straightforward:

1. Less than two weeks ago I came up to Jerusalem to worship (v.11) and to bring social assistance to the poor (v.17).

2. I did *not* create a disturbance (vv.12,18).

3. My accusers are short on proof (v.13).

4. Some Jews from Asia are the ones who incited the Jerusalem mob and are the ones who should be here, but aren't, to accuse me (v.19).

5. My "offence" is that I worship the God of Abraham, Isaac, and Jacob (as my accusers do) in the context of a legal Jewish movement they call "The Way" (v.14).

6. What really rankles some of these accusers is that I believe in resurrection (vv.15,21).

Felix, who Luke says "was well acquainted with The Way" (v.22), deferred his decision and ordered Paul back to a relatively free form of house arrest until "Lysias the commander comes." From time to time he and his wife Drusilla sent for Paul to hear from him, if for no other reason, to converse with someone intelligent and interesting. Paul's emphasis, however, on "justice… self-control… judgement" (v.25) were scary topics for a corrupt leader. Nevertheless he sent for Paul frequently. Luke says he wanted a bribe.

Josephus says (*"Antiquities"* 20:8:9) that it was the complaints of Caesarea's Jewish leaders that led to Felix being recalled in disgrace by Nero. So in Paul's case, aware of those complaints to his boss, Felix tried to ingratiate himself to his detractors by keeping Paul under guard for two years (v.27).

Paul Tried by Festus 25:1–22

Much more than Paul's pesky case, Festus inherited from Felix an infestation of "robbers" (as Josephus calls them) or "sicarii" who murdered people at random with their small, curved swords, and set villages and towns on fire throughout Judea. So his attention was on these insurgents rather than on some minor dispute the Sanhedrin had with a rogue Pharisee. Nevertheless he was forced by the Sanhedrin's importunity to try the case. He wanted to do it in Jerusalem but the prisoner (Paul) wouldn't agree. So he had to try him in Caesarea.

Luke's summary of the trial is brief (vv.7,8). The outcome was as well. Paul, as a Roman, was legally allowed to appeal to Caesar, so he did. Festus was not pleased. In a bit of pique he retorted, "To Caesar you will go!" (v.12). But, as the new procurator, he wanted to please the Jews (after all they had gotten rid of Felix). So he seized the opportunity, when King Agrippa and his wife Bernice came to wish the new governor well, to consult with them about Paul's case.

Agrippa was intrigued. He wanted to meet Paul in person. Festus readily complied (vv.13-22). Even he wanted to hear more about "a dead man named Jesus who Paul claimed was alive" (v.19). If nothing else it had great entertainment value.

Paul and Agrippa II 25:23–26:32

Agrippa was the great grandson of Herod the Great, "King of the Jews". His father was Agrippa 1st. He had Jewish lineage, although his great-great grandfather Antipater was a forced convert to Judaism. Antipater was from Edom, thus he and the Herod line after him were referred to as "Idumeans" ("from Edom"). Like Samaritans who were considered "half-breeds" by the Jews, the Idumean heritage was seen as a blot. There were several moral scandals in Herodian history, not the least being Agrippa's questionable relationship with his sister Bernice. His father, Agrippa 1st, had died in Caesarea (12:19-23), and according to Josephus his memory had been seriously trampled on by soldiers and citizens in both Caesarea and Samaria. For sure, Agrippa 2nd was not happily received in Caesarea. Too many recent memories, too much baggage.

Agrippa 2nd was not happily received in Caesarea. Too many recent memories, too much baggage.

Paul was called from his imprisonment to present his case before Agrippa and Bernice. The pomp and circumstance were impressive (v.23) but not enough to muffle the hint of moral aberration that always accompanied the public appearances of the royal siblings. Nevertheless, monarchy is monarchy. Paul may have found the words sticking in his throat as he respectfully said, "King Agrippa, I consider myself fortunate to stand before you today..." (26:2). He was a lone figure standing before a formidable array of political and religious might. A brave man, to say the least.

With Lysias, Felix, and Festus, Paul was a Roman, with Agrippa he was a Jew. With no hint of half-breed bias he acknowledged Agrippa's Jewishness (v.3) and went on to inform him that he himself was born a Jewish Pharisee (pure blood line implied) and that he had a reputation for strict piety (vv.4,5). He drew Agrippa in as an ally by referring to the hope of "our ancestors" (emphasis on "our"), the hope of resurrection promised to "the twelve tribes" (v.7). Then he positioned himself and Agrippa as defending that hope against the accusations of "these Jews" from Jerusalem. Perhaps raising his voice as he had done when he stood before the Sanhedrin (24:20) he declared, more than questioned, "Why should any of you consider it incredible that God raises the dead?" (v.8). Abraham Lincoln's cryptic comment, "A man who represents himself has a fool for a client" didn't take the Apostle Paul into account. He was a master in his own defence.

In "been-there-done-that" transparency he confessed he had been in the same camp as his accusers opposing "the name of Jesus of Nazareth". Indeed, he admitted being "obsessed" with persecuting "the Lord's people". As a member of the Sanhedrin he had often voted for their deaths. He had been a roving hunter, zealously travelling from foreign city to city, dragging believers in Jesus out of their synagogues. Yes, they were Jews, but they were blasphemers – Paul had been their most feared nemesis (vv.9-11). With the full backing of "the chief priests" (v.12) his "raging fury" (v.11 RSV) had been unassailable.

On his way to Damascus, to ferret out followers of The Way who had escaped his fury in Jerusalem, everything changed. Luke's record of the moment includes detail absent in the other two accounts (cc.9, 22). The blinding light, voice, and prostration are followed by direct words from Jesus that, no doubt, sustained Paul in subsequent persecutions, stonings, deprivations, and adversity on his tireless missionary journeys. First of all he tells Paul to stand which suggests a serious "man to man" communication about to take place. Then Jesus announces that he himself is "appointing" Paul to be "a servant" and "a witness" to this present vision and to future visions. To accomplish this radical transformation and calling Jesus has "rescued" ("delivered, taken out from, chosen") Paul from both the religious sub-culture of Judaism and the secular sub-culture of the Greek-speaking world (in that sense Paul is both Jew and Gentile). Jesus says both subcultures are under "the power of Satan" in that they need "forgiveness of sins" and have yet to be "sanctified by faith in me" (vv.15-18). Paul was to be the trailblazer, the thin edge of the wedge, proclaiming the resurrected Christ to the world.

Appealing directly to Agrippa the Jew, Paul declared he was simply following in the footsteps of the prophets, and even Moses, who foresaw Messiah's day (Dt.18:18; Is.53), and stated his confidence (!) that Agrippa believed the prophets (v.27). Agrippa may have felt both trapped and intrigued, "Almost thou persuadest me to be a Christian" (v.28 KJV). Whereas Festus accused Paul of madness (v.24), Agrippa was moved. He got up, and as he left the room said, "This man could have been set free if he had not appealed to Caesar" (v.32). As for Agrippa it may be that this encounter with Paul had transforming impact. Much later in his reign he made a [16] speech to the leaders of Jerusalem just before the war culminating in its destruction (70AD). It is regarded as a masterpiece. His words are measured, wise, and kind as he counsels Jerusalem to resist any passionate plunge into a war it has no hope of winning. His view of God and his sovereign engagement with the nations of the world demonstrate a spiritual maturity that may have begun that day in Caesarea when Paul proclaimed the risen Savior.

A Perilous Trip to Rome 27:1–28:31

Luke gives a first-person account of a long sea voyage from Caesarea to Malta in ch.27. It was fraught with danger and near death. There is no need to write any summary. It is a very interesting read (vv.1-44) and, according to commentators knowledgeable in such things, it provides excellent insight into ancient nautical protocols. As a "landlubber" I've had to read it several times just to get a sense of what was happening. Suffice it to say that by the grace of God no lives were lost as the bedraggled sailors, soldiers and prisoners managed to swim, float, and wade their way to shore, their ship wrecked on a shoal off the northern coast. Paul, who had been shipwrecked three times (2Co. 11:25), took it all in stride.

Because of fourteen days of lashing winds, towering waves, and constant overcast, the sailors had been unable to navigate. So, only after the welcoming islanders told them where they were did they realize they had made it to Malta. The people and the "chief official of the island" (28:7) made sure they were cared for. After three days some sort of short-term facilities were provided allowing the stranded men to stay for three months (v.11). During that interval Paul, snakebit but healthy (vv.3-6), ministered healing to the sick. There is no record, however, of his teaching anyone. Nor is there any reference in subsequent biblical records of a Maltese Church.

---

[16] Josephus, *Wars of the Jews*, 2:16

The grateful islanders "furnished us with the supplies we needed" (v.10) as Paul, his entourage, the centurion, soldiers, prisoners and sailors "put out to sea in a ship that had wintered in the island" (v.11). The figurehead on this Alexandrian vessel bore the twin gods Castor and Pollux, sons of the legendary Jupiter whose Gemini formation in the stars was believed to be beneficent towards sailors. Paul, unfazed by superstitions, readily boarded the ship and they were on their way to Rome. He knew he would get there – the "angel of God" had told him so (27:23,24).

After a couple of brief stops at ports in Syracuse (Sicily) and Regium (southern tip of Italy) the voyage ended in Puteoli near Naples. Paul connected with some "brothers and sisters" in Puteoli who invited him to stay with them for a week. They probably wanted to hear from him at their next worship gathering. The fact that Julius the centurion allowed this delay suggests that he had developed great respect for his unusual prisoner. Word got to the Church in Rome and some of "the brethren there" travelled several miles down the Appian Way to meet Paul. Rome was next.

Three days after his arrival Paul convened a meeting of Rome's Jewish leaders. He evidently had sufficient stature/fame/notoriety to bring them together. He gave them a brief summary of why he was in Rome and made it clear that he was a Jew, one of them: "My *brothers* although I have done nothing against *our people* or against the customs of *our ancestors...*" (v.17). He had no intention of bringing "any charge against *my own people*" (v.19). Then he raised the bar. This wasn't about him, it was about "the hope of Israel" (v.20), the messianic hope which he saw as inextricably tied to Jesus' resurrection.

His reception was fairly amicable. The Jews were intrigued by "this sect" and arranged a larger meeting. At that event Paul spoke all day (!) "explaining about the Kingdom of God... the Law of Moses... the Prophets" (v.23). As a highly trained Pharisee he was more than able to hold the attention of his audience, many of whom would have been well educated themselves. Many were gripped, even convinced, by Paul's tracing the resurrected Messiah throughout their scriptures. But, when Paul connected Isaiah's prophecy (Is. 6:9,10) with his claim that "God's salvation has been sent to the Gentiles and they will listen!" (v.28), he lost half his audience. "God's salvation" and "the Gentiles" were like oil and water in their view. Indeed, this issue was the fulcrum of Jewish objection to the Gospel wherever Paul preached.

Nevertheless, Jesus was his message. His "rented house" became an ad hoc synagogue for the next two years and Paul boldly preached the Gospel. When he wasn't preaching he wrote letters to the churches and one to a personal friend. In every way he was powerful and prolific.

THE GOSPEL OF JOHN

INTRODUCTION

There are a myriad of Introductions to John's gospel in libraries, bookstores, and on the internet. There is no need for me to give something that is much better given elsewhere. However, there *are* a few observations I'd like to make to help you as you read through this most personal of the four gospels.

Two sentences are key: "We beheld his glory" (1:14) and "these are written that you may believe that Jesus is the Messiah, the Son of God, and that by believing you may have life in his name" (20:31). John combines the personal with the theological, experience with mature reflection, heart with mind.

Unlike Luke, John was an eyewitness of Jesus' life and ministry. He, along with the Twelve, "beheld". They were there. He saw a weary Jesus (4:6), a grieving Jesus (11:35), a dying Jesus (19:30), a risen Jesus (20:19-23). But the ultimate "beheld" occurred on Mt. Hermon at the

Transfiguration (Lk. 9:28-36; Mt. 17:1-8; Mk. 9:2-8). It's a mystery that John does not record that amazing moment when heaven met earth, when the Law and the Prophets conversed with Jesus, when the glory and voice of the Father flattened the Three to the ground. Nevertheless he "beheld" the glory of Christ *personally*. Which meant *in history*.

John's gospel is no exercise in philosophical speculation. It is a record of "that which was from the beginning, which we have heard, which we have seen with our eyes, which we have looked at and our hands have touched... This life appeared; we have seen it..." (1Jn. 1:1,2).

Without this personal, experiential foundation, John's theology would be mere speculation. With it, however, his theology had authority. It had to be strong, not only to push back against the opposition of the synagogue, but to counter the insidious erosion of the Gospel by the rise of the Gnostic heresy. Simply stated Gnosticism was a spiritualized philosophy that taught all matter was evil. There was much more to it, but suffice to say that this view ("Docetism") undercut the incarnation, for how could God who is holy take on flesh which is evil? This is why in the prologue John states, "The Word became flesh..." (1:14). Throughout his gospel he stresses the humanity of Jesus. Yes, he is Son of God, but he is also Son of Man. Both designations are messianic, of course, but there is no question that Jesus the man ate, drank, slept, sorrowed, suffered, and died like any other human being. He bled real blood on the cross.

Many biblical scholars see this gospel as the pinnacle of the New Testament. It truly is glorious. It reveals a Savior who has come to save us – you and me. If we find ourselves bowed in the presence of Christ as we read, John's purpose will have been achieved.

Prologue 1:1–18

James and John were known as "the sons of thunder" (Mk. 3:17). They were the sons of Zebedee, a well-to-do fisherman on the Sea of Galilee. Rough-hewn Galileans, they were direct and aggressive. On one occasion when a Samaritan village refused to host Jesus and his entourage (Lk. 9:51-56) they wanted to "call fire down from heaven to destroy them." Then there was the time when they lobbied Jesus to be his senior cabinet members when he set up his throne in Jerusalem (Mk. 10:35-37). One might say they were both bellicose and pushy, self-seeking and immature. So how could John pen such glorious words as these? Obviously age and experience had fine-tuned his thunder to poetry (tradition says he wrote his gospel in Ephesus sometime toward, some say after, the close of the 1st century). The first sentence stands as one of the most sublime ever written.

"In the beginning" appears both here and in Genesis 1:1. In Genesis it refers to the very first moment of creation. Here it refers to a beginning before all beginning. It transcends time. It is eternity.

The writer to the Hebrews says, "In the beginning, Lord, you laid the foundations of the earth, and the heavens are the work of your hands. They will perish, but you remain" (He. 1:10,11). Time and space are temporal, but "your throne, O God will last forever and ever" (He. 1:8). The "Word" ("Logos" Gk.) has always existed. He has no genealogy, but is eternally "begotten of God", the "image of the invisible God", "the firstborn over all creation" (Cl. 1:15). He is both "Alpha and Omega... who is, and who was, and who is to come, the Almighty" (Re. 1:8).

John, of course, was not trying to be obtuse. He assumed that his readers would at once comprehend the meaning of "Logos". It was common in extant paraphrases of the Hebrew scriptures ("targums"), and very familiar in Jewish and Greek philosophies percolating in Ephesus and Alexandria. Just as the "Wisdom of God" was personified in the Old Testament (eg. Proverbs cc. 8 & 9) the Creator was personified (in Jesus) as the "Logos" – "all things were made through him" (v.3). Or, as St. Paul put it, "in him all things were created: things in heaven and on earth, visible and invisible, whether thrones or powers or rulers or authorities; all things have been created through him and for him" (Cl. 1:16). The Logos is immanent in creation, "without him was not anything made that was made" (v.3b RSV). Indeed, "in him all things hold together" (Cl. 1:17). We're not talking pantheism (God is all and all is God), rather the Logos is both creator and sustainer of the universe. It is separate from him, but remove him and everything collapses. This is theology for the ages, certainly transcending John's thunderous youth. The writer to the Hebrews certainly thought so (see He. 1:1-3).

"Life" and "light" are next (v.4). They are powerful words attributing life-giving power to the Logos. John expresses much the same in Re. 4:11 when he writes, "You are worthy, our Lord and God, to receive glory and honor and power, for you created all things, and by your will they were created and have their being." The Creator creates light even as he creates life – they are interdependent. Mankind must see in order to exist (v.4b). We can choose "darkness" (v.5a) if we will, but that self-imposed void, unyielding and impenetrable, will never obscure the fact that, "the darkness is passing and the true light is already shining" (1Jn. 2:8). Intellect, emotion, and will are all cast in relief by "the light of the world" (8:12). John is calling Jew and Gentile to come out of the shadows.

John is calling Jew and Gentile to come out of the shadows.

He then takes a brief detour to reflect on the ministry of the other John (unlike Matthew, Mark, and Luke he never calls him "the Baptist"). In verses 6-8, and 15 he refers to John as "a man sent from God..." a witness to testify concerning that light who was "surpassed" by the Logos (a theme in John – see 1:24-27,30; 3:28-30; 4:1; 5:36; 10:41). This reminder that John (the Baptist) was eclipsed by Jesus may have indicated the author's awareness, writing in Ephesus, that there was a sect of John's disciples in the city, still holding to John's baptism (see Acts 19:1-6). John wants these well-meaning sectarians to know that the "other John" was *not* the light (v.8). He *was* a valued witness, however, to the emergent Messiah, "the true light..." (v.9a).

This light is "true" as in "exact, accurate". It "was coming into the world", that is, "was ever coming". It pre-exists whereas the "other John" was in the world for only a moment in time. The interaction between eternity and space/time was a constant in John's thinking. The Transfiguration experience had forever impacted him with both the gap and the thin veil between heaven and earth. The Kingdom was less than a breath away.

Yet, "the world that was made through him" not only preferred not to know him (v.10), but couldn't (or wouldn't) "understand" (v.5 KJV) the light of the Logos. And, if there were no unilateral action on God's part (motivated by love) the world would perish (3:16). So the Father sent the Son (Logos) to become one of us, die in our stead, and save us from everlasting alienation from the home and destiny he had planned at the beginning. There was no other option, for "the world by wisdom knew not God" (1Co. 1:21 KJV – see also Ro. 1:18-22).

There is more than a touch of sorrow in John's tone as he writes, "He came to his own home, and his own people received him not" (v.11 RSV). The Greek word is "idios" meaning "one's own, one's home, household, people". Here you have the Creator of all rejected by all. In love he stands at the door and knocks, but the door remains locked shut. It is incomprehensible and tragic.

Nevertheless there was hope. There would be some who would believe in and receive the light (v.12). To those who acknowledged the Logos as Messiah, the Father "gave the right to become children of God". Unlike the Apostle Paul, John did not use the adoption metaphor. Rather, he wrote that the believers in Jesus "were born, not of blood nor of the will of the flesh nor of the will of man, but of God" (v.13 RSV). Later (3:3) he would refer to them as "born again". Even while their feet were planted on terra firma they would be citizens of the heavenly realm. "The Word made flesh" (v.14) who dwells "among us" even as He is God (v.1), has shown and is the way. He personifies the conjunction of heaven and earth.

This multi-faceted prologue to John's gospel is effectively summarized in verses 14-18. As already noted, "The Word became flesh..." undercuts the Gnostic view of the wickedness of all material things (including the human body) by affirming Jesus' humanity. Jesus was conceived, gestated, and delivered in and by a woman; he ate, drank, slept, and suffered all "the slings and arrows" life threw at him; he bled real blood on the cross and died a real death. He was fully man. As a man he "dwelt among us" (v.14) or, "tabernacled" with mankind. When the children of Israel had wandered for forty years in the wilderness the Tabernacle had been the locus of God's presence. For John's mainly Jewish readers the verb "to tabernacle" would immediately resonate, as would the word "glory" (v.14b).

In Israel today there is a common "congratulations" used for birthdays, anniversaries, or any event where someone is being fêted: "kol ha kavod"! ("all the glory" – Heb.). It has its roots in the scriptures where the glory of God is seen as "splendor" or "manifest excellence". In this passage John bears witness to the glory of God he, James, and Peter saw at the Transfiguration. He identified this manifestation as "the glory of the one and only Son who came from the Father" (v.14b). Surely John and the Twelve saw intermittent rays of glory in the miraculous work and stirring words of their Master during three years of ministry. But nothing could compare with the other-worldly awe in seeing Jesus in conversation with Moses and Elijah and hearing (!) the voice of the Father affirming his Son. Yet, human as they were, still beset with nationalistic ideology and personal ambition, "they did not recognize him" (v.10b). Even after the resurrection, with the glorified One standing before them, "some doubted" (Mt. 28:17). In his old age, however, John bore unabashed testimony to "the Word made flesh". Unmitigated grace and transparent truth had won his soul (v.16).

At this point I must take an "uncasual" theological detour. I'll keep it brief, but "the only begotten of the Father" (v.14b KJV) requires a little work.

John refers to Jesus as "the only begotten" on five occasions (1:14,18; 3:16,18; 1Jn. 4:9). It is a "Christological" title unique to his gospel. It stresses Jesus' "one of a kind" status above all space/time and heavenly beings, but even more his saving and life-giving power. Because Jesus can say: "I and the Father are one" (Jn. 10:30) his "begetting" is not an event in time (in a Bethlehem stable) but transcends time. The Christ was not just a tactical intervention in the fallen universe; He was the eternal Son, Creator, Sustainer, and Savior of all. He was "Monogenes

Theos" ("God only-begotten" – Gk.), "God made flesh dwelling among us… full of grace and truth", standing over salvation history as Lord. The Apostle Paul captured this truth in Ph. 2:6-11 when he referred to Jesus:

"Who, being in very nature God,
did not consider equality with God something to be used
to his own advantage;
rather, he made himself nothing
by taking the very nature of a servant,
being made in human likeness.
And being found in appearance as a man,
he humbled himself
by becoming obedient to death -
even death on a cross!
Therefore God exalted him to the highest place
and gave him the name that is above every name,
that at the name of Jesus every knee should bow,
in heaven and on earth and under the earth,
and every tongue acknowledge that Jesus Christ is Lord,
to the glory of God the Father."

The Logos, Monogenes Theos, is Lord of all. Heaven and earth cannot contain him (King Solomon got it right – 1Ki. 8:27), but he has chosen to dwell with humanity for a time, keeping the universe in suspense as it awaits "eagerly for our adoption to sonship" (Ro. 8:22,23). In that sense the designation "Son of Man" is tactical, whereas "Son of God" is strategic. The Father's sovereign plan is unfolding. The Logos is catalyst to its fulfillment.

"The Lamb of God" 1:19–51

As already noted, John does not refer to Jesus' cousin as "John the Baptist". He just calls him "John". But, to avoid confusion I will refer to him as "the Baptist". The Gospel of John begins (after the prologue)

447

with a brief but vital description of the Baptist's testimony re: Jesus. But first, a delegation of "priests and Levites" from Jerusalem came to get clarification as to his identity. "Who are you?" they asked.

John, the rock star baptizer, the man to whom "all the people of Jerusalem" and "the whole Judean countryside" went for baptism in the Jordan River (Mk. 1:5) had become a major force. Everyone, including King Herod, was talking about him. Some said he was the Messiah, others that he was Elijah (v.21), and then there were those who thought he was the Prophet foreshadowed by Moses (Dt. 18:15). John answered, "No, no, and no."

"Then who *are* you?" they insisted. John, who had checked his ego at the door, responded with a humble, "I'm a voice". No name, no claim, just a voice. A lonely voice at that, "in the wilderness". He didn't even claim a unique message. His was Elijah's "Make straight the way of the Lord" (v.27b). When they asked, "Why then do you baptize if you are not the Messiah, nor Elijah, nor the Prophet?" he gave a vague answer about someone who would eclipse him, but gave no name to this unknown stranger (vv.26,27). The next day, however, as he saw Jesus approaching him (and his interlocutors), he made the profound statement, "Look, the Lamb of God, who takes away the sin of the world!" (v.29). "He's the reason I baptize." (See Is. 53:7,8).

The author records no response from the Jerusalem delegation. Perhaps they were still trying to digest this "Lamb of God" announcement. Before they could mutter a response John shocked them further with, "I saw the Spirit come down from heaven as a dove and remain on him... the one who will baptize with the Holy Spirit... God's chosen One" (vv.32-34). He was referring, of course, to what he had witnessed when he had baptized Jesus in the Jordan (Mt. 3:13-17; Lk. 31:21,22). The dove and the voice had convinced him his mission was over and Jesus' ministry was about to begin.

John the apostle then writes that, "The next day John was there again with two of his disciples" (v.35). "There" referred to "Bethany on the other side of the Jordan" (v.28). This location ought not be confused with the home village of Mary, Martha, and Lazarus on the southeast slope of the Mount of Olives. It was an obscure setting a few miles east of the Sea of Galilee that eventually disappeared from historical record. Nevertheless it had historical significance in the early story of Jesus. It is where he called Andrew and John (probably) to follow him. The Baptist apparently did not object to two of his own shifting their loyalties to this newcomer. Indeed it was the Baptist himself who pointed Jesus out to his disciples with that messianic declaration, "Behold, the Lamb of God!" (v.36 KJV). "When the two disciples heard him say this, they followed Jesus" (v.37). There was no "let me think/pray about it", just immediate decision. The Baptist's teaching had prepared them for this moment. The messianic hope had them in its grip.

Nathanael uttered the now famous, "Can anything good come out of Nazareth?"

I wrote a parenthetic "probably" re: the Baptist's unnamed disciple, because the Apostle John does not ever refer to himself in the first person. But the fact that Andrew recruited his brother Simon who became "Peter" (v.42), and Mark mentions James and John as the other brothers comprising the first four disciples (Mk. 1:16-20), suggests that John was more than "probably" the unnamed early trainee. Eight more disciples would soon be called. Philip (from Bethsaida, as were Andrew and Peter) was next (vv.43,44), and he recruited Nathanael (from Cana – vv.47-51). Nathanael, "an Israelite… in whom is no guile!" (v.47) uttered the now famous, "Can anything good come out of Nazareth? (v.46), and then was the first to declare of Jesus, "Rabbi, you are the Son of God! You are the king of Israel!" (v.4a). Jesus responded to this spontaneous outburst with what we might express as, "You ain't seen nothing yet!" (vv.50,51).

Water into Wine 2:1–12

The wedding in Cana (Nathanael's home town) may have been a family affair – why else would Jesus' mother, Mary, and six of Jesus' new friends, Andrew, Peter, Philip, James, John, and Nathanael, have been invited?

Some commentators have suggested it was the Apostle John's wedding! John's mother was Salome (wife of Zebedee) and she was Mary's sister. So a family wedding (if these assertions are true) it might have been. Mary was certainly involved. She seems to have taken personally the embarrassment of running out of wine at such an auspicious family event. She turned to Jesus for help.

For many readers over the centuries, Jesus' response to his mother seems harsh – "Woman, what have I to do with thee?" (v.4). In Jesus' day it was not a rebuke. Again and again he addressed women this way. For example: the Canaanite woman in Lebanon (Mt. 15:28), the woman with "the issue of blood" (Lk. 13:12), the Samaritan woman at the well (Jn. 4:21), a woman caught in adultery (Jn. 8:10), to Mary from the cross (Jn. 19:26), and to a tearful Magdalene (Jn. 20:13,15). The second part of his response, "what have I to do with thee? Mine hour is not yet come," is not impetuous but revealing. Already Jesus was facing the great gulf between the immediate demands of the people and his mission to usher in the Kingdom of Heaven. It was a clash of worldview. It wasn't just Mary, but over the next three years his chosen Twelve would continually, yet unintentionally, try to reduce Jesus to their size. Whether it was wine, or a throne in Jerusalem, the people's vision was myopic. There must have been a tender tone in his voice, however, because Mary, unabashed and confident, turned to the waiters and said, "Do whatever he tells you." Then as a favor to his mother, Jesus performed "the first of the signs through which he revealed his glory" (v.11). His newly minted Six were pumped! (v.11b). In gratitude Mary and her other sons, "brothers", accepted Jesus' invitation to come and visit in Capernaum for a few days (v.12). It was a long walk but the conversation must have been rich.

The Temple Courts Get a Cleaning 2:13–25

Throughout this series of "casual commentaries" I've stated it's not my intention to try to "harmonize" the gospels. Mainly because it can't be done. Each of the four writers have their own perspective and, to use an analogy, they play different instruments in the symphony. I approach each work in its own right, occasionally cross-referencing, but never insisting that it's part of a collaborative effort. Nor will I assume that historical chronology was a value of the writers. The one value, however, was Messiah. Jesus was /is Son of Man and Son of God, the Savior of the world.

Unlike the other gospel writers, John's account of Jesus clearing the temple courts occurs early on (see Mt. 21:12,13; Mk. 11:15-17; Lk. 19:45,46). As required by Mosaic Law, Jesus and his disciples were in Jerusalem for Passover celebrations (Ex. 23:14-17). The epicenter of this huge annual event was the Temple. And, with one hundred thousand or so pilgrims in the city, the Temple was bursting with activity. Its courts contained a massive marketplace, not only for the sale of sacrificial animals, but also for money exchange, food, clothing, and anything else that could be crammed into the sales kiosks. A lot of money was being made, and the Sadducees who controlled the temple economy got a cut of all the profits.

Jesus was incensed at the sight of his Father's house made into a bazaar. He had shown anger before (Mk. 3:5; Lk.13:32; Mt. 16:23) and he showed it again, He snatched some of the leather thongs used by the cattle-drivers, twisted them into a whip, and began swinging it wildly at the sheep, the oxen, the cattle, the drovers, the merchants, and at anything or anyone else who got in his way, shouting, "Get these out of here! Stop turning my Father's house into a market!" (v16). No one resisted this preemptive strike by the furious (not "gentle Jesus, meek and mild") Son of God. What's more, no one dared arrest him.

The dust hadn't settled, however, before "the Jews" (read: the high priests' Sadducean officials) showed up. They must have made some sort of threatening gesture for Jesus responded with, "Destroy this temple, and in three days I will raise it up", referring to his body. John tells us that much later he and the other disciples remembered this after Jesus' resurrection, and it resonated (v.22). Nevertheless, the temple officials melted away. What else could they do? Jesus' signs and wonders (none of which are recorded) silenced them. And, even though many of the people "believed in his name" (v.23) Jesus knew their belief was transient (vv.24,25). In no time these "believers" would be crying, "Crucify him!"

451

Nicodemus and the New Birth 3:1–21

Nicodemus, a Pharisee, impressed with the "signs" that Jesus was doing came to see him at night, perhaps in the Garden of Gethsemane where Jesus often spent a few evening hours in solitude and prayer. He came under cover of darkness because as a member of the Sanhedrin his reputation was at stake. Jesus was not flattered by Nicodemus and cut to the chase.

Much to Nicodemus' puzzlement Jesus declared that the only way to the Kingdom of God was through being "born again" (v.3). A second birth wasn't possible Nicodemus asserted, but Jesus responded by pointing out that one's first birth, "born of water" was "fleshly", but one's second birth, "born of the spirit", was "spiritual" (vv.5,6). He then addressed the look of perplexity in Nicodemus' face by reminding him that he accepted the natural phenomenon of the wind even though its origin and destination was a mystery, so why not accept the mystery of spiritual birth?

Nicodemus still didn't get it (v.9). With a hint of exasperation Jesus said, "I have spoken to you of earthly things and you do not believe; how then will you believe if I speak of heavenly things?" (v.12). Jesus knew what he was talking about, "we testify to what we have seen" (v.11), yet not only Nicodemus, but the "people" refused to "accept our testimony". Nicodemus may have zoned out as Jesus quietly referred to his authority as "the one who came from heaven" and claimed the messianic title of "Son of Man" (v.13). The "eternal life" initiated by the second birth would pivot on his crucifixion (v.14). For the moment these history shaking words were lost on Nicodemus. He walked away, back into the darkness. But, the light would dawn later (7:50;19:39).

John then reflects on the "why" of God's Son coming to earth. He starts with what Martin Luther once called "the Gospel in miniature": "For God so loved the world that he gave his one and only Son, that whoever believes in him shall not perish but have eternal life" (v.16). There is a depth in this sentence that is beyond the capacity of a casual commentary to plumb. But there are a few points to be made.

The love of God for his creation is a constant theme in John's gospel. Here that love for the world is pre-emptive: it is given in order to save mankind from "perishing". We are lost to God and eternal life without a savior. So, God sent his Son to save us. To be "born again" means to be "saved". Belief "in him" is the qualifier. We are not saved by default. As free moral agents we must choose to put our faith in the Son. Our understanding of this salvific mystery may be limited at the beginning of our walk of faith, but so is the knowledge of an infant about life in general. Growth "from faith to faith" (Ro. 1:17) is the key. Indeed this new life generated by the Spirit will see us growing "in the grace and knowledge of our Lord and Savior Jesus Christ" (2Pe. 3:18) until the Day of the Lord. The truth proclaimed by those red neon signs that used to shine over scores of churches in North America's past still prevails: "Jesus Saves".

He came to save, not condemn (v.17). Any condemnation is self-inflicted (v.18), the free choice to reject God's offer of love bears its own consequences. Unbelief prefers the darkness; fear of exposure drives mankind away from the light. Transparency, on the other hand, has no fear of censure. God walks with those whose deeds are "true" (vv.19-21).

John the Baptist Speaks Well of Jesus 3:22–30

Jesus and his disciples left Jerusalem for the rural areas of Judea. He obviously taught and healed in the villages (although John gives no record of this ministry), and (unique to John's gospel) "baptized" (v.22). This is the only reference to baptism other than John the Baptist's (see 4:1,2 where it's noted that Jesus himself did not baptize, but his disciples did). The Baptist's disciples saw this as competition, refusing even to use Jesus' name ("he who was with you..." v.26) when they raised their objections. Regardless, he ignored their pique and affirmed his cousin. He cast himself as the "best man" at a wedding. Jesus was the bridegroom sent "from heaven" (v.27). He had every right to baptize because he was on the ascendancy. John's ministry, to his disciples chagrin, was diminishing (v.30). There was no turning back. The Christ had come.

More Johannine Theology 3:31–36

After the brief anecdote about petty rivalries John returned to the over-arching theme of "He who comes from above…" (v.31 RSV), the eternal Logos who speaks the things of heaven in an incarnate, earthly tongue. The Christ is an eyewitness of the heavenly. His word can be trusted, but "no one receives his testimony" (v.32 RSV). As he wrote, of course, John was an old man reflecting on his own initial intransigence during the events surrounding Jesus' arrest and crucifixion. He and the other disciples soon repented of their desertion, and after Pentecost obeyed Jesus' "great commission" ("Go ye into all the world…") to the end (martyrdom for most). But many of his fellow countrymen turned away from the crucified one. Those, however, who accepted Jesus as Savior "certified that God is truthful" (v.33), and acknowledged the Son as not only "sent" from God but also fully gifted by his Father with "all things" and the "Spirit" (vv.34,35). Salvation from "God's wrath" comes only through belief in that Son (v.36). John minced no words.

The Woman at the Well 4:1–42

At close to 2000 years distant a modern reader is more than out of synch with the historical and cultural context in which the story of Jesus is told. And, when it comes to stories within the story it's even more of a stretch to appreciate the finer points of the narrative. In this case, the woman at the well, something has to be said about Samaritans, women talking to men, the mountains of Ebal and Gerazim, Jacob's well, and "living water", to name a few.

It wasn't a taboo, but it was socially frowned upon for a man to talk to a woman (even his wife!) in public. A well-known rabbinical saying stated, "A man should hold no conversation with a woman in the street, not even with his own wife, still less with any other woman, lest men should gossip." So it was no surprise that the disciples "marvelled that he was talking with a woman" (v.27). Jesus, unperturbed, gave no explanation or apology for his breech of cultural protocol.

The fact that he was talking with a Samaritan was even more surprising. The strong antipathy on the part of Jews to Samaritans was captured a few centuries later by a rabbi who said, "He that eats the bread of the Samaritans is like to one that eats the flesh of swine." It wasn't just their mixed blood due to the resettlement of Samaria with Gentiles by the Assyrians in the 8th century BC, but it was also their insistence that Mt. Gerazim was God's holy mountain (not Mt. Zion in Judea). Their religion was informed exclusively by the Pentateuch (the first five books of the Bible), and religious practice revolved around a temple they had built on Mt. Gerazim. In Deuteronomy 27:4 Moses had instructed the Israelites to build an altar on Mt. Ebal (which faces Gerazim across a valley) but the Samaritans chose Gerazim for their temple because it was the mount of blessing, whereas Ebal was the mount of cursing (Dt. 27:12; 11:29). When attending a modern Samaritan Passover ceremony on Mt. Gerazim a few years ago I looked across the valley to Mt. Ebal. To this day it looks barren, forbidding, and (some would say) "cursed". Nevertheless, rampant racial discrimination combined with the "battle of the holy mountains" meant there was a great gulf fixed between Samaritan and Jew.

Then there was "Jacob's well". This is the only direct reference – the Old Testament says nothing about it. It was (is) located near Shechem (Nablus) and the tradition re: its history, is totally dependent on the words of the Samaritan woman when she told Jesus that "our father Jacob" was the one "who gave us the well and drank from it himself, as did also his sons and his livestock" (v.12). In her day the well was "deep" (v.11), but over time debris and detritus have lessened its depth. It is owned today by the Greek Orthodox Church who oversee the ruins of a 4th century AD church and a 12th century Crusader church built on the site. "Jesus, tired as he was from the journey, sat down by the well. It was about noon" (v.6). One of the most famous conversations in history was about to take place.

From time to time questions arise as to how the gospel writers knew what was being thought or said by the main characters. Some commentators assume that the writer is composing a historical novel, doing due diligence in terms of his own recollections and research. Others see it in terms of speculation and even presumption. Some dismiss the narratives as outright fiction fuelled by religious ideology and enthusiasm. Regardless, there are commentators whose conjectures are biased in terms of anti-supernaturalism, and, on the other extreme, those whose regard for the scriptures borders on bibliolatry. As to the conversation between Jesus and the Samaritan woman at Jacob's well (in the absence of the disciples) my view is that Jesus later recounted it to John, who would have looked askance at later critical critiques. There are three components to the conversation: living water (vv.7-15), true worship (vv.19-24), and Jesus' uncharacteristic claim to messiahship (vv.25,26).

If there had been a bucket on a rope Jesus would/could have drawn water for himself. He didn't but the woman did, so he asked her for a drink (v.7). She was surprised that a Jew would ask a Samaritan for water, but Jesus bluntly stated, "If you knew the gift of God and who it is that asks you for a drink, you would have asked him and he would have given you living water" (v.10). This seems a bit harsh, but it may have been a response to a touch of sarcasm on the woman's part. Tone often meets tone in conversation. Then again, John was not taking dictation when Jesus recounted the conversation. This is probably a summary, and there may have been more said than he records. The fact that she didn't respond to this mild rebuke may suggest that Jesus made the comment "sotto voce", more to himself than to her. She did respond, however, to the "living water" reference. It couldn't come from the well, for Jesus had "nothing to draw with and the well is deep" (v.11), and well water was just water. She would have thought living water to be running water from a stream. So a bit more sarcasm, "Are you greater than our father Jacob…?" (v.12). She was beginning to think this stranger at the well had a high opinion of himself. The "gift of God" talk didn't appeal, but she was intrigued with "living water" (v.15). But she was skeptical too – "Sir, give me this water so that I won't get thirsty and have to keep coming here to draw water" could be interpreted, "Right. Tell me another one!"

She was beginning to think this stranger at the well had a high opinion of himself.

It was what followed next that changed everything. When Jesus referred to her serial monogamies (five husbands) and to her current "live-in" arrangement she declared, a bit of regret for her skepticism in her voice, "Sir, I can see that you are a prophet" (v.19). Then, with hardly a breath, she brought up the age-old divide between Jews and Samaritans re: which holy mountain was truly holy (v.20). She was feisty. Jesus was equally so: "You Samaritans worship what you do not know," in other words, "you worship out of ignorance." But then he boldly stated, "we worship what we do know, for salvation is of the Jews" (v.22). Before she could express a rejoinder he declared that mountains were irrelevant in true worship. God was/is Spirit, and authentic worshippers must do so in and through the Spirit with transparent, truthful lives (vv.21,23,24). Chastened, she shifted focus, passing off her ignorance to the day when the Messiah would clarify everything (v.25). Looking her in the eye Jesus jolted her with the declaration, "I, the one speaking to you – I am he" (v.26).

Just then the disciples returned from shopping in the village of Sychar (vv.4-8), and they were shocked to find Jesus in conversation "with a woman". But they didn't dare question him. The Samaritan woman, perhaps sensing the disciples' disapproval, left for town where she announced to her friends and neighbors that they had to come out to the well to meet "a man who told me *everything* (emphasis mine) I ever did" (v.29). (Again it is clear that John's record of the conversation was a summary. A lot was evidently said that's not recorded.) At this point she was inclined to believe that Jesus *was* Messiah (v29b). The townsfolk went to the well en masse.

While the people were on their way to the well another conversation took place, this time between Jesus and his disciples. It started with the disciples trying to get Jesus to eat something. His blunt reply confused them, "I have food to eat that you know nothing about" (v.32). He had earlier accused the woman of ignorance, now he was doing the same with his men. There is no doubt Jesus was human – thirsty and disappointed, or simply fed up with the general obtuseness of the people (3:12a; 32b). The disciples, as usual, didn't get it. They thought someone else had brought food to him. Jesus made no clarification. He just went on to talk about God's will and harvesting.

"My food is to do the will of him who sent me and to finish his work," said Jesus (v.34). These words echo his response to Satan in the wilderness, "Man shall not live by bread alone" (Lk. 4:4) and "Did you not know that I must be about my Father's business?" (Lk. 2:49 NKJV). Purpose fuels the soul just as food nourishes the body. Jesus' great motivator was to obey and fulfill the will of his Father. The writer to the Hebrews captured this singular focus of Jesus by quoting David (Ps. 40:6-8) when referring to Christ's sacrifice on the cross, "Here I am – it is written about me in the scroll – I have come to do your will, my God" (He. 10:7). God's will was inextricably tied to the coming of his Kingdom. Jesus saw/knew the Kingdom was at the threshold of history, the harvest was "ripe" with willing souls (v.35). Jesus, the "sower", had recruited the disciples, the "reapers" for a bountiful harvest. But these reapers had better keep a sense of perspective in the halcyon days ahead – "Others [had] done the hard work" (v.38 – think Moses, the Judges of Israel, the prophets, now John the Baptist, and Jesus himself). A harbinger of that harvest occurred even as Jesus was teaching his subdued disciples, "Many of the Samaritans from that town believed in him because of the woman's testimony" (v.39). Jesus' teaching over the next two days convinced them, "this man really is the Savior of the world" (v.42). Who knew it would be despised Samaritans who would be the first to acknowledge Jesus as Messiah?! One of the "reapers" (Philip) would bring in a harvest sown by the Samaritan woman (Ac. 8:5) and other reapers (Peter and John) would follow (Ac. 8:14). Jacob's well was a pivot point in salvation history.

A Long–distance Healing 4:43–54

The journey from Judea to Galilee continued. When he arrived "in his own country" (probably Nazareth) he was welcomed, even though he had previously "pointed out that a prophet has no honor in his own country" (v.44). Why the change? Because "they had seen all that he had done in Jerusalem at the Passover Festival" (v.45). Much to Jesus' chagrin the "signs and wonders" factor had made him a celebrity. He much preferred that the people would be drawn to him by his teaching about the Kingdom of God. But no. Later, in Cana, a "royal official" from Capernaum travelled all the way to ask Jesus to heal his sick son. Ruefully Jesus said, "Unless you people see signs and wonders you will never believe" (v.48). Nevertheless, Jesus assured him that his boy would live (v.50). He did live and his entire household (parents, siblings, servants, and slaves) came to faith. John doesn't say how Jesus felt about the whole thing. He simply states this healing (by long distance) was "the second sign" Jesus performed in Cana.

A Healing at a Pool 5:1–15

As previously noted there were three major festivals which all Israelite males were required to attend – Passover, Pentecost, and Tabernacles. Jesus had been to Jerusalem for Passover that year, so "some time later" probably refers to Pentecost, which occurred fifty days afterwards. Like the thousands of other pilgrims, Jesus visited various sites around the city. This day he went to the Pool of Bethesda just a few hundred feet north of the Temple. Perhaps it was one of his favorite locations in that "a multitude of invalids, blind, lame, paralyzed" (v.3) were always there.

The Crusader Church of Saint Anne is one of *my* favorite sites in Jerusalem. Built adjacent to the Pool of Bethesda (or "Bethzatha") it has the finest acoustics of any church I've visited anywhere (Google "Church of Saint Anne"). Standing in the courtyard you can look down into the ruins of a basilica or two built beside the pool over the centuries. The depression itself is fairly steep. There is very little water today.

Most cisterns and urban pools in Jesus' day were cut out of the rock and fed by hewn channels. The collected rainwater was vital for everyday hydration and sanitation of the citizens, especially during a siege by hostile armies. The Bethzatha pool, like the Siloam pool (Jn. 9:7), was seen as a place of healing. This is why there was always a "multitude" of sick and afflicted people gathered there. For centuries there had been a rabbinic tradition that the first person to enter the pool after an intermittent disturbance of the water would be healed. John mentions the "stirring" of the water (v.7) but makes no comment as to its source.

Making his way through the crowd Jesus saw an invalid who had been ill for thirty-eight years. He was partially immobile (perhaps paraplegic – he could make his way slowly to the pool when the water was disturbed, but others always got there before him, v.7). Without assistance to enter the water he had no hope. So he lay on his mat, recognized as a regular, but ignored as a supplicant. Then, Jesus showed up. Without ceremony he healed the man. It was the Sabbath.

Some Pharisees saw the man carrying his mat, a no-no on the Sabbath. The oral tradition included a legalistic spin on Jeremiah 17:21 and Nehemiah 13:19 – no carrying of burdens on the Sabbath allowed! Mind you, that tradition (found in the Mishnah) did allow for a sick or paralyzed person to be carried on their mat, but carrying the mat itself was forbidden. So, this newly healed person was in violation of the Law. They accosted him with his offence, but he passed the buck by saying "The man who healed me" told me to do it (v.11). He couldn't name his healer, so after scolding him his accusers moved on. They caught up with him later in the Temple where he may have gone to offer a thank offering.

Jesus found him there too. Before the Pharisees could harass him further, Jesus gave him a strange, stern warning, "Sin no more, that nothing worse befall you" (v.14). Jesus said much the same to a young paralytic he had healed in Capernaum (Mk. 2:1-5) and would later say to the woman caught in adultery (Jn. 8:1-11). In the Jewish view there was a connection between sinful behavior and adversity. The man he had just healed may, or may not, have been dealing with long-term guilt over some spiritually eviscerating transgression, but whatever the case, Jesus saw a connection and warned him against recidivism. John doesn't say why, but the man immediately found his accusers and gave them Jesus' name.

Jesus Lambastes the Pharisees 5:16–47

The Bethesda healing became a Sabbath controversy with the Pharisees looking "to kill" Jesus. This drastic over-reaction was rationalized with the accusations that he was not only a Sabbath desecrator, but a blasphemer in "making himself equal with God" (v.18). Jesus responds to their charges with several more reasons for their fury to boil, and a few counter-charges as well. This may be Jesus' signature message to all past and present "Pharisees and Sadducees" who "know everything for sure".

Elitism always has its subcultural values. These values create polarities vis a vis: Conservative vs. Liberal, Republican vs. Democrat, Capitalist vs. Communist, etc. Even in Jesus' day sectarian divides existed: Sadducee (Hellenistic liberal) vs. Pharisee (Orthodox conservative), School of Rabbi Shammai (conservative) vs. School of Rabbi Hillel (liberal), the culturally pure (Jew) vs. the culturally impure (Samaritan), the saved (Jew) vs. the damned (Gentile). And, to parse further, there were divides within the divides. But for sure – whatever elite group you adhere to you're right and the others are wrong (or "misled"). Certainty can be a disabling filter. To declare, "the king has no clothes!" is, of course, exactly what Jesus did. His ministry and voice "cleansed the Temple" of the self-righteous. He polarized the polarizers.

I think that anyone of us when faced with those trying to kill us would cut to the chase. Jesus certainly did. Looking his would-be assassins in the eye he answered their charges. In a sense he was saying, "Here's who/what you're trying to kill."

Jesus' enemies were fulminating about desecration and blasphemy, but the issue was much deeper than offence to their religious/cultural sensibilities. Rather, it had to do with authority. I think this is how Jesus saw it, for his answer was all about it. I'm tempted to say, "Just read the text", and move on. But, let's read it together and I will risk the temerity of paraphrasing Jesus' words. Bear with me…

First of all, fellas, you're not dealing with me alone; you're dealing with God. I'm following the Father's lead (v.19). The Father loves me, so much so that he's going to do even more amazing works through me, things that will astonish you (v.20). The Father holds the keys to life and death and has delegated authority to the Son to give life to whomever he pleases (v.21). What's more, the Father has given the Son the right to judge men's character and actions (v.22), and if you do not respect and honor the Son's judgements you are dishonoring God himself (v.23). I will honor those who honor me with eternal life (v.24); even those who have died will hear my words of judgement, and if they, like the living, believe, they too will be raised to eternal life (vv.25, 28, 29). The unbelievers, however, will rise to condemnation (29b). Don't forget that the Son, like the Father, is immanent in creation, all life subsists in them (v.26). The Son is the Son of Man – he is Messiah (v.27). But he hears and judges justly with full accountability to the Father (v.30).

You don't have to take my word for it, there are others who endorse me (v.31,32). For instance, you rushed out to the wilderness to hear my cousin John, and what did you hear? You heard him testifying about me, for I am the Truth. You enjoyed his ministry for awhile because it shone light on the almost buried messianic hope of Israel (vv.33-35). But you missed his point that you were in need of salvation (v.34b). Nevertheless my words and ministry *are* far greater than John's. The signs and wonders that I perform resonate with the Father's authority (v.36). His presence in my works are a sure endorsement, but you don't get it because you don't know him, and even though you pride yourselves in your biblical knowledge you are dead men walking (vv.37-40) with no love of God in your hearts (v.42). That's why I don't need, nor do I want your endorsement. It's more than enough that I have come with the ultimate endorsement, my Father's name (vv.41-43). It's tragic that with all your knowledge of the Law of Moses you don't, or won't, hear what he himself said about me in Deuteronomy 18:15. You don't believe Moses (vv.46,47). How can you then believe me? Regardless, your priority is not God's approval but the approval of your fellow elites.

John doesn't record the reaction to Jesus' words. I dare say there were mutterings, teeth grinding, wrathfully red faces, and more than a few gasps and scornful looks thrown in Jesus' direction. Then again, maybe there was silence. In the presence of authority we tend to keep our mouths shut.

Five Thousand Fed 6:1–14

The gospel writers had little concern for chronology. When John writes, "Some time after this", he might have meant "by and by", or "a few days/ weeks/months later", or "sometime later". Some Bible scholars think up to a year may have passed (Passover to Passover – 2:13; 6:4). But, if John had been concerned about every detail of Jesus' life and ministry in proper order the hyperbolic prospect of the last two sentences of his gospel would have come true: "Jesus did many other things as well. If every one of them were written down, I suppose that even the whole world would not have room for the books that would be written" (21:25). So, "Some time after this" will suffice as merely a transition statement.

Jesus and the Twelve had sailed across the lake to the eastern shore to find a little rest. But no. "A great crowd followed him" (v.2), not in boats, but by walking around the northern shore of the Sea of Galilee. This would have been a distance of about ten miles over a well-worn road. They were not going to let Jesus out of their sight – too many were in need of healing. From one of the mountains on what are today called the Golan Heights Jesus saw the crowd converging on the beach below. Rather than try to escape he decided to feed the crowd.

There has been scholarly conjecture as to why Jesus asked Philip, "Where shall we buy bread for these people to eat?" (v.5). When John writes, "He asked this only to test him" (v.6) it suggests that Jesus saw some need to develop Philip's faith. This was the same Philip whom Jesus rebuked in the Upper Room, "Don't you know me, Philip, even after I have been among you such a long time? How can you say, 'show us the Father'?" (14:9). And it was the same Philip who later became a powerful evangelist to Samaria and, indirectly, to Ethiopia (Ac. 8:4-8; 26-40). Philip, like all the disciples, was a work in progress.

John doesn't say how it happened, but somehow a small boy's humble lunch became available. Two things occur to me: 1. Was Peter being ironic when he drew attention to this feeble fare (five bread rolls and two sardines for upwards of ten thousand people?!). 2. Did the lad overhear the conversation and in a simple act of generosity naively offer what his thoughtful mother had packed for him? Regardless, five thousand men, and probably as many women and children were all fed to the full (v.12) with a lot left over. The people in wonder proclaimed, "Surely this is the Prophet who is to come into the world" (v.14), referring to Moses' prophecy centuries earlier (De. 18:15). While they marvelled Jesus withdrew up to the Golan plateau. He wasn't about to acquiesce to the popular cry to crown him king (v.15).

Jesus wasn't about to acquiesce to the popular cry to crown him king.

Waterwalker 6:16–21

This brief anecdote needs little comment, although it has received massive publicity over the centuries. The very idea of Jesus, or anyone for that matter, walking on water has attracted both childlike belief and cynical disbelief. There is no need to argue. John simply tells the story and moves on six sentences later. If Jesus was who he said he was then he can, and did, do what he chooses. While he rested and reflected on the Golan his disciples battled a storm on the lake. Jesus walked down the mountain and continued across the water, comforted his panicked Twelve, got in the boat, the seas calmed, and they sailed to shore. End of story.

A "Hard Teaching" 6:22–71

What follows is strong drink. It is concentrated Gospel, almost indigestible food. It was taught by Jesus "in the synagogue in Capernaum" (v.59) and managed, not only to polarize the congregation, but to empty the house (v.66). It was a hard teaching with no effort on Jesus' part to soften it. Even as many turned their backs on him he didn't flinch. In his view this was a "live or die" sermon (vv.53,54).

It started with some of the crowd who had been miraculously fed the previous day. They wanted more free food, so they walked back to Capernaum to catch up with Jesus. They were wondering how he had managed to get there in that he had not been in the boat with his disciples (vv.22-25), but Jesus gave no answer. Rather, he entered into dialogue with them, culminating in his teaching about "the bread of life".

He rebuked them for not seeing the "signs" he performed when multiplying the loaves and the fish – all they saw was the food (v.26). Could they not discern the vast difference between the temporal and the eternal? (v.27). Could they not recognize God's seal of approval on his Son? Yes. Some of them could, for they then wanted to know how they themselves could receive God's approval (v.28). It began with belief "in him whom he has sent", Jesus said (v.29).

Their physical hunger was eclipsed by the greater more deeply rooted hunger for the coming of Messiah. Was yesterday's feeding miracle evidence of the fulfillment of the rabbinical teaching that Messiah would bring heavenly bread ("manna") to Israel? So one of the crowd, perhaps a rabbi himself, quoted scripture (Ps. 78:24; 105:40) recalling the miraculous bread in Israel's wilderness wanderings after the Exodus (v.31). The underlying question: You gave us bread for a day, Moses gave us bread for forty years. Is your wonder-working sustainable? Are you the one Moses said would come?

Jesus told them they weren't getting it right. It was the Father, not Moses, who had fed them. What's more, the food – the manna – was not what sustained them. It wasn't the bread from the skies but the bread from heaven – God's sovereign care. They would never have made it

465

to the Promised Land without spiritual food. It is, and was, that bread which "gives life to the world" (v.33). Then he threw them a curve.

In response to "Sir, always give us this bread" he said, "I am the bread of life" (vv.34,35). In the first of the "I am" statements in John's gospel Jesus reiterates the bread of life metaphor four times (vv.35, 41, 48, 51). He not only provides living water (4:14) but living bread (v.51) "to the world" (v.33). This bold statement was hard to take. The crowd in the synagogue "began to grumble" (v.41). Didn't they know this Jesus? Wasn't he Joseph's son? And what's this about his coming "down from heaven"? (v.42). And he's going to "raise us up" at the last day? This is too much. He's out of his mind.

"Stop your grumbling," Jesus said. The issue was not his bold statements, but the Father' sovereign plan. "No one can come to me unless the Father who sent me draws them." And, those who are supernaturally "drawn" will be those whom Jesus "will raise up... at the last day" (v.44). Before the people could remonstrate at this added presumption Jesus quoted Isaiah 54:13, "All thy children shall be taught of the Lord", confronting any accuser with the stern implication that anyone objecting to his claims was beyond heaven's reach. What's more, anyone who has been "taught by God" will "come to me". Why? Because the Father will have taught them that Jesus is not only "from God" but has also "seen" him (vv.45, 46). Once again, Jesus reminded them that the manna in the wilderness was temporal. It sustained the people for forty years, then they died. Jesus, on the other hand, was/is "the bread of life" who provides eternal sustenance (vv.48,50). Eat him ("his flesh") and "live forever" (v.51).

The audience was aghast. "How can this man give us his flesh to eat?" If you and I had been there we would have been scandalized too. We would wince hearing him say, "unless you eat the flesh of the Son of Man and drink his blood, you have no life in you" (v.53). Only those ("taught by God") who understood metaphor could have resisted turning away from Jesus in disgust. For a Jew the very idea of drinking blood was revolting. This time he had gone too far. This was a "hard teaching" indeed. We're "outta here" (v.66).

Aware of the offence he had caused, Jesus threw another curve. This is not about "flesh" but about "spirit" (v.63). Once again the people were not seeing the heavenly reality behind the earthly. They didn't see that Jesus was talking about the Kingdom of Heaven. Nor did they appreciate the sobering truth that he already knew who would believe and who would not (v.64). His real audience was those who had been "enabled" by the Father to believe (v.65). This was offensive too. The idea of predestiny was a hard pill to swallow. So hard that Jesus turned to the Twelve, as scores of his listeners turned away, and asked, "You do not want to leave me too, do you?" (v.67).

The impulsive, outspoken Peter blurted, "Lord, to whom shall we go? You have the words of eternal life. We have come to believe and to know that you are the Holy One of God" (vv.68, 69). Little did he know it but Peter had just confessed what would become the central tenet, the nucleus, of the Church. Nor would he have expected that a year or so later he would regretfully deny the Holy One the same night another of the Twelve would betray him (vv.70,71). Truly, Jesus himself was a "hard teaching".

At the Feast of Tabernacles 7:1–52

The seventh month of the Jewish year (Tishri) was a Sabbath month. The first day of Tishri was a holy day and the tenth day was the Day of Atonement. The Feast of Tabernacles, or "Booths", began on the fifteenth day and commemorated the covenant with God, recalled Israel's wilderness wanderings, and celebrated the autumn harvest. Also called "the Feast of Ingathering" (Ex. 23:16), and "the Feast of the Lord" (Le. 23:39; Jg. 21:19), it was sometimes summarized simply as "the feast" (1Ki. 8:2; 2Ch. 7:8; Is. 30:29). Tabernacles lasted for seven days, followed by a solemn assembly on the eighth, and "Simchat Torah" ("the Joy of the Law") celebrations on the ninth. A brief description of Tabernacles will help us appreciate some of what follows in this seventh chapter of John.

All male Israelites were commanded to "appear before the Lord" three times a year (De. 16:16) for three festivals: "the Festival of Unleavened

Bread" (Passover), "the Festival of Weeks" (Pentecost), and "the Festival of Tabernacles" (Booths). "No one should appear before the Lord empty-handed. Each of you must bring a gift in proportion to the way the Lord your God has blessed you" (vv.16,17). Each man had to construct a booth ("succah") to sleep and eat in for seven days. In the construction of the booth he had to include branches or twigs of myrtle, willow, and palm trees (Ne. 8:13-19). In later times (including today in Israel) these branches are combined with a citron to form a "lulav" which is carried to the synagogue (or to the Western Wall in Jerusalem) and waved before the Lord as the Hallel (Ps. 113-118) is sung. It's a joyful time.

Each day of the Feast a water libation ceremony took place. After walking around the altar at the Temple a priest would perform the libation using two silver bowls, one for water (from the pool of Siloam) and one for wine. On the seventh day the priests would circumambulate the altar seven times as the people cried, "Save us, we beseech thee, O Lord." (Ps. 118:25). "Hosanna" ("hoshianah" – "save now"!) has its roots in this rite.

In the evenings four huge menorahs were lit, their wicks made from used priestly garments. The temple area, in the light cast by these candelabra, hosted a torch dance celebrated by chosen artists who moved to the music of flutes and the chanting of the Psalms of Ascent (Ps. 120-134) by trained Levite singers. Isaiah refers to this nightly ritual in 30:29. The celebration went on well into the night.

Then, each morning, the priest would gather at the eastern gate of the Temple, and in contrition for the sins of their fathers and in response to the Lord's rebuke in Ez. 8:16, they would face the West at the moment of sunrise and recite, "Our fathers when they were in this place turned with their faces toward the East, and they worshipped the sun toward the East; but as for us, our eyes are turned toward the Lord." This act had special significance every seventh year when the Law of Moses was read to the people at the feast (Dt. 31:9-13).

John states that the healing of the lame man at the pool of Bethesda had catalyzed an urgent compulsion on the part of Jerusalem's religious elite "to kill him" (5:18). It had yet to crystallize into a plot, but the antipathy was there. The pressure was mounting and the reports flew throughout Judea and the Galilee that Jesus was a wanted man. So, for a time, Jesus avoided Judea – especially Jerusalem (7:1).

The Feast of Tabernacles was about to be celebrated (v.2), and, like all Israelite males, Jesus was expected to make the pilgrimage to Jerusalem. He appeared reluctant to do so. His cynical brothers tried to bait him, attempting to induce him to go up to Jerusalem and show off his miraculous power (rather like Satan tempting Jesus in the wilderness – see Mt. 4:1-11; Mk. 1:12,13; Lk. 4:1-13). John states boldly that "even his brothers did not believe in him" (v.5 RSV). Jesus simply replied, "You go ahead. You can go whenever you want. As for me, I don't want to go now." Perhaps he saw joining a multitude of pilgrims going up in procession to Jerusalem as something that could devolve into tumult and drama, in that he was being sought by the authorities. He wanted no one hurt. He preferred to wait a few days and go up privately, incognito (v.10).

The Sanhedrin were on the lookout for him from day one of the Feast but he was nowhere to be found (v.11). He didn't show until the fourth day of the celebration (v.14). He performed no miracles but taught in the Temple. His teaching astonished everyone, including the Sanhedrin who had caught up with him. "How did this man get such learning without having been taught?" they asked. This was accompanied by a caustic tone, swiping at his presumed ignorance. It was meant to diminish Jesus in the eyes of his listeners but it had limited impact, "Some said, 'He is a good man', others said, 'No, he is leading the people astray'" (v.12). Polarities stalked him wherever he went.

Jesus ignored the vitriol and continued teaching in a measured way. He shifted to the issue of authority, which was the underlying criticism of the Sanhedrin – he hadn't been "taught". Unlike them he didn't reference rabbinic authorities; rather, his teaching was unilateral, original thought. They had never heard such "chutzpah". But he pressed on.

He immediately disabused them of the misconception re: his originality – "My teaching is not my own. It comes from the one who sent me" (v.16). He wasn't speaking "on his own authority" (v.18 RSV), but the source of his teaching was "from God" (v.17). His teaching was "true", whereas the Sanhedrin's teaching was "false" (v.18b) in that they touted Moses' Law but didn't keep it (v.19.) They were patently hypocritical in their over-reaction to the "miracle" he had performed at the pool on the Sabbath months ago, while blithely performing circumcisions on the Sabbaths whenever the eighth day after a son's birth fell on the "day of rest". Is it more or less a necessity/good work to heal a "whole body" on the Sabbath? (v.23). His detractors changed the subject.

The people, still conflicted (v.12) and somewhat confused, wondered why the Sanhedrin weren't following through on their well-known intent to kill Jesus (vv.25,26a). Was the reason for their inaction a sudden reversal? Did they now believe that Jesus *was* the Christ? But even the people were aware of Malachi's prophecy that the Messiah would appear "suddenly" out of nowhere (Ma. 3:1). So he *couldn't* be Messiah because "we know where this man is from " (v.27). They were thinking Nazareth and Capernaum. But "some of the people" (v.40), better educated in the scriptures, remembered that "the Christ is descended from David and comes from Bethlehem…" (v.42).

"Really? You know me, and you know where I come from?" The tone said, "You don't have a clue!" In fact he declared they didn't even know God, the one who had sent him (vv.28b, 29). The authorities couldn't take this, so "they sought to arrest him" (v.30a), with no success "because his hour had not yet come." This expression was John's explanation of why Jesus was not forcibly removed at that moment. Jesus had used the same language in Cana (2:4) and just a few days previously (7:6). John saw a sovereign plan at work, but in the short term the division in the people (vv.43,44), with "muttering" and controversy (v.31), caused the authorities to hesitate. Jesus then added to the confusion by saying he would soon return "to the one who sent me" and he would be inaccessible (vv.33, 34). The people said, "What? What does he mean?" (vv.35,36).

"On the last day of the feast, the great day" (v.37 RSV), when the priests circumambulated the altar seven times before the water libation, Jesus capitalized on the water imagery by loudly proclaiming in the temple courts, "let anyone who is thirsty come to me and drink.

Whoever believes in me, as scripture has said, rivers of living water will flow from within them." His words may have paraphrased Isaiah 58:11, "The Lord will guide you always; he will satisfy your needs in a sun-scorched land and will strengthen your frame. You will be like a well-watered garden, like a spring whose waters never fail." A matrix of other scriptures would have resonated as well – Is. 12:3; 44:3; 55:1 –

"With joy you will draw water
from the wells of salvation…
"For I will pour water on the thirsty land,
and streams on the dry ground…
"Come, all you who are thirsty,
come to the waters…"

This bold proclamation to the teeming masses in Jerusalem echoed his one-on-one conversation with the Samaritan woman at the well (4:10). His words were interpreted three ways: some said he was "the Prophet" (De. 18:15), others said he was "the Christ", and still others wanted him arrested immediately (vv.40-44). Even the temple police, who had been ordered to arrest him (v.32), were conflicted: "No one ever spoke the way this man does," they said to their superiors (v.46). There was only one voice of reason in the kerfuffle – Nicodemus (vv.50,51). He was mocked by his fellow Sanhedrin members, but he stood his ground.

The Woman Taken in Adultery 7:53–8:11

The earliest and most trustworthy of Greek manuscripts of the New Testament do not include this passage. But, it has been preserved for us and I'm glad it has. Nicodemus had broken the momentum of the Sanhedrin's dispute with Jesus and "they all went home" (7:53). As the muttering mob dispersed, Jesus went to spend the night on the Mount of Olives. This was his preferred place of prayer and rest. Was he sleeping under the stars? Not likely. He usually stayed at his friends Mary, Martha, and Lazarus' home on the southeast slope of the mount. But on the way he undoubtedly spent quality time with his Father in the quietness of the Garden of Gethsemane on the northwest slope. The next morning he was back teaching at the Temple. It was early ("at dawn" – 8:2) with the day-long events of the solemn assembly soon to commence.

Ignoring them he stooped down beside the prostrate woman and began writing words in the dust with his finger.

What happened next had to have been premeditated. A group of men from the Sanhedrin had burst into the home of a woman who was still in bed with someone to whom she was not married. They had grabbed her and forced her out of her house and up to the Temple Mount half-naked and perhaps clutching a bed sheet around her violated body. Her face must have been red with shame even as her self-righteous captors' faces were red with fury. They broke through the crowd gathered around Jesus and threw her down in front of him, demanding that Jesus agree she should be stoned to death. Seemingly ignoring them he stooped down beside the prostrate woman and began writing words in the dust with his finger. Her accusers, of course, would have read the words and were struck to the heart. John doesn't record what he wrote but I think we're safe to imagine that his script captured the secret sins of the men. In the drama of the moment the shift from loud accusations to silence was palpable. "Let anyone of you who is without sin be the first to throw a stone at her," Jesus said quietly. Averting their eyes from Jesus' piercing gaze they slunk away, the oldest of them first (!). Jesus may have helped the woman to her feet as the men disappeared. So, "Where are they?" Jesus asked. "Has no one condemned you?"

"No one, sir," she said.

"Then neither do I condemn you, go now and leave your life of sin."

The crowd of witnesses must have been hugely impacted by this interchange. It was a life lesson they would never forget. For them the next day's "Simchat Torah" ("Joy of the Law") celebration would have been a bit subdued.

Jesus, the Light of the World 8:12–59

John records seven "I am" statements by Jesus: "I am the bread of life" (6:35,48) and "living bread"; "I am the light of the world" (8:12); "I am the gate" (10:7,9); "I am the good shepherd" (10:11,14); "I am the resurrection and the life" (11:25); "I am the way and the truth and the life" (14:6); "I am the true vine" (15:1,5). Just as he employed parables in teaching about the Kingdom of Heaven in Matthew, Mark, and Luke, so too he described himself metaphorically in John, clothing profound truth in accessible, everyday terms. He was comfortable with the vernacular.

His claim to being "the light of the world" (v.12) led to several disputes about who Jesus truly was, culminating in an attempt by the Pharisees to stone him (v.59). Jesus' claims had consequences. Calvary was just steps away.

The same Pharisees who had opposed him over his Sabbath healing of the lame man at the pool of Bethesda were at it again. They accused Jesus of bearing false witness to himself (v.13). "Your testimony is not valid," they sneered. Jesus replied, "Yes it is." He knew where he came from, and where he was going, which was much more than could be said about them. When he said his Father was his "witness" (v.18) they immediately challenged it. Your father? Who is he? Where is he? Jesus responded, "You don't know him, and you don't know me." They didn't understand that "he was telling them about his Father", capital "F" (v.27). This was only the start of something that would come to a boil in the next few minutes.

Let me paraphrase:

Jesus – I'm leaving soon, and your second thoughts about me will be too little too late. You will desperately try to find me but I'll be beyond your reach. Ezekiel's warning about those who refuse to heed the watchman's warning (Ez. 3:19; 33:9) will prove true (v.21).

Pharisees – What? Is he suicidal? (v.22).

Jesus – We are from different worlds, yours the lower, mine the higher. You are blind to the Kingdom of Heaven. In fact, you're as good as dead now, and will be spiritually dead on the Day of the Lord unless you repent and believe in me (vv.23,24).

Pharisees – Who do you think you are! (v.25a).

Jesus – I am who I've said I am all along. But, by the authority of the One who sent me – my Father, the "Holy One of Israel" is whom I've been talking about, though you don't hear me – I tell you your present ignorance will give way to the realization of who the Son of Man is when you crucify him. My Father will vindicate me (vv.26-29).

At this point many in the crowd who had been following this interchange with fascination "believed in him" (v.30). There were many also who "had" believed in him at one point (perhaps Galileans at the Feast who had turned away from Jesus because of his offensive comments about the "bread of life" – 6:25-70). Jesus turned to them with a word of encouragement re: "continue[ing] in my word". If they came back to belief in him they would be made "free" (vv.31,32). But, instead of accepting this conciliatory word they took offence again. They were now on the same page as the Pharisees. "We are Abraham's descendants!" they declared. We're as free as anyone on the planet. How can you be so presumptuous to offer us more than our birthright as Jews?

What followed next needs no paraphrase. As you read it you'll see the radical nature of Jesus' message. Pedigree was no longer enough. Sin is sin, knowing no racial (Jew nor Gentile nor Samaritan) prerequisites. Sinners will be slaves to their father – "the devil" (v.44) – while believers in the Son will become sons of the heavenly Father – God himself. Those opposed to the Son can call him what they like – "Samaritan" and "demonized" (v.48) – but they will "taste death" regardless.

Then came the biggest offence: "Your father Abraham rejoiced at the thought of seeing my day; he saw it and was glad" (v.56). Incredulous, the people retorted, "You are not yet fifty years old and you have seen Abraham!" Jesus replied that not only had he seen Abraham, but even "before Abraham was born, I am!" (v.58). This was too much. They searched furiously for stones, but in the ensuing melée Jesus was able to get away unharmed (v.59).

Jesus Heals a Man Born Blind 9:1–41

Apart from those with sociopathic/psychopathic tendencies all of us have an innate need to see justice served and the problem of suffering addressed. Ever since man first engaged his mind with the imponderables of the universe there have been sincere efforts to address questions like, "If God is good why does he allow suffering and evil?....Why do the innocent and vulnerable suffer most?... Why does sin exist?... Why has my loved one died?" There is a powerful drive within us to right all wrongs, even as we share an impulse to apportion blame for the evils incurred.

In the case of the man born blind the disciples' default, as Israelites, was to accredit his disability to sin, either his own or his parents' (v.2). Sickness was a corollary of sin. Jesus, however, looked beyond this centuries-old belief and said, "Neither this man nor his parents sinned, but this happened so that the works of God might be displayed in him" (v.3). The disciples may have been shocked by this assertion. Hadn't Jesus read the Law where God declares that punishment for sin will extend to the third and fourth generation? (Ex. 20:5; 34:7; Nu. 14:18; De. 5:9). Ignoring the non-verbal rebuke Jesus basically said, "Let's get on with it. This blind man needs our help. The opportunities for ministry won't last much longer" (v.4). Then, reiterating his status as "light of the world" he got on with it, making a paste with saliva and clay, anointing the man's eyes, and instructing him to "Go, wash in the pool of Siloam" (vv.5-7).

This was easier said than done. To get to the pool this blind man would have to tap his way down about two hundred stairs. That stairway is currently being excavated by archaeologists. I've walked it, both up and down, and it is steep and long. The pool of Siloam is hundreds of feet in elevation below the Temple Mount, located at the convergence of the three valleys that define the eastern and western boundaries of the Old City of Jerusalem (the Kidron on the east, the Hinnom on the west, the Tyropoean in the middle). It is a reservoir fed by a subterranean canal (Hezekiah's tunnel) flowing from the Gihon Spring beneath the northeastern slope of the city. "Silwan" in ancient Hebrew meant "Sender". You may ask why the paste and the treacherous descent to the pool? I have no idea. But it must have had something to do with the "display" of the "works of God". That display amazed everyone who knew him "as a beggar" (v.8 RSV). He had climbed those stairs from Siloam without a walking stick, some thought it was a look-alike. "Can't be him," they said.

If a screenplay were being written for a movie, this part of the story might be presented in five vivid scenes:

1. The stir among his neighbors (vv.8-12).

2. The disruption and division among the Pharisees (vv.13-17).

3. The guarded testimony of the man's parents (vv.18-23).

4. A second interview with the man resulting in his ouster from the synagogue (vv.24-34).

5. Jesus seeking him out and he comes to faith (vv.35-38).

The takeaway from this drama was/is one statement: "Whether he [Jesus] is a sinner or not, I do not know. One thing I do know. I was blind but now I see" (v.25). He stood his ground, refused to be intimidated, and gave a classic defence of Jesus' power to heal, a defence which could not be refuted. God truly displayed his glory in him. He stands right up there with the woman who anointed Jesus with the expensive perfume (Mt. 26:6-17), his confession a trumpet blast for the ages.

Jesus turned his attention to the Pharisees who had chased and followed him from the attempted stoning at the Temple. They were conflicted, no doubt, unable to justify their fury at this healer (with the blind man, now seeing and silent, standing beside him). His reference to "judgement" is subtle (v.39). Yes, he is and will be ultimate judge of all, but those who have refused to believe will pass judgement on themselves. Those who confess their spiritual blindness will be saved, those who think they see will perish in their blindness. He was of course directing this to the microcosmic scene of a redeemed beggar and a group of prideful men standing before the Logos, the Lord of Glory. The camera fades to black…

The Good Shepherd 10:1–18

Jesus' choice of a shepherd and sheep analogy had deep roots in Hebrew history. Joseph had said to Pharoah, "Thy servants are shepherds, both we and also our fathers" (Ge. 47:3), and Israel's greatest figures – Abraham, Jacob, Moses, David – were all shepherds. Psalm 23, "The Lord is my shepherd…"; Isaiah 40:11, "He tends his flock like a shepherd; He gathers the lambs in his arms and carries them close to his heart…"; Jeremiah 23:1-4, "I myself will gather the remnant of my flock…" (v.3); Zechariah 11:4-17, "Woe to the worthless shepherd, who deserts the flock!" (v.17), are just a sample of the imagery in the Old Testament which had shaped Israel's self-concept and their view of the God of Abraham, Isaac, and Jacob. And it could very well be that Jesus chose this imagery as an actual flock of sheep passed close by. Many times while walking the streets of Jerusalem I've encountered flocks of both sheep and goats. Shepherding still thrives in Israel.

Mind you, most of us don't resonate with this analogy. We're city dwellers, far removed from agrarian practices and protocols. We need a bit of background, so here are a few pertinent things to keep in mind. A sheepfold was an enclosure bounded by piled rocks comprising a crude fence. Sometimes it was a cave. The entry was blocked with a gate constructed of wood. At night the sheep were herded into the sheepfold, in the morning they were led to pasture. It was not uncommon for more than one shepherd to utilize the enclosure, but there was little confusion when sorting the sheep for the morning because each flock responded only to its shepherd's call. The typical picture is that of a shepherd leading his flock, but sometimes he would drive them from behind. This latter method is the only one I have seen in Israel today.

The sheep were the shepherd's chief asset. So when thieves, stormy weather, or disease struck, he would be at the forefront in their protection. Sometimes a shepherd might even die defending his flock from wild animals or hostile raiders. His life was on the line. Every ram, ewe, and lamb was his personal responsibility. He was on duty 24/7.

So, when Jesus said, "I am the good shepherd; I know my own and my own know me" (v.14), and, "I lay down my life for the sheep" (v.15), the meaning would be clear. When he said, "I am the gate", (v.7), his hearers would know that sometimes a shepherd would lay across the entrance to the fold, becoming a human barrier against danger. Jesus' first priority as Son of God and Good Shepherd was to see his lambs safely home. For him it would mean the way of the cross, where the transgressions of both Jew and Gentile ("other sheep" – v.16) would be atoned for by his death.

Jesus at Hanukkah 10:19–40

After a brief comment re: the "same-old-same-old" criticisms of Jesus by the Pharisees (vv.19-21), John goes on to record the events months later at the "Festival of Dedication" (v.22). It was winter and probably raining (*cold* rain – many winters when we lived in Jerusalem the rain would pour non-stop for weeks with the temperature at or just above freezing). The rain was why Jesus was "walking in Solomon's Colonnade", a covered-in walkway on the east side of the Court of the Gentiles on the temple campus. Everyone would have been wearing extra layers against the cold. The people were at the Temple because it was Hanukkah (as we know it today – Google it.) They were remembering the glorious event when Judas Maccabaeus purified the Temple on Kislev 25 (November to December) 165 BC after its desecration by the Seleucid king Antiochus Epiphanes. It was known as "The Festival of Lights".

Jesus' intrepid enemies, the Sanhedrin members, wouldn't go away. They were at it again, gathering around him in the winter's chill upbraiding him about his putative messiahship (v.24). They wanted a straight answer: Are you Messiah? Yes or no. Their frustration was understandable to a point – in their view Jesus had hinted at it but never declared it publicly. But, in Jesus' view he *had* been clear, for these detractors were the same ones he had been very direct with in the confrontation after the healing of the lame man at the pool of Bethesda (5:31-47). The issue wasn't lack of clarity on Jesus' part, rather, the issue was unbelief on their part (v.25,26). The Samaritan woman (ch.4) and the man born blind (ch.9) *had* believed his direct claims. These two marginalized souls had become Jesus' "sheep" (v.27). But the Pharisees were not his sheep (v.26). They were outside the fold.

Jesus reminded them of what he had told them months previously at the Feast of Tabernacles, and once again they tried to stone him, this time because he claimed to be God (v.33). Jesus responded by quoting Psalm 82:6, "Is it not written in your Law, 'I have said you are "gods"'? (v.34). "If he called them 'gods', to whom the word of God came – and scripture cannot be set aside – what about the one whom the Father set apart as his very own and sent into the world? Why then do you accuse me of blasphemy because I said, 'I am God's Son'"? (vv.35,36). This needs some contextual explanation...

Psalm 82 is only 8 verses long. Here it is:

1. God presides in the great assembly; he renders judgement among the "gods".

2. How long will you defend the unjust and show partiality to the wicked?

3. Defend the weak and the fatherless; uphold the cause of the poor and the oppressed.

4. Rescue the weak and needy; deliver them from the hand of the wicked.

5. The "gods" know nothing, they understand nothing. They walk about in darkness; all the foundations of the earth are shaken.

6. I said, 'You are "gods"; You are all sons of the Most High.'

7. But you will die like mere mortals; You will fall like every other ruler.

8. Rise up, O God, judge the earth, for all the nations are your inheritance.

First of all, Jesus referred to this psalm in the immediate context of an accusation of blasphemy – an accusation from men who had been trained in a rabbinical tradition that rightfully taught them that they were "all sons of the Most High". And, they would have been familiar with the concept of "elohim" – "God" (Heb.) – used occasionally to describe kings, judges, and sometimes angels, with a lower case "g". For example a simple word-for-word translation of verse one might be, "God stands in the assembly of God; He judges in the midst of the gods." In this assembly of gods the Almighty (the upper case "G") chastises these lesser judges, for their unjust judgements of "the poor and fatherless… the afflicted and needy" and their biased "lifting up the faces of the wicked" – in other words they favor the rich at the expense of the poor (no doubt bribes were involved). These "gods" are awash in ignorance ("know nothing" – v.5) and "darkness". The Lord may have called them "gods" but they are mere mortals subject to "die as man" (v.7b in literal Hebrew). Nevertheless it would appear that oral tradition may have been "spun" by the self-righteous to exalt them to inviolable, god-like status in their own eyes. Using scripture to self-aggrandize is an ancient art.

Using scripture to self-aggrandize is an ancient art.

Jesus used this self-aggrandizement just as he had used the coin when challenged about paying taxes to Caesar (Mt. 22:15-22). On that occasion the Pharisees tried "to trap him in his words" (v.15). On this occasion Jesus traps *them* in the manipulation of their own scriptures. In fury "they tried to seize him, but he escaped their grasp" (v.39). He and his disciples walked down to the Jordan Valley, across the river, and up to Gaulanitis where John had baptized (vv.40-42).

The Miracle at Bethany 11:1–44

Jesus and his disciples were a two-day walk away from Jerusalem. About four months had passed since the healing of the man born blind, the weather had warmed, and Jesus' time in Gaulanitis (maybe Perea) had passed relatively peacefully. Then he got word that his dear friend, Lazarus, was ill. His sisters, Martha and Mary, had sent this urgent message to Jesus with the hope that he would come to Bethany immediately and heal him. Jesus took the news calmly and waited two days before setting out. His disciples weren't keen to go back to Judea because, "a short while ago the Jews [religious leaders] there tried to stone you" (v.8). His enigmatic response (vv.9,10) reflected his words re: the healing of the blind man, "Night is coming when no one can work" (9:4). In other words, until the "night" (that is, his arrest and crucifixion) he would keep on doing "the works of him who sent me". Until then he was untouchable.

This unfolding story underscores a point made elsewhere in my casual commentary: there is no effort on the part of the gospel writers to achieve chronological flow or continuity. At best their records are recollections of disparate events and incidents in the three years of Jesus' ministry. By far the critical mass of his life is only hinted at, if at all, in their records. Indeed, "Jesus did many other things as well. If every one of them were written down, I suppose that even the whole world would not have room for the books that would be written," John reflected (21:25). As it turned out there are tens of thousands of volumes in the libraries of the world about Christ, and as far as art is concerned, more paintings on the themes and person of Christ's life and ministry adorn the walls of the world's great museums than any other. Yet, more of Jesus' life is hidden than revealed. Among those unknown factors were his personal friends. Martha, Mary, and Lazarus, a case in point. We know little of the two sisters apart from a brief interlude in Luke 10:38-42, and our only exposure to Lazarus occurs right here in John. He was about to play a critical role in salvation history.

Jesus saw Lazarus' illness (and subsequent death) as another opportunity (like that of the blind man – 9:3) for God's glory to be revealed (11:4). His tardiness was nothing other than timing – he would arrive in Bethany at the exact moment. When he arrived, "Jesus found that Lazarus had already been in the tomb for four days" (v.17). Apparently he was still a few miles from Bethany when Martha came to meet him. She would have been relieved to escape her home for awhile in that the house was crowded with visiting mourners from Jerusalem (v.19), and she probably wanted to mitigate any exposure of Jesus to renewed attacks on his life. He was a wanted man. But, in her grief she could not hold back her disappointment, "If you had been here, my brother would not have died" (v.21). Mary said the same thing a bit later (v.32). Jesus' response was a compassionate promise, "Your brother will rise again." Martha took this as a kind platitude. "Of course he will rise again in the general resurrection" – she was of good Pharisaical stock. Jesus ignored the implicit rebuke. For the first time in his ministry he declared, "I am the resurrection and the life..." (v.25). This was the ultimate "I am" statement, undoubtedly bedrock in John's later description of the Logos, "In him was life, and that life was the light of all mankind" (1:4).

"Do you believe this?" Jesus asked. Martha responded with a three part confession of faith: "I believe that you are the Messiah, the Son of God, who is to come into the world" (v.27). This was the fifth time John recorded confessions of faith in Jesus:

1. Nathaniel – "Son of God"... "King of Israel" (1:49)

2. The Samaritans – "the Savior of the world" (4:42)

3. Peter – "the Holy One of God" (6:69)

4. The man born blind – "the Son of Man" (9:35-38)

Martha's addition, "he who is coming into the world" (RSV) echoed Jesus' statement to the Pharisees on one occasion, "the Kingdom of God is in your midst" (Lk. 17:21). John gives no further detail. He just says that Martha "went back" to her sister to announce that Jesus was on his way.

John states that Mary, Martha's sister, "was the same one who poured perfume on the Lord and wiped his feet with her hair" (v.2). He doesn't record this story, however, till the next chapter (12:1-7), writing several years after the event. His readers would know the story of this Mary. She is not to be confused with Mary Magdalene or the "sinner" of Luke 7. All three are distinct persons. There is no reason to doubt that similar acts of devotion, vis à vis the "sinner" and Lazarus' sister Mary, could have taken place. Perhaps Mary had heard of the "woman in the city who was a sinner" (Lk. 7:37 – read "prostitute") who had so extravagantly expressed her gratitude for Jesus' forgiveness of her sins, and had thought, "How can I do anything less?" Regardless, Jesus evoked powerful feelings in the people he healed and forgave whether it be a much despised Zacchaeus, a woman with "an issue of blood", or a leper who returned to give thanks. Tears of gratitude and joy flooded many an eye in the presence of the Christ.

As he approached the home and its crowd of loud lamenters Jesus recognized many of them as the very same religious leaders who had sought to stone him a few months earlier. They, of course, would recognize him too. He saw them weeping, heard the wailing, and was so indignant at the hypocrisy (knowing they would seek to kill the very man they were mourning! – 12:10) that he actually "snorted" (v.33 – "embrimaomai" – to express hot, vehement agitation – Gk.). This physical outburst may have been a powerful combination of disgust (at the Pharisees) and sorrow for his dear friends. Whatever the case, "Jesus wept" (v.35). He was fully human and felt the pain of loss. Lazarus had been his much-loved friend (v.36), but, even as he wept, the professional weepers muttered resentfully (v.37). Still reeling from the miracle of the blind man's healing, still seeking to dismiss Jesus as a charlatan, they said, "See! He couldn't heal his friend. That blind man's healing was bogus, a one-off. This guy is a phony." Jesus ignored them and went to the tomb, but inwardly was still upset at the two-faced mourners (v.38).

Tombs, or "sepulchres", were sometimes excavated from the living rock (for wealthier persons) or adapted from natural caves. John's reference to a stone "laying on it" suggests this tomb was subterranean with the entrance blocked horizontally. I have been to what is believed to be Lazarus' tomb in Bethany. It is indeed subterranean, and is accessed by a descending stairway of twenty-six steps carved out of the rock (very labor intensive – obviously Martha, Mary, and Lazarus had the means). John calls it "a cave". It surely is, but formed well below the surface. I've been to many tombs in Israel but have seen nothing quite like this one. It's unique, and was/is witness to a crucial turning point in Jesus' story. For Jesus' enemies the raising of Lazarus from the dead would be the final straw.

Whenever possible a dead person's body would be prepared and buried on the day of their death. In the Jewish view the soul of the departed would linger for three days in hope of resuscitation. But, on the fourth day decomposition would begin and the soul would find its way to the Hades. This was the view of the Pharisees who held the hope that one day Hades would release its prisoners at the general resurrection on the "Day of the Lord". The Sadducees, on the other hand, held no such hope. Their theology was limited to the parameters of the Pentateuch (first five books of the Bible) where no mention is made of resurrection. Secular Israelis have a similar view. On the few occasions when one of our friends in Jerusalem died we would see death notices posted declaring, "(*Name)* is no more." For them death was final.

Martha was distressed by Jesus' command to open the tomb (v.39), but Jesus knew what he was about to do. He had done it before. He had not only reminded his questioning cousin John about his messianic power to preach, heal, and raise the dead (Lk. 7:22; Mt. 11:4,5) but he had raised both Jairus' daughter and the son of the widow in Nain (Mk. 5:22-43; Mt. 9:18-26; Lk. 8:41-55; Lk. 7:11-17). In each situation he had revealed "the glory of God" (v.40).

Jesus didn't usually preface his miracles with public prayer, but on this occasion he did so. He wanted the assembled people to know that his power derived from his Father (v.42). He was *not* demon-possessed (10:19) or a super-demon as his religious enemies had tried to make him out to be. He was no magician either. Rather, he was the dependent Son. The Father's glory, not his own, was to be manifest. So, after thanking his Father he shouted, "Lazarus, come out!" And out he came. There was no need for John to describe the astonishment of the mourners. In a matter of minutes word had spread. The Sanhedrin called an emergency meeting (v.47).

The Plot to Kill Jesus 11:45–57

The Pharisees and Sadducees were afraid. They had been trying to trap, silence, and undercut the seditious Galilean without success. He had always bested them. Now he had raised a prominent citizen from the dead! Their frustration knew no bounds. "What are we accomplishing?" There was palpable fear that Jesus would win the country to his purported messianic vision, incite Rome to take severe reprisals, and all would be lost. The Sanhedrin had their protocols for council meetings, but in this case decorum, parliamentary procedure, and hierarchical deferences were lost. It was pandemonium, so Caiaphas, the high priest, raised his voice above the fury, shouting, "You don't know what you're talking about! Be quiet and listen. This man has got to die or else our Temple, our city, and our nation will be lost. Better he should die than all of us at the hands of the Romans!" Little did he know, John reflects, that Jesus would die, not just to save Israel but the whole world (vv.51,52). Caiaphas convinced them and the plot to kill Jesus began.

Word got back to Jesus. "Therefore Jesus no longer moved about publicly among the people of Judea. Instead he withdrew to a region near the wilderness, to a village called Ephraim, where he stayed with his disciples" (v.54). He didn't reappear for several days.

Back in Bethany 12:1–11

In a week Jesus would be crucified. Passover was six days away. Already, people were streaming up to Jerusalem. In spite of the danger to his person, Jesus left his retreat in Ephraim and walked back to Bethany where a thanksgiving meal was prepared for him. There were two guests of honor: Jesus and Lazarus. As they "reclined at table" a large crowd of gawkers gathered outside the home (v.9). If cameras had been invented there would have been several "paparazzi" too. Both men were celebrities.

The guests were reclining at the table because meals were taken in a semi-prone position at a table no more than eighteen inches high. As Martha served, Mary approached Jesus with a vial of expensive perfume.[17] She knelt at his feet, anointing them with the perfume, and, without regard for social correctness, extravagantly and boldly dried them with her unbound hair. Undoubtedly the guests were shocked, while Judas, the pecunious treasurer (v.6), loudly objected, declaring (as unimaginative people have done throughout the ages) that the poor should have been the beneficiaries of something that was worth "a year's wages". Jesus' response? "There is no waste in love." He saw her unbridled act as both love for him and Lazarus, and a prophetic foreshadowing of his upcoming burial (vv.7,8). The poor would always be present, but Jesus had only days to live. "Leave her alone!"

The Triumphal Entry 12:12–19

The raising of Lazarus had heightened the people's view of Jesus as Messiah to a fever pitch. Surely he must be made king! Word quickly spread that he was on his way from Bethany to Jerusalem. "A great crowd" rushed to the roadway to meet him. "Hosanna!" they shouted. "Save now!" (Heb.). The throne would be established in Jerusalem! The Romans would be routed! Justice shall prevail! Hail the king! Shouting with joy and excitement they made way for the "king" as he rode slowly

---

[17] As guests reclined at table a slave would wash their feet. Mary assumes a humble task, even though she is someone of substance.

and mutely on a humble donkey. It was much later that John and the other disciples grasped the prophetic significance of the procession:

"Rejoice greatly, Daughter Zion!
Shout, Daughter Jerusalem!

See your king comes to you,
righteous and victorious,
lowly and riding on a donkey,
on a colt, the foal of a donkey."

—Ze. 9:9

Both "King" and "Suffering Servant" (Is. 53) rode that young beast of burden. No pomp, circumstance, white charger, or heraldic acclaim for this king. No understanding by the people either. The "Hosanna(s)!" would morph into "Crucify him!" within a matter of days.

The Door Opens to Gentiles 12:20–26

While the Pharisees marinated in their slough of fear (v.19), big things (other than parades) were happening in Jerusalem. The significance of the moment may have been lost in the short term, but in the long term it was a seminal watershed: some Gentiles asked to see Jesus (v.21). They were Greek "God-fearers", known by that term because as Gentiles they had been drawn to "the God of Abraham, Isaac, and Jacob". They attended synagogue, observed the Sabbath, and made pilgrimage to Jerusalem three times a year for the major festivals. They were Gentiles in body and Jews in heart. They approached Philip with their request. One or two of them may have known Philip from their business dealings in the Bethsaida region. His name was Greek, as was Andrew's. The two of them brought the request to Jesus. Immediately he recognized the historic turning point the Pharisees had unwittingly prophesied when they stated, "The whole world has gone after him" (v.19). These Gentiles were the thin edge of the wedge. Jesus had come to save both Jew and

Gentile. Time and again the moment had been deferred (2:4; 7:6,30; 8:20), but now, finally, "the hour [had] come for the Son of man to be glorified" (v.23).

They were Gentiles in body and Jews in heart.

It is not clear whether Jesus spoke to the Greeks, the disciples, the crowd, or whether his next few words were more of a soliloquy. He spoke out of a "troubled" soul (v.27) with an agony like the upcoming prayer in Gethsemane (Mt. 26:38; Mk.14:33,34; Lk. 22:44). The "very reason" for "this hour" was that he die for the sins of mankind. He knew he was to be crucified, but he also knew crucifixion to be a horrible death. What agonies awaited! Yet, the goal of his atoning work on Calvary would be greater than saving the world, ultimately it was to "glorify the Father's name" (v.28). The pain would have to be.

As he cried, "Father, glorify your name!", his Father responded. Only at Jesus' baptism by John, and at the Transfiguration, had a voice been heard from heaven. "I have glorified it, and will glorify it again," the heavens thundered. The crowd heard the voice but not the words (v.29), and Jesus told them that the voice was for their "benefit" not for his. The mighty crack of thunder signalled the beginning of the day of salvation (v.32) and the ending of Satan's rule of sorrow (v.31). But for those who really heard him they knew, perhaps with dismay, that "when I am lifted up" meant the cross (vv.32,33). After encouraging them to "believe in the light" (v.36), Jesus, the "Logos" in whom "was life, and that life was the light of all mankind" (1:4), returned to Bethany where he "hid himself from them". Jesus' public ministry was over.

John summarizes Jesus' Pubic Teaching 12:37–50

John may have been a bit depressed by the apparent fruitlessness of Jesus' public ministry. As he wrote towards the end of the 1st century he would have been encouraged by the growth of the Church in the Gentile world, but his thoughts as he looked back were sad. Yet, even in this darkness he harkened back further to the words of Isaiah's prophetic vision. It was comforting to know that God had seen the public unbelief that would surround his Son. In his omniscience the Almighty also knew that there would be those who *would* believe and be saved.

He laments that even "though [Jesus] had done so many miracles… yet they believed not on him" (v.37 KJV). He himself had written of only six miracles, most of them performed in Judea. In his view these should have been enough to convince the people, but they were obdurate. It was too easy to attribute Jesus' power to the demonic or magical, especially when he refused to fulfill their intransigent demand that he establish a throne in Jerusalem and "save now!" ("hosanna").

Then John finds relief in Isaiah:

"Who hath believed our report?
And to whom has the arm
of the Lord been revealed?" (Is. 53:1 KJV)

"Make the heart of this people fat,
and make their ears heavy,
and shut their eyes; lest they
see with their eyes and hear
with their ears, and understand
with their heart, and convert
and be healed." (Is. 6:10 KJV)

John's relief is that the unbelief in the Logos was a fulfillment of prophecy. Isaiah's vision (Is. 6) had shown him the glory of the Lord, "high and lifted up". It had also warned him that unbelief would all but decimate the land. Nevertheless there would be a budding of new life in the "stumps" of the terebinth and oak trees (Is. 6:11-13). Isaiah doesn't question God's sovereignty. Perhaps he remembered that at the time of Israel's exodus from Egypt it was written that God hardened Pharoah's heart (Ex. 9:12). But then again, it was also written that Pharaoh hardened his own heart (Ex. 8:15,32). Whatever the case may be, a hardened heart is a hardened heart. God has given mankind the freedom to reject his grace. In this grim truth John found solace. And, in the uplifting truth that many of Jesus' religious opponents came to faith in him, John was encouraged. He even cut them some slack for keeping their belief secret (vv.42,43). Jesus was no taskmaster. No divine energy was spent on micro-managing freedom of choice.

What follows is not chronological. Jesus had already "hid himself from them" (v.36). So, either this teaching was anecdotal or it may have been a collage of several didactic moments. Regardless, it's a pungent portrayal of Jesus' essential message. Here it is point by point:

1. Belief in Jesus is belief in the Father (v.44 – see also 5:36,37; 7:16; 8:19, 42; 13:20).

2. Seeing Jesus is seeing the Father (v.45 – see also 1:18; 10:30,38; 14:9).

3. Jesus is "light of the world" (v.46 – see also 8:12; 9:5).

4. Jesus is a savior, not a judge (v.47. – see also 3:17; 5:45; 8:15,50).

5. Rejection will result in judgement for unbelief "at the last day" (v.48 – see also 6:39,40,44).

6. Jesus does not speak on his own authority (v.49 – see also 5:30; 6:38; 7:16,17; 8:28; 10:18; 14:10).

7. Jesus' message of eternal life is given in obedience to the Father's commandment (v.50).

THE UPPER ROOM 13:1–17:26

The Last Supper 13:1–30

Much more qualified biblical commentators than I have hazarded opinion on why John did not include a record of what became known as the "Eucharist" ("thanksgiving" – Gk.) in his account of the Last Supper. It is baffling to be sure. Only John himself can explain the omission. We, of course, cannot.

What John *did* include, however, was a startling act on Jesus' part: washing the feet of the disciples. Knowing that the Passion was about to begin (signalled by Judas' decision to betray him – v.2), and fully aware of who he was as Son of God, and anticipating his return to his Father (v.3), Jesus shocked the Twelve by removing his outer garments and wrapping himself in a towel (v.4). Then, assuming the role of a slave, he knelt at the feet of the reclining men and began to wash their feet with water from a basin (v.5). Foot washing of dinner guests was common currency in those days, but it was always performed by slaves of the host. Jesus did not own slaves – so who would do the washing? According to Luke's gospel there had been a dispute already over which of them was "to be greatest". Thus, they all may have been looking sidelong at each other, but not one of them would assume the lowly position of foot-washer. Ego prevailed. Jesus chose not to scold them. He had on another occasion referred to himself as "among you as one who serves" (Lk. 22:24-27). Whereas Luke makes no mention of the foot washing, John highlights it. It was a non-verbal rebuke. The abiding lesson: "You should do as I have done for you" (Jn: 13:15).

Jesus, Peter, and Judas 13:18–38

In the conversation to that point Jesus had ignored Peter's bluster ("you shall never wash my feet" – v.8) but had referred to one of them who was not clean (v.10) – a clear reference to Judas (v.11). "I know those I have chosen," Jesus said (v.18). "Chosen" is a challenging word, for Jesus had "chosen" the Twelve, which included Judas. But now it appears that Jesus' choice was multi-faceted. To be a disciple was not necessarily equivalent to being an "apostle". An apostle was a "sent one". Jesus was about to send eleven of the Twelve out to the world to evangelize, but Judas would perish, an unwitting fulfillment of David's lament, "Mine own familiar friend, in whom I trusted, which did eat of my bread, hath lifted up his heel against me" (Ps. 41:9 KJV). Jesus was the Father's "sent one" (v.20b) and his acceptance by the Eleven was their assurance of acceptance by the Father. Similarly those who accepted Jesus' "sent ones" (v.20a) were accepting/being accepted by Jesus himself. It's unlikely that Judas ever accepted Jesus as the "sent one" of God. He wanted the King of the World, not King of Heaven and Earth.

Jesus Foretells the Betrayal 13:21–30

John records that Jesus was troubled in spirit" ("tarasso" – Gk. – "to agitate, unsettle, perplex") as he reluctantly informed the disciples that one of them was about to betray him (v.21). This was not the first time John had seen Jesus troubled (see 11:33, 35, 38; 12:27), but there may have been a pallor on his face that John had never witnessed. There is something about being betrayed by a friend that stabs like a knife.

The disciples were struck with consternation and self-doubt. Each knew in his heart that he might have enough residual weakness and conflicting thoughts to be a betrayer of this enigmatic leader. So, "they stared at one another" (v.22). They saw in each other a hollow, troubling capacity for complicity.

As mentioned earlier, people in those days reclined at a low table when eating. With due respect to Leonardo da Vinci's classic painting, "The Last Supper", Jesus and his disciples were not sitting on benches or chairs. Each was lying on his left side, resting on his left arm propped on cushions, his legs stretched out at an angle, his right arm and hand free to take the food and drink, each head near the torso of the one reclining beside on the left. Seems awkward but it worked.

Peter was probably on John's right even as John was on Jesus' right. This enabled the silent communication with Peter motioning to John non-verbally or in a whisper, "Ask him which one he means" (v .24). John then easily turned to Jesus with a sotto-voce, "Lord who is it?" (v.25). Jesus responded that the one to whom he was about to pass a piece of matzah was the one. He looked across the table to Judas, their eyes met, and the bread was passed. At that moment whatever visceral turmoil may have been afflicting Judas vanished – "Satan entered into him", says John. He rose from the meal and with Jesus' words, "What you are about to do, do quickly", left. The disciples thought Jesus had sent him for more food, or to distribute alms to the poor (v 29). The die was cast. Judas entered and was enveloped by a dark night of the soul.

The New Commandment 13:31–35

The departure of Judas was a watershed for Jesus. With a sigh of relief and anticipation, as if he were saying, "Now we can get on with it!" he declared, "Now the Son of Man is glorified and God is glorified in him. If God is glorified in him, God will glorify the Son in himself, and will glorify him at once" (vv.31,32).

Just as Jesus' obedience had brought the Father "glory on earth by finishing the work you gave me to do" (17:4), so now the cross would glorify him (12:27,28). Jesus had "come to do thy will, O God" (He. 10:7 KJV), and had done it to perfection. Now the Father would glorify the Son in his own heavenly glory (v.32), in answer to Jesus' prayer, "And now, Father, glorify thou me in thy own presence with the glory I had with thee before the world was made" (17:5). Jesus' incarnation was a mere blip in the unfolding of an eternal plan, but that moment in time was to produce a harvest of chosen souls as his "possession" (17:6) who would have "the power to become the sons of God" (1:12 KJV). Salvation was more than freedom from the curse of sin, it was freedom to explore and "reign" (2Ti. 2:12) in the coming "new heaven and new earth" (Re. 21:1).

There would be a hiatus, however, before these newly minted "Sons of God" accessed the eternities. Jesus would make the way (through death and resurrection) but the disciples could not follow "now" (v.37). Their day would come, however. In the meantime they were to obey a new commandment: "Love one another" (v.34). Indeed, their love for one another would be the signature of true discipleship (v.35). It was to be a constant, guileless love, like that of "little children" (v.33).

This command formed the epicenter of Christian ethics, stressed by John himself in his epistles:

"Dear friends, ... I am writing you a new command...
anyone who loves their brother and sister lives in the light...
But anyone who hates a brother or sister is in darkness..."

—1JN. 2:7-11

"For this is the message you heard from the beginning:
We should love one another."

—1JN. 3:11

"And this is his command: to believe in the name
of his Son, Jesus Christ, and to love one another
as he commanded us."

—1JN. 3:23

"I ask that we love one another."

—2JN. 5B

John took it a step further, describing the roots of the ethic of love as sourced in the nature of God himself:

"Dear friends, let us love one another,
for love comes from God. Everyone who
loves has been born of God and knows
God. Whoever does not love does not

*know God, because God is love. This is how God
showed his love among us: He sent
his one and only son into the world that we might
live through him. This is love: not that we
loved God, but that he loved us and sent his son
as an atoning sacrifice for our sins. Dear
friends, since God so loved us, we also ought to
love one another. No one has ever seen God
but if we love one another, God lives in us and
his love is made complete in us."*

—1Jɴ. 4:7-12

Jesus' new commandment has had ramifications to this day.

A "Heads Up" to Peter 13:36–38

Peter, who among his virtues also had his faults, not the least being impulse control, was quickly put in place by Jesus. "Will you really lay down your life for me? Very truly I tell you, before the rooster crows, you will disown me three times!" Self-preservation would eclipse loyalty.

Jesus Says "Good-Bye" 14:1–16:13

The Way, The Truth, The Life 14:1–14

It's not surprising that the disciples were "troubled" (v.1). Peter had just been warned that he would disown Jesus at the coming dawn, Judas had just rushed off with traitorous intent, Jesus himself was troubled – the atmosphere in the Upper Room was beset with anxiety. But, Jesus didn't call on them to calm down, rather he called them to belief. This may have been a tough call in that the disciples were already feeling orphaned ("whither I go, you cannot come" 13:33). How does one respond positively to someone you depend on who says, "Trust me", while they abandon you? Their hopes were being dashed. Insecurity was gripping their hearts. What's going on here?!

It's not surprising that the disciples were "troubled". Jesus himself was troubled – the atmosphere in the Upper Room was beset with anxiety.

Jesus addressed their fear of abandonment immediately. You will go to where I'm going but not right away. There needs to be preparation (v.2b), but you will join me in "my Father's house". There is more than enough room. You will not be overlooked, forgotten, or lost. My Father knows your name and no one can fill the place he has for you other than you. Yes, I'm going away, but I'm coming back. When I do I'll gather you and we'll go to my Father's house together.

Thomas asked, "How do we get there?" Jesus responded with another of his "I am" statements, "I am the way, and the truth, and the life. No one comes to the Father except through me" (v.6). There would be no Gnostic journey or esoteric pathways. All one had to do was to "believe in God… also in me" (v.1). That was enough. The way to God was personified in Jesus. The truth was Jesus. All life was in Jesus. Little wonder early Christianity was known for decades as "The Way". Jesus was everything – " in him was life, and that life was the light of all mankind" (1:4).

Philip, like Thomas, still troubled in heart, asked another basic question, "Lord, show us the Father and that will be enough for us" (v.8). These questions weren't spontaneous. They had been simmering for some time. The suddenness of events and Jesus' statements brought them to a boil. Uncertainty always bursts through when unexpected pressure is brought to bear. Peter, James, even our author John, and the others felt an unnerving disappointment in Jesus which would culminate in a wholesale desertion a few hours later. You say you and the Father are one? Really? We wonder…

Jesus picked up on this nascent unbelief (vv.9,10) and reminded them of his teaching "words" (v.10b) and his "works" (v.11b). Then he made two statements which on the surface, seem stupendous: "he who believes in me will also do the works that I do; and greater works than these will he do…" (v.12 RSV) and "Whatever you ask in my name, I will do it" (v.13). For the humble pilgrim these promises are both intimidating and discouraging. Only the spiritually egotistical or high maintenance navel-gazers can self-deceive themselves into thinking they can do greater than Christ and get whatever they want on a whim, as if Heaven is their personal candy store. Most of us make little impact on the world and often find the heavens as brass when we pray. Yet, Jesus said it. What did he mean?

> *Only the spiritually egotistical or high maintenance navel-gazers can self-deceive themselves into thinking they can do greater than Christ and get whatever they want on a whim, as if Heaven is their personal candy store.*

To plumb the meaning we have to look at the qualifiers that are hidden in plain sight: "because I go to the Father… in my name… that the Father may be glorified in the Son…". First of all everything is predicated on belief: "he who believes in me" (v.12a). The "greater works" refer to greater scope, not greater personal power. Jesus ministered in postage stamp Palestine. He did not travel to Italy, Egypt, China, or Mesopotamia. These great civilizations were untouched by his presence.

But, after his resurrection, ascension, and the outpouring of his Spirit at Pentecost ("because I go to the Father"), the disciples spread the seeds of the word "to the ends of the earth." And, as to asking anything in prayer, wish fulfillment is off the table. To ask "in my name" means to ask as Jesus himself asked of his Father. His were no specious, selfish petitions. He asked according to his Father's will with the endgame being his glorification. Heaven is deaf to personal agendas. "*Thy* kingdom come, *Thy* will be done" opens the door to the Father's heart. 'Tis far better to remember that Jesus prays for us! (v.16a).

Jesus Introduces the Comforter 14:15–31

After belief (v.12a) comes love and obedience (v.15). True discipleship pivots on those three. The Eleven would have to learn to believe, love, and obey a soon to be departed Master. To assist them in this steep learning curve Jesus introduced a "Counsellor, Advocate, Comforter", the Holy Spirit (v.16), who would teach them "all things" and remind them of all that Jesus had taught them (v.26). He would not leave them orphaned (v.18).

The Greek word for advocate is "parakletos". In legal terms it means "legal assistant". It was also translated "intercessor, advisor, helper", sometimes "defender" by various rabbinical authorities. As John presents him, the Holy Spirit is sent by God (v.26; 15:26; 16:7), given, and received (14:16,17). He brings help. Some commentators think that "Helper" is the best English translation of "parakletos". He is actively engaged as "the Spirit of Truth" in the lives and work of those who believe, love, and obey. Interestingly John even refers to Jesus himself as "parakletos" in 1John 2:1,2: "we have an advocate with the Father – Jesus Christ, the Righteous One". The Helper convicts the world of guilt (16:8-11), teaches about Jesus (14:26), bears witness to Jesus (15:26), and lives in and with the disciples (v.17). What's more, unlike Jesus, He is not spatially limited. He goes with the disciples to the ends of the earth *and* the end of the world (v.16b), enabling them to do "greater things" than Jesus was able to do in the flesh. He tends and fuels the fire set by the resurrection. Without him the Church dies.

Jesus returned to his disciples' "troubled hearts" (v.27b). First of all, he reminds them that their sense of loss must be moderated by his promise that he will "come again" (v.28a KJV), and secondly they should be happy for him because their loss will be his gain – "I go to the Father" (v.28b). Then he said something that has fuelled controversy over the centuries: "the Father is greater than I" (v.28c).

There is no way that this casual commentary can revisit centuries of theological dispute, church councils, heresies, and controversies over the relationship between God the Father and God the Son; nor over the nature of Christ as Son of God and Son of Man. To do so would require a huge library of books and expert guidance from men and women much more academically/theologically adept than I. And it would require study of the myriad histories of Orthodox, Eastern Orthodox, North African, Russian, Serbian, Greek, Albanian, and so many other organized theologies. It's amazing what a domino effect six seemingly innocuous words can create. Try Googling "Council of Nicaea" (if you dare!) and follow the rabbit trail throughout the centuries.

Nevertheless something "casual" must be said, but in doing so I defer to St. Paul:

"In your relationships with one another have the same
mindset as Christ Jesus:
Who, being in very nature God,
did not consider equality with God something
to be used to his own advantage;
rather, he made himself nothing
by taking the very nature of a servant,
being made in human likeness."

—Ph. 2:5-7

This passage continues through to the eleventh verse but the statement, "he made himself nothing" is intriguing. In the Greek it means, "he divested himself of his prerogatives", or, "he abased himself". Theologians call this the "Kenosis". As fully God and fully man Jesus was able to "empty himself" of the independent exercise of attributes such as omnipresence, omniscience, and omnipotence to facilitate the incarnation. He didn't adopt human nature, he *was* human. He was not a mere theophany, he *was* God. But as a human he was, for a period of time, a willing and obedient son. In that sense "the Father was greater" than he. So, in obedience to his Father's will he would submit to "the prince of this world" (Satan) who was about to crucify him, but that submission came out of strength, not weakness. His willingness to endure suffering and the cross was evidence of his love, both for the world, and ultimately for his Father (vv.30,31).

Jesus is the Vine 15:1–17

This passage presents the powerful analogy of the vine and the branches as the relationship between Christ and his Church. The key point: "apart from me you can do nothing" (v.5c). Any effort on the part of the followers of Christ to "extend the Kingdom" without his Spirit leading and empowering it will come to nothing. It is too easy to have, "a form of godliness but denying its power" (2Ti. 3:5), nothing but mere religion, a hollow facsimile, a pious but empty shell. Apart from the vine the branches are dry, withered sticks (v.6). They don't even make a decent fire.

There has been much speculation on the part of commentators as to why Jesus chose the imagery of the vine. Some think it may have been a vineyard on the slopes of the Kidron Valley as he and the disciples walked to Gethsemane. Others suggest there may have been a vine growing at one of the windows in the Upper Room. Then there are those who venture that the cup of wine at the meal was the stimulus. John doesn't say. It could be, however, that the "Kiddush" (the blessing – Heb.) pronounced before the drinking of the wine may have sparked the thought:

"Blessed art Thou, O Lord our God, King of the Universe,
who brings forth fruit from the vine."

This blessing is given every "Kabbalat Shabbat" ("Welcoming the Sabbath" – Heb.) as Jewish families begin their sacred meal. A similar blessing accompanies the breaking and distribution of the bread. And, of course, these blessings are pronounced each year at the Passover meal.

Regardless, Jesus referred to himself as the "true vine" when the group reassembled (probably at Gethsemane). In the same sentence he referred to his Father as "the farmer" or "gardener", the owner of the vine who cultivates and trains it. Both vine and branches are under his care.

The disciples are "already clean" (v.3) in that they are newly budded. When they are grown, however, the expectation is that they will be fruitful. If not, or if stunted, the farmer will prune them (v.2) and most often pruning is painful. The key to fruitfulness is "to remain" in Christ (v.5). Only then can the life of the vine flow into the branches. Fruit, of course, is the outflow. A significant aspect of that fruitfulness is effective prayer (v.7). And why not? If the life of the believer flows from the vine, then prayer will be according to the will of the life-giver. "Not my will but thine…" will be the signature of all petitions. A vineyard cannot tolerate any rogue branch that seeks its own way. The farmer will be quick to cut off any self-seeking or self-aggrandizing fungus. The branches must remain "clean" for the vineyard to be sustainable. (The concept of clean – "kosher" (Heb.) would not be lost on these Jewish "branches").

Jesus referred to "the great commandment" again and tied obedience to love (v.10). Loving words must be accompanied by loving actions. Step one is to love one another (vv.12-17). He knew that the integrity of the future Church would rise and/or fall on this principle. Sadly, the "farmer" has had to do a lot of pruning over the centuries…

The ultimate expression of love for one another is to "lay down one's life for one's friends" (v.13). This was what Jesus was about to do. And, what the disciples were now commanded to do was rooted in the Father's will (v.15b). Jesus had taught them everything they could comprehend, so now it was up to them to follow through. They had been "trained" as branches to bear "fruit that will last" (v.16).

Hated by the World 15:18–25

When Joseph and Mary brought the baby Jesus to the Temple "to present him to the Lord" (Lk. 2:22b), an old prophet named Simeon "took him up in his arms", blessed him, and prophesied, "this child is destined for the fall and rising of many in Israel, and for a sign that will be spoken against… that the thoughts of many hearts may be revealed" (vv.34,35 NKJV). He was so right. Jesus' teaching, his miracles, and his adroit handling of his enemies laid raw "the thoughts of many hearts". Even while the common people ("am ha aretz" – Heb.) flocked to hear him, attributing messianic stature and calling on him to "save now" ("Hosanna!"), the religious elite called him "demon" and tried to kill him. In the end even the "am ha aretz" turned on him, replacing "Hosanna" with "Crucify!" Yes, Simeon was *so* right. The world "hated" Jesus (v.18). Jesus warned the Eleven that his rejection by the world would soon happen to them as well (v.19). And he made the shocking statement that those who hated both him and the disciples did so, ultimately, because they hated the Father (v.23).

This hatred sprang out of ignorance (v.21b). If Jesus had not "spoken" (v.22) mankind would not be culpable, with God "winking" at their ignorance (Ac. 17:30). But no. The "Light" had come into the world and they who hated "without cause" (v.25 – see Ps. 35:19; 69:4) were "without excuse" (v.22b).

More About the Comforter 15:26–16:15

In a former book, *Theology for Non-Theologians* (Google it), I devoted an entire chapter to a discussion of the Trinity entitled, "One Plus One Plus One Equals One", which was, at best, a cursory glance at a *huge* theological concept. The Trinity, as such, is never mentioned in the Bible, and if it hadn't been for these four chapters in John (cc.14-17) we likely would never have begun to explore it. We have Jesus to credit for the mysterious and captivating view of God as Father, Son, and Spirit.

The disciples were still "troubled" (16:6), especially as Jesus warned them about the persecution that was to come their way. It was bad enough that he was leaving them, but to hear him say they too would be killed (v.2) would have been more than upsetting. Then, what were they to think of this new person, "the Comforter" whom Jesus was sending to counsel and help them (15:26)? The last thing they thought they wanted was a stranger in the group. And, they wouldn't understand the significance of his being "the Spirit of Truth" until the Day of Pentecost fifty days later. Jesus bluntly told the Eleven that his troubling words, painful in the short term, were intended to bolster them in the long term, "so that you will not fall away" (v.1). During ensuing crises they "will remember" his warnings about the blind-sides that were sure to come their way (v.4a).

"Grief" (v.6a) had eclipsed the disciples' memory of former questions asked by Peter (13:36) and Thomas (14:5) re: where Jesus was going (16:5). They were focused on their sorrow, not on the joy awaiting Jesus upon his return to "him who sent me". Like children they had little concern for the needs of the parent – it's all about me. This was why Jesus had given them only child-sized bits of revelation during the three years they had accompanied him (v.4b). But now the deep learning curve to spiritual adulthood would be forced upon them. They would need a "Helper" to coach and empower them for the long road ahead (vv.7-11). The "Personification of Truth" would be killed, buried, and then would rise again, ascending to the Father before the "Spirit of Truth" could descend to empower the Church for evangelizing the world.

As noted earlier "paraklete" can be interpreted as "Advocate, Counsellor, Comforter, Helper". The "Advocate" role can be inferred as Jesus spoke of the Holy Spirit "convicting" the world about sin, righteousness, and judgement (v.8). The point of the "conviction" is to precipitate repentance, but the free moral choice each person has been gifted with by their Creator allows them to continue in sin. If they refuse to repent they have, at least, been warned, and will be "without excuse" on the Day of the Lord when the Holy Spirit (the Spirit of Christ himself) will "judge the living and the dead" (1Pe. 4:5). The Advocate's power to convict the soul of sin was demonstrated early on in the people's response to Peter's sermon on the Day of Pentecost – "When the people heard this, they were cut to the heart and said to Peter and the other apostles, 'Brothers, what shall we do?'" (Ac. 2:37). The Spirit will convince the world that Jesus truly was "the Righteous One" by bearing witness through the apostles to the resurrection and ascension. In that sense he will convince the world that Jesus was the personification of righteousness, and judgement will fall on those who through unbelief crucified the Lord of Glory. The ultimate judgement will see "the prince of this world" (Satan) condemned (v.11).

The everlasting era of the Kingdom is here.

Jesus then shifted gears (vv.12-15) with a further comment about the Holy Spirit. To paraphrase: Okay. Enough for now. When the Spirit of Truth comes he will fill in the blanks. But remember, he'll be telling you what I could have told you before you were ready to hear it. His words will be my words. Our words are the Father's words. The everlasting era of the Kingdom is here.

Weeping Will Turn to Joy 16:16–24

Jesus confused the disciples with his next statement: "In a little while you will see me no more, and then after a little while you will see me" (v.16). There are two kinds of seeing here (v.16a,16b). Two different Greek verbs are used, one suggests seeing "in the flesh" and the other "in the spirit". For example, we can look at an individual wondering what his/her story might be; once we've heard the story we say, "Oh. Now I see..." We can see what presents itself, and we can see what lies behind it.

Jesus tells the disciples that he is "going to the Father, where you can "see" me no longer, but "the Spirit of Truth... will guide you into all truth... and will tell you what is yet to come" (vv.13). In other words, the "Helper" will help the disciples see what lies beyond. This is why "it is good for you that I am going away" (v.7).

The disciples still didn't get it (vv.17,18). So Jesus simply acknowledged their present sorrow and troubledness, and using a birth analogy, promised them that the Father (through the Spirit) would make things clear (think Day of Pentecost) "in a little while", and their grief would turn to complete joy (vv.20-24). The Spirit would truly bring them comfort, closure, and power to pursue the far horizon.

It's Time for Plain Speaking 16:25–33

One wishes sometimes that Jesus would have spoken plainly to the disciples. His "figures" (v.25) can be vague and wearying. The Greek word "paroimia" has a number of meanings: "byword, proverb, adage, enigma, obscure saying, parable, similitude, figurative discourse." Here, Jesus admits to obscure speaking and says, "I will no longer use this kind of language but will tell you plainly about my Father." It's time to be clear. "In that day" refers to the Day of Pentecost when the "Spirit of Truth" would descend on the disciples. This "descent" would be dependent upon the "ascent" referred to in v.28: "I came from the Father and entered the world; now I am leaving the world and going back to the Father". In this sentence Jesus refers to his pre-existence, incarnation, death and resurrection, and ascension. Once the Holy Spirit has come there will be no need for Jesus to pray for them (v.26b) other than those times when they need an "Advocate with the Father" because of sin (1Jn.2:1). Their access to the Father will be predicated on their love for his Son and belief that he *is* the Son (v.27). From now on it's family.

But, every family has its issues. In this case the disciples, who prematurely exclaim, "Ah! Now we get it!" and "Now we believe!" (vv.29,30), are brought up short by Jesus saying, "Really? Now you believe?" (v.31). He then goes on to say that in a few minutes ("The hour is coming, indeed it has come..." v.32 RSV) they will desert him, leaving him alone. The warning is not a scold, merely a statement of fact. Regardless, they will "have peace" even in the midst of much trouble to come, because he, Jesus, has "overcome the world" (v.33).

Jesus Prays for Himself 17:1–5

This is the beginning of what is often called "The High Priestly Prayer". Before praying for his disciples, and then for the unity of the Church that they will lead in the world, he calls on the Father to "glorify me in your presence with the glory I had with you before the world began" (v.5). It's as though he is asking that the "kenosis" (the "self-emptying" of Philippians 2:6-8) be reversed, and that he return to "the fullness of the Godhead..." (Cl. 2:9). He's accomplished "the work you gave me to do" (v.4), his disciples now are beginning to know the Father (v.3), and he's coming home. One gets the sense that he can hardly wait.

Jesus Prays for the Disciples 17:6–19

When interpreting the words of Jesus we must never lose touch with the underlying spiritual/cultural context. Jesus and the disciples, the Pharisees and Sadducees, the common people, the Sanhedrin, indeed *everyone* was Jewish. The history was Jewish. The scriptures were the Jewish scriptures. God was understood as "the God of Abraham, Isaac, and Jacob". Salvation history was rooted in a covenant with Israel. And everything pivots on "the Name". Some biblical scholars refer to this as the "Name Theology" of Israel.

One must go back to God's dealings with Moses to trace the genesis of this "Name Theology". At the "burning bush" (Ex. 3:1-15) God revealed his name for the first time in history. In that momentous theophany the Lord told Moses who he was, "the God of Abraham, Isaac, and Jacob", even as Moses hid his face in fear. Then the Lord told him that he was sending him "to Pharaoh to bring my people the Israelites out of Egypt." Moses finally found his voice and asked God for his name. "I Am Who I Am" was the response. Never before had anyone heard the name of God – "YHWH" ("Yaweh" – Heb. – also meaning "I Will Be Who I will Be", and abbreviated to "I Am" – v.14). Later God had referred to himself as "God Almighty" ("El Shaddai" – Ex. 6:2-4) but YHWH was personal. So personal that to pronounce it meant invoking the very presence of God, which meant death (Ex. 33:20). To this day Orthodox Jews will not pronounce YHWH at any time, even when reading the scriptures aloud in synagogue services. They substitute "Adonai" ("Lord") when reading, and in conversation refer to God as "Ha Shem" ("The Name"). When writing the name "God" they write "G-D". The Lord takes his name very seriously too. Read Ezekiel ch. 36 to see that he has attached his "Name" to Israel – their failures are seen as his failures, so he will save them, not for their sake, but "for the sake of my great Name".

So when Jesus says, "I have manifested thy name to the men whom thou gavest me out of the world…" (Jn. 17:6 RSV) it is no small matter. The Father's glory, word, truth, and gifting of these men to his Son, are all bound up in "the Name". The major task assigned to Jesus had been to "protect them" and keep them "safe by that name you gave me" (v.12). Indeed, the very sustainability of the Church would depend on, "Holy Father, protect them by the power of your name…" (v.11b). That protection would be vital both in terms of the world's hatred (v.14) and the wiles of "the evil one" (v.15). The "Name" was/is everything.

Jesus Prays for the Church 17:20–26

Indeed, the "Name" is foundational to Jesus' prayer for the future Church. The last sentence of his prayer captures the essence of his vision: "I made known to them thy name, and I will make it known, that the love with which thou hast loved me may be in them, and I in them" (v.26 RSV). The unity of the Church for which he prays (vv.21, 22, 23) is to be both present and future in dynamic tension, a work in progress – the Name is "known" (v.26a) and is being made known (v.26b). In the present/future Church its unity will convince the world of the truth of Christ (v.23b) who, in the near present (resurrection) will be glorified as Son of Man, but in future will be glorified in Heaven as Son of God with the "glory which thou hast given me in thy love for me before the foundation of the world" (v.24b RSV). In reading this prayer one gets the sense that Jesus' three years of ministry was a mere snapshot of what is to come. The unity of the

Church, inextricably united to the "Name", indeed with the eternal DNA of the unity of Father and Son, empowered by the coming "Counsellor", is a percolating mass of spiritual energy (rather like the pre-ferment starter for sour dough bread) that will culminate in a holy people ready to "rule and reign" in the "new heaven and new earth" (2Ti. 2:11-13; Re. 21). St. Paul's prayer for the Ephesian Church captures much of Jesus' vision:

> *"For this reason I kneel before the Father, from whom every family in heaven and on earth derives its name. I pray that out of his glorious riches he may strengthen you with power through his spirit in your inner being, so that Christ may dwell in your hearts through faith. And I pray that you, being rooted and established in love, may have power, together with all the Lord's holy people, to grasp how wide and long and high and deep is the love of Christ, and to know this love that surpasses knowledge – that you may be filled to the measure of all the fullness of God."*
> —Ep. 3:14-19

There's no avoiding the fact that the Church has been fraught with conflict and division throughout history. Thankfully we have "an advocate with the Father" (1Jn. 2:1 NKJV), "Jesus Christ the righteous" whose blood "keeps on cleansing us" (Gk.) from all sin (1Jn. 1:7). He has continued to cleanse throughout the centuries even as he has continued to make the Father known (v.26) to his recalcitrant Church.

FROM GETHSEMANE TO CALVARY 18:1-19:42

I have spent a lot of time in the Garden of Gethsemane. During the seven years my family and I lived in Jerusalem, then later filming television commentaries, Gethsemane was a favorite venue for quietness and prayer. Often when sitting in the shade of a centuries-old olive tree, leaning against the gnarly trunk, I would imagine that night of Jesus' arrest, the violence and injustice juxtaposed with the serenity of the place, a few of the oldest trees silent witnesses to the betrayal of the Son of God.

John doesn't record the agonies of the Garden suffered by Jesus in prayer. Rather he proceeds directly to the arrest. Judas' arrival with "a detachment of soldiers and some officials from the chief priests and the Pharisees" (v.3) would not have taken Jesus and the disciples by surprise. They would have watched them for twenty minutes or so as they proceeded down from Mount Zion through the Kidron Valley and up to Gethsemane, their lighted lanterns leading the way through the night. Rather than retreat, Jesus went out to the Garden's entrance to meet them (v.4).

Jesus had started something back when he referred to himself as the Good Shepherd, "Therefore my Father loves me, because I lay down my life that I may take it up again. No one takes it from me, but I lay it down of myself. I have power to lay it down, and I have power to take it up again..." (10:17,18). Many theories have been put forward by scholars and commentators as to why all those who had come to arrest Jesus "fell to the ground" when Jesus offered himself saying, "I am he" (v.6). Could it be that his "power to lay it down" was released in that moment of submission? This was no magic trick. The Son of God, maker of heaven and earth, commander of myriads of angels, capable of destroying all his enemies with one word, chose to yield. Those who had come to take him by force were forcefully thrown to the ground. It's a wonder they didn't run away. Peter, no surprise, swung his sword.

Thirty years ago I happened to be recording a television commentary, with our cameras set up on a hill a few kilometers south of the Old City of Jerusalem, near what is now "the Promenade", a beautiful walkway/terrace commanding a stunning view of Zion. At one point I looked down into the valley beneath and saw a familiar sight, an archaeological team setting up for a dig. During a break I walked down to the site and stopped to talk to one of the archaeologists who was stringing a taped barrier from tree to tree. I asked him, in my broken Hebrew, what he hoped to find.

"We think this may be the burial site for the family of Caiaphas. You know, the priest the experts have been telling us never existed," he said.

I was back in North America when I read the news. The Israeli Antiquities Authority announced they had indeed discovered Caiaphas' family plot and published a beautiful photograph of what they called "the Caiaphas ossuary", an ornate stone casket holding the bones of "Joseph, son of Caiaphas". He had been sixty years old at death. And the myth of Caiaphas' non-existence was laid to rest.

Indulge me a further reminiscence. Before this discovery of Caiaphas' family burial plot, the "house of Caiaphas" situated just a few hundred meters below the Zion Gate of the Old City, was described as a "possible" site, an excellent "visual aid", but not authentic. Now it's taken more seriously. It is a walled housing complex, with a minor palace surrounding a large courtyard. My lasting memory of visiting the place is the deep cistern beneath one of the lavish apartments where high-profile prisoners were kept. They had to be lowered and retrieved by a very long ladder or a rope. It's likely that many prophets were interned there over Jerusalem's tumultuous history.

Annas, former high priest, father-in-law to Caiaphas the current high priest, probably lived in one of the apartments. The soldiers brought Jesus, as dawn was breaking, to Annas, the elder, before going across the courtyard to Caiaphas' apartment. There would have been quite the commotion with soldiers, slaves, and household servants shouting and milling about, the entire scene shrouded in charcoal smoke from a fire in the courtyard and the mists of dawn filtering the early rays of the rising sun. John, who for some reason was known by the palace staff, was allowed into the compound, Peter was not (v.16). John had to use his influence to convince the servant girl at the gate to allow him in. Peter may have been a bit furtive telling the girl that he was *not* one of Jesus' disciples, perhaps because he was expecting Malchus (the man whose ear Peter had severed) or one of his acquaintances to discover him and avenge the wound. So he blended in with those warming themselves by the fire, keeping his face in the shadows. He would have been easy to miss in that all the attention was on the notorious prisoner from Galilee.

Meanwhile Jesus was brought before Annas. John calls him "high priest" in an honorific way, much like we refer to former presidents as

"Mr. President". The interchange was brief, with one of the officials slapping Jesus' face. There was no resolution, so Annas sent Jesus, still bound by ropes, across the courtyard to his son-in-law's apartment. They would have passed the fire and in the shuffle someone asked Peter if he was one of Jesus' disciples. "I am not", he replied. Then one of Malchus' relatives, who may have been in the group who had arrested Jesus at Gethsemane, challenged, "Didn't I see you with him in the garden?" Peter totally denied it, and "a rooster began to crow" (vv.26,27).

Jesus and Pilate 18:28–19:16

I have mentioned before in this commentary that it is not my concern to attempt to "harmonize" the synoptics (Matthew, Mark, Luke) with the Gospel of John. I take each book as it is written, with full regard for the unique perspective each author brings to the history for Jesus' life and ministry. So I will make no comment on the date or the nature of the Last Supper as John remembers and records it. Nor will I comment on the divergence of detail re: the Passion that subsists in the four accounts. It is *John's* history before us here, not Matthew's, Mark's or Luke's. So let's carry on.

John chose not to record any detail about Jesus' appearance before Caiaphas and the Sanhedrin. But he did provide a unique description of Jesus and Pilate in conversation, with intermittent interaction between Pilate and Jesus' accusers. If it were a Shakespearean play, it might have been presented as interplay between the principal actors and a chorus. There are six scenes:

1. Pilate annoyed vv.28–32

For one thing, it was early morning. Pilate may not have had his coffee. For another, this raucous crowd of accusers were flaunting their moral/religious superiority by refusing to enter Pilate's "hall of judgement" (v.28 KJV) because it was "unclean". Instead they shouted from the courtyard. This would have been more than off-putting. Further, it seemed that the ruckus was "much ado about nothing", a mere religious dispute that had nothing to do with him as Roman proconsul. "Deal with him yourselves!" he shouted. "We can't," they replied, "because we want him executed and only you have the power to do that." If they had had the power to kill him they would have stoned him for blasphemy (see 8:59; 10:31), but they could/would not pick up a stone on a Sabbath (Passover was a *major* Sabbath). They wanted him dead *now*. Crucifixion was the Roman punishment for sedition, high treason, or threat to the Emperor, so their plan was to convince Pilate to execute Jesus as an insurrectionist. John observes that Jesus had already predicted the cross (v.32 – see 3:14; 12:32).

> *If they had had the power to kill him*
> *they would have stoned him for blasphemy*
> *but they could/would not pick up a stone*
> *on a Sabbath. They wanted him dead now.*

2. The interrogation vv.33–38a

Caiaphas and the Sanhedrin had condemned Jesus as a blasphemer, but before Pilate they accused him as a messianic want-to-be, which explicitly positioned him as a threat to Rome because *the* Messiah would be "King of the Jews". They knew this charge would get Pilate's attention. But Pilate was flummoxed. He hadn't heard the term before. "Are you the King of the Jews?" he asked Jesus quizzically. "I'm not Jewish you know. What's up with your chief priests and this spurious charge?"

Jesus acknowledged that he was a king, but his Kingdom was not political. His was a Kingdom built on "the truth" (vv.36, 37). "Really?" Pilate shrugged, "So, what is truth?" (v.38a).

3. Pilate tries to dodge vv.38b–40

Pilate tried a maneuver by reminding the angry crowd (which was growing by the minute) that the Romans honored the tradition of releasing a prisoner at Passover. Then, lacking impulse control, he suggested that he release "the King or the Jews", knowing no doubt this would infuriate the people. Which it did. "Give us Barabbas," they roared.

4. Another Maneuver 19:1–7

Pilate was really annoyed by now. This early morning intrusion by people with whom he had had previous run-ins was too presumptuous and obnoxious by half. Maybe if I flog this strange man and humiliate him before the people they'll back off and go home. So, after scourging Jesus and wrapping a purple robe (mocking his "royalty") around his bloody back and shoulders, he presented him, crowned with thorns, with a derisive "Here's your king!" The people raged, "Crucify! Crucify!" Pilate shouted, "Do it yourselves! In my judgement he's innocent." But then the people said something that struck a chord of fear in Pilate's superstitious soul, "He has made himself the son of God" (v.7).

5. Pilate afraid vv.8–12

Like all Romans, Pilate would have believed in gods and demi-gods whose offspring possessed supernatural powers. He also believed these gods sometimes took on human form and patrolled the earth (see Ac. 14:11,12). Some of what he had heard about Jesus' supernatural powers now came to the fore. Son of God they say? What if he is?

With a knot of fear in his chest he took Jesus back into the judgement hall and tremulously asked, "Where are you from?" Jesus remained mute. Pilate lashed out, "You dare not answer? Don't you know I have the power of life and death over you?" Jesus calmly replied, "Your power is delegated" (he could have said much more). Pilate, conflicted, went out to the crowd again, declaring he intended to release Jesus. The crowd retorted, "If you let this man go, you are no friend of Caesar..." (v.12).

6. Pilate caves vv.13–16

By this time Pilate was close to emotional exhaustion. He brought Jesus back out to the mob, sat on the "judgement seat", gathered his dignity and declared, "Here is your king!" Raising his voice above the shrieks,

"Crucify!. Crucify!" he shouted, "Shall I crucify your king?", at which point the chief priests cast aside their national pride, their theology, and their messianic hope by crying, "We have no king but Caesar!" (v.15). Both Pilate and the people had caved. Calvary awaited.

Jesus is Crucified vv.17–37

John's account of the crucifixion is brief, some would say stark. He describes it in two short sentences (vv.17,18). "Golgotha" is a transliteration of the Aramaic "galgalta" or "gulgulta" meaning "skull" ("cranion" – Gk.; "calvaria" – Lat.). The place of public executions (stoning by the Jews, crucifixion by the Romans) was probably a quarry with part of a limestone hill cut away by stone cutters for construction purposes. So there would be a man-made cliff-face with gouged out crevices creating a skull-like look. The "Garden Tomb" outside the Damascus Gate in the Old City of Jerusalem abuts such a hill. Not many insist that this is Calvary but the society that manages the site refers to it as "an excellent visual aid". Such a quarry provided limitless stones for stoning, and level ground for the placement of crosses. And a location outside a major gate provided public exposure, a valuable tool for mitigating blasphemous or seditious behavior. It also allowed mean-spirited souls to throw rocks at a law-breaker or spit in a crucified criminal's face (those being stoned would be hunched over or collapsed, those being crucified were at eye-level). Calvary was a nasty place.

Pilate, still smarting after his acquiescence to the chief priests, got back at them by placing a "titlos" (Gk.) or "titulus" (Lat.) on the cross, stating in Hebrew (local language), Latin (Roman language), and Greek (world language) that "Jesus of Nazareth" was "King of the Jews" ("INRI" – "Iesus Nazarenus Rex Iudaeorum"). This trilingual placard announced to the world who Jesus was (much to the displeasure of the chief priests – v.21). Pilate had no idea that his fit of pique would be prophetic.

As Jesus hung on the cross the four Roman soldiers whose duty that day was to crucify criminals divided what was left of Jesus' clothes (this was a perquisite – obviously these men were poorly paid). They did not quarter his undergarment ("chiton" – Gk.) because it was seamless and valuable. So they cast lots for it (John notes the fulfillment of Ps. 22:18).

John refers to the women standing near the cross: Jesus' mother Mary, her sister (traditionally identified as Salome, mother of James and John), Clopas' wife Mary, and Mary Magdalene (v.25). There is a touching scene where Jesus gives responsibility for his widowed mother to John ("the disciple whom he loved"). John writes, "from that time on, this disciple took her into his home" (v.27). Then Jesus called for a drink, declared "It is finished", and died. John makes no passionate or even theological summary statement. Later, on the Isle of Patmos, writing "the Revelation", he describes "thousands upon thousands" of angels in heaven singing,

"Worthy is the Lamb, who was slain,
to receive power and wealth and wisdom
and strength and honor and glory and praise!"

—RE. 5:12

These words have been forever immortalized in Handel's Messiah. The Logos is "the Lamb slain from the creation of the world" (Re. 13:8). Jesus saves.

Fridays were the "Day of Preparation" for the Sabbath which began at sundown. The chief priests, frustrated by Pilate's intransigence re: the placard, insisted that Jesus and the two miscreants crucified on either side be taken down before the weekly Sabbath began. To take them down, however, required their deaths, so to hasten the process, they asked that the soldiers break their legs (v.31,32). This would force their bodies to slump down, compressing their lungs, causing suffocation. Pilate complied. The soldiers broke the legs of the men beside Jesus, but when they got to him he had already died. One of the soldiers thrust a spear into his side to be sure. John declares he saw it with his own eyes (v.35). He also saw another two prophecies fulfilled (Ps. 34:20; Ze.12:10).

Jesus is Buried vv.38–42

While the soldiers were removing the bodies of the two thieves Joseph of Arimathea arrived, having sought and received permission from the beleaguered Pilate to remove, prepare, and bury the body of Jesus. Nicodemus also arrived to help, bringing "a mixture of myrrh and aloes, about seventy-five pounds" (vv.38,39). Both men were members of the Sanhedrin, and secret disciples or Jesus. Their act of love for the Master forever stigmatized them – first, for defiling themselves by touching a dead body, and second, for publicly demonstrating their devotion to Christ. For sure they were subsequently removed from the synagogue, and stripped of their membership in the Sanhedrin. Near Calvary there was a garden with a new tomb hewn from the living rock. They gently laid him there just as the sun set.

HE IS RISEN! 20:1–29

When my family and I lived in Jerusalem one of my ministry responsibilities was broadcasting the Gospel from a small radio station located in an abandoned customs house in southern Lebanon. It was called "The Voice of Hope". Its signal covered lower Lebanon and upper Galilee. For years I drove every week from Jerusalem, down to Jericho, through the Jordan Valley, past the Sea of Galilee, and up to the border between northern Israel and Lebanon. At the border I showed my military pass (provided by the Israel Defence Forces) and I was waved into Lebanon. One of the biblical sites I drove through on the way was Magdala, the home village of Mary the Magdalene.

In the 1980's Magdala had a road sign and not much else. There was evidence of an ancient village between the highway and the shore of Kinneret but it was a nondescript ruin. Today, however, it is one of the most fascinating archaeological digs in the region. The excavation began in 2006 and now boasts an amazing discovery of a coastal town, majoring in fish processing, with the oldest Galilean synagogue ever uncovered. The centerpiece of this beautiful house of worship is the

Magdala Stone with a carved menorah, the most ancient of any outside Jerusalem. I recorded a television commentary there recently, awed by the beauty and authenticity of the place. My focus for the video, as you would expect, was Mary Magdalene, the first witness of the Resurrection.

Unfortunately she has suffered much mythologizing. Suffice it to say she is *not* the woman with the costly vial of perfume, nor is she the sister of Martha and Lazarus and there is *no* record of her being a prostitute. What we *do* know is that Jesus healed her of a serious spiritual affliction (Lk. 8:2) and that she was one of many women who accompanied the Twelve and Jesus in their various itinerations. She was loyal and courageous. When the Eleven had fled Gethsemane, later to hide out, she had the inner strength to risk her personal safety to not only attend the crucifixion and burial of Jesus, but to walk in early Sunday darkness to the tomb by herself. She was a force.

John writes that she arrived at the tomb in the dark, and seeing that the stone "had been removed from the entrance" (v.1) she quickly ran back to where the Eleven were staying. Breathlessly she told Peter and John, "They have taken the Lord out of the tomb, and we don't know where they have put him!" ("we" suggests a few other women had met up with her). All three ran to the tomb (John got there first), undoubtedly incensed that grave robbers had stolen Jesus' body away. Peter saw John looking in, pushed by him and went in, both of them struck by the orderly placement of the burial cloths (vv.4,6). Robbers would have left a mess. John was so amazed at the sight (it looked like Jesus' body had simply dematerialized leaving the grave cloths and head piece intact) that "he believed" (v.8). Only later was he able to address the wonder scripturally (v.9).

John calmly states, "Then the disciples went back to where they were staying" (v.10). Mary had returned. Weeping, she took another look into the tomb. The narrative is so astonishingly matter-of-fact that one wonders if John for some unexplained reason was playing it down – "She saw two angels in white" (!). Without any mention of fear (usually biblical characters were *always* afraid when they saw an angel) Mary says the same thing to them as she had said to the disciples. She then turned around and there was the gardener (or so she thought. v.15). She didn't recognize his voice until he said her name (vv.15,16). In total shock and awe she must have fallen at his feet and thrown her arms around him. "Stop clinging to me" (Gk.), he said, as if she could convince him with such urgency to stay. No, there was much to do, "ascending to the Father" (v.17) being top priority. Was this ascent a present or future event? Perhaps, in his glorified body, Jesus was already freely transitioning from the earthly Kingdom to the heavenly and back again. John gives us no explanation. We can only wonder.

Mary's was the first eye-witness testimony to the resurrection: "I have seen the Lord".

Mary rushed (?) back to the Eleven. Her's was the first eye-witness testimony to the resurrection: "I have seen the Lord" (v.18). So understated. So wonderful. That confession became the historical bedrock on which the preaching of the Gospel would be built – "If Christ be not risen, then is our preaching vain, and your faith is also vain." (1Co. 15:14 KJV), wrote St. Paul. Without the empty tomb we are "yet in our sins" (1Co. 15:17b).

He Appears vv.19–29

The post resurrection appearances of Christ to many eye-witnesses over forty days are critical to the integrity of the Gospel. There are four vital components that are all rooted, not in mystery, but in history:

1. Christ died.
2. He was buried.
3. He rose from death.
4. He was seen.

This is the theological DNA of the Apostle Paul's Gospel (1Co. 15:1-8). And even though "least of the apostles" (1Co. 15:9) the historical sustainability of the faith demonstrates that Paul got it right.

The disciples were in hiding "with the doors locked" when suddenly Jesus appeared among them. They must have been astonished, let alone terrified (a ghost?!), but John gives no detail. He showed them his wounds, assuaged their fear – "Peace be with you!" – then imparted the Holy Spirit ("he breathed on them") as he commissioned them to apostolic ministry. They were now duly empowered "sent ones" with the authority to mediate between heaven and earth for those to whom they ministered (vv.21-23).

John records that Thomas was not there at the time. When the other disciples told him what had happened he refused to believe it. If he couldn't see Jesus for himself, even to the point of touching his wounds, there was no way he was going to be drawn into this fantasy (vv.24,25). Eight days later Jesus appeared behind those same locked doors. This time Thomas was there. Without a rebuke Jesus invited Thomas to touch his wounds. Thomas answered, "My Lord and my God!" Then came the rebuke – "Because you have seen me, you have believed; blessed are those who have not seen and yet have believed" (v.29). Nevertheless Jesus must have imparted his Holy Spirit to Thomas (perhaps privately) for he founded a vibrant church in southern India which thrives to this day (there are five thousand churches in the city of Chennai alone!). Christian Indians see him not just as an apostle, but a saint.

John then concludes his gospel (ch.21 is an appendix). He basically says he's chosen only some of "the signs" Jesus did, but they should be enough to convince the readers that "Jesus is the Messiah, the Son of God" and come to faith (vv.30,31). Believe in the Logos and live!

The Appendix 21:1–25

This brief epilogue recounts the miraculous catch of fish at the Sea of "Tiberias" (the Sea of Galilee), the sense of insecurity as to who this person on the beach was who gave the order to cast the nets on the other side of the boat, the restoration of Peter to favor, and a final affirmation of John, "the beloved disciple."

There are two points of difficulty: Why didn't the seven disciples recognize Jesus immediately? And what did Jesus mean when he said about John "If I want him to remain alive until I return what is that to you?" Both questions require speculation. I'll leave it to you.

John concludes by reminding the reader that his gospel is a collection of just a few of the marvelous things Jesus said and did in his brief time on earth. But, as he said in 20:31, this is more than enough evidence for belief.